INTRODUCTION TO LITERARY CONTEXT

American Short Fiction

INTRODUCTION TO LITERARY CONTEXT

American Short Fiction

SALEM PRESS

A Division of EBSCO Information Services, Inc.
Ipswich, Massachusetts

GREY HOUSE PUBLISHING

Publisher's Cataloging-In-Publication Data
(Prepared by The Donohue Group, Inc.)

Introduction to literary context. American short fiction /
  [edited by Salem Press].—[1st ed.].

    p. : ill. ; cm.

  Includes bibliographical references and index.
  ISBN: 978-1-61925-212-7

1. Short stories, American—History and criticism. I. Salem Press (Salem, Mass.) II. Title: American short fiction

PS374.S5 I58 2013
813/.0109

First Printing

PRINTED IN THE UNITED STATES OF AMERICA

CONTENTS

PUBLISHER'S NOTE

American Short Fiction is a new title in Salem Press's *Introduction to Literary Context* series. This series is designed to introduce students to the world's greatest works of literature—including novels, short fictions, novellas, and poems – not only placing them in the historical, societal, scientific and religious context of their time, but illuminating key concepts and vocabulary that students are likely to encounter. A great starting point from which to embark on further research, *Introduction to Literary Context* is a perfect foundation for *Critical Insights*, Salem's acclaimed series of critical analysis written to deepen the basic understanding of literature via close reading and original criticism. Both series – *Introduction to Literary Context* and *Critical Insights* – cover authors, works and themes that are addressed in core reading lists at the undergraduate level.

Introduction to Literary Context: American Short Fiction is the second title in the series. The first covered post-modernist American novels, and future volumes will cover poetry, British fiction and world fiction.

Scope and Coverage

American Short Fiction covers 40 works written by American and Canadian authors and published in the 19th and 20th centuries. The list of authors is diverse, including Edgar Allen Poe, considered one of the first short story writers, Antiguan–American author Jamaica Kincaid, and Pulitzer Prize winner Alice Munro, considered the master of the contemporary short story. Other than being described as a concentrated form of narrative prose fiction, short fiction has no clear, distinctive characteristics. Even its length, traditionally defined as being readable in one sitting, is not predictable in today's speedy culture.

Organization and Format

The essays in *American Short Fiction* appear alphabetical by title of the work. Each is 6–8 pages in length and includes the following sections:

- Content Synopsis – summarizes the plot, describing the main points and prominent characters in concise language.
- Historical Context – describes the relevance to the story of the moods, attitudes and conditions that existed during the time period that the work took place.
- Societal Context – describes the role that society played within the piece, from the acceptance of traditional gender roles to cell phone etiquette.
- Religious Context – explains how religion—of the author specifically, or a group generally, influenced the short story.
- Scientific & Technological Context – analyzes to what extent scientific and/or technological progress has affected the story.
- Biographical Context – offers biographical details of the author's life, which often helps students to make sense of the story.
- Discussion Questions – a list of 8–10 thoughtful questions that are designed to develop stimulating and productive classroom discussions.
- Essay Ideas – a valuable list of ideas that will encourage students to explore themes, writing techniques, and character traits.
- Works Cited

Introduction to Literary Context: American Short Fiction ends with a general Bibliography and subject Index.

ABOUT THIS VOLUME

The literary history of all nations and cultures is founded on the short story. Although the novel ultimately may be lauded as the pinnacle of an individual author's literary achievement, the short story is the writers' stepping stone to mastering their craft, and all renowned novelists have honed their skills and developed their singular styles through producing short fiction. The once flourishing literary journals presented the short works of writers who would find permanence or fade to obscurity, so it has been the short story that proved the gauntlet that defined the literary artists of each generation. Many of the writers presented in this volume gained initial fame in such publications. While many were bound for glory in both the long and short form, many 19th-century masters represented in this collection continued to create short fiction after launching successful careers as novelists.

For students running the gamut from grammar-school fledglings through doctoral candidates, the short story retains its relevance as a learning tool throughout the course of education. The same holds true for the writer. The short story is the classroom of both the author producing the work and the student studying the finished product. Children learn reading through what essentially amounts to illustrated short stories: even the most rudimentary volumes with a single word adorning each page qualify. Thus, the short form is as ingrained in our literary DNA as eye color in the human genome.

Noted American literary scholar Malcolm Cowley, outlined what he asserted were the stages of short story creation from the germination of the original idea to the finished product in an interview with *The Paris Review*. Cowley's take is interesting because it's more concerned with the emotion and psychological preparation involved rather than the physical act:

For short-story writers the four stages of composition are usually distinct…. Before seizing upon the germ of a story, the writer may find himself in a state of 'generally intensified emotional sensitivity…when events that usually pass unnoticed suddenly move you deeply, when a sunset lifts you to exaltation, when a squeaking door throws you into a fit of exasperation, when a clear look of trust in a child's eyes moves you to tears.' I am quoting again from Dorothy Canfield Fisher, who 'cannot conceive,' she says, 'of any creative fiction written from any other beginning.' There is not much doubt, in any case, that the germ is precious largely because it serves to crystallize a prior state of feeling. Then comes the brooding or meditation, then the rapidly written first draft, then the slow revision; for the story writer everything is likely to happen in more or less its proper order. For the novelist, however, the stages are often confused. The meditation may have to be repeated for each new episode. The revision of one chapter may precede or follow the first draft or the next.

The stories covered in this volume are an amalgam of 19th- and 20th-century examples from the top authors producing short fiction in their respective times. The 19th century is of particular interest as the period in which American fiction began to take form. Despite its hard-won independence, Americans continued to look to England and the continent for its artistic leads in the post-Revolutionary period and into the early 1800s. Britain remained the center of English-language publishing, and while America had a thriving market for newspapers, pamphlets, and journals, those outlets were almost exclusively the kingdom of nonfiction with a smidge of poetry as the only form of creative writing. Fiction publishing was almost a nonentity as American authors had yet to find a voice.

Most scholars accept Washington Irving's *The Sketch Book*, published in installments throughout 1819 and 1820, as the first popular short story collection by an American author, although, ironically, the stories and essays in the volume were written in England and are dominated by English themes. However, the collection also contained the distinctly American tales *Rip Van Winkle* and *The Legend of Sleepy Hollow*, two classics still widely read today. Their vast popularity proved that an American market for short fiction was possible although it would be several more years before it fully flourished.

In 1837 Nathaniel Hawthorne assembled the short stories he'd previously published individually to little avail for a collection dubbed *Twice Told Tales*. Born and raised in New England, Hawthorne wore the yoke of Puritanism that prevailed throughout the Northeast. The majority of his well-known stories concern sin and guilt, recurring themes which crescendo in his most famous work *The Scarlet Letter* (1850). Hawthorne's sea captain father died when he was young, leaving the family with the ample financial resources to allow Nathaniel to pursue a writing career after graduating college without ever laboring in a profession. He toiled for years in near monkish seclusion writing and honing his fiction while developing his themes and perfecting his style. Scholars believe that he published stories under pseudonyms while continuing to refine the texts until he could improve them no further and burning the earlier, imperfect drafts. *The Minister's Black Veil*, covered in this volume, is among his initial successes. Steeped in Puritanism, the story, which Hawthorne labels "A Parable," follows the Reverend Mr. Hooper's donning of a black veil covering all but his mouth

and chin and the exaggerated turmoil it creates in the community. The veil seems symbolic of the sin we all possess, and while Hooper wears his openly (acknowledging his sin), those around him are oblivious to the invisible veils they wear themselves.

Although a contemporary of Hawthorne, Poe—alcoholic, addicted to gambling, and worldly—was the austere New Englander's antithesis. As Hawthorne's stories are sermons in morality, Poe wrote to entertain his audience. His tales of the macabre riveted readers, and he is accepted as the father of the mystery; the most prestigious award bestowed to works in that genre by the Mystery Writers of America bears his name and likeness—the Edgar. Like Hawthorne, Poe also lost his father at a young age but was adopted by a wealthy family. Raised as a gentleman, he initially pursued a military career including several years attending West Point. Poe's stepfather, however, later remarried, dashing Edgar's chances of inheriting the family fortune and forcing him to struggle through a string of odd jobs that proved as unsuccessful as his military endeavors. Poe also spent much time in seclusion perfecting his craft.

Hawthorne's *The Minister's Black Veil* and Poe's *The Tell-Tale Heart*, one of the many Poe creations covered here, are as opposite as their creators, yet close analysis reveals similarities. Hawthorne's Reverend Hooper's decision to hide his eyes from humanity propels the story, while the nameless old man in Poe's murder story loses his life solely because he "had the eye of a vulture—a pale blue eye, with a film over it." Both characters seemingly are innocents who have done nothing to warrant their fates and have been harshly judged by others for their physical appearance. Scholars assert that Hooper's veil is a symbol of his sin-deformed soul, while the old man's deformity is physical. But if the eyes are the window of the soul, as popular adage suggests, perhaps the old man's spirit is as corrupt as his orb.

Zora Neale Hurston is one of ten women writers included in this volume. Her short story *Sweat* was published in 1926 in the only issue ever produced of *Fire*, a planned quarterly magazine for young African-American writers. *Sweat* was never collected in an anthology or republished during the author's lifetime (1891–1960). Hurston brings authenticity to the story about the decaying marriage of a woman and her abusive, philandering husband through dialogue written in vernacular and the use of real locations like Joe Clarke's store where Hurston herself shopped. Protagonist Delia Jones initially seems the typical weak, cowering woman afraid of her brutal husband, Sykes. Readers, however, quickly discern that Sykes has lost his power to dominate his wife. In the story's opening scene, Delia is separating the washing she takes in to earn her living when Syke's drops his coiled up bullwhip on her shoulders. Thinking it is a snake, which she deathly fears, "a great terror [takes] hold of her" and it is "a full minute" before she realizes her husband's vicious joke. Although it appears that Sykes dominates his wife, Hurston describes the whip, long the instrument of black suppression, as "long, round, limp and black," giving it phallic overtones: Sykes has been Delia's oppressor for years, but she has found a new strength and self-worth rendering Sykes impotent and powerless.

Although not a sermon in the manner of Hawthorne, *Sweat* has distinct religious symbolism. Syke's attempt to drive away Delia by bringing a real snake into her house is replete with Biblical overtones that Hurston makes obvious by having the woman refer to the serpent as "ol' satan" and "ol' scratch." And like the narrator of Poe's tale who seals his own fate by confessing his crime to the police, Sykes also is the author of his own demise as the viper ultimately kills him instead of Delia. Also remarkably reminiscent of *The Tell-Tale Heart*, Delia's final vision of the dying Sykes is his "open eye shining." The themes presented by Poe and Hawthorne in the 1800s still flourished in

20th-century short stories. However, *Sweat* is an excellent illustration of how 20th-century fiction became distinctly American. Both Hawthorne's *The Minister's Black Veil* and Poe's *The Tell-Tale Heart* could as easily be set in England or Europe, while Hurtson's use of ethnic dialogue roots her story firmly in the soil of the American South.

Hurston introduces another facet into the story as does Jack London in *To Build a Fire*, included in this volume: place and its physical elements as an integral factor of the short form. Not just the purview of novels, location can play a paramount role in setting the mood and tone in short fiction as well. Several authors are so connected to a single location that the geometry becomes a character. This perhaps is best personified by James Joyce's use of Dublin, Ireland, as the setting for all his writings—his sole short story collection isn't called *Dubliners* because he failed to conjure another title! Setting often gives a story or a novel its personality. While this is more prevalent in the alternate worlds of science fiction and fantasy, readers of all genres need to be immediately aware of a story's setting in order to fully comprehend the author's intent.

As stated above, Poe and Hawthorne are prime examples of stories with universal settings which can broaden their appeal to a wider array of readers as the location doesn't set the story's tone. *Sweat* is rich with Biblical symbolism, which the author amplifies through setting it in a stifling hot South Florida. Hurston gives readers the triple whammy of a serpent, Satanic references, and Hellish heat. London uses the Yukon's frozen landscape to set his story's mood. London, however, goes further by employing the –70F temperature as the story's antagonist and third character along with the man and the dog. The unnamed protagonist is locked in a to-the-death struggle against the murderous cold in a duel as lethal as any fought with a sword or pistol. London also utilizes an element so far not seen in the previous shorts: presenting a story completely through narration sans dialogue.

Another interesting feature of London's story is the dog. The animal is described as a "wolf-dog," a combination of the wild and the domesticated. The "dog" easily can be seen as representing nature as London instills it with intelligence, as well as instinct: the dog understands that it's too cold to travel, a fact the man repeatedly acknowledges yet foolishly ignores. The dog is the rational, the man the irrational. At the story's conclusion, the dog survives while the man succumbs to the killing cold.

Spring-boarding into the mid 20th century, John Updike's *A & P,* included here, brings a new ingredient to the study of short fiction: humor. While many stories have been written solely to deliver laughs, Updike, as well as J.D. Salinger, also included in this collection, follows in the footsteps of Mark Twain and others by lacing otherwise dramatic outings with humor. It is interesting to note that Updike's story is set in a small area a few miles outside of Boston, the exact local where Hawthorne lived and arguably set his fiction. The Puritan spirit that pervaded that area clearly has departed. While Hawthorne's characters were aghast at anything in the realm of sex or immodestly, *A & P* delivers the sexual desire of a young man toward three equally young women who enter the supermarket where he works wearing only bathing suits that display much flesh. Although the young man never directly expresses any sexual desire, he, like London's protagonist, surrenders to the illogic although he realizes it clearly is folly that may destroy his future.

As depicted in these highlighted stories, as well as numerous others in this collection, short fiction holds all the wonders of novels. Short fiction has it all.

Michael Rogers

A & P

by John Updike

"Fiction is a tissue of lies that refreshes and informs our sense of actuality. Reality is-chemically, atomically, biologically-a fabric of microscopic accuracies."

John Updike

Content Synopsis

Set in a small town north of Boston five miles from the beach on a Thursday afternoon, this story opens famously: "In walks three girls in nothing but bathing suits" (15). Revising the tried-and-true Arthurian plot, "Sammy is on a romantic quest: In the name of chivalry, he acts to save the "queen" (and her two consorts) from the ogre Lengel. At the same time, Sammy is tempted by the three Sirens from "the Point," (Peck). Updike offers us a young 'knight' as a check-out clerk and the damsel in distress as an inappropriately dressed teenager. According to Blodgett: "Updike pokes gentle fun at Sammy because he succumbs to the girls who are cast in the roles of the legendary Sirens—the mythological temptresses who lured unwary males to their destruction." The intersections between class and gender, the humor and the unforgettable narrative point of view all make this story a classic.

From the first line, readers are drawn into Sammy's world and perspective. The in media res beginning of "A & P," adds to the realism of the piece as the first line catches readers hook, line and sinker. The conversational and often confessional tone encourages identification with Sammy's plight despite the rather large flaws in his personality. The word "I" or "my" occurs eight times in the first paragraph alone, firmly establishing the point of view of the nineteen-year-old protagonist. Within that same opening paragraph, Sammy's range of attitude towards women is illustrated via his objectification of a young, desirable "Queen" in a bathing suit, and his scorn at an older woman at the checkout, clearly past her sexual prime referred to as a "witch." Later in the text, the wives and mothers in the store are referred to as houseslaves. When Updike shifts the narration into second person point of view, it sometimes has the effect of making the reader complicit in the thoughts and actions of chauvinistic Sammy.

The three girls: Plaid, Big Tall Gooney Gooney and the Queenie are all subjected to Sammy's gaze, for better or for worse. While Plaid is too chunky and Gooney Gooney's chin too long for his taste, Queenie is just right. She quickly becomes the central focus of Sammy's attention as he collects and provides details like the exact shade of her hair color, the way her feet touch the ground, and the condition of her bathing suit.

The store is a full five miles away from the beach, positioning the bathing suit clad girls as out of context "under the fluorescent lights" in the market, testing their sexual power and flaunting the 'rules' of the establishment.

Sammy's reaction to the girls arguably begins to shift when they approach the meat counter only to be ogled by McMahon the butcher. As they walk away from his counter "all that was left for us to see was old McMahon patting his mouth and looking after them, sizing up their joints. Poor kids, I began to feel sorry for them" (17). The physical break (in extra line spacing) at this point signals the reader that something important has occurred. Some readers believe that Sammy simply shifts his attitude from chauvinistic to patronizing towards the girls, no longer objectifying them, but not perceiving them as equals either. Other readers' claim Sammy's rite of passage begins in this moment, as he watches an older man mirroring his own slavering over the girls. He decides he doesn't want to be 'that guy' and shifts his feeling from exploitative to protective or what he perceives as 'heroic'. His 'transformation' is not as clean as some would suggest. Sammy does not switch a pitchfork for a halo at this point in the story. The comments he provides as Queenie pulls her money out from the bathing suit top which he felt "was so cute," and her hands "bare as God made them" signal both a shift in his lecherous view to a more seemingly innocent one, but he fails to lose a superior tone. Although he envisions himself as their "unsuspecting hero" he still refers to Queenie's breasts as "scoops of vanilla" (19), and refers to the three as "my girls." Thompson's view of whether or not Sammy should be considered a hero, illustrated in The Explicator is that "Sammy must… remain an employee until he can find a reason to justify his quitting. Though masking his actions as chivalry, Sammy uses the girls; for they act as catalysts that precipitate his well-considered decision to resign" (Thompson).

Stokesie, Sammy's fellow check-out clerk and friend, watches the girls alongside Sammy but is described as acting like the "responsible married man." In the second slot to Sammy's third, Stokesie is more invested in his career at the A & P, hoping to one day become manager. Along with Lengel the manager, Stokesie represents more adult male figures whose responsibilities (one to a family, the other to a job) dictate their actions, unlike the relatively unencumbered Sammy.

As the girls approach Sammy and hand over their purchase, Kingfish 'Fancy' Herring Snacks, Lengel, the manager, appears and berates the girls for their dress. The girls leave quickly and whether or not they hear Sammy say "I quit" is debatable. The reason Sammy gives Lengel for quitting, that making the girls feel badly was uncalled for, is not the only motivation for his departure. Sammy times the statement "quick enough for them to hear" thinking they will…what? Stop and gather him into their flock? Date him? Thank him? It is unclear what Sammy wants out of his action aside from some external approbation that his action was 'good' or 'right.' Sammy's justification "It seems to me that once you begin a gesture it's fatal not to go through with it" reveals not only his personality but also his limitations. Sammy is still locked in a stage of development in which he would rather 'save face' than think about repercussions of his hasty actions.

In the story's final lines, the statement "I felt how hard the world was going to be to me hereafter" allows for several interpretations. They could be a reference to the financial difficulty he will experience as a result of his job loss; to a feeling of being singled out and stuck in a working-class job where his every move is monitored and controlled; or could refer to the fact that if Sammy continues to make snap decisions without realizing the consequences of his actions, he will continue to be 'out of a job'. Sammy's character must learn that actions beget consequences.

The answer to the question 'Does Sammy reach maturity or change as a result of his experience?' is not clear by the end. Told in retrospect, after the events (perhaps years after) occurred, Sammy comments near the end that "now comes the sad part of the story…but I don't think it's sad myself" (17) leaving the reader wondering if Sammy eventually recognizes that this action was beneficial even though at the time it felt like a mistake.

Historical Context

Set in the 1950s, perhaps as much a decade after the end of WWII, and shortly after the Korean War, Sammy talks about Stokesie having two kids "chalked up on the fuselage" already. An innocuous enough sounding comment, the chalking up reference obliquely alludes to handmade, painted or stenciled war-time markings made on governmental aircraft by airmen. While some fuselage markings were of personal insignias, more prevalent were 'kill marks' which denoted the number of enemies 'hit'. The connection between Stokesie's family unit 'marks' and 'kill marks' both develops Sammy's perspective on fatherhood and emphasizes the little ways in which images of a war seep into contemporary consciousness.

Sammy makes another off-hand comment about the A&P someday (in 1990) becoming The Great Alexander and Petrooshki Tea Company. Set during the Cold War, this reference comes out of growing tensions about the spread of Communism and McCarthy-era paranoia. The explosion of debate over whether Communism offered real class change or a 'red menace' during this historical time period find their way into the text subtly: in a short reference; in a hint at class struggle; in the touch of rebellion offered by both Sammy and the girls. Both Sammy and the girls attempt to disrupt order in the market, and whether they are conscious of it or not, they respond to the civil unrest of the day.

Published about 17 years after George Orwell's "Animal Farm," Updike also uses animals (though only as descriptive devices) to explore the dangers of or problems with collectivist instinct, power and authority. Animals are used repeatedly in the text by Sammy to help describe the patrons in the A & P. Sammy 'smoothes' the 'feathers' of a female patron he then describes as 'snorting.' Speaking directly to the reader, Sammy wonders about girl's brains: "Do you really think it's a mind in there or just a little buzz like a bee in a glass jar?" (16). The shoppers are compared to chickens (feathers), sheep, and pigs, all farm animals. In the end, the fact that both groups blend, have no distinct personalities, are easily led and easily spooked, dooms them in the sense that each becomes a 'victim' of an increasingly consumer-driven economy—one group literally, the other, metaphorically.

Societal Context

Published in the early 1960s, but set in the 1950s, Updike's story of initiation reflects the kinds of contemporary social and familial situations Sammy must navigate in order to be successful as a character. Sammy's family is developed as typically working class, drinking out of beer insignia glasses and depending on his job for additional income. He must explain his actions to his family, accepting responsibility for what he has done. Sammy must also decide how he wishes to perceive and interact with women in the future.

Class difference is represented in various ways, most prominently through tension between working members of the local community and the wealthy patrons from "the Point." Illustrated via the attitude of Queenie who "remembers her place, a place from which the crowd that runs the A & P must look pretty crummy" (18) and "didn't walk in her bare feet much," (16) Sammy appears, through his actions, to attempt to join the group of girls whose social position allows them considerably more freedom than his own. Sammy wistfully imagines a cocktail party in Queenie's living room with the men dressed in suits and the women in sandals holding "drinks the color of water with olives and sprigs of mint in them" (18), illustrating his desire for more and at the same time revealing that Sammy doesn't know mint is not a martini garnish. His family's scorned 'beer culture' is pitted against Queenie's family's 'martini culture,' and suffers in the comparison.

Gender issues and the emergence of feminist consciousness are represented when Lengel states the rules that proclaim the girls be "decently dressed"—coding the norms of the day for correct dress and behavior for women—while Queenie returns "we are decent." The miscommunication in which the girls hear Lengel's comment as an ad hominem attack reflects a defensive stance and reactionary response. The dialogue highlights the emerging ideas about expectations for women's behavior, as much as it explores the teenage girls both 'owning' their sexual power while asserting their 'decency.'

The effects of a growing consumer culture are described, according to Thompson, as Sammy details the girls' bodies "in terms of common items found in the supermarket; by drawing a parallel between the store's commodities and the girls, Sammy suggests that they, like the commodities, are merely objects to be observed, handled, and used. He describes one girl as having 'a soft looking can with those two crescents of white just under it' (187), and the other as having 'one of those chubby berry faces' (188). Most significantly, he views Queenie's breasts as 'the two smoothest scoops of vanilla [he] had ever known' (Thompson).

Religious Context

Although Updike himself suffered a crisis of faith during the period in which this story was written, there is no real point at which this seeps into the text. Religion appears in only a few scattered references. Used as a conduit to developing character and setting, Lengel's traditional and 'authoritarian' stance is illustrated via the fact that he teaches Sunday school. Organized religion appears in the "congregational church" that sits at the town center, surrounded by real estate offices and the market, each representative of consumer consumption. Blodgett asserts that "Sammy impulsively assert[s] principles in a cultural climate that has put the supermarket in place of the church"). Sammy's offhand comment near the end of the story that Queenie's hands were "bare as God made them" (18) may signal not only a shift in Sammy's gaze but also allude to the 'bareness' of Eve in Eden before the fall, juxtaposing sexual desire with religion.

Scientific & Technological Context

Because the story focuses almost exclusively on Sammy's situation in the market, there is little or no direct reference to science or technology in the text. The small markers of progress: the cash register and the 'electric eye' that allows the market's doors to open appear to refer to the continuing development of consumer culture. The advertising and packaging of food parallels the advertising and 'packaging' of the girls. The electric-eye and register that Sammy hears saying "pee-pul" are both examples of a conflation of human/machine.

Biographical Context

John Updike, an only child, was born in rural Pennsylvania in 1932. His mother was also an author, writing short stories and novels. Although the family suffered financial difficulty, Updike's grades allowed him to receive a full scholarship to attend Harvard University where, in 1954, he graduated summa cum laude. In that same year, he published his first short story in the New Yorker Magazine. In an interview conducted in 1976, Updike addressed what critics perceive as his penchant for writing from experience and the difficulty of dealing with the line between fiction and autobiography in the comment "I suppose there's no avoiding it—my adolescence seemed interesting to me," while at the same time asserting "the work, the words on the paper, must stand apart from our living presences…I really don't think I am alone among writers in caring about what they experienced in the first eighteen years of life" (Charters 1525–1527). Pessimistic about the fate of literature in the twentieth century, Updike commented to an interviewer in 1999, "If you could draw a diagram of the average head, literature would have a smaller area of it then it did even in the 1950s" (Rogers).

Tracy M. Caldwell

Works Cited

Blodgett, Harriet. "Updike's A & P." *The Explicator* 61.4(2003): 236–237. Academic Search Premier. EBSCO. 12 Sept. 2005.

Charters, Ann. "John Updike." Biographical note in *The Story and Its Writer: an Introduction to Short Fiction*. Boston: Bedford books of St. Martin's Press, 1991.

Peck, David. "A & P." *Masterplots II: Short Story Series*. MagillOnLiteraturePlus. EBSCO. 15 Aug. 2005.

Rogers, Michael. Interview with John Updike. "The Gospel of the Book: LJ Talks to John Updike." *Library Journal* 124.3 (1999): 114–117.

Thompson, Corey Evan. "Updike's A & P." *The Explicator* 59.4(2000): 215–217. Academic Search Premier. EBSCO. 12 Sept. 2005.

Updike, John. "A & P." *Literature: An Introduction to Fiction Poetry and Drama*, X. J. Kennedy and Dana Gioia, Eds. New York: Pearson and Longman, 1985.

Discussion Questions

1. Have you ever been in a situation where your feelings for an object of your attraction influenced you to make poor decisions? Do you think these decisions will affect you in years to come?
2. Explore the evidence on both sides to answer the question is Sammy a hero or not?
3. If someone's actions result in positive change, does it matter whether or not their motivations were selfish or unselfish? Think about this in terms of Sammy's real reasons for quitting versus what might result in Lengel's re-evaluation of his conversation with the girls.
4. How does this story deal with emerging feminist thought in direct opposition to traditionally established views of women? Do the girls break the rules and argue with Lengel because they are making a 'political' statement or do they have other motivations?
5. Does this text, set in the 1950s, still seem to reflect issues today's teenagers face in terms of expression via clothing and the interactions between teenagers of opposite sexes?
6. Discuss the men in the text (Sammy, Lengel, McMahon and Stokesie) in terms of what general attitude each represents about women during the time period.
7. How do you interpret the actions of the three girls? Do you think they are intentionally taunting the men in the store, desiring objectification, or do you think they have some other motive?
8. Looking at the narration, discuss how old you think the narrator is when he narrates his story. What evidence can you gather via specific descriptions and word choice to advance an argument that the story is told immediately or soon after the event, or years later as an adult. Does it matter when the narrator is narrating?
9. Does it seem, via the narration and ideas, that Sammy was able to escape a blue-collar existence by the time he narrates the story? How does that matter in terms of the themes of the story?
10. How is irony used by Updike to clue the readers into details about Sammy that would be more apparent in a third-person account even though Sammy is the narrator?

Essay Ideas

1. Write an essay exploring the ways in which the Arthurian concept of chivalry is used in the story both ironically and as contemporary revision.
2. Write an essay that analyzes the development of Sammy's personality through his actions, thoughts, and speech in the text. Identify Sammy's epiphany and argue about the extent to which his experience in the A&P will influence him in the future.
3. Write an essay that explains the meaning behind major symbols in the text.
4. Write an essay exploring the ways in which this story resembles a modern day adaptation of a fairy tale (find a tale with which to compare the plot of "A&P").
5. Write a personal essay in which you explain how your own life experiences are similar to either Sammy's or the girls'.

An Occurrence at Owl Creek Bridge

by Ambrose Bierce

Content Synopsis

"An Occurrence at Owl Creek Bridge" opens in Alabama during the Civil War as Peyton Farquhar, with wrists bound and a rope around his neck, is about to be executed. He is described as a thirty-five-year-old farmer with kind eyes; not the type of man one would expect to see at a military execution. Bierce describes Farquhar to show how indiscriminate war is against man. The soldiers are depicted as stiff and unemotional; standing guard in "a formal and unnatural position." Farquhar surveys the scene around him and contemplates where he could go if he managed to escape. He hears a loud, striking noise that he later realizes is the ticking of his watch.

Section II opens with a flashback that reveals that Farquhar was a wealthy planter who, for reasons not disclosed, could not join the Confederate army. He tried to help the South during wartime as best he could. Even though he was still a civilian, he was a soldier at heart. One night, Farquhar and his wife were approached by a Yankee spy disguised as a Confederate soldier. He claimed that Union soldiers had secured Owl Creek Bridge and threatened to hang any civilians caught trying to cause trouble with the railroads or the bridge but suggests that there might be a way to "elude" the soldiers and sabotage the bridge (470).

Section III flashes forward to Farquar falling through the bridge and the reader can assume that Farquhar attempted to help the South win back the bridge and is being hung as a result. Farquhar loses consciousness for what feels like a long time and when he awakens he experiences great pain from his neck downward. As he is swinging from the bridge, the rope miraculously breaks and Farquhar sinks into the stream. He frees his hands, then tears the rope from his neck and swims to the surface desperate for air. Once above water, Farquhar's senses are keen. He sees every tree, leaf and insect on each leaf and hears even the "humming of the gnats" (471).

Farquhar is snapped out of his reverie as he realizes that he is being shot at by the Union soldiers whom have realized he has escaped. Senses still alert, he dives under water and can hear the water rushing in his ears as well as the "thunder" of gunfire above the surface (472). As Farquhar gets further downstream, he is blinded by a giant wave and realizes that they are now firing a cannon to get him. He eventually makes it to shore and rejoices in the sand which he thinks looks like "diamonds, rubies, emeralds" (472). At the sounds of another cannon shot, Farquhar runs into the forest and tries to make his way home.

He walks all day and by nightfall finds a long uninhabited road heading in the right direction. He is disturbed by the wall of trees on both sides of the road and the unfamiliar noises, "whispers in an unknown tongue," which he hears (473). He starts to feel thirsty and his neck is sore and swollen. As

7

he walks on, he can no longer feel the road beneath his feet. Suddenly, Farquhar has arrived at home and figures he must have fallen asleep walking. His house looks "bright and beautiful" and he sees his wife looking lovely and joyous coming down the walk to greet him. The fantasy is over as Farquhar reaches out to hold her and suddenly feels "a stunning blow upon the back of the neck" (473). He is hanged and his escape was nothing more than an illusion.

Symbols & Motifs

As Farquhar is about to hang, he is tortured by the slow shrieking noise which turns out to be his watch. The watch ticking "as slow as the tolling of a death knell" symbolizes the subjective nature of time (469). Time feels as if it has slowed down to Farquhar as he awaits his hanging. The ticking also represents the acuteness of the senses at crucial moments in a person's life; or in this case, the end of a person's life.

The soldiers in the story are a symbol of the coldness and brutality of war. They stand unemotional at Farquhar's hanging and when Farquhar escapes, they act only as vehicles of destruction, shooting guns and firing cannons in his direction. The soldiers lack humanity; they are merely stony figures that "might have been statues" acting out the insensitive roles of war (468).

Nature is represented as the one pure thing in the story. Farquhar rejoices at the sight of sand, the smell of flora and the sound of insects beating their wings. The stream and the woods protect Farquhar from man and his brutal weaponry, at least in his mind.

Historical Context

When the Civil War (1776–1781) began, most people believed it would be quickly resolved (Elements of Literature 476). Unfortunately, the war lasted four years and with over 600,000 people killed, it claimed more American lives than all other wars combined (476). Ambrose Bierce was a young man during the Civil War. He fought hard in the Union army and was injured in battle. Later in life, Bierce revisited the sites of the battles in which he fought (Grenander). As a result of the war, his views on life were drastically altered by his experience. In 1889, after his son was killed in a shootout with another young man, Bierce poured his grief into his writing (Grenander). The stories he wrote were not directly about his son but about his experiences with death during the Civil War. The collection, titled "Tales of Soldiers and Civilians," was published in England under the apt name of "In the Midst of Life" in reference to the passage "in the midst of life, we are in death" (Grenander).

Societal Context

Ambrose Bierce wrote with contempt for what he thought was the disillusionment of humans to have hope and sentimentality for life (466). His own view of life was much darker and his writing focused on the cruelty and barbarity of war and its complete disregard for human life. Bierce can be associated with both the realist and naturalist literary movements (466). He was an anti-Romantic and did not believe that life has neither redemption nor gratification to offer. In "An Occurrence at Owl Creek Bridge," Bierce creates sympathy for Peyton Farquhar as he attempts to escape execution by the cold, inhuman Union soldiers. However, as the reader's hopes for Farquhar's freedom reach their pinnacle, Bierce yanks them away. The hope was a farce, as Farquhar's journey was only in his mind.

Religious Context

"An Occurrence at Owl Creek Bridge" does not have a specific religious context.

Scientific & Technological Context

In "An Occurrence at Owl Creek Bridge" Ambrose Bierce contrasts the dangers of technology, complete with rifles and cannons, to the peacefulness of the natural surroundings in which Peyton Farquhar finds himself upon escape. War is represented as an entity in conflict with nature that has the power to turn human soldiers into hard, unfeeling killing machines themselves.

Biographical Context

Born in 1842 to an unsuccessful farmer in Miegs County, Ohio, Ambrose Bierce was the tenth of thirteen children (Elements of Literature 466). Later, the family moved to a farm in Indiana (Grenander). Beirce was raised in a log cabin and received little formal education (466). He learned mainly by reading the books in his father's extensive library (466).

At the start of the Civil War, when he was nineteen, Bierce enlisted in the Union Army with the Ninth Indiana volunteers. He fought in many battles and was severely wounded (466). After the war, Bierce reenlisted in the army but left after a few years and went to work at the United States Mint in San Francisco (466). While working there, he contributed satirical pieces to local newspapers. His popularity led to a job as editor of the San Francisco *News Letter* which propelled Bierce into the San Francisco literary community where he met famed humor writer Mark Twain (466). Bierce wrote with scorn about war and the corruption of the times and eventually acquired the nickname "Bitter Bierce" (466).

He moved to England in 1871 after getting married and lived there for four years while writing for humor magazines (466). In 1876, he returned to San Francisco where he wrote a regular column for which he became famous on the West Coast (466).

He never did receive wide recognition for his fiction during his lifetime (466). Bierce and his wife separated in 1888, after he discovered some love letters from another man (Grenander). Shortly after their separation, their son died tragically in a gunfight over a girl (Grenander). He and his wife divorced in 1905, and she died a few months later, an event from which Bierce never fully recovered (Grenander). In 1905, Bierce published "The Devil's Dictionary," which was a collection of ironic and humorous definitions. For example, he defined war as, "a by-product of the art of peace" and peace as a "period of cheating between two periods of fighting" (466).

Bierce moved to Mexico alone in 1913 to report on its revolution (466). He believed that dying in the midst of revolution was better than dying of old age or disease; Bierce disappeared shortly after the move. It is most likely that he was killed in the Battle of Ojinaga on January 11, 1914 (Grenander).

Jennifer Bouchard

Works Cited

Ambrose Bierce. *Elements of Literature: Fifth Course, Literature of the United States.* Holt, Rinehart and Winston, 2003. p.466–467, 474–476.

Bierce, Ambrose. "An Occurrence at Owl Creek Bridge." *Elements of Literature: Fifth Course, Literature of the United States.* Holt, Rinehart and Winston, 2003. p.469–473.

Grenander, M. E. "Ambrose Bierce." *Dictionary of Literary Biography, Volume 186: Nineteenth-Century American Western Writers.* Ed. Robert Gale. Pittsburgh: University of Pittsburgh, 1997.

Discussion Questions

1. What is the significance of the story's title? What does the word "occurrence" suggest?
2. What effect does Bierce achieve by personifying death as a dignitary on the first page?
3. How does the point of view at the beginning of the story mimic the perspective of a camera recording the opening scene of a movie?
4. How do time and sound change in the moments before Farquhar's hanging?
5. What point of view does the writer use a few seconds before Farquhar dies? Why is this suitable?
6. Was Bierce trying to get the reader to sympathize with the Union or the Confederate side of the war, or neither? Explain.
7. What does the story suggest about the nature of war?
8. How would you describe the ending of the story? Did you feel that the ending was credible and powerful or did you feel cheated?
9. What does this story reveal about the psychology of a person in a life-or-death situation?
10. What are the main themes of the story?

Essay Ideas

1. Describe and analyze Bierce's literary style. Focus on the structure of his narrative, shifts in point of view and descriptive details.
2. Write a brief narrative in which you explore the mind of a character who is in the midst of a crisis.
3. Write an essay in which you analyze how the theme of illusion versus reality is woven throughout the story.
4. Research and write a paper on one of the topics relevant to this story (e.g. life-or-death experiences, spies in the Civil War, wartime executions).
5. Examine the portrait of Ambrose Bierce by J.H.E. Partington. Write an essay in which you describe and analyze how the artist captures Bierce's enthrallment with death and the human mind.

The Bear

by William Faulkner

Content Synopsis

"The Bear," a novella that is the centerpiece of Faulkner's 1942 collection "Go Down, Moses," follows the young Ike McCaslin through several seasons of hunting Old Ben, an ancient and indomitable bear, through a hundred-square mile tract of virgin forest known as the big woods. One strand of the novella could be read as a coming-of-age story. Ike starts out as a green boy of ten, but by sixteen, under the tutelage of the Native-American and African-American Sam Fathers, he has learned to be a better tracker and woodsman than most of the adults who make up the annual hunting party. "The Bear" is also a story of the end of an age, for Old Ben represents the primeval forest itself, and to hunt and kill him is to assert man's dominance over nature. Ike is growing up in the decade after the Civil War, when men are steadily encroaching on the last of the South's true wilderness. As an adult, Ike McCaslin will eventually choose to ally himself with primal nature, giving away his land and possessions in order to live with an utter simplicity.

Both Ike and Faulkner's novella as a whole are concerned not only with the vanishing American frontier, but with the weight of history that the McCaslin family's slaveholding past represents. If the first half and final pages of "The Bear" are a relatively straightforward narrative, the long middle of the novella is a stream-of-consciousness exploration of the legacy of slavery that is epic in scope. By poring over his slaveowning father's, uncle's, and grandfather's ledger books, Ike follows the black and white sides of his family down the generations, grappling with what slavery means for his own future as well for that of his country. Ike's eventual renunciation of his inheritance represents an act of atonement: he first attempts to bequeath part of his wealth to his African-American relatives, and when that is not enough, he gives up his own share of it. His return to nature aims to redress the unnatural practice of slavery that his ancestors brought to the land.

"The Bear" is a triumph on many levels. The sections concerning the hunting party contain masterful descriptions of men, animals, and the woods themselves. The long fourth chapter of "The Bear," on the other hand, is a bravura Modernist, stream-of-consciousness performance in which Faulkner works on the widest canvas possible. That Faulkner was able to fuse the two very different halves of "The Bear" into a single work speaks to his genius as a writer.

Historical Context

The time that Faulkner wrote and reflected upon, the 1940's, was an important part of American history. Because Ike is a generation or two older than Faulkner, he has a more direct connection to the frontier, and to the men who were part of it, than the author himself would have. Ike also has a more direct connection to the legacy of slavery. Again and again, Faulkner would return not just to the Civil War period, but to the decades of transition that followed it. The southerner in Faulkner's fiction lives among battlefields and monuments that keep him from ever forgetting the weight and pressure of history. As Faulkner's protagonist Gavin Stephens says in "Sanctuary," "The past is never dead; it isn't even past."

Ike McCaslin, like so many Faulkner protagonists, feels the weight of history bearing down on him. Taking down from the shelf his slaveholding grandfather's journals, he engages with a terrible history that is at once particular to his family and shared by the entire nation. As he follows the chronicle of slaves bought, sold, and born, and reads between the lines, Ike is able to piece together his grandfather's sexual relationships with slave women—one of whom is his own daughter—Ike takes personal responsibility for acts committed before he had even been born. The slave records become part of his own identity:

> He would never need look at the ledgers again nor did he; the yellowed pages in their fading and implacable succession were as much a part of his consciousness and would remain so forever, as the fact of his own nativity (271).

Ike's subsequent quest to bestow part of his inheritance on his grandfather's African-American descendents, and his eventual decision to renounce his own inheritance altogether, is the young man's attempt to atone for his family's history. He must sacrifice himself to make up for "the white man's curse" (259).

In the wide-ranging fourth chapter of "The Bear," Ike and his cousin debate the nature of history itself, arguing about whether the course of human events hinges on the decisions of men, a predestined order decreed by God, or a random set of happenstance events. In one fascinating passage,

Ike lists a series of accidents that might be credited as winning the Civil War for the North: the Yankee discovery of the "lost dispatches" (a copy of Lee's battle plans found wrapped around a bunch of cigars), Stonewall Jackson's accidental death to friendly fire, and Jeb Stuart's unnecessary and avoidable absence at the start of the Battle of Gettysburg (286). It is a fascinating list of historical accidents that proved highly important in the shaping of history. Elsewhere in this running argument, Ike presents a stream-of-consciousness account of the history of Reconstruction in the south (289–292). Ike's broad vision and sweeping pronouncements represent a radical reinterpretation of history that a modern reader may find at turns fascinating and exasperating. He argues, for example, that it is the Northern "carpetbaggers"—men who relocated to the South in the wake of the war in pursuit of profit—who would become within a few generations the most virulent oppressors of African Americans. The carpetbaggers…

> …in another generation would be engaged in a fierce economic competition of small, sloven farms with the black men they were supposed to have freed and the white descendents of fathers who had owned no slaves anyway…and in the third generation would be back once more in the little lost county seats as barbers and garage mechanics and deputy sheriffs and mill-and gin-hands and power-plant firemen, leading… in an actual formalized regalia of hooded sheets and passwords and fiery Christian symbols, lynching mobs against the race their ancestors had come to save (290).

In this passage, among others, Ike seems to displace responsibility for the inequality and oppression that characterized the Jim Crowe South onto the North. Elsewhere Ike—horrified as he is by slavery—seems to mount a strained justification for the merits of the system. The long argument that makes up the center of "The Bear" is therefore one that the reader ought to engage in and question rather than merely accept. The purpose of Ike and his cousin's conversation is not merely to get a series of historical facts straight, but to get at the use and purpose of history itself.

Societal Context

Major de Spain and General Compson's hunting party, which forms each year in the big woods, represents an alternative to the social order that prevails in the town of Jefferson and in the rest of the south. The hunting camp is a society without women, where men are able to drink, smoke, curse, and dress and act roughly. It is, to use an old canard, Eden without Eve. Ironically, this absence of women requires the men to take on the domestic roles that they would normally expect their wives, daughters, or servants to perform. They cook, clean, mend clothing, and otherwise preside over their temporary home. It would therefore be a mistake to see the hunt as a hyper-masculine ritual, for the men actually take on a wider range of roles and responsibilities in the woods than are available to them in town.

The camp is also a place where the stark divisions between men of different races and social classes become blurred. Ike's friendship with Sam Fathers, who is African American and Native American, and with Boon Hoggenbeck, who is simple-minded and unmannered, is possible in the woods in a way it would not be in the town. Faulkner's narrator is explicit about this leveling quality: in the woods, Ike's companions are "men, not white nor black nor red, but men, hunters" (191). Being a hunter trumps all of the divisions that separate men in town. The two strands of "The Bear"—Ike's love of nature and his hatred of slavery and its legacy—intersect in this Edenic vision of the big woods as a place where men live in peace with nature and each other.

Yet beneath the surface, Faulkner's depiction of the hunting party and of Ike's efforts to locate and remunerate his grandfather's African-American descendents may reinforce the very racist assumptions that they seem to challenge. For example, the episode in which Ash, an African-American cook, tries his hand at hunting is played for pure comedy. Ash has spent much of his life accompanying Major de Spain to the woods, but has learned nothing about the actual practice of hunting. His parodic attempt at joining Ike in the hunt seems to make the point that Ash's place is in the kitchen.

A comparable dynamic is at work in Faulkner's depiction of the African-American man who marries Fonsiba, Ike's African-American cousin. A northerner, he is strikingly different from the African-Americans who grew up in the slave-holding southern states. Ike describes the stranger this way:

> He looked past McCaslin and saw the man, the stranger, taller than McCaslin and wearing better clothes than McCaslin and most of the other white men the boy knew habitually wore, who entered the room like a white man and stood in it like a white man, as though he had let McCaslin precede him not because McCaslin's skin was white but simply because he lived there and knew the way, and who talked like a white man too... (274).

When Ike sees the northerner some months later, however, on the Arkansas homestead that he and Fonsiba are attempting to cultivate, everything has changed. Ike finds the man

> Reading... before that miserable fire for which there is not wood sufficient to last twenty-four hours, in the same ministerial clothing in which he had entered the commissary five months ago and a pair of gold framed spectacles which... did not even contain lenses, reading a book in the midst of that desolation, that muddy waste fenceless

and even pathless… and over all, permeant, clinging to the man's very clothing and exuding from his skin itself, that rank stink of baseless and imbecile delusion. (278).

The African-American man who had proudly born Fonsiba away is revealed to have been operating under a "baseless and imbecile delusion" that he could live self-sufficiently. It is hard not to interpret this as indicting the enfranchisement of the South's African-American population. Faulkner sets up the figure of the proud, free-born black man only to reduce him to folly and madness. The former slaves and their children, Faulkner seems to imply, are not truly capable of taking care of themselves.

Religious Context

Ike and his cousin, McCaslin, speak of the legacy of slavery and of man's relationship to nature in explicitly Christian terms; the two are attempting, in their protracted debate, to justify the ways of God to men. It is appropriate, therefore, that much of Ike's moral struggle centers on his interpretation of the books that his grandfather has passed down to him. The ledgers have some of the power and significance of a holy book. Ike imagines…

It was as though the ledgers in the scarred crack leather bindings were being lifted down one by one in their fading sequence and spread open on the desk or perhaps upon some apocryphal Bench or even Altar or perhaps before the Throne Itself for a last perusal and contemplation and refreshment of the Allknowledgeable (261).

The ledgers track his grandfather's and his uncles' history of purchasing, trading, and managing their slaves, and also hint at darker episodes, revealing which of the slave children were fathered by Ike's grandfather. In reading the ledgers, Ike becomes a witness to these acts; he resembles the Recording Angel of medieval tradition. Yet the ledgers also serve to indict him, for the land and wealth that he has inherited are themselves the legacy of slavery. In Ike and Faulkner's estimation, slavery is America's original sin.

Ike's struggle to understand the ledgers is matched by his struggle to interpret the Bible. When McCaslin cites the Bible as a defense of slavery, identifying the African-American slaves as "the sons of Ham," Ike objects (260). He makes a distinction that stands in sharp contrast to fundamentalism or scriptural literalism: "There are some things He said in the Book, and some things reported of Him that He did not say" (260). Ike knows how to distinguish between what is true and what is not in the Bible:

How will we choose which is truth? You don't need to choose. The heart already knows. He didn't have his book written to be read by what must elect and choose, but by the heart (260).

Ike has read the Bible and his grandfather's ledgers, and his heart has led him to reject not only the principles that justified slavery, but the inheritance that slavery has bequeathed him.

Like his namesake, Isaac, Ike is a child of his father's old age. In the Book of Genesis, Abraham is called on to sacrifice his son Isaac to God. Faulkner's novel reverses this logic, for Ike McCaslin instead sacrifices his patrimony. Giving up his inheritance is an attempt to atone for the curse of slavery that his father and grandfather have left him. Ike is a child of old age, but also a child of a new age, and his self-sacrifice allies him both with the sin of Adam and the salvation of Jesus Christ.

Scientific & Technological Context

Perhaps no innovation was more central to America realizing its vision of Manifest Destiny than the railroad. A town that boasted a railroad station—or even just a flag-station along the rails—was connected with the rest of American, and goods and people could flow to and from it. The railroad stood for progress and for civilization, for man asserting himself over nature. In "The Bear," the railroad is the harbinger of doom both for the big woods and for the primal society that the hunting party constituted. Although the train had long been a presence in the woods, it "had been harmless then" (320). One narrow track could not really make a difference to all that trackless wilderness; the train ran with an "illusion of frantic rapidity between the same twin walls of impenetrable and impervious woods" (320). On Ike's last visit to the big woods, however, soon after Major de Spain has sold his land to a logging company, Ike finds that everything has changed. The train has "brought with it into the doomed wilderness even before the actual axe the shadow and portent of the new mill" (321). The primeval forest falls to the train and the mill, its old trees being sawed up into new boards. Ike understands "why Major de Spain had not come back, and that after this time he himself, who had had to see it one time other, would return no more" (321). The woods stand in the way of progress, and the old forest and the old way of life that it engendered are coming to an end.

Ike, however, has already decided to ally himself with nature and the past rather than with progress and the future. In a self-determined rite of passage, Ike sets out into the woods alone and unarmed. After having walked for nine hours, he realizes that something still separates him from the primeval forest:

> He stood for a moment—a child, alien and lost in the green and soaring gloom of the markless wilderness. Then he relinquished completely to it. It was the watch and the compass. He was still tainted. He removed the linked chain of the one and the looped thong of the other from his overalls and hung

them on a bush and leaned the stick beside them and entered it (208).

Leaving his watch and compass behind means abandoning the last of the aid that modernity might provide him. He relinquishes these objects in order to be entirely accepted by nature itself, and it is only after doing so that he sees Old Ben emerge from and disappear back into the woods.

Biographical Context

"The Bear" emerged during a period in the early 1940's (1942) when Faulkner was supporting himself by writing stories for magazines. He wrote and sold a story called "Lion," which contained much of the material about Boon training a hunting dog that would be a match for Old Ben. The story drew on Faulkner's own experience hunting as a boy and a man. He then went back and expanded the story, adding Ike McCaslin's character and focusing on the young man's initiation into the hunt. At that point, Faulkner had a long story that essentially consisted of the first three sections of "The Bear."

Faulkner put the story down in order to write a treatment for a screenplay and to work on a few other Hollywood projects. But "The Bear" seemed still to hold his attention. He wrote to his friend and editor Robert Hass, saying "There is more meat in it than I thought, a section now that I am going to be proud of and which requires careful writing and rewriting to get it exactly right" (Blotner 432). He began to write part four of the novella; the stream-of-consciousness section in which Ike and his cousin McCaslin argue over Ike's giving up his share of their grandfather's patrimony. It was a decision that would give "The Bear," which had begun as a simple story of a hunt, its sweeping, epic scope. In the fifth section of the story, Faulkner returns to the big woods and to Ike's final hunt before the logging company destroys the virgin forest. In its final form, "The Bear" successfully integrates two forms of storytelling that are radically different in scale and import. Comparing the various stages by which Faulkner constructed the novella gives one rare insight into his creative process and his powers of accretion and synthesis.

When Faulkner received the Novel Prize in 1949, he used "The Bear" as source material for his acceptance speech. The novella was indeed something Faulkner was "proud of" and had gotten "exactly right."

Matthew J. Bolton

Works Cited

Blotner, Joseph. *Faulkner: A Biography*. New York: Random House, 1984.

Faulkner, William. *Go Down, Moses*. New York: Random House, 1942.

Discussion Questions

1. Is Ike right to consider himself culpable for the sins of his father and his grandfather? What obligation does he have to his grandfather's African-American descendents?

2. Do some strains of Ike's philosophy and some aspects of his way of life amount to a defense of the status quo in race relations? What is Ike's vision for redressing the legacy of slavery?

3. What does Old Ben represent? How would you describe the relationship between the bear and the men who hunt him?

4. Contrast Lion, Boon's hunting dog, with Old Ben. Are they both forces of nature, or is Lion somehow less connected to nature than the old bear?

5. Based on your reading, trace out the white and black branches of the McCaslin family tree.

6. How do the tragic and comic elements of this novella intersect? Is a character like Boon meant to be a tragic figure or a clown?

7. Is the fourth, stream-of-consciousness section of "The Bear" meant to be easily reconciled with the rest of the novel? How does Faulkner create meaning through disrupture and juxtaposition?

8. How does the complexity of the fourth section of the novel reflect the complexity of the family relations and historical legacy with which Ike grapples? Explore the relationship between content and form.

9. What is the role of women in this novel? Pay particular attention to the scene between Ike and his wife in their boardinghouse bedroom.

10. Discuss the novel's final image: Boon Hoggenbeck guarding a tree full of squirrels. What might this scene be meant to represent?

Essay Ideas

1. Contrast the various representations of the Native Americans in "The Bear" or in Faulkner's other work. Do Sam and Boon represent a basic dichotomy in depictions of Native Americans: the Indian as either noble savage or violent manchild?

2. Explore the logic behind Ike's hunting an animal that he sees as the spirit of the woods itself. Is his hunting the bear a consummation or a betrayal of the hunter's way of life?

3. Is the hunting party opposed to or complicit in the notion of Manifest Destiny as represented by the train and the lumber mill?

4. Read "The Bear" in comparison with one or more of the great nineteenth-century American novels, such as "Moby Dick," "Uncle Tom's Cabin," or "The Last of the Mohicans."

5. Read Hemingway's "In Our Time" and compare his treatment of Native Americans, hunting, and the woods to Faulkner's.

6. Contextualize Faulkner's view on the legacy of slavery by reading it in light of historical documents or accounts. Consider comparing Ike's vision of American history to that of Abraham Lincoln as articulated in The Emancipation Proclamation.

7. Ground Ike's mythic stream-of-consciousness account of slavery, the Civil War, and reconstruction in the context of a historical account of the period. How accurate is Ike's conception of, for example, the relationship between the influx of carpetbaggers and the rise of the clan?

8. Identify Biblical symbols and parallels in "The Bear." Discuss the woods as a second Eden, the legacy of slavery as a form of original sin, or the bear itself as a religious symbol.

9. Read Faulkner's Nobel Prize speech alongside the passages of "The Bear" from which he drew the speech's material. What does comparing the two reveal about Faulkner's process of editing or of reinventing his own work? What choices did he make in transforming the passage into a speech?

10. Consider any one of the five sections of "The Bear" as a self-contained story. How does Faulkner create a story arc and satisfying conclusion in this individual section? To what extent should "The Bear" be read as a series of self-contained episodes?

Bluebeard's Egg and Other Stories

by Margaret Atwood

Content Synopsis

Published in 1983, "Bluebeard's Egg and Other Stories" is Margaret Atwood's second short-story collection.

The first story, "Significant Moments in the Life of My Mother," is based on Atwood's own mother. It is a series of vignettes of the narrator's mother's life, from when she was a child growing up in Nova Scotia, through marriage and the narrator's childhood. The vignettes might also be read as a lesson in how a writer forms character, in that they reveal not the "big" moments such as weddings, births, and deaths, but incidents that are more revealing about the woman telling the story, such as the first vignette in which the mother inadvertently killed some baby chicks given to her at Easter. Retelling the stories is, for the narrator, a struggle in understanding. She understands that her mother "had as much fun as possible," yet this concept of fun was far different than it is now. The messages of the stories, as well as where and when they are told, also reveal older attitudes about differences between genders, since some stories are only told among women, in the kitchen, to spare men from the details. The progression of stories ends with a depiction of the narrator as becoming quieter, more withdrawn, settled into her "gloom," while her mother keeps busy around her; there are few stories to tell of this time. The lack of story illustrates the gulf between them as the narrator becomes an adult and a separate person from her mother: "I had become a visitant from outer space."

Another autobiographical story, "Hurricane Hazel," depicts the narrator in the tenth grade with a boyfriend named Buddy, whom she describes as an "accident" since he'd been "handed over" by a friend who was dating Buddy's cousin (34). She describes Buddy as living in a world with "a long list of things that could never be changed or fixed" (33). When the narrator goes away for the summer to her family's primitive cabin, she is "surprised and horrified" when Buddy, Charlie, and Trish show up for a visit. They take her out on a picnic and Buddy gives her his identification bracelet. When the narrator returns to school she continues her relationship, but Buddy becomes more of an "obligation" (54). The relationship ends when she refuses to go out with him because of an impending storm, which turns out to be a hurricane. The disappointment of the storm's wreckage is compared with her lack of feeling about the breakup, likening it to the "flatness of the water, the melancholy light" (58).

In "Loulou; or, the Domestic Life of the Language," a successful potter lives in a house of current and ex-lovers, all of whom are poets. She houses and feeds the poets, yet they constantly regale her with sarcasm and petty word plays. In contrast to the poets, Loulou dislikes talk. She seduces her accountant. Fearful of money and behind on her taxes, the accountant represents someone who might take care of her. She also likes the way the accountant sees her: as creative and successful, in contrast to the way the poets treat her as a dim-witted mother. She worries that they do not seem to really know her and in fact make up things about her; they even talk about her in the third person in her presence. She worries that maybe she is what they say she is; "maybe she has only… their words, for herself" (82). Perhaps she is also trying to escape the observations of lovers who know her too well, since they tease her, unknowingly, about seducing the accountant. In the end, though, she and the poets seem to come to some truce; she suggests they order out for pizza, and then she realizes that they accept her as she is. They require no more, no less.

In "Uglypuss," Joel, a street-theater artist, leaves his apartment just when he knows his ex-girlfriend, Becka, is coming over to try to reconcile with him. He meets a woman in a bar and sleeps with her. When he returns, he finds his apartment destroyed and his cat, Uglypuss, gone. Becka has put it in a bag and sprayed it with boot spray. She directs her anger at the cat because she identifies its masochistic tendencies with herself, to demonstrate how she believes she was treated by Joel.

The next two stories feature a woman named Emma who believes she is invincible. She believes this because, as explained in "The Whirlpool Rapids," she survives an accident on a trip down the Niagara whirlpool rapids. Surviving the accident not only makes her fearless, it also makes her what others perceive to be selfish, because she comes to realize "how very little difference she makes in the general scheme of things" (129). In the second story, "Walking on Water," Emma goes with her older, married lover and former college professor, Robbie, to a Caribbean island. Here she mistakenly lures Robbie into her world of optimism and invincibility. Looking for a challenge, Emma decides to undertake a walk on an underwater ridge to a nearby island and persuades Robbie to come with her. She gets ahead of him and he nearly drowns. Here Emma finally confronts her vulnerability: not for her own life, but for those she loves.

In the title story, "Bluebeard's Egg," Sally is a middle-aged woman contemplating her marriage to Ed. Ed is a heart surgeon yet Sally regards him as a simpleton, largely because he seems clueless when it comes to women. He cannot tell why his previous two marriages ended in divorce; he seems impervious, for the most part, to other women's charms. In truth, she is troubled that he "is a surface, one she has trouble getting beneath" (167). Sally is supposed to rewrite the Bluebeard fairy tale from a contemporary viewpoint for a night class. She decides to make Ed the egg which the young women have to keep safe, but she gives up on this idea, instead moving to her preparations for a party. At the party, she catches Ed touching her friend inappropriately. Both Ed and the friend act as if nothing has happened. Sally then panics, wondering if she's been duped all this time: "Possibly Ed is not stupid. Possibly he's enormously clever" (182). The thought is so shocking to her she hears a roaring sound in her head. Just as the women in the Bluebeard story are victims of their curiosity, Sally finds her whole world changed when she actually gets some insight into her husband.

"Spring Song of the Frogs" focuses on Will, who is divorced. Will seems bewildered and disappointed by the world of women. A date disappoints for her predictability; a niece is in the hospital for an eating disorder. An old girlfriend comes to visit him in his country home and they sit outside to listen to the frogs, but the thrill of it falls flat, as he realizes there "aren't as many frogs as there used to be," evoking, perhaps, the narrowing of his options as he grows older.

In "Scarlet Ibis," a family of three are in the Caribbean and go on a special tour to see the scarlet ibis, a rare red bird. Christine and Don are clearly in a tense time in their relationship. Don is "under a lot of pressure," and Christine wonders if it has to do with her. Christine fantasizes of being able to tell him to stay sitting in his seat to just look at her, a fantasy she finds herself unable to act upon. While they are on the tour boat, it springs a leak, though their guide ignores it. The tourists then scramble to save themselves, plugging up the leak and bailing water. The hole in the boat is fixed by a large woman sitting on the leak. When they see the birds, it is enough to make them momentarily forget their problems. Don even holds Christine's hand and later, Christine dismisses the difficult time in their relationship as a phase.

Alma, the mother of a young child separated from her husband, is making a salt garden in the story "The Salt Garden." The salt garden summons up a childlike curiosity for Alma. This curiosity was not necessarily a scientific one, as her father had thought and hoped, but one that invited her to imagine a more magical world. Perhaps it is this magical world that she is trying to escape to when she has seizure-like episodes, which she calls hallucinations. Alma experiences these episodes with both Mort, her estranged husband, and her lover, Theo, a dentist. Both men regard themselves as the cause. Alma thinks of herself as "doing nothing," referring to her care-taking of the house and her daughter. The only concern she seems to express about the future comes with her fantasy of escaping into a root cellar to avoid a nuclear attack. What seems to most plague Alma is her inability to make decisions. Most notably, she does not want to choose between Mort and Theo. Rather, she seems to want to stay in the kind of relationship "limbo" she's in for as long as possible. It becomes apparent that this is just another fantasy when Theo makes a comment that someday their affair will end. The story ends with another one of Alma's episodes. When she comes to, she says that she thought perhaps it was "the real thing"—presumably, she means death. In a sense, something does die: her fantasy world.

Thus the salt garden becomes a metaphor for the enduring nature of her life, despite the inevitable changes: "After everything is over, she thinks, there will still be salt" (259).

"In Search of the Rattlesnake Plantain" returns the reader to the autobiographical territory of Atwood's parents in the northern woods, with the narrator, her parents, and her friend Joanne. The narrator observes that she fears loss, contrasting her reason why to her friend. The narrator observes her friend's loss of a pair of binoculars and reflects that, while she may not be as well-equipped as Joanne, having something means that you can lose it. Her father is preoccupied with a different kind of loss: the disappearance of various species in the natural world. The rattlesnake plantain, a plant they are searching for, is one of these. Their "search" serves as a metaphor for the threat of the loss of her parents, as she and Joanne get separated from her parents, thinking they've found a short cut, they find her parents have reached home first. The story sets the stage for an event that happens some time afterwards, when the narrator returns home to help with her ill father, who is suffering mental deterioration from an earlier stroke. The father offers up some hopeful tidbits, including the observation that the rattlesnake plantain is making a comeback.

In "The Sunrise," a woman artist named Yvonne approaches strange men to ask if she can paint them. She is an established artist, who had a show once closed down for displaying erect penises on her pictures. Yvonne has had to learn to live alone: she's "like a plant… a rare one, which can flourish and even live only under certain conditions" (282). Though to everyone else Yvonne seems satisfied with life, there is an undercurrent of sadness, such as when she meets a former lover and observes that she misses the sensations he aroused in her. Yvonne has mostly closed herself up, evoking an image of a flower closing its petals. The one offering she makes to this former lover is one of her "secrets," she gets up every morning to watch the sun rise. Later, when she asks a man with an orange Mohawk haircut if she can paint him, she seems to be somewhat shaken out of her complacency. The man nearly forces himself on her and disparages her work. He shows her his artwork, which consists of cut-up pictures of women's naked body parts. She makes love to him, then afterwards questions her whole existence, based on the man's assertions: "… if art sucks and everything is only art, what has she done with her life?" (296). The last two passages of the story juxtapose possible tools for suicide that Yvonne keeps in her apartment (pills and a razor blade) with a scene of a sunrise, a sign she has retained hope and faith in herself and in her art.

"Unearthing Suite," the fourth of Atwood's autobiographical quartet, is also the last story in the collection. Again, she writes of her parents and their inevitable deaths. Here they announce to the narrator that they've bought their urns. The story celebrates the unique natures of each parent. As depicted in "Significant Moments," the mother is a high spirit, someone who seeks pleasure and speed and takes up ice-dancing at an old age. The father pursues his life-long interest in nature and science, prowling through the woods. Their difference, and perhaps complementarity, can be summed up in the two phrases, "My father likes projects. My mother likes projects to be finished" (307–8). The "unearthing" of the title is conveyed through the father's unearthing of the creatures found in the earth, and of the "earths" she describes as their various homes or "seasonal dens" (306). The story ends with the parents relating an event they find nearly miraculous: the finding of a dropping that they identify with that of a fisher, an animal that has become rare and has never before been seen in that area. To her parents, the dropping is a sign of something miraculous, of "divine grace," a sign of momentary radiance in their "mundane, familiar, much-patched" lives (323).

Historical Context

"Hurricane Hazel," as an autobiographical story, is shaped by Atwood's own experiences of being a teenager in the 1950s, the time when "dark melancholy figures suddenly surfaced on the movie screens," a time marked by conformity and very specific roles for men and women (Sutton 73). The hurricane of the title also corresponds to an actual natural event which provides "the emotional metaphor for the ending of the narrator's relationship with Buddy" (Sutton 73).

Time and place shape the characters of Atwood's parents in her other autobiographical stories (see Biographical Context). As products of the early part of the twentieth century, they also stand as contrasts to the social conventions of that time, especially Atwood's mother, who prefers her life in the "bush" with Carl Atwood over a "fate worse than death: antimacassars on the chairs" ("Unearthing Suite" 312). References to the natural landscape in these same stories also document the encroachment of civilization on the northern wilds of Canada. One narrator notes the changing forest that is becoming "more and more like a curtain, a backdrop behind which is emptiness, or a shambles. The landscape is being hollowed out" ("In Search of the Rattlesnake Plantain," 271).

Many of the stories illustrate the tensions of changing mores for women and men in the aftermath of the Women's and Civil Rights Movements of the 1960s and '70s, such as in "Uglypuss," "The Sunrise," and "Bluebeard's Egg." (See Societal Context.)

Societal Context

While Atwood's work might be labeled as feminist, she does not resort to easy solutions of women triumphing over men. Instead, she looks squarely at the various tensions in relationships. While in "Bluebeard's Egg," Sally has a smugness about her husband Ed, she finds that he's smarter than he seems. "Uglypuss" puts an ugly twist on female revenge, and while "The Salt Garden" depicts a very human woman as both a wronged wife and the "other woman," she lives in a fantasy world. Even in "Hurricane Hazel," the narrator likens Buddy giving away his identification bracelet with the giving away of his identity. Perhaps the most feminist of her stories are her autobiographical ones, depicting her own mother as rebelling against the conventional role of suburban housewife. In "The Salt Garden," Alma makes a salt garden for her daughter and recalls her fascination with science as a young girl, an interest encouraged by her father, who thinks she exhibits scientific curiosity when what she is really interested in is how it ignites her imagination.

Still, the two stories depicting men as the main characters ("Uglypuss" and "Spring Song of the Frogs") do not depict them very sympathetically: both seem locked into their own self-absorbed worlds, unable to make the step out into vulnerability with women close to them.

"The Sunrise" takes up issues of the woman as artist that, according to Rosemary Sutton, was a difficult issue for Atwood as a young woman. Much of Atwood's work "is known for its feminist critique of the canonical, white male Tradition" (Cooke 24). Yvonne is a painter of men, of male bodies, performing a "revision" of the tradition of using the female form as the subject. That Yvonne is single is not incidental; for a female artist coming of age in the 1950s and '60s, a choice had to be made between marriage and art. "Loulou" similarly takes up complicated issues of the woman as artist versus woman as householder. In this story, the two roles seem to have reached a kind of compromise.

Religious Context

While not immediately obvious, several of the stories address themes of religion and spirituality, particularly rooted as they are in Christian values of humility and redemption. Emma, the character

featured in two connected stories, seems to believe she has been "chosen" in some special way to survive life-threatening ordeals. She does not express this belief in any overtly religious way, however. "Walking on Water," the second of these stories, is a classic example of hubris, the belief that one can take on god-like powers. Certainly the act of "walking on water" evokes images of Jesus parting the waters in the Bible. While Emma does succeed in her challenge, she does so at the expense of her lover, therefore exposing her vulnerability.

In "Scarlet Ibis," another story that takes place in the Caribbean, Christine (whose name certainly invites a religious reading) meets a woman on a tour who identifies herself as a Mennonite missionary. She is uncomfortable by the woman's identification of herself in this way: "Religious people of any serious kind made her nervous" (214). She is made even more uncomfortable by the woman's disclosure that one of her children is dead, not commenting for fear that the woman might say something "about the will of God, and she didn't want to deal with that" (214). Later, when the boat they're on springs a leak, it is the Mennonite woman who offers a solution: she sits her large bottom on top of the hole, acting, in a comedic way, as the savior. This woman serves as a contrast to Christine, who, though virtuous in not throwing her Pepsi can into the water, steers clear of anything that would call attention to her. She reflects that she would have never done what the woman had done. She cringes at the woman's comment that you could look at the ibis "forever": "Forever was loaded" (224). Her body is even a contrast: while she feels "fragile and empty, like blown glass," the Mennonite woman is "luminous and pink and round as a plum" (225). While in retrospect, Christine talks about her experience as you would any story of your vacation, with the funny anecdotes sprinkled in, it obviously has had a more profound effect on her, perhaps even a spiritual one. Spirituality might be expressed as an understanding that one is just a small piece of a larger, mysterious whole, and if so, this can be seen in her observation of the scarlet ibis, when she glimpses another world, "not real but at the same time more real than the one on this side" (225).

Scientific & Technological Context

Informed by her own upbringing as the daughter of an entomologist and having spent much time in the Canadian northern woods, the connection between Atwood's fiction and science is primarily that of one concerned with the natural world. Nature performs not only a backdrop, but also powerful metaphors for the characters in her stories. A hurricane marks a break-up in "Hurricane Hazel." A woman braves first a whirlpool than an underwater ravine in "Two Stories about Emma." The scarlet ibis, a rare bird, is a sign of hope for a married couple, as a sunrise is for a single woman artist ("The Scarlet Ibis" and "The Sunrise"). A salt garden is made by Alma in a story by that name, and also acts as a metaphor for both her fantasy life and for the feeling of solidity in her life. Both "In Search of the Rattlesnake Plantain" and "Unearthing Suite" comment obliquely on the ecological devastation of humanity, yet remain hopeful, with the father's observation that the rattlesnake plantain is making a comeback and with the mother's discovery of a fisher scat on the roof of a house.

Biographical Context

Born in 1939 in Ottawa, Canada, Atwood is the daughter of unconventional parents. Her father was a field entomologist and her mother was something of an adventurer, preferring life in the bush. The family spent winters in various cities and the rest of the year primarily in the remote areas of northwestern Quebec. Atwood did not spend a full year in school until she was in the eighth grade and her family moved to Toronto.

Atwood attended Victoria College at the University of Toronto and, after graduating in 1961 with a BA in English literature, she went on to Radcliffe College at Harvard University to study for her M.A. and PhD. She received her M.A., and then took a teaching job in Vancouver. She returned to Harvard in 1965, but did not finish her dissertation. She married a writer, Jim Polk, whom she divorced after six years. After some travel, she eventually settled in Toronto, where she still lives now with writer Graeme Gibson. She and Gibson have a daughter named Jess.

Influential and prolific, Margaret Atwood is known worldwide and has the distinction of being one of the few literary writers who can command a wide audience. An author of poetry, prose, nonfiction, criticism, screenplays, and children's books, Atwood has been publishing work since her poetry collection "The Circle Game" appeared in 1966. (An earlier chapter-book, "Double Persephone," was self-published while she was in college, in 1961.) Her first novel, "The Edible Woman," was published in 1969. Her most recent book is "The Penelopiad," a retelling of the story of Penelope, the wife of Odysseus. Her other short-story collections include "Dancing Girls" and "Wilderness Tips." Another collection, "The Tent," was published in early 2006.

"Bluebeard's Egg and Other Stories" contains four "quasi-autobiographical" stories, some of the few autobiographical pieces published by Atwood (Sutton 33). These include "In Search of the Rattlesnake Plantain," which, according to Nathalie Cooke, is an accurate portrayal of Atwood's father's stroke, one that began his decline until his death in 1993 (4). Biographer Rosemary Sutton attributes the description of the brother's Greek lessons in "Hurricane Hazel" to real life experiences with Atwood's brother, Harold (33). "Significant Moments in the Life of My Mother" is based on Atwood's mother, also named Margaret.

"Unearthing Suite" is the fourth, more fully developing her parents as characters and the importance of nature in their lives. In these stories Atwood evokes her relationship with her parents as well as the natural environment of the Canadian Northwood's that had such an impact on her growing up.

As many writers do, Atwood undoubtedly drew on life experiences in other stories. As noted in "Social Context," "The Sunrise" takes up conflicts similar to ones that Atwood experienced as a young woman writer, in which she was faced with choices between love and art. Another female artist is featured in "Loulou, or the Domestic Life of Language," which also presents a house of male poets, perhaps drawing on Atwood's own experiences with male poets in the 1950s and '60s. One of the places Atwood frequented as a college student was the Bohemian Embassy, a private club/coffee shop in Toronto that featured young writers. Rosemary Sutton describes the atmosphere at the Embassy as "hypocritical" towards women. "All the propaganda still insisted that creativity was male," Sutton observes, quoting Atwood as saying that "'Not even the artistic community offered you a viable choice as a woman'"(103).

Alyssa Colton

Works Cited

Atwood, Margaret. *Bluebeard's Egg and Other Stories*. 1983. New York: Fawcett Crest, 1986.

Cooke, Nathalie. *Margaret Atwood: A Critical Companion*. Westport, Connecticut and London: Greenwood Press, 2004.

Lannon, Mary. "Margaret Atwood." *Writers Online* 3.1 (fall 1998). Albany: New York State Writers' Institute. 23 November 2005.

Sutton, Rosemary. *The Red Shoes: Margaret Atwood Starting Out*. Toronto: HarperCollins, 1998.

For Further Study

Margaret Atwood Reference Site http://www.owtoad.com

Margaret Atwood Society Homepage http://www.mscd.edu/~atwoodso/

Ridout, Alice. "Temporality and Margaret Atwood." *University of Toronto Quarterly* 69.4 (fall 2000): 849–871. Academic Search Premier. 6 December 2005.

Wilson, Sharon Rose. *Margaret Atwood's Fairy-Tale Sexual Politics*. Jackson University Press of Mississippi, 1993.

Discussion Questions

1. What was the most significant difference between the narrator and the mother that was observed in the story, "Significant Moments in the Life of My Mother"?
2. Why do you think the narrator in "Hurricane Hazel" was drawn to Buddy? What did their relationship consist of?
3. Do you think the relationship Loulou has with the "poets" is one based on equality? Why or why not?
4. Who is the more sympathetic character in "Uglypuss"? Who do you identify with?
5. In "Two Stories about Emma" the main character feels invincible. What are the advantages and disadvantages of this attitude?
6. Discuss how "Bluebeard's Egg" uses the original fairy tale, and whether or not this story is a "rewriting" of it.
7. How do the various descriptions of women serve to characterize the main character, Will, in "Spring Song of the Frogs"?
8. At the end of "Scarlet Ibis," Christine reflects that her "tensions with her husband were" just a phase. Is there anything in the story to suggest that there are other reasons why their marriage improved?
9. What is the significance of Alma's "hallucinations" in "The Salt Garden"? What purpose do they serve in the story?
10. What is the significance of the rattlesnake plantain in the story "In Search of the Rattlesnake Plantain," especially considering that the purpose of the characters' walk is to find a bog?
11. Do you think Yvonne is satisfied with her life in "The Sunrise"? Why or why not?
12. What is the meaning of "suite" in the title of the story "Unearthing Suite"?

Essay Ideas

1. Choose two stories in the collection and compare and contrast their depictions of women or men.
2. Choose one story and explain the role of nature imagery in it.
3. Analyze how stories and storytelling are commented on in "Significant Moments in the Life of My Mother."
4. Analyze the use of fairy tale in "Bluebeard's Egg" and what it says about the theme of the story.
5. Analyze the depiction of romantic love—or the lack of it—in one of the following stories: "Bluebeard's Egg," "Hurricane Hazel," "Uglypuss," "Walking on Water," "Scarlet Ibis," or "The Salt Garden." What is Atwood saying about the nature of love in the story?

The Cask of Amontillado

by Edgar Allan Poe

Content Synopsis

This popular and often-anthologized short story takes place in Italy and is told fifty years after the events depicted have occurred. It begins with a startling declaration: "The thousand injuries of Fortunato I had borne as best I could, but when he ventured upon insult I vowed revenge" (310). Thus the reader is thrust immediately into the action, and into the cunning mind of the narrator, Montresor. Like "A Tell-Tale Heart," "The Cask of Amontillado" directly addresses its readers-putting us, in effect, in the uncomfortable position of Montresor's confidants and making us feel like accessories to his crime. "You, who know so well the nature of my soul," he continues in the story's second sentence, "will not suppose, however, that I gave utterance to a threat. At length I would be avenged […]" (310). While we learn a great deal about Montresor in these first few sentences (for instance, he's proud, methodical, and vengeful), the exact nature of the "insult" Fortunato has supposedly inflicted upon Montresor remains unclear to us, though it appears that the former has somehow hurt the latter's family or family honor. In any event, Fortunato fails to recall Montresor's coat of arms or family motto-which latter, appropriately, is "Nemo me impunelacessit" (313) or "No one provokes me with impunity." Whatever Fortunato's transgression, Montresor seeks revenge for it in a bizarre

and terrible fashion, as the story's plot unfolds together with his plan.

Before Fortunato arrives on the scene, Montresor explains his strategy for vengeance. He "must not only punish but punish with impunity"; he must reveal himself as an "avenger" to his victim; and he must use duplicity to achieve his end: "It must be understood that neither by word nor deed had I given Fortunato cause to doubt my good will. I continued, as was my wont, to smile in his face, and he did not perceive that my smile now was at the thought of his immolation" (310). More perceptive than his adversary, Montresor has discerned Fortunato's "weak point," which is the great pride he takes in his "connoisseurship of wine" (310). Because Montresor, himself "skilful in the Italian vintages" (310), shares Fortunato's knowledge of and pleasure in wines, he is well positioned to exploit his victim's vulnerability.

Once he has introduced himself and his foe, Montresor establishes the story's setting: "It was about dusk, one evening during the supreme madness of the carnival season, that I encountered my friend" (310). (Montresor's use of the word "friend" exemplifies his taste for irony, which he indulges throughout the rest of his tale). Appropriately, Fortunato is dressed in "motley," wearing the "parti-striped dress" and the "conical cap and bells" (311) of a fool or court jester. Caught up in celebration, he has "been drinking much" (310) and

27

is therefore particularly susceptible to Montresor's machinations. Montresor tells Fortunato that he has bought "what passes for Amontillado" (a pale dry sherry) and has been "silly enough to pay the full Amontillado price" (311) without asking for his friend's advice. "As you are engaged, I am on my way to Luchresi," he lies. "If any one has a critical turn it is he" (311). Fortunato exclaims that "Luchresi cannot tell Amontillado from Sherry," and Montresor quickly exploits his condescending remark: "And yet some fools will have it that his taste is a match for your own" (311). After this clever stab at his pride, Fortunato naturally insists upon accompanying Montresor to his wine cellar, despite the latter's protestations that the "vaults are insufferably damp" and will aggravate his companion's "severe cold" (311).

In an ironic twist, Montresor has given his servants "explicit orders not to stir from the house" during the carnival, thereby ensuring "their immediate disappearance, one and all" (312) and eliminating any witnesses to the crime he plans to commit. He and Fortunato descend into the vaults that contain his wine which, significantly, also function as the "catacombs of the Montresors" (312). After Fortunato suffers a coughing fit, Montresor announces that they must leave the noxious vaults. His ironic declaration at once provides further insight into Fortunato's apparent offense against him, eases his own conscience somewhat, and makes certain they will remain where they are: "'Come,' I said, with decision, 'we will go back; your health is precious. You are rich, respected, admired, beloved; you are happy, as once I was. You are a man to be missed. For me it is no matter. We will go back; you are ill, and I cannot be responsible. Besides, there is Luchresi....'" (312). Fortunato refuses to return, of course, and avers that he "shall not die of a cough." Montresor responds with characteristic irony: "True-true" (312). He then offers Fortunato some wine (ostensibly to bolster his health, but in reality to inebriate him further), and the two continue.

After Fortunato remarks that the catacombs are "extensive," his companion replies that the "Montresors [...] were a great and numerous family" (313). He reminds Fortunato of their motto and their coat of arms. After they pass "long walls of piled skeletons, with casks and puncheons intermingling, into the inmost recesses of the catacombs" (313), Montresor again asks Fortunato to consider his health and leave. Fortunato again refuses, and he again drinks some wine.

At the end of the catcombs, they reach a smaller crypt whose "walls had been lined with human remains, piled to the vault overhead" (314). One wall has been cleared of bones, and within it there is "a still interior crypt or recess, in depth about four feet, in width three, in height six or seven" (314). Montresor asks his companion to proceed into this space, telling him that within is the Amontillado. Once Fortunato does so, Montresor immediately enchains him and begins sealing the niche with the stones and mortar he has hidden nearby for this purpose. While he works, he enjoys Fortunato's struggles and screams—at one point even echoing the latter and outdoing them "in volume and in strength" (315). Before Montresor places the final stone, Fortunato acts as if the situation were a practical joke and says, "Let us be gone" (316). Montresor echoes him, and Fortunato cries, "For the love of God, Montresor!" (316). "Yes," his murderer replies, "for the love of God!" (316). From this point Fortunato is silent. Montresor concludes his masonry work and replaces "the old rampart of bones" (316). He concludes his tale by noting that "[f]or the half of a century no mortal has disturbed them. In pace resquiescat!" (316).

Symbols & Motifs

The vaults: The vaults under Montresor's house function as wine cellar, family crypt, prison cell, and torture chamber. In this fashion, many of the story's principal topics—wine, death, family honor, and punishment—are symbolically linked by its setting. The surface region, full of celebration and merriment, seems to contrast dramatically with the subterranean one, marked by gloom and horror. In psychological terms, these two realms can be interpreted as the conscious and unconscious minds; in mythological terms, as the world and underworld. The two spaces are not quite as different as they appear, however, for above the ground the public "madness of the carnival season" (310) rages, while beneath it Montresor's private madness reigns; furthermore, both worlds are characterized by self-indulgence and masquerade.

Doubles: Montresor and Fortunato have a good deal in common. Both are proud, both are connoisseurs of wine, both are aristocrats. Moreover, at several points throughout the tale Montresor echoes Fortunato's words and actions. By drawing parallels between these two characters, Poe employs a common Gothic device which he also uses in "William Wilson" and "The Fall of the House of Usher"—that of the doppelganger or evil twin. It is noteworthy that Montresor seems to lose the heart for his grisly task and hurries to complete it after he and his double cease mirroring each other, that is, when he twice calls out "Fortunato!" and receives no verbal response from his companion (316).

Historical Context

In describing his family crypt, Montresor references "the great catacombs of Paris" (314). Strictly speaking, the term "catacomb" applies to vast underground cemeteries for the early Christians and Jews of classical antiquity. The so-called catacombs of Paris are actually former limestone quarries that became burial grounds only in the late eighteenth century. These subterranean crypts, which comprise extensive and complex networks of tunnels, are described by Victor Hugo in his novel "Les Misérables." Bona-fide catacombs of the sort Montresor and Fortunato pass through have existed

throughout Italy since the time of ancient Rome. The fact that most of the story's action takes place in a milieu so heavily weighted with history, and death, underscores the potentially fatal influence of the past upon the present and future.

It is impossible to determine precisely when the story is set. Montresor's reference to Parisian catacombs implies a late-eighteenth- or early-nineteenth-century setting. Montresor's emphasis on his family's coat of arms and his own membership in the Freemasons, however, suggests his tale could take place much earlier—perhaps as early as the Italian Renaissance, a period marked by tremendous conflict and intrigue between both noble families and independent city-states. During the Renaissance, the fortunes of families such as Fortunato's and Montresor's might easily rise and fall dramatically within a generation or two. In any event, by leaving his tale's temporal setting open to interpretation, Poe enhances its nightmarishly disorienting quality.

Societal Context

In Italian society, family honor has always been of considerable importance. Accordingly, Montresor's family motto and coat of arms play a key role in the story. The coat of arms—a colorful and symbolic design associated with a specific individual or family, often of noble status—derives from patters marked on the armor and shields of medieval knights to identify them during battles and jousts. The Montresor family's coat of arms suggests both combat in general and conflict between the two men in particular. The "huge human foot d'or, in a field of azure" that "crushes a serpent rampant whose fangs are imbedded in the heel" (313) signifies Montresor's destroying Fortunato after being wronged by him. The design also implies that this injury might have poisoned Montresor. Furthermore, that Montresor knows so well the symbols associated with his family, while Fortunato fails to remember them, indicates not only the former's emotional investment in his family honor but also the extent to which the latter ignores it, at his peril.

The Montresor family motto, "Nemo me impunelacessit" (313) or "No one provokes me with impunity," illustrates the Italian tradition of the vendetta (from the Latin vindicta or "vengeance"), an inter-familial feud usually provoked either by a murder or by a grave insult of some sort. The vendetta often operates in societies, for instance, medieval Italy, in which power is fairly decentralized and held by a few prominent families. When Montresor picks up his trowel and begins work with his bricks and mortar, he literally and figuratively takes vengeance out of the law's hands and into his own. The feudal (and feuding) society in which he and Fortunato live allows him to seek his vengeance "with impunity" (310).

Religious Context

The story is set during the time of carnival, a religious festival that takes place before Lent—a period before Easter marked by prayer and penance—in Roman Catholic (and some Christian Orthodox) countries. Carnival has always involved masquerade, and in Venice masks have been especially significant. Prior to the eighteenth century and the beginning of Austrian hegemony, residents of Venice were permitted to wear masks from the festival of St. Stephen at the start of carnival until midnight on Shrove Tuesday.

Religion—specifically, Roman Catholicism of the sort most likely practiced by Montresor and Fortunato—may also be involved in the story's narrative structure. An intriguing question posed by the first-person point of view is, "To whom is Montresor telling his story, and why?" It seems unlikely that, after "half a century" (316), Montresor would be confessing to the authorities whom he has planned so carefully and subtly to avoid. He might be boasting to an old friend, but such self-congratulation would be at odds with the regret revealed (though denied) in the final

lines of his tale: "My heart grew sick; it was the dampness of the catacombs that made it so" (316). (Just as Fortunato is ultimately endangered not by the damp but by Montresor, so Montresor is finally sickened not by the damp but by his own lethal vengeance.) Perhaps the most likely auditor is a father-confessor, a Catholic priest from whom he seeks forgiveness in the final years of his life. This reading is supported by Montresor's addressing his audience as "You, who so well know the nature of my soul" (310). If Montresor has indeed decided to confess at last his long-ago sin to a priest, this line becomes as ironic as those he delivers to Fortunato.

Scientific & Technological Context

As Montresor guides Fortunato through the vaults, he calls upon him to "observe the white web-work which gleams from these cavern walls," which his companion identifies correctly as nitre (313). Later, Montresor again draws Fortunato's attention to this substance: "'The nitre!" I said; 'see, it increases. It hangs like moss upon the vaults. We are below the river's bed. The drops of moisture trickle among the bones. Come, we will go back ere it is too late. Your cough-'" (313). Nitre, or potassium nitrate, may be found in crystal form upon cave walls, as in Poe's story. Its presence in Montresor's vaults not only indicates how damp and therefore unhealthy they are, but also, because nitre can be used to create gunpowder, implies the potential explosiveness of the situation.

Biographical Context

Edgar Allan Poe was born to traveling actors in Boston in 1809. His father vanished, and his mother died two years after his birth. A Richmond merchant, John Allan, took young Edgar into his home but never adopted him. Their already-tense relationship became yet more difficult after Allan refused to honor his foster son's sizable gambling debts, thereby compelling him to withdraw from the University of Virginia less than a year after his enrollment in 1826. Poe enlisted in the army in 1827 and entered West Point in 1830, but he was dishonorably discharged a year later. He then worked as a newspaper and magazine editor in Richmond, Philadelphia, and New York. In 1836 he married his thirteen-year-old cousin, Virginia Clemm, who died in 1847 after a long struggle with tuberculosis. In 1839, to generally favorable reviews, Poe published "Tales of the Grotesque and Arabesque," which contained twenty-five tales. Poe gained a reputation first as a literary critic and then, after "The Raven and Other Poems" was published in 1845, as a writer. He died in Baltimore in 1849.

"The Cask of Amontillado" first appeared in the November 1846 issue of *Godey's Magazine and Lady's Book*. Those in the publishing world of the time interpreted it as Poe's response to attacks made upon him by his onetime friend Thomas Dunn English in the New York *Evening Mirror*—which included a charge that Poe was a heavy drinker. Moreover, Poe (who often entered feuds with other literary figures) had been involved in a dispute with William Evans Burton, the founder of *Burton's Gentleman's Magazine*. In a letter Poe wrote to Burton five years before "The Cask of Amontillado" was published, he rebukes his correspondent for overreacting to a perceived slight. As Poe explains to Burton, "no real injury, or attempt at injury, have you ever received at my hands." He

then anticipates the Montresor family motto: "If by accident you have taken it into your head … that I am to be insulted with impunity I can only assume that you are an ass" (Silverman 316).

If we read "The Cask of Amontillado" biographically, it is worth noting that the Montresor family motto is also the national motto of Scotland, that the "Scotch" John Allan, like Fortunato, was an oenophile and a member of the Masons, and that the word "Amontillado" comprises the name "Allan." Thus the story may be read as an attack upon Poe's stepfather who, like Fortunato, was "rich, respected, admired, [and] beloved" by all save his stepson (Silverman 316–17).

Jamil M. Mustafa

Works Cited

Hayes, Kevin J., ed. *The Cambridge Companion to Edgar Allan Poe. Cambridge Companions to Literature.* Cambridge: Cambridge UP, 2002.

Kennedy, J. Gerald, ed. *A Historical Guide to Edgar Allan Poe.* Oxford: Oxford UP, 2001.

Poe, Edgar Allan. "The Cask of Amontillado." *In The Fall of the House of Usher and Other Writings: Poems, Tales, Essays and Reviews,* ed. David Galloway. London: Penguin, 2003. 310–16.

Silverman, Kenneth. *Edgar A. Poe: Mournful and Never-ending Remembrance.* New York: Harper Perennial-Harper Collins, 1991.

Discussion Questions

1. Examine the story for instances of irony. What role does irony play in this tale?
2. What has Fortunato done to Montresor and his family? Does Fortunato's punishment fit his crime?
3. Are we meant to sympathize with Montresor? How would the story differ if told by Fortunato?
4. Why does Montresor end his tale with "In pace resquiescat!" ("Rest in peace!")?
5. To whom is Montresor telling his story? Why does he wait fifty years to tell it?
6. Why does Montresor echo Fortunato's screams and last words?
7. Why does Montresor twice ask Fortunato to turn back and leave the vaults?
8. What is the significance of clothing and costume in the story?
9. What does wine represent in the story? Why is the tale entitled "The Cask of Amontillado," though there is no such cask?
10. Does Montresor feel any regret for murdering Fortunato?

Essay Ideas

1. Compare and contrast the characters of Fortunato and Montresor.
2. Analyze the significance of the text's first-person point of view.
3. Analyze the story's symbolism and other figurative language.
4. Explore the role played by pride in this tale.
5. Compare this story to any text mentioned above in terms of theme, character, figurative language, or other literary elements.

Cathedral

by Raymond Carver

"If the writing can't be made as good as it is within us to make it, then why do it? In the end, the satisfaction of having done our best, and the proof of that labor, is the one thing we can take into the grave."

Raymond Carver

Content Synopsis

"Cathedral" appeared in Carver's collection of the same name in 1983 and has since been heralded as his "masterwork" (Boyle 119). At first glance, the story is deceptively simple, detailing the events of a single evening's interactions between an unnamed couple and the wife's blind friend, Robert. Information about past experiences of each of the characters peppers the text as the story progresses. The first paragraph establishes the narrator/husband's perspective on a number of things: his wife, her friends, and, perhaps unwittingly, his narrow-minded perceptions of the world around him. The flat tone that he employs when describing events like Robert's wife's death add to the reader's understanding of the two-dimensional nature of his character, a man with little or no human interaction whose ideas about people and places are developed via television and the movies:

"In the movies, the blind moved slowly and never laughed. Sometimes they were led by seeing-eye dogs. A blind man in my house was not something I looked forward to" (269). Robert's blindness "bothered me," explains the narrator in the first paragraph, and "he was no one I knew" (269). His ignorance and prejudice is compounded by a later statement about Robert's dead wife: "Beulah! That's a name for a colored woman" (271).

The relationship between his wife and Robert, a man for whom she worked reading aloud from papers and other printed material not available in Braille, culminated in her last day in his office where he "asked if he could touch her face" (269). This simple example of human contact and the ways in which it deepened her relationship with Robert are lost on the narrator, perhaps until the very end when he experiences a similarly physical connection with the blind man. The wife's prior relationship experience is important terms of why she stays with her husband, and why she has stayed in touch with Robert over the years. Her first marriage to a commissioned officer ended badly, as the isolation and continual relocation of military wifehood coupled a sense of being "cut off from people" caused her to attempt suicide before finally divorcing (270).

Robert's visit clearly bothers the narrator on several levels. His discomfort with a social situation (dinner) is compounded by thinly veiled jealousy and defensiveness that belies anxieties about the state of his marriage. Before Robert arrives, the wife says matter-of-factly to her husband: "If you love me, you can do this for me. If you don't love me, okay" (273). This exchange culminates in the wife throwing a potato at her husband who, shortly thereafter, begins drinking.

The issues in the marriage between the narrator and his wife are illuminated via details of three other relationships, the narrator's wife and her first husband, the narrator's wife and Robert, and Robert's relationship with his deceased wife. The narrator relates, somewhat sneeringly, that Robert and Beulah were "inseparable" and wonders at the idea that the couple lived their lives together without Robert "ever having seen what the god-damned woman looked like" commenting "it was beyond my understanding" (271). He begins to feel badly for Beulah whom he imagines had a very dissatisfying relationship, describing, without a hint of irony, that she "could never see herself as she was seen in the eyes of her loved one," and was a woman "who could go on day after day and never receive the smallest compliment from her beloved" (271).

The narrator's character is developed via his conversations and his narration of events, both essential to understanding his epiphany near the end. His wife notes that he doesn't have any friends. He is continually surprised as his ideas of blindness are, one by one, demolished during his actual encounter with a blind person. His incredulity that Robert wears a beard, smokes and does not use a cane or wear dark glasses, the way he eats his food, his drinking and agreeing to smoke marijuana, all come as revelations to the husband. Robert exudes patience when dealing with the con-versational blunders of the narrator: "Which side of the train did you sit on?" he asks Robert, won-dering what scenic view the man enjoyed on his train trip (272). Robert's character, described as a man who was "a regular blind jack-of-all-trades,"

enjoys several diverse occupations, as well as a hobby operating a ham radio through which he communicates with others as far away as Guam and Tahiti (275). In contrast, the husband describes his job of three years as one he doesn't like, yet makes no effort to leave.

The large amounts of alcohol consumed by all: the narrator's drink before they arrive, the three big glasses of Scotch they enjoy when Robert enters their home, two more drinks before dinner, sev-eral drinks after dinner, and another while smok-ing two joints, lubricates conversation and allows the husband's walls to come down. However, the deep problems the husband faces in actually con-necting with others in a meaningful way are still present. Even after Robert agrees to try smoking marijuana with the narrator, he still "didn't want to be left alone with a blind man" (275). The hus-band's attitude does shift once his wife falls asleep and the husband says to Robert, "I'm glad for the company," following with an internal monologue "and I guess I was. Every night I smoked dope and stayed up as long as I could before I fell asleep. My wife and I hardly ever went to bed at the same time" (276).

As the two watch/listen to television programs, Robert delivers a line of dialogue that provides the narrator with a philosophy of life in contrast to his own: "I'm always learning something. Learning never ends. It won't hurt me to learn something tonight. I got ears" (276). Robert appears to be the catalyst for change in the lives of both the wife and husband, by offering them an opportunity for gen-uine connection and/or by subtly using statements to influence the two. When the program on cathe-drals begins, the narrator describes the images to Robert, and in a moment of inspiration the husband realizes, "Something had occurred to me. Do you have any idea what a cathedral is?" (277). Robert is able to respond with a laundry list of descrip-tive details but ultimately decides that he didn't really "have a good idea," urging the narrator to explain instead, valuing direct human communication over the impersonal narration of the television. The challenge of describing a building whose importance relies not only on its architecture but also on its emotionally connected function as a holy space proves difficult to the husband, who is unaccustomed to expressing any real emotions aside from bitterness and sarcasm. The husband takes on the request with a kind of obsession: "Say my life depended on it" (277), which in a sense it does. After unsuccessfully attempting to explain the cathedrals, Robert hits on a problem, asking the narrator, "Are you in any way religious?" (278). Thinking about this question, the husband confesses his lack of belief in religion, which he recognizes makes it impossible for him to fully describe a cathedral. Robert, unwilling to give up on their project, asks the husband to find some paper and draw a cathedral with him. The narrator who, for the bulk of this short encounter has repeatedly expressed distaste for Robert and a desire for him to go upstairs, suddenly roots around the house for paper, and sits on the floor with Robert, Robert's hand over his, and begins to draw. This intimate moment in which the husband has the first real physical contact with anyone in the story initiates his epiphany; his realization that there is more to life than an unrewarding job and marriage, self-imposed isolation and views predicated on third party sources instead of real life experience.

The wife wakes up while they are drawing, unable to understand what they are doing or why. In an interesting twist, she is suddenly left out of the loop as the relationship between Robert and the narrator becomes the focus. Robert explains: "we're drawing a cathedral, me and him," emphasizing the connection between the two men (279). Robert instructs the husband to close his eyes and continue drawing. The narrator's description that, "his fingers rode my fingers as my hand went over the paper. It was like nothing else in my life up to now," presents a very different persona than the narrator of a few hours ago who didn't even want Robert in his house (279).

After they finish drawing, instead of looking at what they created, the narrator chooses to keep his eyes shut, savoring the moment and seeming to understand that the real accomplishment was not in the product but rather in the process of creating. Many critics have suggested, focusing on the husband closing his eyes and keeping them that way the husband's epiphany comes in the form of realizing what it means to be blind. While this certainly is true, the statement fails to explore the arguably deeper epiphany of the protagonist hinted at in his last lines: "I was in my house. I knew that. But I didn't feel like I was inside anything," alluding to the opening up of the narrator to new possibilities with further implications than understanding the blind experience (279).

Historical Context
Carver usually focuses on the microcosm of everyday life and its everyday challenges rather than the macrocosm of political and historical struggles and their effects. Although the early 80's were rife with important historical and literary moments, Carver, for the most part, does not cite any historical happening as influencing his writing of "Cathedral." Stull points out that "In life, art, and even death, Raymond Carver's double, mentor, and companion soul was Anton Chekhov" (qtd. in "Biography"). This time period saw the emergence of literary trends towards experimental and what would be termed minimalist, postmodern or realist fiction, yet it is difficult to separate how the styles influenced Carver versus how Carver influenced these movements. According to Stull, "[Carver] laid the groundwork for a realist revival in the 1980s. ("Biography").

Societal Context
The issues involved with alcoholism and how it can be destructive to individuals and relationships

are explored in this story. The narrator's disaffected state of being seems exacerbated by his turn to alcohol and drugs, which he uses both to provide a comfort level during Robert's visit and as a strategy to deal with his frequent nightmares. The narrator seems more comfortable with maintaining the 'status quo' of a life described as pretty unsatisfying. The reader is left to question whether or not the narrator's lack of motivation and unhappiness are caused by or are the cause of his substance abuse. As a long time alcoholic, Carver often creates characters with various addictions, specifically alcohol. The fact that Carver was finally sober when he wrote this story directly affects the ending in which he is able to imagine a kind of optimistic hope for the narrator, whereas in earlier writing his darkened vision would arguably have left his protagonist in a more ambiguous position.

Religious Context

Near the beginning of the story, the narrator says Grace before they eat: "Now let us pray…pray the phone won't ring and the food doesn't get cold" (273); a sarcastic and irreverent comment that elicits a frown from his wife. The most obvious religious reference in the story is the television special on cathedrals and the shared drawing made by the narrator and Robert. The drawing project in which the husband seems to recognize that aspects of his life are empty as a result of his lack of faith in anything is central to the development of his emerging consciousness. When Robert asks him to comment on his religious beliefs, the husband replies, "I guess I don't believe in it. In anything. Sometimes it's hard…cathedrals don't mean anything special to me. Nothing." (278). The superficial way in which the husband approaches his cathedral description mirrors his shallow view of the world. The fact that a cathedral is a location where people gather to share meaningful contact makes it an important symbol in the story,

exemplifying yet again the ways in which either the narrator's life is devoid of human connection or he is simply ignorant of the benefits of human connection to others.

Scientific & Technological Context

The most important technological reference in the text is to the television. The television is discussed during the initial conversation between the three characters when they compare models and whether or not they have black and white or color screens. A double-edged sword, the television certainly arguably serves a connective purpose. Much like the first radio broadcasts, television provided people with the opportunity for a shared experience in the sense that they all viewed the same images at the same time, even though they did not occupy the same physical space. However, the television, like the computer, while offering a space in which individuals can interact, excerpts human contact from this connective opportunity. Thus, throughout the story, the reader must consider the importance of both modes of connection, identifying the fact that a lack of balance can be destructive to an individual's development of empathy, and insert its own ideas in the place of learned experience on the part of the viewers.

Biographical Context

Carver's early history is almost as interesting as his vast cache of stories and poetry. Born in Clatskanie, Oregon in relative poverty with a family whose members did not attend school beyond the eighth grade, Carver spent his life moving from place to place, occupying many diverse jobs including hospital custodian, textbook editor, lumber mill worker, and prescription deliverer. Carver was essentially always on the move, settling for only a few years in any one place.

Carver married 16-year-old Maryann Burk in 1957, and the couple had two children shortly thereafter. Experiencing "blue-collar desperation on terms more intimate than most American Writers," Carver turned his life experiences and need for cash into arguably some of the best short literature of the century (Kennedy and Gioia 99). After receiving his degree from Humboldt State College in 1963, Carver continued to be plagued by personal and financial problems that restricted his writing time: "getting milk and food on the table, getting the rent paid, if a choice had to be made, then I had to forego writing" (qtd. in Charters 209).

In 1967, Carver met Gordon Lish, who published several of his stories in *Esquire*. Carver achieved his style of stripped down fiction through intense revision, sometimes as many as "twenty or thirty drafts" (Charters 209) and is one of the few writers who revised a published story significantly and published it as well ("The Bath" and "A Small Good Thing"). John Gardner, Carver's mentor at Chico State, instilled the value of revision by requiring at least ten drafts of any story handed him. Gardner also gave Carver keys to his office, where in isolation he was able to "under[take] my first serious attempts at writing" (qtd. in Charters 1418).

Carver survived one failed marriage, several bankruptcies, and an alcohol addiction which he overcame in 1977, the same year he met his future wife, Tess Gallagher. His success in battling alcohol addiction was one of his great achievements, of which he stated: "I am prouder of that, that I quit drinking, than I am of anything in my life" (qtd. in Kennedy and Gioia 269). Like many authors who write realistic fiction, Carver was frequently asked if his experiences inspired his writing. Carver once responded: "None of my stories really happened, of course…but there's always something, some element, something said to me or that I witnessed, that may be a starting place" (qtd. in Gioia and Gwynn 1750). Tess Gallagher states in the introduction to Carver Country, that the story "Cathedral" was inspired by the visit of

blind friend Jerry Carriveau to their home (Gioia and Gwynn 1750-51). According to Esquire editor Tom Jenks, the incident was almost identical to the story: "Tess had fallen asleep and then a program on cathedrals came on. The blind man had no idea what a cathedral looked like, and in the end, Ray sat on the floor with him, holding his hand, drawing a cathedral" (qtd. in Gioia and Gwynn 1751). T. C. Boyle identifies Carver as "foment[ing] a revolution in American letters similar to the effect the work of certain seminal punk bands had on the epicene of rock music of the late seventies" (119).

A self-described "cigarette with a man attached to it" (Stull "Biography"), Carver died of lung cancer at the age of fifty on August 2, 1988, just two months after his marriage to Gallagher. The wedding "took place in Nevada, in the Heart of Reno Chapel, and Carver described it with gusto as a 'high tacky affair.' True to the tragicomic occasion, Gallagher went on to a three-day winning streak at roulette (Stull, "Biography"). One of the most oft quoted pieces of poetry by Carver is his poem "Gravy" published posthumously in *All Of Us*, the poem represents Carver's attitude about his impending death. The last few lines sum up:

"I'm a lucky man.

I've had ten years longer than I or anyone expected. Pure gravy. And don't forget it."

Tracy M. Caldwell

Works Cited

Boyle, T. C., Ed. *Doubletakes: Pairs of Contemporary Short Stories*. Massachusetts: Thompson Wadsworth, 2004.

Carver, Raymond. "Cathedral." *The Longman Anthology of Short Fiction: Stories and Authors in Context*. New York: Longman, 2001. 269–279.

Charters, Ann, ed. *The Story and Its Writer: An Introduction to Short Fiction*, 3rd ed. Boston: Bedford Books of St. Martin's Press, 1991.

Gioia, Dana and R. S. Gwynn, Eds. *The Longman Anthology of Short Fiction: Stories and Authors in Context*. New York: Longman, 2001.

Kennedy, X. J. and Dana Gioia, Eds. *Literature: An Introduction to Fiction, Poetry and Drama*, 4th Ed. New York: Pearson Longman, 2005.

Stull, William L. "Prose as Architecture: Two Interviews with Raymond Carver." *Clockwatch Review* Inc., 1995–96. 25 Sept. 2005.

_____ "Biographical Essay." 1 Nov. 2005.

Discussion Questions

1. How do you feel about the narrator at the opening of the story? Why? Do your feelings about him change during the course of the story? Why?

2. Does the narrator feel like a 'real' character, or a caricature? What details provided in the story support your assertion?

3. Explain the relationship between the narrator's wife and himself. Would you call them happy?

4. Discuss how the relationship between the narrator's wife and Robert differs from her relationship to her present husband and previous one.

5. Why do you think the wife stays with the narrator?

6. Do you think religion has a significant part in the development of the story? For example, did the subject of the drawing have to be a cathedral or could it be something else?

7. Carver explores his style "it's possible… to write about commonplace things and objects, using commonplace but precise language, and to endow those things, a chair, a window curtain, a fork, a stone, a woman's earring—with immense, even startling power" (qtd. in Kennedy and Gioia 111). Where do you see this in the story "Cathedral"?

8. How is suspense created and sustained through this story that takes place during a few short hours one evening during a simple dinner party?

9. Explain what the narrator means by the last line that he "didn't feel like [he] was inside anything"?

10. Where do you see the narrator's feelings about Robert begin to shift? Why? Do you think it is only the alcohol and marijuana that forge the connection between the two men, or is it something deeper?

11. Is it possible for a person to have a life changing experience in the course of one evening? Do you think the narrator will change as a result of the experience with Robert, or will he remain the same?

Essay Ideas

1. Look at the relationships provided in the story: Robert and his wife, Robert and the narrator's wife, the narrator's wife and her first husband, and compare them to the relationship between the narrator and his wife. How do all the relationships in the story serve to develop the suspense and growth of the narrator through the story?

2. Analyze the changes in the narrator's character as he moves towards his epiphany. Explore three or more moments that exemplify stages in his development. Discuss where you believe the epiphany is in the story and how it will change the narrator.

3. Dialogue is essential in this piece to both move the plot forward and provide three-dimensional portraits of each character. Choose representative quotes from each character and analyze how they clue readers in to the conflicts in each speaker's life.

4. Write an essay that argues either for or against an interpretation of the narrator as an antihero.

5. The main action of the story involves eating, drinking and smoking. How do these actions become essential in terms of setting up a situation in which human interaction is highlighted?

Everything That Rises Must Converge

by Flannery O'Connor

Content Synopsis

Written in 1961, "Everything That Rises Must Converge" is unlike most stories by Flannery O'Connor in that it focuses on "topical issues" ("Habit," 436) more than religious themes. She wrote that she was "highly pleased" with the story and she asked that the title be used for her second collection of stories, which was not published until after her death in 1964.

The central character, Julian, sees himself as an intellectual and a liberal. He has graduated from college and wants to be a writer, but he sells typewriters and lives with his mother. Because her ancestors owned plantations and slaves, the mother sees herself and her son as members of the Southern aristocracy, even though she now rents an apartment in a deteriorating neighborhood and worries about having spent $7.50 on a new hat. She bought it, she says, echoing the words of the sales clerk, because she "won't meet [herself] coming and going" (406). She claims to have "great respect for [her] colored friends" (409), but refers to her childhood nurse, Caroline, as an "old darky" (409). Furthermore, she believes that African Americans were "better off" when they were slaves," and that while they should rise, they should rise "on their own side of the fence" (408). She is racist and segregationist, but she is not malicious.

Julian, who fancies himself to be intellectually and morally superior to his mother, shows no appreciation for the sacrifices she has made for him so he can have straight teeth and a good education. He believes that he is intelligent in spite of his "third-rate college" and that "in spite of all her foolish views, he was free of all prejudice and unafraid to face facts" (412). Yet the narrator also shows that he secretly shares some of his mother's values. When she speaks of the large house of her ancestors, which he had seen only after it was decayed and inhabited by a black family, we are told, "He never spoke of it without contempt or thought of it without longing" (408).

Julian accompanies his mother as she rides a city bus to a weight-loss class downtown because her doctor has ordered her to "lose twenty pounds on account of her blood pressure" (405). She has insisted that he accompany her at night since the buses have been fully integrated. When they first board the bus and sit on one of the benches in the front that was formerly reserved for white riders, no African Americans are on the bus. As she puts it, "I see we have the bus to ourselves," (410), which causes Julian to cringe. After she initiates a trivial conversation with a fellow passenger, Julian withdraws into "the inner compartment of his mind where he spent most of his time" (411). From within this "mental bubble" he looks down on his mother as his mental and moral inferior, and he believes he is "emotionally free" (412) of her.

When a well-dressed African American man sits on the bench across from them, Julian moves across to sit next to him, knowing the action will provoke his racist mother. He tries to start a conversation by foolishly asking the man for a match despite the "No Smoking" sign and the fact that he does not have any cigarettes. His mother says nothing, but her face turns "unnaturally red, as if her blood pressure had risen" (413). Despite his own foolishness and her looks of reproach, he feels that "he could with pleasure have slapped her as he would have slapped a particularly obnoxious child in his charge" (414). Julian fantasizes about ways to "teach her a lesson" by bringing home a black friend or a "beautiful suspiciously Negroid woman," but he has never had any success in "making any Negro friends" (414).

A "sullen-looking colored woman" enters the bus and, to Julian's "annoyance," squeezes into the seat next to him while her little boy sits next to his mother. When he realizes that the black woman's hat is identical to his mother's, he thinks she will learn a lesson about her pettiness, but instead she seems to find it funny. Considering all children to be "cute," she plays games with the child, much to the displeasure of the boy's mother. When Julian's mother says, "I think he likes me" and smiles with "the smile she used when she was being particularly gracious to an inferior," the boy's mother yanks him back to her "as if she were snatching him from contagion" (417). Yet the white woman continues to play games with the boy.

Both sets of mothers and sons get off at the same stop. When, out of habit, Julian's mother offers the boy a penny, the other woman explodes at her racist condescension, hitting the white woman with her bulging pocketbook. Julian helps his mother up and begins to lecture her: "[T]he old world is gone. The old manners are obsolete and your graciousness is not worth a damn" (419). But she continues to walk off in the wrong direction, saying she is going home and adding, "Tell Grandpa to come

get me" (420) and then "Tell Caroline to come get me" before she collapses, apparently the victim of a stroke. Her last appeal, then, is not to her son but to the black nurse of her youth.

The story ends with Julian's awareness of his dependence. He cries, first, "Mother," then "Darling, sweetheart, wait," and then "Mamma, Mamma"(420), but she apparently dies, and "The tide of darkness seemed to sweep him back to her, postponing from moment to moment, his entry into the world of guilt and sorrow" (420).

Symbols & Motifs

The title: O'Connor said she took the title for the story from Teilhard de Chardin, a theologian who said that evolution led to the progress of species into higher forms of consciousness, which would eventually converge into a unified consciousness (Walters 127). John May points out the positive meaning of the title: "In each of the levels of conflict, there is a higher level of convergence that reflects the forward thrust of the evolutionary process," even if the process is "painful and gradual" (97). With her death, Julian's mother does receive his love and respect, and Julian is painfully awakened to "the complexity of racial tension. The condescending heart is less dangerous than the martial mind" (May 97).

The hats: As Dorothy Walters points out, the coincidence of the hats represents not only the doubling of the black and white women, reinforced by the exchanging of sons, but it also indicates the "the blacks' economic stature is rapidly overtaking that of the whites' and that blacks have won as much freedom to pursue absurdity as the whites" (129).

Clothing more generally is significant of social status. Julian's mother makes a point of wearing gloves to her exercise class, and when Julian makes a display of removing his tie, she insists that he not disgrace her in such a way. The business attire of the black man on the bus further indicates the economic progress being made by some African Americans.

Historical Context

The "threat" of desegregation, as it was perceived by segregationists in the United States, created social and political turmoil throughout the 1950s and early 1960s. After the Supreme Court decision declaring segregated schools to be unconstitutional, governors and legislators in many Southern states found ways to postpone the integration of schools, despite repeated rulings against them by federal courts.

The issues of integrating public transit came to national attention with the arrest of Rosa Parks in December, 1955, for refusing to yield her seat in the middle section of a bus in Birmingham, Alabama, to a white man. At the time, the front of the bus was reserved for whites and the back for blacks, with seats in the middle available for blacks only if white people did not want them. Her arrest led to the boycotting of buses by black patrons, led by Dr. Martin Luther King, and an appeal of her conviction to the U.S. Supreme Court, which banned segregation in public transportation.

However, in Atlanta, the city O'Connor likely saw as the setting for the story, the integration of buses stalled until after similar arrests of six black ministers in 1957, and even then it took another two years before courts ordered integration of Atlanta buses and trolleys (Myrick-Harris and Harris). Therefore, at the time O'Connor wrote the story in 1961, the issues involved would have continued to reverberate.

Societal Context

Racism was so deeply ingrained in the Southern states that attempts to overcome it and the Jim Crow laws that institutionalized and helped perpetuate white racism faced huge obstacles. For generations, whites and blacks in the South had lived in a legal and social system based on the assumption of white superiority and black inferiority. Maintaining separate schools, with far more resources going to the white schools, made it difficult for black students to gain an education comparable to that of most whites. The use of separate train cars for African Americans and, with the coming of motorized buses, of a system requiring them to sit only in the back of the bus, served to reinforce the sense of superiority among whites and of inferiority among blacks. The institution of lynching, which continued into the 1940s, particularly dehumanized African Americans. Whites participating in lynchings often saw them as festive occasions, memorialized in celebratory photographs and the taking of the victims' body parts as souvenirs.

The depth of the entrenchment of racism is reflected in the obstacles presented in attempting to integrate institutions. For example, the Catholic Church had reached out to both black and white parishioners, but with separate churches and schools for the races. In 1957, the bishop of the diocese in Atlanta, Francis Hyland, suggested to a group of priests that the Catholic high schools should be integrated rather than exist as two separate institutions, one for white and one for black students. But the advisors talked him out of the proposal, arguing that it would hurt the Church's attempts to win new parishioners and perhaps provoke the state of Georgia to retaliate by taxing the schools and taking away teachers' credentials. Even in 1961, when Bishop Hyland joined the bishops from Savannah and Charleston in a public announcement that the parochial schools would be integrated as quickly as could be safely achieved, many Catholics reacted angrily and withdrew from the Church. Catholic schools were not integrated until after the public schools (Moore).

Religious Context

This story is rare for O'Connor because it does not carry a clear religious message. Virtually all of her stories combine satire of the characters with themes about the need for religious faith and the power of grace to change the characters' perceptions of themselves and their world. In her letters, she refers to "Everything that Rises Must Converge" as her "topical story" (436, 537), and she implies that she wrote it because she needed an artistic change: "I've been writing for sixteen years and I have the sense of having exhausted my original potentiality" (468).

However, "Everything that Rises Must Converge" has much in common with her overtly religious stories, particularly the characters whose pride blinds them to their need for insight until a dramatic, often tragic, event leaves them at forces outside their control.

Scientific & Technological Context

This story offers little in the way of scientific or technological developments. However, the use of a bus for the setting is significant because public buses were one place in which people of different races were brought together in close proximity. In the mid-twentieth century, buses were commonly used by the middle class in urban areas as well as by the economically disadvantaged. Unlike trains, on which different cars could be designated for different races, to maintain segregation on a bus required that different areas of the bus be segregated. Jim Crow laws commonly required African Americans to sit in the back so whites could have access to the more convenient seats closer to the door. It is this degrading segregation that has ended shortly before the beginning of "Everything That Rises Must Converge."

The coincidence of the two women wearing the same hat reflects the use of mass production of clothing as well as the fact that an African American woman could afford and have access to a hat that Julian's mother found disturbingly expensive.

Biographical Context

Mary Flannery O'Connor grew up in a segregated South, so she knew first-hand the depth of racist attitudes and the complexities that would result from desegregation. Born on March 25, 1925 in Savannah, Georgia, O'Connor spent the first thirteen years of her life across Lafayette Square from St. John's Catholic Cathedral, which was appropriate in light of her solid Catholic beliefs. She was known as a bright girl, but somewhat eccentric even at an early age, as is shown by her pride at having taught a chicken to walk backwards, which was memorialized on a newsreel.

Her parents, Francis O'Connor, Jr., and Regina Cline O'Connor, were both of Irish–Catholic heritage, and her early education was in parochial schools. When her father was diagnosed with lupus, the family moved to Milledgeville, where her mother had deep family roots and the Cline family continued to be socially distinguished. Milledgeville had been the state capital through the mid-1800s, and the family house is on the same block as the former governor's mansion. When her father died in 1941, O'Connor found herself in an uncommonly matriarchal family (Cash 28–29). She attended a girls' high school and then the Georgia State College for Women (now Georgia College and State University) from 1942–1945. She majored in English and sociology and was active on the student newspaper, primarily as a cartoonist.

After graduation, she attended the Iowa Writers' Workshop, where she started publishing stories from what was to be her first novel, "Wise Blood." Then she was accepted into the Yaddo artists' colony at Saratoga Springs, New York. After a few months in New York City, she lived with Robert and Sally Fitzgerald in Connecticut until she was struck with lupus on a trip back to Milledgeville early in 1951.

From that time, she lived with her mother on a family farm called Andalusia, outside Milledgeville. Regina managed the farm, overseeing both white and black workers. In her letters, Flannery critically records some of her mother's racist and condescending statements about her black workers, but Regina also acted benevolently toward them (Cash 149). O'Connor's own attitudes are somewhat ambiguous. In some of her earliest stories she, treated black characters sympathetically, but she also used the word "nigger" occasionally, usually in dialogue but sometimes in the narrator's voice. She sometimes satirizes her black characters, but no more so than she does the whites. Her letters show her to be aware of the inevitability of social change while also aware of her own social environment. In a letter from 1959, she notes that she would be willing to meet James Baldwin, a noted but controversial African American writer, in New York, but that "[i]t would cause the greatest trouble and disturbance and disunion" for her to see him in Georgia ("Habit" 329). Yet she saw integration as inevitable, and saw the need to approach the changes with "mutual charity and forbearance" (Cash 155).

Through the 1950s and early 1960s, *O'Connor* produced two novels, *Wise Blood* and *The Violent Bear It Away*, and a steady series of short stories that would make up two collected volumes. When her health allowed, she traveled to give readings at colleges throughout the eastern U.S. She continued to write while her health deteriorated and she succumbed to lupus in the summer of 1964, at the age of 39.

Michael L. Schroeder

Works Cited

Brinkley, Douglass. *American Heritage History of the United States*. New York: Viking, 1998.

Cash, Jean W. *Flannery O'Connor: A Life*. Knoxville: U of Tennessee P, 2002.

May, John R. *The Pruning Word: The Parables of Flannery O'Connor*. Notre Dame, IN: Notre Dame P, 1976.

Moore, Andrew S. "Practicing What We Preach: White Catholics and the Civil Rights Movement in Atlanta." *Georgia Historical Quarterly* 89 (2005): 334–367. Academic Search Premier.

Myrick-Harris, Clarissa, and Norman Harris. "Retrenchment and Redirection (1950–1959)." *Atlanta in the Civil Rights Movement*. Atlanta Regional Council for Higher Education. 2002. 26 May 2006.

O'Connor, Flannery. "Everything that Rises Must Converge." *The Complete Stories*. New York: Farrar, Straus, and Giroux, 1964. 405–420.

——. *The Habit of Being. Letters*. Ed. Sally Fitzgerald. New York: Farrar, Straus, and Giroux, 1979.

Walters, Dorothy. *Flannery O'Connor*. Boston: Twayne, 1973.

Discussion Questions

1. While the story is less explicit in its religious elements than most by O'Connor, some religious allusions are used. What are the suggestions of the statement that Julian is "waiting like Saint Sebastian for the arrows to begin piercing him" (405)?

2. Discuss the use of foreshadowing in the story. What are some of the hints of both what will happen to Julian's mother and his response?

3. Find and discuss examples of hypocrisy or small-mindedness in the depiction of Julian.

4. The point of view is more complex than might first be noticed, with an outside narrator filtering Julian's thoughts and observations. We do not directly see what Julian's mother thinks except through what she says. Discuss whether this point of view creates an obstacle to understanding the mother.

5. Julian's mother believes that one should dress and act in certain ways, not to impress others but for oneself, because "true culture" is "in the heart," and "how you do things is because of who you are" (410). In contrast, Julian pulls off his tie as a result of an "evil urge to break her spirit" (409), and in other ways he uses appearances to be rebellious or try to teach his mother a lesson. Do you agree with the mother that one's appearance should be a reflection of how one sees himself or herself?

6. Julian's mother says, in reference to racial integration, "With the world in the mess it's in, … it's a wonder we can enjoy anything. I tell you, the bottom rail in on the top" (407). She later returns to the metaphor of the fence with "They should rise, yes, but on their side of the fence" (408). Discuss how this metaphor relates to the theme.

7. Julian's mother insists on the importance of her ancestors being Godhighs, and that one of her ancestors was a governor and others were plantation owners. Consider the implications of the name "Godhigh," and discuss to what degree one's ancestry is important in determining one's character.

8. Examine the description of the neighborhood on page 406, and discuss the impression O'Connor creates and the details and word choices she employs to create the impression.

9. Early in the story we are told, from Julian's perspective, that "he had cut himself emotionally free" of his mother (412), and throughout the story he wants to treat her as a child. Discuss how the ending shows him to be self-deluded about his relationship with his mother.

10. Discuss whether Julian will be significantly changed by the apparent death of his mother. Why or why not? If he will be changed, in what ways?

Essay Ideas

1. Discuss your attitude toward Julian. Do you see him positively, as a potential force for change, or do you see him to be self-centered and hypocritical? Consider the narrator's irony, with which the narrator might be ridiculing Julian for his attitudes and perceptions even as Julian ridicules his mother's attitudes and beliefs.

2. Read some of the other stories in which O'Connor includes intellectual children who think they are superior to their parents, such as "The Enduring Chill" and "Good Country People," and write an essay exploring how O'Connor uses the conflicts to contribute to her themes.

3. Write an essay presenting your views of Julian's mother (who remains nameless). Do you see her negatively because she is racist, or well-meaning but misguided, or do you focus on some other trait? Use examples and short quotations to illustrate your points, keeping in mind that much of the story presents Julian's views, not an objective depiction of the mother.

4. The conflict in this story is built around divisions between generations as well as divisions between races. Write an essay in which you explore the relationship between Julian and his mother. Are his feelings of superiority commonly felt by grown children toward their parents? You might want to consider the image of her mother that O'Connor creates in her letters in "The Habit of Being."

5. Write an essay in which you explore what you see to be O'Connor's purpose in writing the story. Is the story primarily arguing for social change, or is it more a humorous depiction of types of people and their attitudes? Is it more concerned with conflicts between races, between generations, or between the old and the new? Whatever you see the primary purpose to be, develop your opinion with specific examples and short quotations from the story itself.

Edgar Allen Poe was an American author, and one of the earliest short story writers. Poe, shown here as a young man, is best known for his tales of mystery and the macabre, and is thought of as the inventor of the detective fiction genre; nine of his short stories are included in this volume. Photo: Library of Congress, Prints & Photographs Division, LC-DIG-pga-04119.

The Fall of the House of Usher

by Edgar Allan Poe

Content Synopsis

This often-anthologized short story is considered Edgar Allan Poe's masterpiece. It begins on "a dull, dark, and soundless day in the autumn of the year" as the narrator stands before "the melancholy House of Usher" (90). He inspects the mansion closely and notices, among its other idiosyncrasies, "a barely perceptible fissure" (93) extending from the roof of the building to its base. From the moment he sees the house it disturbs him, and he studies it for some time without determining exactly why he is so troubled—though he believes he discerns "about the whole mansion and domain" a "pestilent and mystic vapour" (90). This narrator, like others in Poe's tales, is unnamed and possibly unreliable. We learn from the outset of the story that he has been a "reveller upon opium" (90); thus, his peculiar response to the house of Usher and his account of the bizarre goings-on there might be explained by drug use—or it might not. In this story, as in others, Poe allows us to choose between a psychological and a supernatural explanation for the plot.

The narrator arrives at the Usher mansion after receiving a letter from his childhood friend, Roderick Usher, whom he has not seen in many years and who has succumbed to a peculiar malady described as both a "bodily illness" and a "mental disorder" (91). The sickness, which Roderick terms "a constitutional and a family evil," manifests itself in his extreme sensitivity to stimuli of any kind, a "morbid acuteness of the senses" (95). This strange sickness is paralleled by that of Roderick's sister, Madeline, who suffers from a mysterious disease that involves a "settled apathy, a gradual wasting away of the person" (97), and catalepsy—a death-like state of immobility and unresponsiveness.

Roderick feels he will ultimately "abandon life and reason together, in some struggle with the grim phantasm, FEAR" (96). He also believes that his house is somehow alive and malevolent, and that his health has deteriorated under its unwholesome influence. The narrator attempts to minister to his friend by painting and reading with him, and by listening to his peculiar musical performances. Soon, however, he realizes "the futility of all attempt at cheering a mind from which darkness, as if an inherent positive quality, poured forth upon all objects of the moral and physical universe" (97). Rather than leading Roderick toward health, the narrator becomes increasingly involved in his friend's dark fantasy life and fascinated by his weird artworks, books, and music. One of Roderick's ballads, "The Haunted Palace," serves as an allegory for the precarious state of his mental health, as the troubled dwelling of the title symbolizes "the tottering of his lofty reason upon her throne" (98).

One evening, Roderick tells the narrator that Madeline is "no more" (101), and he asks for assistance in briefly entombing her within the house.

Roderick explains that his request is motivated by fear of grave robbing, given "certain obtrusive and eager inquiries on the part of her medical men" and "the remote and exposed situation of the burial-ground of the family" (102). The two men place her coffin in a vault deep within the house, a "region of horror" that once served "in remote feudal times, for the worst purposes of a donjon-keep" (that is, it functioned as a prison and a torture chamber), and "in later days, as a place of deposit for powder, or some other highly combustible substance" (102). While helping Roderick to put Madeline in her temporary tomb, the narrator notes a "striking similitude between brother and sister," and Roderick informs him that "the deceased and himself had been twins, and that sympathies of a scarcely intelligible nature had always existed between them" (102). Before Madeline is sealed into the vault, the narrator observes that the "disease which had thus entombed the lady in the maturity of youth, had left, as usual in all maladies of a strictly cataleptical character, the mockery of a faint blush upon the bosom and the face, and that suspiciously lingering smile upon the lip which is so terrible in death" (102–03).

As the days pass, Roderick becomes more agitated, and the narrator ponders whether he is struggling with "some oppressive secret" or simply exhibiting the "inexplicable vagaries of madness" (103). In either case, he begins to share his friend's anxiety. One night, during a powerful storm, he is awakened by "low and indefinite sounds" from some unknown source and experiences "an intense sentiment of horror, unaccountable yet unendurable" (104). Roderick enters his bedroom, throws open the window, and the two men see that the "under surfaces of the huge masses of agitated vapour, as well as all terrestrial objects" are "glowing in the unnatural light of a faintly luminous and distinctly visible gaseous exhalation" (104–05). The narrator draws Roderick away from the window, crying, "You must not—you shall not behold

this!" and tries to rationalize the bizarre and noxious atmosphere surrounding the house as the result of either "merely electrical phenomena" or else mist rising from the stagnant "tarn" (small lake) alongside the mansion (105).

The narrator attempts to calm Roderick by reading aloud a medieval tale of the knight Ethelred, but the recital has unintended consequences. When Ethelred smashes the door to a hermit's dwelling, the narrator believes he hears the "noise of the dry and hollow-sounding wood" (106) echoing "from some very remote portion of the mansion"—yet he attributes this noise to his "excited fancy" (106). When the knight confronts not a hermit, but a dragon, which emits "a shriek so horrid and harsh," the narrator becomes aware of "a low and distant, but harsh, protracted, and most unusual screaming or grating sound" (106) somewhere in the house. Finally, when a shield falls before Ethelred "with a mighty great and terrible ringing sound," the narrator hears "a distinct, hollow, metallic, and clangorous, yet apparently muffled reverberation" (107), as if the event had indeed occurred.

Leaping to his feet, the narrator rushes to Roderick's chair to find him murmuring to himself and revealing his awful secret:

> "We have put her living in the tomb! [...] Ethelred-ha! ha!-the breaking of the hermit's door, and the death-cry of the dragon, and the clangour of the shield!-say, rather, the rending of her coffin, and the grating of the iron hinges of her prison, and her struggles within the coppered archway of the vault! [...] I TELL YOU THAT SHE NOW STANDS WITHOUT THE DOOR!" (108).

The narrator is horrified to witness the door slowly open to reveal "the lofty and enshrouded figure of the lady Madeline of Usher," with "blood upon her white robes, and the evidence of some bitter struggle upon every portion of her emaciated frame" (108). Suffering "her violent and now final death-agonies," she totters upon the threshold for a moment before collapsing upon Roderick and bearing him "to the floor a corpse, and a victim to the terrors he had anticipated" (108).

At this point the narrator flees from the house. Once he has put some distance between himself and the doomed mansion, he turns to observe the "blood-red moon" (109) shining through the fissure in the building. As he watches, the fissure widens quickly, the mansion collapses, and the lake closes "sullenly and silently over the fragments of the 'HOUSE OF USHER'" (109).

Symbols & Motifs

The title: As the narrator explains, the phrase "House of Usher" includes "in the minds of the peasantry who used it, both the family and the family mansion" (92). Just as the house is ancient and upon the verge of collapse, so too is the family. The title thus describes the literal fall or dissolution of the mansion and the demise of the Usher family, as Roderick and Madeline are the last of their line. It is appropriate that the story's action takes place "in the autumn of the year" (90) (that is, in the fall), and that everywhere are images of death and decomposition as, for instance, in the "few white trunks of decayed trees" (90) outside the mansion that represent the moribund Usher family tree. The narrator refers to these as "ghastly tree-stems" (91) and later notes that "the stem of the Usher race […] had put forth, at no period, any enduring branch," so that "the entire family lay in the direct line of descent" (92). In other words, the Ushers have become identified with their mansion because they have always lived there; and they have remained there because the Usher name and estate have passed directly from father to son, with no "collateral issue" (92)—that is, no other branches of the family tree.

Doubles: When the narrator examines the house, he tries to make some sense of its uncanny effect upon him by looking at its reflection in the "black and lurid tarn" (91); but he finds the "inverted images" (91) even more troubling than the originals. Here the motif of doubling is introduced, and this topic is repeated throughout the tale, for example, when the Ethelred story is echoed by Madeline's struggles to free herself from the tomb. The most significant instance of doubling is of course the fact that Roderick and Madeline are twins. The Usher twins are unhealthy, and Roderick describes his own illness as "a constitutional and a family evil" (95) that is worsened by his house (by implication, both his mansion and his family). It appears that members of the Usher family have been too closely related for too long, and that Roderick and Madeline's illnesses result from centuries of inbreeding. In fact, the "sympathies of a scarcely intelligible nature" (102) between Roderick and Madeline may well be incestuous, hence his motive for burying her prematurely in order to rid himself of the guilt caused by their unnatural relationship.

Historical Context

Precisely where and when "The Fall of the House of Usher" occurs is impossible to determine, as readers are given few geographical or temporal markers. Like many of Poe's tales, its setting is somewhat dream-like and universal. That said, Roderick's apparent anxiety that Madeline's doctors will disinter and study her corpse suggests that the story might be set in the first decades of the 1800s, as this period "saw a proliferation of medical schools and a concurrent explosion in demand for cadavers" (Tward). The narrator's references to opium also indicate an early-nineteenth-century setting, since during this era opium was available in the United States and Europe and was used recreationally by writers such as John Keats and Thomas De Quincey.

While the story's plot may unfold in the early nineteenth century, its milieu—the House of Usher, its environs, its inhabitants, and its contents—is distinctly medieval. To get over the tarn, the narrator crosses "a short causeway to the house" (93) reminiscent of a drawbridge over a moat before entering "the Gothic archway of the hall" (93). He also informs us that the house possesses "turrets" (104) of the sort found on castles. Moreover, he describes those living in the vicinity of the Usher mansion as "the peasantry" (92) and refers to Roderick's sister as "the lady Madeline" (97). In an act both ghastly and appropriate, Madeline is entombed in a vault that "had been used, apparently, in remote feudal times, for the worst purposes of a donjon-keep" (102)—that is, as a medieval torture chamber. This emphasis on the medieval is most apparent when the narrator describes Roderick's taste in literature. Roderick's song, "The Haunted Palace," takes place "in the olden / Time long ago" (99); Roderick delights in "an exceedingly rare and curious book in quarto Gothic—the manual of a forgotten church" (101), and many of the books he reads were written in the Middle Ages.

The story's references not only to the medieval in general, but to the Gothic in particular, are significant. The term "Gothic" refers to an architectural style common in the Middle Ages that enjoyed renewed popularity during the nineteenth century in both design and literature. (The term "Medieval Revival" is used to describe the Victorians' enthusiasm for the Gothic.) To Poe and his contemporaries, the Gothic was associated with artistic power and peculiarity; thus, it makes sense that Roderick—whose painterly and musical performances are of a potent yet "fantastic character" (98)—would live surrounded by "sombre tapestries" and "phantasmagoric armorial trophies" (93).

Societal Context

Having lived in Virginia and South Carolina, Poe was quite familiar with southern society and culture. Moreover, a magazine he edited, the "Southern Literary Messenger," published pieces that both affirmed and questioned the "peculiar institution" of slavery. Accordingly, some critics have argued

that "The Fall of the House of Usher" describes the decline and fall of the American South. Harry Levin interprets it as "an allegory of feudal plantation culture in the death throes" (160), while David Leverenz believes the plantation owner John Landolf served as a model for Roderick Usher (218).

If we view "The Fall of the House of Usher" as a prescient allegory for the South's demise, it is worth considering the bond between mistress and slave as represented by Madeline and Roderick. From this perspective, Madeline might well be seen as a moribund southern belle; at once a lady in decline and a metaphor for a fading civilization. While there are no actual slaves in the tale, the narrator does metaphorically describe Roderick as "a bounden slave" to "an anomalous species of terror" (95) namely, that he will die of fright. Ultimately, Roderick's deadly fear is Madeline; thus, figuratively speaking, Roderick is a slave and Madeline is his mistress. Moreover, their relationship is characterized by "sympathies of a scarcely intelligible nature" (102) similar to those Poe attributed to the mutually dependent relationship between master and slave. That said, the fact that Madeline falls upon Roderick and kills him—after he has buried and tried to destroy her—might suggest that the South will ultimately collapse under the burden of slavery.

Religious Context

While religion does not figure prominently in Poe's tale, the text does include religious references. Roderick's peculiar composition, "The Haunted Palace," associates "good angels" and "Spirits moving musically" with the palace in "the monarch Thought's dominion" (99). If we read the ballad as an allegory of Roderick's deteriorating mental state, these spirits living in harmony might represent his sanity. Conversely, the demonic "evil things, in robes of sorrow" that "move fantastically / To a discordant melody" (100) might signify his madness.

In addition, Roderick's library includes volumes on religion. Roderick's "chief delight" is "found in the perusal of an exceedingly rare and curious book in quarto Gothic—the manual of a forgotten church-the Vigiliae Mortuorum secundum Chorum Ecclesiae Maguntinae" (101). While this tome appears to be an invention of Poe's, others in Roderick's collection do exist. The narrator notes that he and his host "pored together over such works as […] the Belphegor of Machiavelli" and "the Heaven and Hell of Swedenborg" (101). Machiavelli's "Belphegor" concerns a demon, while Swedenborg's "Heaven and Hell" is a work of eschatology and mysticism. "One favorite volume," the narrator confides, is "a small octavo edition of the "Directorium Inquisitorium," by the Dominican Eymeric de Cironne" (101)—an instruction manual for priests interrogating suspected heretics and, ironically, a list of forbidden books of the type Roderick favors.

Scientific & Technological Context

"The Fall of the House of Usher" depicts medical doctors as crafty yet incompetent. The narrator mistrusts "the physician of the [Usher] family," whom he describes as having a "sinister countenance" (102) marked by both "low cunning and perplexity" (93). Moreover, the "disease of the lady Madeline" has "long baffled the skill of her physicians" (97), who appear to be more interested in dissecting her corpse than in treating her illness and have made "obtrusive and eager inquiries" (102) regarding an autopsy. Madeline's malady, characterized by a "settled apathy, a gradual wasting away of the person, and frequent although transient affections of a partially cataleptical character" (97), calls to mind consumption (tuberculosis) and catalepsy (rigidity of the limbs and insensitivity to stimuli). These are two disorders that appear frequently in nineteenth-century literature and that were of great interest to contemporary physicians and researchers. Roderick might also suffer from hypochondria, a diagnostic category described by medical writers of the nineteenth century.

Biographical Context

Edgar Allan Poe was born to traveling actors in Boston in 1809. His father vanished, and his mother died two years after his birth. A Richmond merchant, John Allan, took young Edgar into his home but never adopted him. Their already-tense relationship became yet more difficult after Allan refused to honor his foster son's sizable gambling debts, thereby compelling him to withdraw from the University of Virginia less than a year after his enrollment in 1826. Poe enlisted in the army in 1827 and entered West Point in 1830, but he was dishonorably discharged a year later. He then worked as a newspaper and magazine editor in Richmond, Philadelphia, and New York. In 1836, he married his thirteen-year-old cousin, Virginia Clemm, who died in 1847 after a long struggle with tuberculosis. In 1839, to generally favorable reviews, Poe published "Tales of the Grotesque and Arabesque," which contained twenty-five tales (including "The Fall of the House of Usher"). Poe gained a reputation first as a literary critic and then, after "The Raven and Other Poems" was published in 1845, as a writer. He died in Baltimore in 1849.

The Usher name is drawn from that of Noble Luke Usher and Harriet L'Estrange Usher, who performed onstage with David and Eliza Poe, Edgar's parents. Some critics believe there are autobiographical elements in "The Fall of the House of Usher," and see Madeline and Roderick, an ailing woman and a tortured artist, as evoking Virginia and Poe himself.

Jamil M. Mustafa

Works Cited

Hayes, Kevin J., ed. *The Cambridge Companion to Edgar Allan Poe. Cambridge Companions to Literature.* Cambridge: Cambridge UP, 2002.

Kennedy, J. Gerald, ed. *A Historical Guide to Edgar Allan Poe.* Oxford: Oxford UP, 2001.

Leverenz, David. "Poe and Gentry Virginia." *In The American Face of Edgar Allan Poe,* ed. Shawn Rosenheim and Stephen Rachman. Baltimore: Johns Hopkins UP, 1995. 210–36.

Levin, Harry. *The Power of Blackness: Hawthorne, Poe, Melville.* New York: Knopf, 1958.

Poe, Edgar Allan. "The Fall of the House of Usher." In *The Fall of the House of Usher and Other Writings: Poems, Tales, Essays and Reviews,* ed. David Galloway. London: Penguin, 2003. 90–109.

Tward, Aaron D. and Hugh A. Patterson. "From Grave Robbing to Gifting: Cadaver Supply in the United States." *MSJAMA* 287 (2002): 1183.

Discussion Questions

1. What does the narrator's description of, and reaction to, the House of Usher tell us about him, and about the house?

2. What are the functions of art, literature, and music in this story? Why are the narrator and Roderick so involved in these pursuits?

3. What is the significance of Roderick's extreme sensitivity? Can he really hear Madeline's struggles in her tomb?

4. Why does Madeline never speak? What role does she play in this tale? How would you characterize her relationship with her brother?

5. Is the narrator of this tale reliable? Why or why not?

6. Why is Madeline entombed in the dungeon? What does the narrator's description of this chamber tell us about her character, his, and Roderick's?

7. Does Roderick realize that Madeline is alive when he entombs her? Does the narrator? If so, consider the implications. Why would Roderick or the narrator want to bury her alive?

8. Is the House of Usher really alive and evil? Are the events that occur on the night of the storm natural or supernatural?

9. What significance does the story of Ethelred hold? How does it correspond with the story of Roderick and Madeline?

10. Why does the story end as it does?

Essay Ideas

1. Analyze how Roderick, Madeline, and the narrator relate to one another.

2. Analyze the significance of the story's setting.

3. Argue for the narrator's (un)reliability.

4. Explore the role played by illness in this story.

5. Compare this story to any text mentioned above in terms of theme, character, figurative language, or other literary elements.

Jamaica Kincaid is an award-winning Antiguan-American author, whose writing is known for its angry tone; her short story *Girl* is included in this volume. Photo: Kincaid at the Miami Book Fair International in 1999; Wikipedia.

Girl

by Jamaica Kincaid

Content Synopsis

A strictly descriptive summary of "Girl" can easily be accomplished in a single sentence: an older woman instructs a girl, almost certainly her daughter, on how to behave like a lady, take care of the household, and interact with men. The entire short story itself consists only of a single long paragraph; in fact, according to Kincaid's punctuation, it is comprised entirely of a single, very long sentence.

One remarkable feature of the story is the complete absence of a traditional narrator. Unlike a typical story, the text never explicitly identifies who the characters are or where the story is set. Nor is there any action. Indeed, the only thing it contains is a monologue by the older woman, which is briefly interrupted twice by the girl, leaving the reader responsible for gleaning the facts from what the characters say.

At first, the mother's advice and admonitions seem rather unexceptional. They include instructions on how and when to wash the clothes, how to "cook pumpkin fritters," and how to "walk like a lady" (3). What does become quickly apparent is that the story's setting is not likely twenty-first century America. When the girl washes the white clothes, for instance, the mother tells her to "put them on the stone heap"; she teaches her daughter how to choose "cotton to make yourself a nice blouse"; and, at one point, she demands to know of the girl, "Is it true that you sing benna in Sunday school?" (3). While the first two examples suggest a more labor-intensive and less consumerist culture than the current-day United States, the mention of "benna," a form of folk music popular in Antigua, provides strong evidence that the story is set in the Caribbean. Another telling piece of information—the mother's warning to the girl to "soak your little cloths right after you take them off" (3)—reveals that the girl has reached puberty and may explain why she is now receiving this lecture on behaving like a woman.

What begins as a simple list of instructions and prohibitions takes on a deeper significance when the mother begins to weave in commentary on the girl herself, such as when she offers, "on Sundays try to walk like a lady and not like the slut you are so bent on becoming" (3). Harsh evaluative judgments like this one are not in any way differentiated from the rest of the flow of the mother's advice. While commenting, almost offhandedly, several times on the girl's destiny to become a "slut," the mother continues her enumeration of typical household tasks ("this is how to sew on a button" and "this is how you sweep a whole house"), good manners (how to "set a table for tea" and how to "smile to someone you don't like too much"), and even regional superstitions ("this is how to throw back a fish you don't like, and that way something bad won't fall on you") (4–5).

Interspersed among this everyday and utilitarian counsel, however, are some surprising bits which reveal some of the gritty reality of the life which awaits this girl as she grows into a woman. The mother, for instance, advises her that "this is the way to bully a man," "this is how to love a man, and if this doesn't work, there are other ways, and if they don't work don't feel too bad about giving up," and "this is how to make a good medicine to throw away a child before it even becomes a child" (5).

The titular character speaks only twice, once in protest—"but I don't sing benna on Sundays at all and never in Sunday school" (4)—and once in question—"but what if the baker won't let me feel the bread?" (5). The story ends with the mother's somewhat ambiguous reply to her daughter's question about feeling the bread: "you mean to say that after all you are really going to be the kind of woman who the baker won't let near the bread?" (5). The most obvious meaning of the mother's question is the implication that the girl will, indeed, grow up to be a "slut" and, therefore, due to her lack of virtue, will not be allowed to handle the bread. It is, however, also possible to interpret it as the mother's shock that her daughter, whom she has been so certain will grow up to be promiscuous, will, in fact, be such a virtuous and unavailable woman that she will be unable to entice the baker into letting her touch his bread with all the sexual connotations therein implied.

Historical Context

Antigua's history is inextricably tied up with British imperialism and the British slave trade. The British established a colony on Antigua in the mid-seventeenth century, and, shortly thereafter, introduced sugar cane farming to the island. As the sugar trade boomed, the British shipped increasing numbers of enslaved Africans to Antigua to work the plantations. When the Caribbean sugar market began to wane and social pressures to end slavery began to mount in England, the Act of Emancipation was passed and, by 1838, all forms of African slavery in Antigua were finally ended.

Antigua remained a colony of England until 1981, however, and "[f]ormal emancipation, of course, did not mean equality for the ex-slaves, nor did it effect a transformation in social and power relations in the region. The white elites continued, by and large, to monopolize ownership of the major economic resources, to exercise political ascendancy (subject to the colonial powers), and to enjoy the greatest social prestige" (Brereton and Yelvington 6). The world which the mother and daughter of "Girl" inhabit is one much removed chronologically from slavery but is still one in which social relations and economic and cultural power are divided along racial lines. Many of the mother's commands to the girl seem to be aimed at teaching the young girl how to ingratiate herself with the colonial powers that be and how to exorcise, or at least hide, those aspects of herself that are most African and Antiguan in nature.

On the subject of the effects of England's long colonial rule over Antigua, Kincaid writes, "what I see is the millions of people, of whom I am just one, made orphans: no motherland, no fatherland, no gods, no mounds of earth for holy ground … and worst and most painful of all, no tongue" ("Small" 305). Bitterly, she asks her reader, "Have I given you the impression that the Antigua I grew up in revolved almost completely around England? Well, that was so" (306).

Societal Context

The two characters of "Girl," the mother and the daughter, embody opposing strands of thought about the roles of women which characterized post-emancipation and post-colonial Antigua. The mother's concerns lay in making a "lady" out of daughter, teaching her how to dress modestly, set a table for tea, show the proper respect based on the social class of one's guests, and maintain her sexual purity at all costs. The particular form of gender ideology she espouses sounds very familiar because it has its origins in British polite society and is an offspring of that apotheosis of high moral periods, the Victorian Era.

After the emancipation of the slaves in Antigua, the majority of women left the fields for the domestic sphere. According to Bridget Brereton, their primary motivation was not so much to emulate the lifestyles of their British colonizers as to escape the sexual abuse they often suffered in the labor gangs; however, "[a]ntislavery activists, clergymen, officials and British policymakers all shared a basic assumption: the ex-slaves should model their domestic lives on the middle class Western family" and began a century-long propaganda campaign to convince the former slave women to accept "lifelong monogamy based on Christian marriage," the dependency of women on their husbands, and the necessity of maintaining a "decent, comfortable, Christian home" (102). Over time, many of the middle-class Antiguans, such as the mother of "Girl," adopted this British model of gender ideology.

As much as some women may have come to aspire to their colonizers' codes of behavior, other currents ran strong as well, and the tensions between the more natural Antiguan culture and the high-minded British model can be seen in the mother's advice. Though she seems obsessed with her daughter's sexual propriety, and especially with insuring that the girl devote her sexual attention to a single man, she also reveals to her, "this is how to bully a man" and "this is how to make a good medicine to throw away a child before it even becomes a child" (5). She likewise instructs her on "how to spit up in the air if you feel like it," a decidedly unladylike pursuit (5). These seemingly contradictory teachings suggest that the mother, as much as she would like to buy into the British ideologies,

cannot completely cut ties with her own Antiguan heritage.

Despite the whites' attempts "to impose European cultural forms on the people and to weaken or denigrate forms which derived partly or wholly from African, Amerindian, or East Indian elements," the Antiguans often refused to abandon fully their own cultural traditions (Brereton and Yelvington 8). In particular, the Caribbean women often "rejected European notions about marriage and family patterns. They cherished several different family forms, and the evidence suggests that many, if not most, declined to adopt the model of lifelong, monogamous marriage" (9). The resistance to "Christian marriage" was serious enough in the eyes of the whites that, in the period in which "Girl" is most likely set, the 1950s, the Caribbean was beset by "Mass Marriage Movements" which tried, without success, to increase the rates of "legitimate" marriages (21).

Seen in this context, the degree of the mother's obsession with steering her daughter away from becoming a "slut" can be understood because it is an attempt to make her Antiguan daughter behave in an un-Antiguan way. It is on par with her forbidding her to sing benna, also a part of her native culture. The nature of the mother's agenda is hinted at by the way the story opens: "Wash the white clothes on Monday," a literal "white-washing" of her daughter's heritage (3).

While the daughter has almost no voice in the narrative, she can be associated with the generation to which Jamaica Kincaid herself belongs, a generation to grow up in the post-colonial era and to be prepared to reject the imposed British culture and to embrace the underlying Antiguan culture at last. And the fact that both of the daughter's brief interruptions begin with the word "but" further suggests that she has ideas which contrast with her mother's and that she might not be willing to submit to the status quo as her mother apparently has.

Religious Context

Because Antigua spent over 300 years as a colony of Great Britain and did not achieve full independence until 1981, its religious landscape, not surprisingly, has long been dominated by the Church of England. When the mother of "Girl" rebukes her daughter, "don't sing benna in Sunday school" (3), the Sunday school service she refers to almost certainly is Anglican. Given what we know of the mother and her desire to make her daughter into the perfect "imitation of a proper English lady" (Paravisini-Gebert 51), her reasons for forbidding the girl to sing benna may have less to do with the sometimes bawdy nature of benna and more to do with the Afro-Caribbean nature of the folk music which sharply contrasts with the rigid formality of the ritualistic Anglican mass and which identifies its singer as Afro-Caribbean rather than British.

Surprisingly, however, the mother's restriction may not reveal as much of a rejection of black Antiguan culture—especially religious culture—as might be expected. She prohibits her daughter not from singing benna altogether, just from singing benna in Sunday school. As much as the mother exhibits an anglophilic obsession with genteel manners and upward social mobility, she does not utterly reject all things Afro-Caribbean. Lizabeth Paravisini-Gebert argues that the "importance of appearances—the hiding of the true nature of things—is a central theme of this story, where the mother feels charged with the task of teaching her daughter the need for hypocrisy as a tool of survival" (52). Religion is one area in which the mother appears to accept her Afro-Caribbean heritage, even if out of the view of the British colonizers.

As Paravisini-Gebert argues, "[t]he one element of the native culture the mother openly embraces is Obeah, the African-based system of beliefs that involves the supernatural, witchcraft, sorcery, and magic and acknowledges the power of spells to inflict harm or help in healing" (53). In contrast to all of the mother's exhortations designed specifically to anglicize her daughter, there are several which reveal her connection to Obeah spirituality: "don't pick people's flowers—you might catch something; don't throw stones at blackbirds, because it might not be a blackbird at all … this is how to throw back a fish you don't like, and that way something bad won't fall on you" (5). In addition to these superstitions, the influence of Obeah in these characters' lives is suggested by the mother's medicinal lessons: "this is how to make a good medicine for a cold; this is how to make a good medicine to throw away a child before it even becomes a child" (5). Like most folk religions, Obeah spiritualism includes a familiarity with herbalism.

The girl in the story, then, is suspended between two very different religious systems. Judging from the mother's warnings, she sees no direct contradiction in practicing both Obeah and Anglicanism; rather, the important lesson is make a show of following the religion of the colonial power while learning the craft of Obeah to survive day-to-day life.

Scientific & Technological Context

One notable aspect of the life depicted in "Girl" is the obvious absence of the technologies which are, more or less, taken for granted in Western culture today. The opening lines, "Wash the white clothes on Monday and put them on the stone heap" (3), immediately signal a culture without laundromats or washers and dryers in the home. Even running water cannot be taken for granted, as the mother admonishes the girl to "be sure to wash every day, even if it is with your own spit" (4). Modern medicine, too, is absent, and the girl is taught "how to make a good medicine for a cold" as well as how to make a medicine to abort a fetus (5).

During Kincaid's childhood, Antigua ranked as one of the wealthiest of the Caribbean islands, but by the standards of highly-industrialized nations like the United States, Antigua was still quite poor and underdeveloped. Though from a "moderately prosperous" family, relatively speaking, Kincaid herself grew up in a home which "had no electricity, bathroom, or running water," privations which "were the result of the slow development of the Antiguan urban infrastructure" rather than her family's personal circumstances (Paravisini-Gebert 2). Even many years later, when Kincaid returned to Antigua to visit her dying brother, she noted upon driving away from the hospital that there was a "major crossing where there was a stoplight that was broken and had been broken for a long time but could not be fixed because the parts for it were no longer made anywhere in the world" ("My Brother" 12–13).

The effects of having such a technologically-deprived culture help to perpetuate both the colonial and the patriarchal power structures. Because everyone had to work so hard just to survive, the British could generally count on the Antiguans being too busy, too tired, and to poor to organize and mount any sort of serious insurrection. Likewise, because the women's domestic work—as revealed in "Girl"—involved a great deal of very time-consuming physical labor, most women would be thoroughly consumed simply trying to keep up with everything that needed to be done, leaving little time or energy for them to try to improve their position in society.

Biographical Context

Jamaica Kincaid was born Elaine Cynthia Potter Richardson in St. John's, Antigua in 1949. She grew up with her mother, a homemaker, and her stepfather, a carpenter. Though she has described her family as "poor, ordinary people" (qtd. in Paravisini-Gebert 1), they were, in fact, in relative terms "moderately prosperous, part of the genteel lower-middle class" (2). Because of Antigua's lagging infrastructure, Kincaid's early life consisted of domestic chores, including "arranging for the 'night-soil' men to collect and replace their outhouse tub when full, fetching buckets of fresh water in the morning and early evening, trimming, cleaning, and replacing the kerosene in the oil lamps, and later helping her mother care for her three younger brothers" (2).

By all accounts, Kincaid was an extremely intelligent and curious girl who did very well in school and loved reading. Her life changed drastically, however, when her three brothers were born one after another and her stepfather became ill. When she was thirteen years old, her mother took her out of school to help take care of her siblings, and Kincaid began to feel like her future was being taken away in order to provide futures for her brothers; "she witnessed with growing disillusionment her mother and stepfather's great expectations for her brothers' professional futures and what she saw as indifference to her own prospects" (Paravisini-Gebert 4). The sense of betrayal she felt came to a head one day when, charged with watching over one of her brothers, Kincaid lost herself in her reading and neglected her sibling; when her mother found out, she gathered together all of Kincaid's beloved books and burned them. In her later writing, Kincaid recreates this scene "as the traumatic moment when her Edenic world [was] shattered, and the 'paradise of mother' [was] dramatically ruptured" (Burrows 94).

At the age of seventeen, in order to help with the family finances, Kincaid moved from Antigua to New York to work as an au pair. Once physically distanced from Antigua and from her mother, she began to think in terms of her own freedom and self-fulfillment. She broke off contact with her mother for a few years, took the name Jamaica Kincaid, and began to write. "Girl" was her first piece of fiction, written in a single afternoon after reading Elizabeth Bishop's poem, "In the Waiting Room." She has claimed that when she wrote "Girl" she "found her voice as a writer—a voice that turned out to be that of her mother" (Paravisini-Gebert 51). In her later fiction, she returns to the same themes present in "Girl" time and again and has, in fact, said herself, "I've never really written anything about anyone except myself and my mother" (qtd. in Burrows 94).

Kim Becnel

Works Cited

Brereton, Bridget. "Family Strategies, Gender and the Shift to Wage Labour in the British Caribbean." *The Colonial Caribbean in Transition: Essays on Post emancipation Social and Cultural History.* Ed. Bridget Brereton and Kevin A. Yelvington. Gainesville, FL: UP of Florida, 1999. 77–107.

Brereton, Bridget and Kevin A Yelvington. "Introduction: The Promise of Emancipation." *The Colonial Caribbean in Transition: Essays on Post-emancipation Social and Cultural History.* Ed. Bridget Brereton and Kevin A. Yelvington. Gainesville, FL: UP of Florida, 1999. 1–25.

Brown, Stewart. "Introduction." *The Oxford Book of Caribbean Short Stories.* Ed. Stewart Brown and John Wickham. NY: Oxford UP, 1999. xiii–xxxiii.

Burrows, Victoria. *Whiteness and Trauma: the Mother-Daughter Knot in the Fiction of Jean Rhys, Jamaica Kincaid, and Toni Morrison.* NY: Palgrave Macmillan, 2004.

Kincaid, Jamaica. "Girl." *At the Bottom of the River.* NY: Farrar, 1983. 3–5.

_____. "My Brother." *Transition: An International Review.* Winter 1996: 4–34.

_____. "A Small Place." *Life Notes: Personal Writings by Contemporary Black Women.* Ed. Patricia Bell-Scott. NY: Norton, 1994. 300–308.

Kurlansky, Mark. *A Continent of Islands: Searching for the Caribbean Destiny.* Reading, MA: Addison-Wesley, 1992.

Paravisini-Gebert, Lizabeth. *Jamaica Kincaid: A Critical Companion (Critical Companions to Popular Contemporary Writers).* Westport, CT: Greenwood, 1999.

Discussion Questions

1. It is clear that, if not literally impoverished, the girl and her mother live on the edge of poverty. Why, then, is it so important that the girl learn the "proper" way "to set a table for tea"?

2. Why do you suppose the mother is so obsessed with her daughter's sexuality?

3. What do you see as the significance of the mother's prohibitions on singing benna at Sunday school and on speaking with "wharf-rat" boys? What is she protecting her daughter from?

4. How does the lack of technology affect the day-to-day life of the Antiguans? And, specifically, of the Antiguan women?

5. Antiguan society, according to Kincaid, is marked by a gaping divide between the white British colonizers and the black Antiguan colonized. Is there evidence of these racial inequalities in "Girl"?

6. The directions the mother gives to the girl seem, at times, overwhelmingly meticulous: "This is how you sweep a corner; this is how you sweep a whole house; this is how you sweep a yard" (4). Why are there so many specific instructions?

7. Interspersed among the mother's more practical instructions are several superstitious warnings: "Don't throw stones at blackbirds, because it might not be a blackbird at all," for instance (5). What do all of these superstitions have in common? What do they tell us about the mother? About Antiguan culture?

8. Why does the mother, on one hand, try to convince her daughter not be become a "slut" and then, on the other, teach her several ways to "love" a man? Is there a mixed message here? Why?

9. What is the significance of the mother teaching the girl how to make a medicine to cause a miscarriage? Is the mother simply convinced that the girl will, indeed, become promiscuous and will therefore need such a medicine, or are there other reasons?

10. Why is "Girl" written entirely as a monologue (or dialogue, if you count the daughter's two brief protests)? What does this format achieve that a more traditional story might not?

Essay Ideas

1. Look at the mother's final statement—"You mean to say that after all you are really going to be the kind of woman who the baker won't let near the bread?" (5). In the context of all else that she has said, what exactly is the mother implying here? Write an essay in which you argue for your specific interpretation of this line.

2. What does the type of advice and instruction the mother offers tell us about life for women in Antigua during this time period? If the daughter does take her mother's warnings to heart, what kind of woman will she turn out to be? Is the mother teaching her daughter simply how to submit within the context of a patriarchal, and colonial, world, or does she give her some ways to empower herself? Write an essay in which you explore the mother's ultimate agenda.

3. Assuming that this story is set in the 1940s or 50s, examine the relative lack of technology in Antigua as suggested by the mother's monologue. Consider how much more technologically advanced American and British life was at this time. As a colony of Britain, why would Antigua not share comparable technological infrastructure? How does the lack of technology affect the Antiguans' lives? How does it affect their relationship with the British?

4. Kincaid says that she sat down and wrote "Girl" in one afternoon after reading Elizabeth Bishop's poem, "In the Waiting Room." Read Bishop's poem and try to find what in that poem must have inspired Kincaid to write her story. Write an essay comparing and contrasting the two works.

5. Among the lessons imparted by the mother is one about how to create an herbal medicine to induce a miscarriage. Why does the mother expend so much energy trying to keep her daughter from becoming promiscuous only to offer her a way out of the possible consequences of that promiscuity? What does that suggest about her hopes for her daughter? About the possibilities available to women? The mother also teaches her various ways to please a man. Why the contradictory advice? Write an essay in which you explain why the mother offers seemingly contradictory advice.

Go Down, Moses

by William Faulkner

Content Synopsis

William Faulkner's "Go Down, Moses" is a collection of linked short stories exploring the relationships between the black and white descendents of a slaveholder named Lucius Quintus Carothers McCaslin. McCaslin was born before the American Revolution, and the two branches of his family—one legitimate and one unacknowledged—represent a microcosm of American history itself. Slavery, in Faulkner's cosmology and in that of his protagonist Ike McCaslin, is America's original sin. The Civil War may have ended slavery itself, but the legacy of the "peculiar institution" continued to color everyday life for whites and African Americans alike. Ike, realizing this, will give up his inheritance and return to nature in an attempt to atone for his grandfather's sin. Yet, the same logic that justified his ancestors in keeping slaves justifies his contemporaries in exploiting and taming the wilderness around them, so that Ike over the course of his lifetime must watch the virgin forest that he loves fall to the axe and the planing mill. By the same token, Ike witnesses history repeating itself when he finds that his great-nephew Carothers 'Roth' Edmonds has gotten pregnant an African-American woman who is herself a descendent of their common great-great-grandfather, McCaslin. A hundred years and some five generations have passed, but the white man still has power over his black neighbors—a power he still heedlessly abuses.

Historical Context

The seven stories in "Go Down, Moses" represent a series of different historical periods. The first story, "Was," is set in the 1860's, while the last two, "Delta Autumn" and the eponymous "Go Down, Moses," are set in 1940. The collection as a whole therefore encompasses the eighty–year period from the end of the Civil War to the time in which Faulkner was writing. This span of time is roughly co–equal with the lifespan of two McCaslin descendents: the white Ike McCaslin and the black Lucas Beauchamp. Ironically, the McCaslin land and legacy will fall to neither man, for Ike renounces his claim to it while Lucas, as a black man, has no claim to make beyond the thousand dollars that McCaslin left him. Instead, it is the Edmonds family that holds the McCaslin land and fortune. Yet Ike and Lucas's names themselves proclaim their history, for Ike is the only living McCaslin, while Lucas bears a name that might serve as a genealogical roadmap of his part of the country: he is Lucas Quintus Carothers McCaslin Beauchamp.

Many of the characters in "Go Down Moses" are intensely conscious of history itself, spending their time and energy reconstructing how their fathers lived and the legacy they have passed on to them.

Ike, for example, pores over his family's slave ledgers in an attempt to understand his grandfather's and his uncles' history as slaveholders. When Ike learns that his grandfather had a sexual relationship with several slave women—one of whom was his daughter—he takes on the weight of history and sets about to make some kind of recompense for his grandfather's crimes. Ike might agree with Joyce's Stephen Dedalus that "history is a nightmare from which I am trying to awake."

Lucas Beauchamp, too, possesses a historical consciousness. He sees himself and his own status in terms of his descent from old Carothers McCaslin. He stops hunting rabbits and opossums, for example, because the practice:

> Was no longer commensurate with his status as not only the oldest man but the oldest living person on the Edmonds plantation, the oldest McCaslin descendent even though in the world's eye he descended not from McCaslins but from McCaslin slaves, almost as old as old Isaac McCaslin who lived in town… almost, as old Isaac was, coeval with old Buck and Buddy McCaslin who had been alive when their father, Carothers McCaslin, got the land from the Indians back in the old time when men black and white were men (37).

Lucas can trace his own genealogy, and in so doing can draw clear connections between himself and his white cousins and ancestors. It doesn't seem to matter to him that "in the world's eye" he should lay no claim to being a McCaslin; he has written his own history. Like Ike, and perhaps like Faulkner himself, Lucas believes in an Edenic time before history in which black men, white men, and American Indians lived without clearly demarcated racial lines. This theme returns in "The Old People" and in "The Bear," where hunting in the woods allows men to live according to a different social order than the one that prevails in town.

The penultimate story in the collection, "Delta Autumn," shows history repeating itself as Roth Edmonds impregnates a young woman who is herself an African-American descendent of old McCaslin. Roth has asked Ike to tell the woman "no" and to give to her a bundle of money (355). Appalled by his cousin's behavior, Ike nevertheless gives her the money and Roth's message. Yet he also gives to the woman's child the horn that General Compson had left him. The act seems to acknowledge both that Roth's child is part of the McCaslin line, and that Ike has not yet atoned for his family's history.

Societal Context

"Go Down, Moses" is an exploration of what race means in America. Race is as much a social construct as it is an objective reality, and the collection dwells on how individuals build their own identity as well as the identities of those around them. "Whiteness" and "blackness" can change weight and meaning from one situation to another. "Was," for example, begins with Uncle Buck and Uncle Buddy, sons to old McCaslin, pursuing one of their runaway slaves, Tomey's Turl, to a neighboring plantation. The relationship is simple enough: the white men own the black man, and will get back their property. Over the course of the story, Uncle Buck becomes entangled in a series of bets with his neighbor, Mr. Hubert, and also—having wandered into the wrong bedroom at night—finds himself obliged to marry Hubert's spinster sister. Buddy comes to redeem his brother by playing a game of poker against Hubert. With money, marriage, and ownership of the fugitive slave on the line, Hubert looks from his cards, to Buddy, to the man who has dealt them:

> 'Who dealt these cards, Amodeus?' Only he didn't wait to be answered. He reached out and tilted the lampshade, the light moving up Tomey's Turl's arms that were supposed to be black but were not quite white, up his

Sunday shirt that was supposed to be white but wasn't quite either… and on to his face; and Mr. Hubert sat there, holding the lampshade and looking at Tomey's Turl. Then he tilted the shade back down and took up his cards and turned them face down and pushed them toward the middle of the table. "I pass, Amodeus," he said (29).

Turl's arms are "supposed to be black," but looking at him across the card table, Hubert understands that the man is not only Amodeus "Buddy" McCaslin's slave, but his half-brother. When the chips are quite literally down, Hubert acknowledges that racial identity and relationships across the races are more fluid and nuanced than a white man would normally admit.

Elsewhere in the collection the strict lines that divided the races during slavery and segregation become blurred. In "The Bear," white men, black men, and American Indians live together in a hunting camp that allows for a fluidity in their identities and relationships that would not be possible in town. It is a romanticized vision of the woods as a place where men of different races are "men, not white nor black nor red, but men, hunters" (191). Yet in so many other instances, race becomes a monolithic, all-important aspect of identity. In "Delta Autumn," Ike McCaslin has a long conversation with the mother of Roth's child. He has assumed that she is a white woman, but when she refers to her family taking in laundry, he realizes with a start that she is African-American. His response to the biracial child is telling:

Now he understood what it was she had brought into the tent with her… the pale lips, the skin pallid and dead-looking yet not ill, the dark and tragic and foreknowing eyes. Maybe in a thousand or two thousand years in America, he thought. But not now! Not now! He cried, not loud, in a voice of amazement, pity, and outrage: "You're a nigger!" (361).

Ike, in many respects, has been presented as a saintly figure who sees slavery as the country's original sin and who gives up his own inheritance to make amends for it. Yet he is viscerally appalled by the sight of a child who has both black and white heritage. According to Ike, the country may be ready to accept such a biracial person in "a thousand or two thousand years." The scene and the worldview it represents feel particularly relevant in light of the recent election of Barack Obama as the nation's first African-American (and first biracial) president. The kind of change that Ike thought would be a thousand or two thousand years coming, came instead within a single lifetime.

Religious Context

Faulkner drew the title for his collection from the nineteenth-century Negro spiritual of the same name:

The Lord, by Moses, to Pharaoh said: Oh! let my people go.

If not, I'll smite your first-born dead—Oh! let my people go.

Oh! go down, Moses,

Away down to Egypt's land, And tell King Pharaoh to let my people go.

The spiritual tradition, like that of its counterpart the hymn, involves expounding on a line or verse from the Bible. "Go Down, Moses" refers to God's command to Moses in the Book of Exodus: "And the Lord spoke unto Moses, go unto Pharaoh, and say unto him, thus saith the Lord, let my people go, that they may serve me" (5.1). When Pharaoh refused to free the enslaved Israelites, God visited a series of plagues and punishments on the Egyptians. Moses would eventually lead his people out of Egypt to the freedom of the Promised Land. The Exodus story was a powerful archetype in African-American culture, for it tells of the bondage and eventual freedom of the chosen people.

Faulkner's choice of titles therefore casts his collection in explicitly Christian terms. The legacy of slavery is not merely a historical reality, but a religious and spiritual one. Nor are the enslaved Israelites the only Biblical parallels informing Faulkner's treatment of race in America. The white American may be Pharaoh, who has enslaved God's people, but he is also Adam, who was given dominion over paradise but fell from grace and left to his children the stain of original sin. Lucius Quintus Carothers McCaslin is such an Adamic figure. "The Bear," the longest work in "Go Down, Moses," centers on Ike McCaslin's struggle to atone for some of his grandfather's sins by restoring to the African-American line of the McCaslin family some of the inheritance they are owed. Ike—named for Isaac, whom God called on Abraham to sacrifice—sacrifices himself for the sins he has inherited from his grandfather. This raises yet another Biblical parallel: Ike, like so many of Faulkner's protagonists, is a Christ-figure.

The final story in "Go Down, Moses," brings the collection's title into the world it describes. Molly Worsham, an African-American descendent of McCaslin, visits lawyer Gavin Stevens to ask him to bring the body of her son, who has been executed for shooting a police officer, back home to be buried. She tells Stevens: "Roth Edmonds sold my Benjamin. Sold him in Egypt. Pharaoh got him" (371). She will return to this refrain several times over the course of the brief story. In bringing home to the Edmonds estate the body of the executed man, Stevens is helping to bring to a close the legacy of Carothers McCaslin himself. The collection ends, fittingly, with the Christian rite of burial.

Scientific & Technological Context

One might read "Go Down, Moses" through the lenses of two very different formulations of racial identity: nineteenth- and early twentieth-century pseudo-scientific theories of racial difference and the modern scientific practice of DNA analysis. In Faulkner's south, whiteness and blackness were viewed as monolithic, inalienable qualities. The state of Louisiana, for example, long defined as "colored" anyone who had "a trace of black ancestry." In 1970, a challenge to this statute caused the state to clarify their definition: now a person was "colored" if they were at least 1/32nd of African descent (Daniel 20). The implication of such a statute—which was not overturned until 1983—was that whiteness was a sort of "pure" state that could be "colored" by even the smallest trace of non-white blood. This paradigm was supported by pseudo-scientific fields of study such as phrenology, which posited that the shape and structure of the head and the facial features indicated intelligence, moral character, and other traits. Eugenics, which is perhaps most closely associated with Hitler's Third Reich and its obsession with Aryan racial purity, was likewise put to service to justify the enslavement of African-Americans.

Modern science presents a very different perspective on race. First, real science has displaced the bodies of pseudo-scientific writing and "research" that sought to assert that the white race was genetically superior to others. Today, DNA analysis allows scientists to trace a person's lineage back many generations and hence to identify the complex pattern of their genetic inheritance. "African-American Lives," a 2006 PBS documentary hosted by historian Henry Louis Gates, Jr., helped put such an undertaking into the public light. Using both genealogical research and DNA analysis, the series explored the heritage of prominent African-Americans, including Oprah Winfrey. By identifying the incredibly broad range of ancestors that any one person may claim, such research further invalidates the idea that whiteness and blackness are distinct and monolithic qualities.

Biographical Context

A life-long Southerner, Faulkner was the descendent of slaveholders who had fought for the confederacy in the Civil War. The legacy of slavery and the war, as well as the dynamics of race relations in the present-day south, and in America as a whole, was never far from his mind. African-American characters figure prominently in many of his greatest novels, including "The Sound and the Fury," "Absalom, Absalom!," and "Light in August." Yet "Go Down, Moses" may represent Faulkner's most explicit treatment of relationships between black and white southerners who share not only a common history, but a common ancestry.

Faulkner dedicated the collection to Caroline Barr, the African-American woman who had worked as a servant for Faulkner's family and who had therefore helped raise him. Barr, incidentally, is the inspiration for Dilsey in "The Sound and the Fury." Barr died early in 1940, and two years later Faulkner would publish "Go Down, Moses." Faulkner's dedication reads:

To Mammy

CAROLINE BARR

Mississippi [1840–1940]

Who was born in slavery and who gave to my family a fidelity without stint or calculation of recompense and to my childhood an immeasurable devotion and love.

Faulkner's dedication speaks to the complicated, conflicted picture of race relations that emerges from "Go Down, Moses" as a whole. Ike McCaslin is one of several Faulkner protagonists who mounts the argument that race relations in the south were characterized not only by the oppression of slavery, but by genuine human relationships of the sort lacking in the north. Above the Mason-Dixon Line, indifference and "calculation of recompense" kept whites and African-Americans at a distance from each other. This may seem like a backhanded rationalization of slavery and of Jim Crow policies, but Faulkner's dedication makes clear the inherent contradictions that he faced as a white man who considered an African-American woman his "mammy."

Caroline Barr's death may have been the impetus and organizing principle for Faulkner's collection. In 1940, he was churning out stories at a steady clip. In need of money, as he so often was, Faulkner's sights were set on publishing in magazines that would pay him $500 or $1,000 for a single story. Yet somewhere in the midst of this "pot boiling," as he called it, Faulkner's genius asserted itself. He saw that so many of his new stories touched on the themes of race and history; that by drawing connections among the disparate periods he was exploring, he could trace the legacy of slavery across the generations. Faulkner, like several of the critics who first read "Go Down, Moses," considered the work to be a novel rather than a collection of short stories. The dedication to Caroline Barr, whose own lifespan almost exactly corresponds to the century that "Go Down, Moses" concerns, makes explicit and makes personal the governing idea behind Faulkner's novel.

Matthew J. Bolton

Works Cited

Blotner, Joseph. *Faulkner: A Biography.* New York: Random House, 1984.

Daniel, G. Reginald. *More than Black?: Multiracial Identity and the New Racial Order.* Philadelphia: Temple University Press, 2002.

Faulkner, William. *Go Down, Moses.* New York: Random House, 1942.

Discussion Questions

1. Faulkner drew the title for his collection from the Negro spiritual "Go Down, Moses." How does the collection rework the Biblical theme of the exodus and the journey to the promised land?

2. What are the other religious tropes or themes that serve as organizing principles for the collection? How does the Adam and Eve story, for example, play itself out in Faulkner's mythos?

3. Faulkner wrote "Go Down, Moses" a decade before the civil rights movement got underway. Where in the collection is he at his most progressive or his most reactionary?

4. Does the world of "Go Down, Moses" allow any of its characters to maintain a bi-racial identity, in which they are somehow able to claim both their white and their African-American heritage?

5. Is "Go Down, Moses" a tragedy, a comedy, or both? What are some of its most purely tragic or purely comic moments?

6. What did the Big Woods represent for Ike, Boon, and the other hunters? What is the relationship between the loss of the Big Woods to logging and development and the changing relationships between whites, African-Americans, and American Indians in the south?

7. Discuss the importance of place and land as an organizing principle in this collection.

8. Refer to Faulkner's maps of Yohknaptawpha county. How do these maps change or inform your reading of "Go Down, Moses."

9. To what extent have Faulkner or his protagonist's observations and formulations about race become outdated? To what extent are they still relevant?

Essay Ideas

1. Compare any two members of the extended McCaslin family, be they across the generations or across the white and black branches of the family tree.

2. Identify the significance of given names in one or more of the stories, discussing the name's antecedents in the Bible and in the McCaslin family.

3. Read the collection in light of Faulkner's other novels. How does "Go Down, Moses" inform the relationships between black and white characters in a novel such as "The Sound and the Fury," "Absalom, Absalom!," or "Light in August"?

4. Study one of the historical periods in which Faulkner's stories are set, such as the era of reconstruction. How faithful is Faulkner to historical accounts of the period? Where does his reading of history depart from that of most historians?

5. If "Go Down, Moses" is, as Faulkner often called it, a novel, who is the novel's protagonist? Make a case for old McCaslin, Ike, Lucas, or another of the characters as the collection's main character.

6. Compare Faulkner's representation of slavery with that of Frederick Douglass or another African-American writer who experienced enslavement first hand.

7. Deconstruct one of the novel's comic scenes—such as Uncle Buck's chasing down the runaway Tomey's Turl—by reading it as a serious or even a tragic episode. How does Faulkner's perspective on the scene render it comic, and what light might a different perspective shed on the scene?

8. Compare Faulkner's genealogy of the two branches of the McCaslin family with that of an actual mixed-race family. Annette Gordon-Reed has detailed genealogies of the Hemingses family, notably the line descended from Thomas Jefferson and his slave Sally Hemings, in her books "Thomas Jefferson and Sally Hemings: An American Controversy" and "The Hemingses of Monticello."

9. Compare Faulkner's construction of multi-racial identity or African-American identity with that of a contemporary author. Consider James McBride's "The Color of Water" or Barack Obama's "Dreams for my Father" as two memoirs about coming to terms with one's multi-racial heritage.

10. Analyze Faulkner's maps of Yoknapatawpha County or one of his commentator's genealogical charts of the McCaslin family. Write an essay discussing how these para-textual documents shed light on "Go Down, Moses."

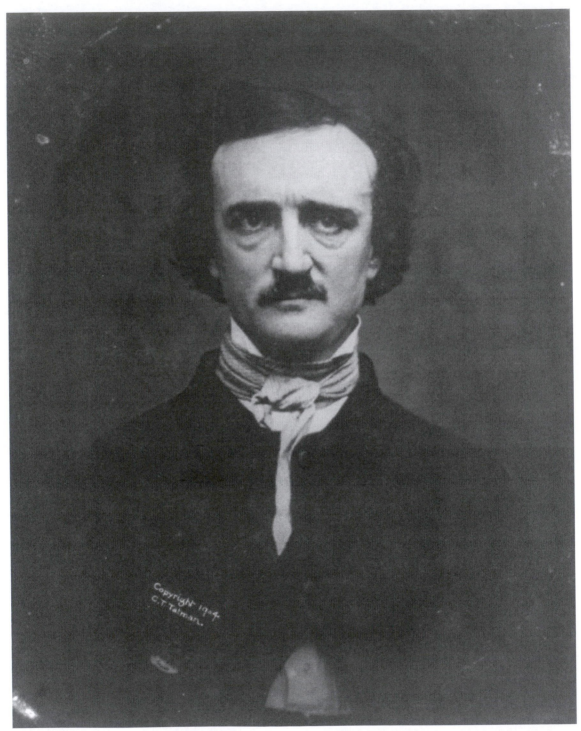

Edgar Allen Poe was an American author, and one of the earliest short story writers. Poe, shown here, shortly before his death at age 40, is best known for his tales of mystery and the macabre, and is thought of as the inventor of the detective fiction genre; nine of his short stories are included in this volume. Photo: Library of Congress, Prints & Photographs Division, LC-USZ62-10610.

The Gold-Bug

by Edgar Allan Poe

Content Synopsis

This essay presents a plot summary and analysis of Edgar Allen Poe's short story "The Gold-Bug." The essay contextualizes the story through a discussion of historical, societal, religious, scientific and biographical information. Centered heavily on Poe's interest in cryptography and ratiocination through its depiction of ciphers and symbols, the story also plays with societal issues like race, status, and wealth.

The story opens as a narrator, a physician who lives in Charleston, South Carolina, describes his longtime friend, Mr. William Legrand, who was born in New Orleans to a wealthy family, but now lives in a hut on Sullivan's Island, a long, sandy barrier island near Charleston, with only his former slave Jupiter for company. Legrand passes the time hunting and fishing and seeking new species of insects and seashells. The hut is empty when the narrator arrives to visit his friends on a chilly late-October day, but Jupiter and Legrand soon return with some marsh-hens to cook for dinner and news of a new insect, a scarabaeus or dung-beetle, that they discovered that day on the beach. Legrand is chagrined that he has returned without the "bug" itself—he has lent it to a friend, Lieutenant G—and after trying to describe it to the narrator, he pulls from his pocket a dirty scrap of what looks like foolscap, sketches the bug upon it, and hands the sketch to the narrator.

The narrator is jostled towards the blazing fire when Legrand's Newfoundland dog rushes in and jumps up to greet him, and the narrator is puzzled when he finds that the bug drawing does not resemble Legrand's earlier description. No antennae are visible in the drawing, which looks to the narrator like an ordinary death's-head or skull.

When the narrator remarks on this discrepancy, Legrand demands to see the drawing. When he scrutinizes it, his face grows red and he sinks abruptly into a mood of abstraction. The narrator, puzzled by this sudden change of mood, decides not to spend the night and returns to Charleston.

More than a month later, the narrator is surprised when Jupiter appears at his door, looking "dispirited" (287). Jupiter persuades the narrator to accompany him back to Sullivan's Island, where Legrand is suffering from some strange ailment that makes him act strangely and "cipher" all the time. Jupiter is certain that this illness has resulted from Legrand's being "bitten" by the gold-bug, and hands the narrator a note from Legrand begging him to come upon business "of the highest importance" (289). The scene is enlivened by Jupiter's comic misconstructions of Legrand's elaborate language and by the fact that the former slave has threatened to "beat" his disobedient master with a stick. The narrator agrees, and is surprised to find a scythe and spade in the Jupiter's boat. These tools, says Jupiter, have been ordered by Legrand, and will apparently be essential to the mysterious business ahead.

When they arrive, Legrand is flushed with excitement and promises that "this bug is to make my fortune" (291). He brushes off the narrator's concern that he is ill, and points out that he is merely excited. The narrator is eventually persuaded to accompany Legrand and Jupiter. They set off late in the afternoon, equipped with digging tools, the dog, dark lanterns, with Legrand swinging the gold-bug on a piece of whipcord "with the air of a conjuror" (293). After two hours' walk they pause; Legrand orders Jupiter to climb an enormous tulip-tree, and a comic scene ensues in which the reluctant Jupiter continues to ascend through the branches of the tree until he reaches a limb where he finds something strange indeed: a human skull nailed to the branch. Legrand orders Jupiter to climb out on the branch and drop the gold-bug, still on its string, through the skull's left eye. Jupiter complies; the bug is lowered towards the ground, and Legrand carefully marks its trajectory on the ground, then counts off a number of strides. Shovels are distributed and the three seekers dig a large hole in the ground by lantern-light. When they reach the depth of five feet without finding anything, Legrand and Jupiter wordlessly begin to pack up their belongings to return home, gravely disappointed. Suddenly, however, Legrand has an insight: he asks Jupiter to identify his left eye, and when Jupiter identifies his right eye instead, Legrand orders him to re-ascend the tree and perform the operation again—this time correctly. They again mark the bug's trajectory, count off paces, and dig, but this session of digging yields a different result. First, the dog begins to bark frantically; the men muzzle him, and are frustrated when he continues to yelp through the muzzle. After two hours and increasing yelps of excitement from the dog, they find two complete human skeletons and remnants of clothing, a knife, and coins. Ten more minutes of frenzied digging reveal an enormous

trunk, too large for three men to lift, filled to the brim with gold, jewelry, and other pieces of booty.

Jupiter reminds the two white men that, if not for the gold-bug, they never would have found the treasure. The three men leave behind the dog, which Jupiter sternly charges with protecting the treasure, and return to the hut for a few hours of sleep. The next day, armed with sacks, they return to retrieve the treasure. They divide the spoils evenly and return again to the hut, exhausted and exhilarated. After carefully emptying the box and inventorying its contents, the men eventually estimate the total value of the treasure at more than a million and a half dollars.

Legrand finally explains to the narrator, Jupiter, and the reader how he knew where the treasure was buried. He admits that he began to be excited when the narrator returned his drawing of the gold-bug and he found, on its reverse, a picture of a death's head that was not present when he made the original drawing. On closer scrutiny, he finds that the "paper" is actually vellum, or parchment, and thus both expensive and durable, and acting upon his knowledge of invisible writing, he exposes the parchment to the fire's warmth and more designs appear, including the figure of a baby goat, or kid. Recollecting that the notorious pirate Captain Kidd had once frequented the environs of Sullivan's Island, Legrand grows increasingly excited, connecting the "kid" to the death's head (a traditional pirate symbol). More exposure to the fire reveals a paragraph of mysterious characters, comprising letters, numbers, and punctuation marks. Legrand explains that he used the principles of cryptography—which involves substituting one symbol for another systematically—to decode the cipher, enlisting principles of probability such as the frequent use of the letter "E" in English.

Having decoded the paragraph, however, Legrand still has work to do. The instructions themselves are written in a kind of code, referring to locations like "Bishop's Hostel" and "the Devil's

Seat." After puzzling over these mysteries, Legrand consults with elderly locals, who recognize the names and point him towards the landmarks they reference.

The astonished narrator reproves Legrand for his earlier "grandiloquence" and mysterious, obnoxious behavior while the three men were searching for the treasure. Legrand admits that he was annoyed by the accusations of insanity and had resolved to punish the narrator. The narrator concludes the story by asking Legrand the provenance of the skeletons found in the hole. Legrand is uncertain, but proposes that because Kidd must have had help in burying the heavy trunk; the bodies may well be those of his compatriots, who were not as lucky as the narrator and Jupiter. Instead of sharing his secret with his associates, Legrand surmises, Kidd may well have murdered them with the very tools they had used to dig the hole.

Historical Context

"The Gold-Bug," which won a $100 prize and publication from the *Philadelphia Dollar Newspaper* in 1843, is deeply rooted in history. Calling up a legend of pirate treasure from the seventeenth century; a legendary beetle reputed by the ancient Egyptians to symbolize eternal life; and eerily anticipating the California gold-rush that would begin in January 1848, the story asks readers to look both backward and forward. In a veiled way, it also addresses issues of racism and inequality that would result in the American civil war less than fifteen years later.

Americans at mid-century were coming to terms with their colonial past, which had left its traces in barbaric or "peculiar" institutions like piracy and slavery. William Legrand, as a child of New Orleans aristocrats who through "a series of misfortunes" have been "reduced … to want," recalls the familiar mythos of the New World emigrant who leaves the homeland to regain a lost fortune in a new, hostile place, largely through

intelligence and hard work. The physical traces of this past—evident in the "manumitted" or freed slave Jupiter and the buried pirate treasure—are redeemed by the actions of Legrand. Though he operates mysteriously, even "insanely" in the eyes of the narrator, there is method in his madness. Legrand emerges from poverty not from simple hard work or passive virtue, but because of his ability to interpret and make use of a series of coincidences. These coincidences are laughably small. A beetle is found on the beach; when it bites, Jupiter picks up a piece of parchment to contain it; Legrand, having loaned the bug, creates a makeshift drawing of it; the drawing is jostled near the fire on an unexpectedly chilly day; and so forth. It is Legrand's ability to interpret these coincidences in a flexible and creative way that is the heart of his success. His educational background has prepared him to understand the parchment's likely historical context and to solve the cipher using mathematical probability. His practical intelligence leads him to ask local elderly people, some of them African-American, for advice about the strange place-names suggested in the cipher. Tolerance for frustration comes in handy when Jupiter forgets the difference between right and left.

Legrand performs his most important gesture when time comes to claim the treasure. "A little after four we arrived at the pit, divided the remainder of the booty, as equally as might be among us," says the narrator, and this is the last we hear of the distribution. Unlike Captain Kidd, who more than likely murdered the associates who helped him bury the chest, Legrand agrees to divide the treasure three ways, evenly, between himself, the narrator, and Jupiter. Legrand's willingness to give two-thirds of the treasure to his friends, one of them a servant and former slave, is radically egalitarian in that it effectively mitigates the violence inherent in the treasure, which represents innumerable thefts not only of money but of personal jewelry that undoubtedly had emotional value for its owners.

Societal Context

Poe's presentation of Jupiter, the freed African-American slave who has followed his "massa" from New Orleans to South Carolina, has been criticized as crude and racist. He speaks in a funny, phonetic version of Legrand's language, he can't tell his right from his left, he mistakes the bug for one made of "real gold." On closer inspection, however, the figure of Jupiter emerges as more than simply a racist caricature. In fact, he is emblematic of the story's deeper themes concerning language, interpretation, and intelligence.

Jupiter's language is a garbled version of Legrand's, as he regularly substitutes familiar "ordinary" words for Legrand's more elaborate choices, as when he refers to an "epistle" (letter) as a "pissel" (farm slang for penis). Other mix-ups, such as his substitute of "siphon" for "ciphering," defamiliarize the intended word and force the reader to pronounce the word aloud in order to "crack" the code of Jupiter's speech. This elementary process of code-cracking, in which the reader must guess what "correct" word to substitute for Jupiter's dialect version, is part of the fundamental lesson of the story—that interpretation is not optional but essential, and that "codes" like Jupiter's language deserve not to be ignored, but to be scrutinized and translated.

Though Poe uses Jupiter to provide comic relief, the ex-slave is also presented as more "master" than Legrand himself. Though Legrand frequently upbraids Jupiter for minor mistakes, he knows his servant's participation is essential and he values the work Jupiter provides. Legrand is presented as a mentally unbalanced young man who is supervised, and even threatened with beatings, by his former slave, the true "master" of the situation. Finally, as Jupiter does not hesitate to point out, the intrinsic value of the gold bug was first recognized by himself, when, having been bitten, he glanced around for a piece of jetsam to use as a container for the ill-tempered, but beautiful bug.

Religious Context

Poe was not an overtly religious man, devoting his most powerful energies, especially in his horror tales, to the depiction of supernatural influences that existed outside of Christian cosmology. Poe's use of the scarab beetle in "The Gold-Bug," however, recalls an earlier religious tradition. The ancient Egyptians worshiped the scarabaeus sacer, or dung-beetle, as an emblem of transformation and immortality. The hieroglyph that represents the beetle is a trilateral phonetic that translates roughly into "to come into being" or "to transform." Scarab beetles roll dung into spheres that are sometimes many times their own body size; the Egyptians thought that these balls resembled the sun in its daily transit and identified the beetle with the sun's rise and fall, extending the metaphor to the life span of humans. Scarab jewelry was an indispensable element of Egyptian funerary rites, and scarab ornaments were crafted of priceless gems and metals and often inscribed with inscriptions or cartouches.

Poe uses the scarab beetle of the story, which is shiny, golden, very heavy, and bad-tempered, as a powerful, multivalent symbol. Jupiter interprets it literally, asserting that the bug itself is solid gold, while Legrand admires it first as a possibly unique specimen and then as a clue to an important mystery. The narrator believes neither of these assertions, but is concerned that Legrand has caught "the gold-bug," a term for a person obsessed with seeking riches. By the end of the story, each man's interpretation has been proven at least partly true, though the beetle itself turns out to be what in detective fiction is known as a "red herring" or "macguffin"—a promising clue that eventually turns out to be valueless or misleading.

Readers might compare the scarab to a Christian cross, a symbol that is often made into jewelry and treated as a talisman—an object with religious significance that is thought to bring good luck or divine protection to its owner. Just as ancient

Egyptians felt that the scarab offered them divine protection ("heart scarabs" were inlaid over the hearts of mummies to protect their souls in the afterlife), modern Christians may wear or keep in their house a cross that symbolizes their faith and protects them from harm. Poe, whose classical education was extensive, was undoubtedly aware of the Egyptian lore associated with the scarab, and in this story defamiliarizes the talisman by demonstrating that, though no magic or supernatural intervention may be involved, talismans nonetheless provide good luck and protection to those who believe in their powers.

Scientific & Technological Context

Circumstances, and a certain bias of mind, have led me to take interest in such riddles, and it may well be doubted whether human ingenuity can construct an enigma of the kind which human ingenuity may not, by proper application, resolve (311)

"The Gold-Bug" envinces Poe's strong interest in cryptography and ratiocination. In the 1840s, the telegraph had come into wide use in the United States, and its influences spread far and wide. The substitution of one set of symbols for another, as in Morse code, intrigued Poe, who had always recognized the arbitrariness of language and from childhood onward had been fascinated by symbolic systems like linguistics and mathematics. Poe articulated his interest in cryptography as early as 1839, when he published a series of unsigned articles in Alexander's Weekly Messenger describing the principles of what he termed "secret writing." He challenged readers to come up with cryptographs, boasting that he could solve any substitution puzzle, and continued to solve and publish these in the magazine until he left the Messenger in 1840.

In "The Gold-Bug," Poe brings together the competing discourses of science and religion in the symbol of the beetle itself, which humans have valued for its metaphorical and spiritual significance and for its possible uniqueness as a scientific specimen. The cartouches, or hieroglyphic inscriptions, on the back of scarab jewelry also served as "codes" to early Egyptologists, as they learned to interpret the ancient codes. At mid-century, biologists were intent on classifying the world's innumerable plant and animal species, and Legrand's fascination for entomology is presented as part of this "fad." Yet his belief in the value of the beetle turns out to have a larger metaphorical significance, suggesting that the activities of scientists are intrinsically valuable, leading us to a new appreciation of "true gold."

Biographical Context

Edgar Allan Poe had a difficult, unhappy, and brief life, but in spite of many obstacles, left behind a rich body of literature including poetry, fiction, and criticism. Born in Boston in 1809 to actor–parents, Poe quickly found himself without resources when his mother died of tuberculosis and his father deserted the young family. Poe and his siblings were given as foster children to several different families, Poe to the Allan family of Richmond who were affluent and able to provide him with an excellent early education. He grew very close to his foster mother, Mrs. Frances Allan, but had a more testy relationship with John Allan. The Allans moved to England, where young Poe excelled at school in London, and when they returned to Richmond, he enrolled at the University of Virginia. He wrote poetry throughout his adolescence and early adulthood and published two books before he was 23. But soon Poe was forced to withdraw from the university because his foster father refused to pay his expenses. Poe then sought a military career, enlisting first in the army and enrolling at West Point in 1830. Again, however, though he excelled academically, Poe was dishonorably discharged within a year. His third book, *Poems*, was published in 1830, partly with money raised by his fellow students at West Point.

Poe was repeatedly alienated from and reconciled with his foster-father, who was both tight-fisted and rigid, and eventually sought work as a journalist and editor in Richmond, Philadelphia, and New York. He was an effective editor, but his high standards and occasionally judgmental reviews won him both friends and enemies. He found himself in a new family in the mid-1830s when he married his young cousin Virginia Eliza Clemm, who at the time was only fourteen. Poe's relationship with Virginia and with her mother Maria Clemm, a mother-figure whom Poe playfully called "Muddy," were warm and companionable, and it is likely that the marriage was not consummated until Virginia was an adult. Poverty was a constant problem for this unusual menage, and when Virginia died of tuberculosis in 1847, while they were living in New York, Poe was devastated. Always susceptible to the effects of alcohol, he began to indulge in increasingly serious drinking binges, and his erratic behavior alienated employers and cost him substantially.

Poe continued to write poems and fiction while working as a journalist and editor. His output, in spite of obstacles, was astonishing. After publication of *The Raven and Other Poems* in 1845, he began to experience fame as a writer, something he had always sought. He reunited with his teenage sweetheart, Elmira Royster, in 1848, and undertook a lecture and reading tour in 1849. But at the age of forty, he was found unconscious in the street in Baltimore, Maryland, possibly from alcohol poisoning, and never recovered consciousness. The exact cause of Poe's death has never been determined.

Lisa Jadwin

Works Cited

Auerbach, Jonathan. *The Romance of Failure: First-Person Fictions of Poe, Hawthorne, and James.* New York: Oxford UP, 1989.

Kennedy, J. Gerald. *Poe, Death, and the Life of Writing.* New Haven: Yale UP, 1987.

Knapp, Bettina L. *Edgar Allan Poe.* "His Life and Legacy." New York: F. Ungar, 1984.

Poe, Edgar Allan. *The Fall of the House of Usher and Other Writings.* Ed. and intro. David Galloway. London: Penguin Classics, 1986.

Poe, Edgar Allan. "The Gold-Bug." In *The Fall of the House of Usher and Other Writings* 283–319.

Rosenheim, James. *The Cryptographic Imagination: Secret Writing from Poe to the Internet.* Baltimore: Johns Hopkins UP, 1997.

Walker, I. M., ed. *Edgar Allan Poe: The Critical Heritage.* New York: Routledge & Kegan Paul, 1986.

Woodberry, George E., and R. W. B. Lewis. *Edgar Allan Poe.* New York: Chelsea House, 1997.

Discussion Questions

1. Why does Legrand choose to feign insanity?
2. How does the story's epigraph relate to the story itself?
3. Discuss Poe's portrayal of nature in this story.
4. How does the setting of the story contribute to its major theme of code-cracking?
5. What does the phrase "le grand" mean in French, and why is it an appropriate name for the story's protagonist?
6. "Jupiter" was the name for the chief god of the Roman pantheon, called "Zeus" by the ancient Greeks. Why did Poe choose this name for Legrand's "valet" in this story?
7. What errors do the three men make as they search for the treasure?
8. Surprisingly, the Newfoundland dog plays an important role in the story. Discuss the clues he provides that make the discovery of the treasure possible.
9. What is it about the parchment that convinces Legrand that the document must be valuable?
10. Describe some modern uses of code-cracking.

Essay Ideas

1. Make a list of Jupiter's word substitutions. What patterns do you see in the choices he makes? Which of Legrand's words does he mistake, and why?

2. Why did Poe chose to make the narrator nameless?

3. Compare Legrand, whose strange behavior makes him seem insane, with other characters from literature, such as Hamlet. How is Legrand similar to, and different from, these other characters?

4. Comment on the use of humor in this story. Where does it appear, and what functions does it serve?

5. The story is divided into two parts—the first, an account of actions, and the second, an explanation of those actions. Why did Poe structure the story this way?

A Good Man is Hard to Find

by Flannery O'Connor

Content Synopsis

A disconnected family goes on a vacation from Atlanta to Florida. The children, John Wesley and June Star, are wild and inconsiderate; their parents apathetic. The grandmother complains about the changing times and lack of respect of people today. She tries to convince her son Bailey to take the family to Tennessee instead of Florida so she can visit relatives. She brings up the fact that an escaped convict called The Misfit is on the loose and headed towards Florida, but he ignores her and they take their trip. To spite Bailey and comfort herself, the grandmother brings her cat and hides it in a basket. While driving through Georgia, the grandmother reminisces about the people and places from days gone by. They stop at an old-fashioned barbecue for lunch and the grandmother and the restaurant owner, Red Sam, shake their heads over the changing times and how hard it is to trust people. Red Sam declares that, "a good man is hard to find" (O'Connor 681).

As the family drives on, they pass a dirt road, and the grandmother remembers an old plantation house from her younger years and asks Bailey to drive by it. She exaggerates about secret compartments in the house to get the grandchildren interested in seeing it. They kick and scream until Bailey finally relents and turns down the dirt road she thinks the house is on. As they travel down the long, desolate road, the grandmother realizes that the house she was thinking of was actually in Tennessee, not Georgia. As she remembers, her cat jumps out of the basket onto Bailey and he crashes the car into a ditch. Everyone is relatively unharmed but they are now stranded. The children shout excitedly, "We've had an ACCIDENT!" while the adults shake with fear (O'Connor 683). While they await assistance, a car with three men inside approaches them. The driver of the car, a shirtless middle-aged man in "scholarly" looking wire-rimmed glasses, turns out to be The Misfit (O'Connor 684).

The Misfit's two sidekicks, Hiram and Bobby Lee, take Bailey and his son off into the woods and gunshots are heard shortly after. The grandmother grieves for him shouting, "Bailey boy!" but then tries to flatter The Misfit to save herself (O'Connor 686). She tells him that he is not a bit "common" and asks him if he prays. When he says no, she tries to convince him that prayer will help to set him on the righteous path. The Misfit then has Hiram and Bobby Lee take the mother, her baby and June Star off to the woods and three shots are heard. The grandmother continues to try to save herself. She begs The Misfit to pray and spare her life. She has a moment of heartfelt empathy for him at the end when she reaches out to touch him and calls him one of her babies, but he shoots her three times and has his partners throw her body in the woods (688). The story ends as The Misfit declares, "It's no real pleasure in life" (689).

Symbols & Motifs

The aptly named character of The Misfit serves as a symbol both of evil as well as a symbol of the villain's inability to fit into society. The family also represents a bunch of misfits as demonstrated through their ungratefulness and disregard for other's emotions. The mother ignores her children except for her baby; the children have no qualms about littering and talking back to adults. The family is living without really being aware of the fact that life is precious.

The vacation that the family is taking also has symbolic significance as a journey away from their familiar surroundings. The fact that the family is going further South might be indicative of the direction they are heading in the afterlife. Even their stop along the way at Red Sam's resembles a place of purgatory ("Flannery O'Connor and 'A Good Man is Hard to Find'"). The grandmother revisits moments of her life as the family drives along on their way to Florida and is the only family member who seems to learn anything on the road of life.

The characters' names act as symbols as well. John Wesley, the hostile, loud-mouthed child, is named after the founder of the Methodist religion ("Flannery O'Connor and 'A Good Man is Hard to Find'"). June Star, the bratty, selfish sister of John, has a name that resembles a starlet of the 30's or 40's, aptly demonstrated at Red Sam's in her demand for a song she could dance to ("Flannery O'Connor and 'A Good Man is Hard to Find'"). The children's mother ironically is given no name and their father is given a generic one. The grandmother is not given a name as her identity is that of the family elder.

Historical Context

Flannery O'Connor takes special care in presenting the differences between the old generation of Southern gentility and the current (1950's) generation, which is more abrasive and fast-paced. A personal history is explored as the grandmother reflects on plantation homes, unpaved roads and formal clothing while riding with her son and his young family on a highway to the trendy vacation spot of Florida. The grandmother appears to be struggling with the changes occurring throughout the time period. These changes are reflected in her children and grandchildren.

In the 1950s, the population was growing and expansion of cities and suburbs was occurring across the country while farmland began to decrease. The advent of rock n' roll music fed the desire of the nation's young people to rebel against their parents' traditional values. Clothing became more colorful and casual. Restaurant and entertainment chains multiplied, leaving the traditional "mom and pop" joints, like Red Sam's, to fade away. In addition, the rise of communism and the threat of espionage and nuclear war led to a population filled with fear and uncertainty.

Societal Context

This story presents a contrast between the grandmother's generation and that of her children and grandchildren. Both generations are depicted as imperfect. The grandmother is unknowingly racist; the children are unknowingly inconsiderate to their elders. The grandmother tells her grandchildren that they have no respect for anything these days, which is true as seen in their speech and actions such as trying to throw trash out the car window. However, in the next breath the grandmother shouts, "Oh look at the cute little pickaninny!" and "Little niggers in the country don't have things like we do" in reference to a black child they happen to drive past (O'Connor 679). Flannery O'Connor acknowledged in her essay "The Element of Suspense in 'A Good Man is Hard to Find'" that the old woman resembles a Southern stereotype and said that most Southern readers have an older relative who resembles the grandmother. She retains elements of Southern hospitality and manners, but it is exclusive to non-common folk and those of the white race. She is ignorant of her own ignorance.

The fact that the whole family dies at the hands of The Misfit and his random violence parallels the author's own belief that society (in the 1950's) was going fiercely downhill. Even the innocent baby is murdered. The Misfit is the epitome of everything that is wrong with society. He lacks faith, manners, and has no respect for laws and moral standards of any kind. His appearance is a contradiction in itself. He is middle-aged, graying and wearing scholarly glasses, yet he is shirtless and is wearing tight jeans. He agrees with the grandmother on many levels and entertains her talk of Jesus but shoots her without thought as soon as she tries to get close to him. He represents the hypocrisy of both the older and younger generations, but his dominance in the story reveals an apocalyptic glimpse of the future.

Religious Context

Flannery O'Connor was known to be a devoutly pious Roman Catholic and Christian principles are present in all of her work. In "A Good Man is Hard to Find" O'Connor wrestles with the nature of good and evil, but even more so, presents the reality that most people stumble through life on a less than righteous path. Bailey and his wife and children appear consumed with their own desires and have little concern for others. The grandmother, as unlikable as she is, is the only character reflective enough to see how far removed society is from what really matters in life. In her essay on this story, O'Connor states, "The heroine, the Grandmother, is in the most significant position life offers the Christian. She is facing death. And to all appearances she, like the rest of us, is not too well prepared for it" (O'Connor 704). "A Good Man is Hard to Find" is a story that reminds the reader that evil does exist in the world and the day

of judgment is always just around the corner. The story forces the reader to take a second look at his or her own life and ask the question—am I ready?

This story first appeared in a collection by the same name with the following quote from St. Cyril of Jerusalem as an opening, "The dragon is by the side road, watching those who pass. Beware lest he devour you. We go to the father of souls, but it is necessary to pass by the dragon" (Drake 187). Whether the dragon is the devil or Christ is up for debate, but regardless, according to O'Connor, this figure is watching and judging us all.

The Misfit and his sidekicks represent the embodiment of evil and The Misfit could be compared to the devil, but even he seems more human and complex than that. The Misfit is troubled by the evil in the world even though he is a contributor. He more likely represents one more troubled soul on earth that lacks religion.

Scientific & Technological Context

"A Good Man is Hard to Find" does not have a specific scientific or technological context.

Biographical Context

Mary Flannery O'Connor was born in Savannah, GA in 1925 and spent much of her life in Milledgeville, GA until her death in 1964 (Goia & Gwinn 677). She graduated from Georgia State College for Women in 1945 and earned her MFA from the University of Iowa in 1947 (Goia & Gwinn 677). In 1950, she was diagnosed with lupus and shortly thereafter she moved in with her mother in Milledgeville (Goia & Gwinn 677).

Even though she was raised in the South, which is predominantly Protestant, Flannery O'Connor was a devout Roman Catholic (Goia & Gwinn 677). Her religious views colored her work as she viewed contemporary Southern society with growing disdain. The voice in her work is extremely moralist, wryly satiric and highly critical of the decline of Southern "mysteries and manners" (Goia & Gwinn 677).

She has been described as a Southern Gothic writer because of the violence and moral confusion of her characters (Goia & Gwinn 677).

In her lifetime, O'Connor published two novels, "Wise Blood" in 1952, and "The Violent Bear It Away" in 1960, as well as a collection of short stories, "A Good Man is Hard to Find" in 1955. After her death, the short story collection, "Everything that Rises Must Converge" was published in 1965 and a collection of essays "Mysteries and Manners" was published in 1969. "The Complete Stories of Flannery O'Connor" won the National Book Award in 1971.

Jennifer Bouchard

Works Cited

Clark, Beverly Lyon. *Flannery O'Connor.* Georgetown University. 15 January 2008.

Drake, Robert. "The Bleeding Stinking Mad Shadow of Jesus in the Fiction of Flannery O'Connor." *Comparative Literature Studies,* Vol. 3, No. 2, 1966, pp. 183–96.

"Flannery O'Connor's A Good Man is Hard to Find: Who's the Real Misfit?" *National Endowment for the Humanities.* 15 January 2008.

"Flannery O'Connor and 'A Good Man is Hard to Find.'" *Tyler Junior College.* 15 January 2008.

Gioia, Dana and R.S. Gwynn, eds. *The Art of the Short Story.* New York, Pearson Longman, 1992.

O'Connor, Flannery. "A Good Man is Hard to Find." Eds. Dana Gioia and R.S. Gwynn. *The Art of the Short Story.* New York, Pearson Longman, 1992.

O'Connor, Flannery. "The Element of Suspense in 'A Good Man is Hard to Find'" Eds. Dana Gioia and R.S. Gwynn. *The Art of the Short Story.* New York, Pearson Longman, 1992.

Discussion Questions

1. How would you characterize the grandmother?
2. How would you describe the rest of the family?
3. What is the significance of the title of the story, "A Good Man is Hard to Find"?
4. What purpose do names serve in this story? Who is not given a name? Why?
5. What are some examples of foreshadowing in the family?
6. How does O'Connor describe the cultural and physical landscape of the setting?
7. How does O'Connor distinguish between the old and new South?
8. What are some differences between the grandmother and the mother?
9. Who is the real Misfit in the story?
10. What is the significance of the discussion of Jesus?
11. What are the main themes of the story?

Essay Ideas

1. Write an essay in which you argue that the grandmother is the hero of the story. Use examples of the text to support your claims.

2. Analyze O'Connor's use of humor in "A Good Man Is Hard To Find." Be sure to discuss how she balances humor with the grotesque.

3. Investigate O'Connor's use of symbolism in the story. Be sure to include The Misfit and the road as symbols.

4. Discuss the presence of contrasts in the story. What purpose might these contrasts serve in terms of the overall message of the story? Use examples from the story to support your analyses.

5. Write an essay in which you analyze all of the Christian allusions and images in the story. Discuss how they contribute to the key themes.

Greasy Lake

by T. Coraghessan Boyle

I have indeed been to Greasy Lake on innumerable occasions, and [...] the stupidities engaged in by the characters in the story can't begin to match the stupidities that I perpetrated in real life.

T. Coraghessan Boyle

Content Synopsis

"Greasy Lake" is set on a June night and early morning; the opening words, "There was a time," imply a fairy tale-like timelessness for the action. It is narrated in the first person by an unnamed man looking back to his days as a nineteen year old, "when it was good to be bad"; he and his friends "were all dangerous characters then" (129). Their town (unnamed) is located near a lake, called Wakan by the "Indians," "a reference to the clarity of its waters" (129). These waters are now murky, its shores garbage-strewn, and its island denuded of vegetation: "it looked as if the air force had strafed it" (129), which is the first of many military references in the story. The site has become a teenage hangout, a place to "drink beer, smoke pot, howl at the moon," but also to "snuff the rich scent of possibility on the breeze" and "savor the

incongruous full-throated roar of rock and roll against the primeval susurrus of frogs and crickets. This was nature" (129). It is, at any rate, as close to nature as one can get in a technological age in which the natural world is increasingly buried in human waste, though this irony becomes clear only as the story progresses.

On the night in question, the narrator and his friends Digby (a student at Cornell who wears a gold star in his right ear) and Jeff, who is considering leaving school to "become a painter/musician/ head-shop proprietor" (129), drive to Greasy Lake in the narrator's mother's Bel Air, after cruising the strip, visiting various bars, eating fast food, and egging mailboxes and hitchhikers while "looking for something we never found" (130). Such details suggest that their concept of what constitutes a bad character is naïve. What they do find at Greasy Lake is a parked motorcycle, "like the exoskeleton of some gaunt chrome insect" (130), and a parked 1957 Chevrolet they mistake for the car of a friend, Tony. They decide to have some fun with Tony and the girl they assume he has with him by hitting them with their lights, honking their horn, and leering in the car windows at them.

However, the car is not Tony's but rather the car of "a very bad character in greasy jeans and engineer boots" (130) who bursts out of the car and attacks the three. Unfortunately, the narrator drops the car keys when getting out, "a tactical error, as damaging and irreversible in its way as Westmoreland's decision to dig in at Khe Sahn" (130). The narrator is kicked several times, chipping a tooth, and Digby is laid out by a roundhouse punch. The fight is imaged, somewhat comically, in the hyperbolic terms of combat; they have a battle cry ("motherfucker"), and the narrator imagines himself as a "kamikaze" (131). He grabs his tire iron from underneath the seat (where all bad characters carry such a thing, he tells us) and, "mindless, raging, stung with humiliation—the whole thing, from the initial boot in the chin to this murderous primal instant involving no more than sixty hyperventilating, gland-flooding seconds," brains the "bad greasy character" (131).

The narrator and his friends here have their first confrontation with mortality. The greasy character collapses. "Wet his pants. Went loose in his boots" (131). "A single second, big as a zeppelin, floated by" (131). They believe they have killed him, and the narrator imagines the inevitable involvement of the police and his trip to the electric chair.

At this point, "the fox," the woman in the car, leaps out, half undressed, calling the narrator and his friends animals (132). They do indeed seem transformed by this point into genuine bad characters, and set on her, seeing her as "already tainted" because she has painted toe nails (132). The narrator likens himself, Digby, and Jeff to the rapists in Bergman's "Virgin Spring," (a grim morality tale in which three men rape and kill a girl, only to be killed in turn by her father), as they come at her, "panting, wheezing, tearing at her clothes, grabbing for flesh" (132). They are prevented from raping her by the arrival of another car, a Trans Am, with "two guys—blond types, in fraternity jackets" (134) in it. The narrator and his friends flee.

The narrator enters the lake, planning to swim for it, when he has the central experience of the story, "one of those nasty little epiphanies for which we are prepared by films and TV and childhood visits to the funeral home" (133): he comes

upon a corpse in the water. Indeed, he literally falls face forward upon it. He believes he has just killed one man, and now he encounters the corpse of a second. Only after his recognition of the corpse in the water does he experience the "joy and vindication" of learning he is not a murderer, when he hears "the verbal virtuosity of the bad greasy character" (133) again challenging him and his friends.

The narrator stays hidden in the shallows of the lake. On shore, the bad greasy character, who we now learn is called Bobbie, takes out his frustration on the narrator's car, aided by the fraternity boys. As they smash the car (with the narrator's own tire iron!) and fill it with "bottles, rocks, muck, candy wrappers, used condoms, poptops, and other refuse" (134), the narrator is left to consider his plight and that of the nameless corpse: "I thought about him, fog on the lake, insects chirring eerily, and felt the tug of fear, felt the darkness opening up inside me like a set of jaws. Who was he, I wondered, this victim of time and circumstances, bobbing sorrowfully in the lake at my back. [...] My car was wrecked; he was dead" (134).

Eventually, Bobbie and the frat boys leave. As the sun rises on the next morning, there "was a smell in the air, raw and sweet at the same time, the smell of the sun firing buds and opening blossoms" (134). The narrator emerges from hiding and contemplates the wrecked car: "It lay there like a wreck along the highway, like a steel sculpture left over from a vanished civilization. Everything was still. This was nature" (134). Nature here has become something rather different from what it was at the beginning of the story. Then, nature was the background to superficial acts of rebellion, a dumping ground that nevertheless offered vague, inchoate promise. Now, it is not only much more intensely alive but also a stark reminder of death and destruction. Nature now includes the human artifact, and all it implies about human nature.

Only now can the narrator find the lost car key, a clearly symbolic discovery, as well as a literal necessity. The car is damaged but still drivable, since the tires have not been slashed. Just as the three are about to drive off, having cleared the junk out of the car, yet another vehicle pulls in: a silver Mustang driven by two girls, "Tight jeans, stiletto heels, hair like frozen fur" (135). One of them approaches and says they are looking for Al, owner of the abandoned chopper and evidently the corpse in the lake. The narrator says they haven't seen anyone, but the girl is not particularly concerned. She notes, "'you guys look like some pretty bad characters'" (136)—echoing their self-perception from earlier in the story—and offers them some drugs and an opportunity to party with her and her friend. The narrator tells us, "I thought I was going to cry" (136), they decline the offer, and drive off, the sun shining on the lake and the girl left behind, "watching us, her shoulders slumped, hand outstretched" (136).

The story is superficially simple, a direct, linear narrative of a single event in the narrator's life. It is deeply indebted to the initiation story, in which the "protagonist encounters a sudden Joycean epiphany, a new awareness of the reality of human existence" (Walker). However, it rewards careful attention in the complex ways it invokes that tradition and in its thematic and symbolic elements. Here are some major story elements worth further consideration.

Symbols & Motifs

The title: The title focuses our attention on the setting as a key component. Greasy Lake was once known "for the clarity of its waters," but now it is "fetid and murky, the mud banks glittering with broken glass and strewn with beer cans and the charred remains of bonfires" (129). It is a "festering murk" (129), "feculent" (132), covered with "mats of algae that clung to the surface like scabs" (132). It is also "primeval" (129), "dark, rank, mysterious" (130). It may be a party site, but it is associated with decay and destruction; it is a once

beautiful environment desecrated by the white culture that displaced the "Indians" (itself a term that redefines those whom it names from a European perspective) to whom it was Wakan, the clear lake. We should not be surprised, therefore, to find it the site of manifestations of the darkness hidden beneath the veneer of civilization, the "mindless" "primal" murderousness (131), the "lust and greed and the purest primal badness" (132) that emerges quickly and almost irrepressibly in the characters. The confrontation with nature in this story brings the narrator face-to-face not with a romantic nature but rather a heart of darkness.

Water: Water is a common symbol of transformation and purification. The narrator undergoes submersion, which we might expect to symbolize cleansing and rebirth. However, rather than a source of life and regeneration, Greasy Lake is, or has become, a site of death. The narrator encounters a corpse floating in the shallows. He lies in the water, "the bad breath of decay all around me, my jacket heavy as a bear, the primordial ooze subtly reconstituting itself to accommodate my upper thighs and testicles" (134). The primordial ooze, original source of life, is here instead tied to decay, ironically surrounding his thighs and testicles, his own generative organs being subsumed. The narrator does not emerge from the lake cleansed and renewed but rather with a grim insight into what lies beneath the surface: the "darkness opening up inside me like a set of jaws" (134).

Self-consciousness: Boyle's fiction generally is "highly self-conscious" (Zimmerman 66). Throughout the story, the narrator contextualizes the action in relation to works of fiction, from the opening words reminiscent of fairy tale to his consistent citation of literary, filmic, or televisual comparators for their experience. He and his friends model themselves on the poetry of André Gide. When he hits the greasy character with the tire iron, he images the character's collapse as a Hollywood stunt man's pratfall.

When he thinks he has killed the greasy character, he imagines the clichés of crime fiction. He compares himself and his friends to characters in a Bergman film, and himself to a character in "The Naked and the Dead." Indeed, the repeated description of himself, his companions, and even Bobbie as "bad characters" invites us to see them all as characters performing roles cast for them in various fictional constructs. In short, an important element of the story is its consciousness of its status as a story, as the conversion of experience into narrative. It is, one might say, a story about initiation stories as much as it is an initiation story itself.

Historical Context

Boyle is deliberately vague about when the story is set. It is June, "the third night of summer vacation" (130), but no year is given. Boyle has said,

> I tried to keep the "punks" universal, rather than pin them down to a timeframe. Actually, the story was written in 1981, during the punk era, and the styles, of course, were simply recycled (with the addition of straight-pins, etc.) from an earlier period. The beauty of "Greasy Lake" is that we have all been there, no matter the era, and you can take the "greasy" reference for what you will.
> (Qtd at "All About T. Coraghessan Boyle Resource Center").

However, Boyle has indicated that the story has autobiographical elements. The boys are listening to "Toots & the Maytals" on the radio. Boyle would have been the protagonist's age in 1968, when Toots & the Maytals had their first hit, and Westmoreland's stand at Khe Sanh (cited by the narrator as a comparison to his first big mistake in the story) took place in late 1967, so it may not be unreasonable to associate the story with that time period. Boyle's point that "we have all been there, no matter the era," though, is suggested in the ways the story likens the action to events

across a wider historical spectrum. The historical contexts invoked, however, are consistently associated with war or at least violence. The reference to Khe Sanh invokes a battle technically won but which marked the turning point in the Viet Nam conflict; Westmoreland may have won the battle but in a larger sense, he lost the war, a fact with ironic resonances in the pyrrhic victory the protagonist wins in the story. In addition to Vietnam, Boyle also cites the rape of the Sabine women (part of the myth of ancient Rome: Rome, winning the wars against its neighboring enemies but lacking women, invited its Sabine neighbors to a religious celebration and abducted their women there ("Rape of the Sabine Women"), the sacrifice of Christian martyrs, and, repeatedly, modern war. The narrator uses aerial strafing as a simile (potentially any twentieth-century conflict), images himself as a kamikaze (World War II), references Mailer's "The Naked and the Dead" (World War II), and images himself and his companions as "war veterans" (135) and the steering wheel of his car as "the ejection lever of a flaming jet" (135), and so on. In short, the rather comic violence and attempted rape in the story is contextualized against a broad tapestry of human violence across the ages but especially in the highly technologized twentieth century.

Societal Context

Every city or town has its own Greasy Lake and its disaffected youth enacting what they think are acts of defiance and rebellion against parents and authority. The youths in this story are clearly rebels without much cause and without much real need for rebellion. They are clearly not the genuinely bad characters they think they are, as, by contrast, Bobby and the dead Al most evidently are (or were). The narrator tells us, "When we wheeled our parents' station wagons out onto the street we left a patch of rubber half a block long" (129). The key detail is the car: the family station wagon, or one's mother's car (the narrator indicates specifically that he was driving on his fateful June night), is not the car of a genuine rebel or outcast. The 1957 Chevy driven by Bobby is a more genuine muscle car, what a "bad character" might drive, as is Al's chopper (the biker is an easily recognizable exemplar of the rebel outlaw). Digby's gold star in his right ear is calculated to irritate a parent, perhaps, but is hardly a major symbol of rebellion, and his rebellion is largely subverted by the fact that he "allowed his father to pay his tuition at Cornell" (129). Jeff's artistic pretensions make him an equally unlikely bad character. Indeed, as the narrator indicates, these suburban rebels are poseurs deriving their stance from art and imitation: "We read André Gide and struck elaborate poses to show that we didn't give a shit about anything" (129). They may well not give a shit about anything, but the story stresses their disaffectation as a pose rather than a genuine marker of outcast status. Indeed, the narrator is almost as worried about what he can tell his mother about what happened to her car as he is about anything else. His sense that the dead Al "was probably the only person on the planet worse off than I was" (134)—this from someone who moments before was referencing the Vietnam conflict—underscores his superficiality and the limits of his vision. Indeed, the extent to which this story suggests that the narrator experiences anything like a real epiphany and undergoes the sort of initiation, or growth to maturity we would expect to follow such an experience, is open to doubt, as Michael Walker argues (in the only specific study of "Greasy Lake" published as of 2005). This is a story of callow, pampered youth who seems to learn little from his experience, though Boyle's own comment on the story is instructive:

"It seems to me that the narrator wants to cry because something has been revealed to him about the nature of life, its dark accidents

and the limitations of hip. There is always a badder character than you. And what are you searching for anyway? Death? Yes, but for an accident of fate, he could have been the guy bobbing in the lake.

(Qtd at "All About T. Coraghessan Boyle Resource Center")

Boyle writes about "the banality and bestiality of contemporary society" (Adams 281), both of which are evident in the narrator's account of his adventures.

Religious Context

Boyle's background is Irish Catholic, and though "Greasy Lake" is not an overtly religious text, it invokes Christian, and some specifically Catholic, motifs. The first clear example is the narrator's assertion that the lost car keys would be "my grail and my salvation" (131) if he could find them. The Holy Grail, of course, can be found only by the purest of knights, who then cannot return it to Arthur's court. The Grail represents, especially in this story, an impossible salvation, as is clear when the narrator is finally able to find the keys only after his anti-baptism. The baptismal implications of submersion, ironically inverted here, have already been discussed under "Symbols & Motifs," but there are further noteworthy points. The narrator describes his discovery of the corpse as an epiphany, a term which in context probably calls to mind novelist James Joyce's concept of the epiphanic moment in literature. Joyce used the term "epiphany" to describe a character's moment of insight or self-revelation, but the religious root of the word is noteworthy: the epiphany refers literally to the revelation of the infant Christ to the wise men and therefore to the gentile world and it is also associated with the baptism of Christ. While in the water with Al's corpse, the narrator describes it as "three-days-dead" (133). There is no way he can know how long Al has been dead, but the reference to three days of death (and the story occurs on the characters' third night of searching for "something we never found" (130)) suggests Christ's time in the tomb. However, there is no real epiphany, baptism, or resurrection in this story, only the recovery of Bobbie; the greaser the narrator thinks he has killed rises up precisely when the narrator describes Al as three days dead. The "rush of joy and vindication" (133) he feels is not the result of a literal resurrection but merely of the discovery that he is not a murderer.

Even the story's intertextual references have religious references. The Bergman film "Virgin Spring," for instance, tells the story of a young woman raped and murdered by three men while on her way to church, the vengeance taken by her devoutly Christian father, and his penitential act accepted (perhaps) by God, as indicated by the appearance of a "virgin spring" (Bamber). The parallels, as well as the contrasts, to Boyle's story are evident. Boyle also cites the murders of Christian martyrs (along with the rape of the Sabine women and the capture of Anne Frank, acts with their own religious overtones) when the narrator describes the screams of the intended rape victim as he flees into the water. Again, though, the narrator fails to complete any such martyrdom (either as perpetrator or victim), so his story lacks the transformative and transcendent overtones of the stories he invokes in parallel to his own.

Scientific & Technological Context

Environmentalism is a major and recurring element in Boyle's work. He has described the consumption of oil and its contributions to global warming, clear-cutting, and other excessive consumption of natural resources as "raping the environment" (Durer). These concerns are not foregrounded in "Greasy Lake," but Boyle's association of violence and sexual assault with the setting underscores his ecological concerns. "Greasy Lake" itself has been the victim of human attack; its island "looked as if the air force had strafed it" (129). Its shores and waters

have been polluted and contaminated. Nature has been technologized. Indeed, the story's interest in car culture renders technological development a major feature in the narrative. Nature has been replaced by the machine, the chopper resembling "the exoskeleton of some gaunt chrome insect" (130), the wrecked car "like a steel sculpture left over from a vanished civilization" (134) being part of "nature" as the narrator comes to understand it by the end of the story. The destructiveness of technological culture to the environment and to humans is implicit in the story. Boyle has said, "I wonder when enough is enough, though. And I wonder when there [will be] enough of us big apes that we not only destroy all of the other creatures but destroy ourselves as well" (Durer). The teens in "Greasy Lake" act out in microcosm what western culture has enacted macrocosmically.

Biographical Context

T. C. Boyle was born in Peekskill, New York, in 1948 to working-class Irish immigrant parents. (Adams 281). He was born Thomas John Boyle but adopted the middle name Coraghessan at 17 ("All About T. Coraghessan Boyle Resource Center"). He claims never to have read a book before he was eighteen (Adams 281). Despite the good values he says his parents taught him, he rebelled against their advice and "was just a wild hooligan and vandal" (Ulin 151) as a teenager. He drank and did drugs excessively; one early short story, "The O. D. and Hepatitis Railroad or Bust," about shooting heroin, "was a way for me to convince myself to not do it anymore" (Ulin 151). He took a job teaching high school in Garrison, near his home town, to avoid the Viet Nam war (Adams 281). After four years and the publication of his first short story, he entered the Iowa Writers' Workshop in 1972, earning a MFA in 1973 eventually earning his Ph.D in 1977 ("All About T. Coraghessan Boyle Resource Center"). In that year, he won a creative writing fellowship from the National Endowment for the

Arts. His first book, "Descent of Man" (1979), won the St. Lawrence Award for Short Fiction (Adams 281). He has since won numerous literary awards, including a second NEA grant, a Guggenheim Fellowship, the PEN/Faulkner Novel of the Year Award, the O. Henry Award, and numerous others. Boyle has taught creative writing at the University of Southern California since 1978, where he is now a full professor ("All About T. Coraghessan Boyle Resource Center"). He is the author of 10 novels and seven short story collections (including his collected stories).

Dominick Grace

Works Cited

Adams, Michael. "T. Coraghessan Boyle (1948–)." *DLB Yearbook: 1986.* Ed. J. M. Brook. Detroit: Gale, 1987. 281–86

"All About T. Coraghessan Boyle Resource Center." *auteurs.net.* 23 April 2001. 12 December 2005.

Bamber, Martyn. "The Virgin Spring." *Senses of Cinema.* August 2004. 12 December 2005.

Boyle, T. Coraghessan. "Greasy Lake." *The Longman Anthology of Short Fiction: Stories and Authors in Context.* Compact ed. Ed. Dana Gioia and R. S. Gwynn. New York: Longman, 2001. 129–36

Durer, Gregory. "A Conversation with T. Coraghessan Boyle." *Salon.com.* 15 December 2000. 12 December 2005.

Rape of the Sabine Women. 6 August 2003. 12 December 2005.

Ulin, David L. Interview with T. Coraghessan Boyle. *The Bloomsbury Review* 9.6 (1989): 4–5, 16. *Rpt. in* Short Story *Criticism.* Vol 16. Ed. David Segal. New York: Gale, 1994. 149–52.

Walker, Michael. "Boyle's 'Greasy Lake' and the Failure of Postmodernism." *Studies in Short Fiction* 31.2 (1994): 247–55. *Literature On-Line.* 12 December 2005.

Zimmerman, Shannon. "Boyle, T. Coraghessan (1948–)." *The Facts on File Companion to the American Short Story.* Ed. Abby H. P. Werlock. New York: Facts on File, 2000. 66–68.

Discussion Questions

1. Why is the story called "Greasy Lake"?
2. Listen to Bruce Springsteen's "Spirit in the Night" (from which the epigraph is drawn). Why does the story use a rock song for its epigraph? How does the story invoke, echo, or respond to the song?
3. Why does the narrator not reveal his name?
4. The narrator claims that he and his friends were "bad characters." Is this true? What evidence is there in the story to support your view?
5. The story unfolds on a June night through to dawn the next day. How is this temporal setting important?
6. How are women imaged in the story? How are they important to it?
7. What do you think would have happened if the frat boys hadn't shown up when they did? What evidence from the story supports your view?
8. In one night, the narrator almost kills one "bad character" and encounters the corpse of another in the lake. How plausible are these events? Does their plausibility matter?
9. What does the repeated sentence "This was nature" mean? Does its meaning change over the course of the story?
10. Why does the narrator feel like crying when the girl offers him the pills near the end of the story?

Essay Ideas

1. Compare/contrast this story with another coming of age or initiation story.
2. Analyze the tone of the story. How does Boyle use tonal variation to influence our responses to the story?
3. Boyle employs several strategies to invite us to contextualize the story against other forms of fiction-Hollywood movies, television shows, even fairy tales. Analyze the effects of these strategies.
4. Write a detailed analysis of how the setting-both geographical and temporal-informs the meaning of the story.
5. Analyze Al's role in the story.

The Haunting of Hill House

by Shirley Jackson

Content Synopsis

The novel begins with a disturbing glimpse of Hill House, which for "eighty years" has "stood by itself against its hills, holding darkness within" (3). The focus shifts to Dr. John Montague, an anthropologist with an interest in the supernatural who has "been looking for an honestly haunted house all his life" (4). Dr. Montague has contacted a group of people who have "been involved in abnormal events" (5) and has invited them to join him at Hill House.

Foremost among these would-be psychic researchers is the novel's protagonist, Eleanor Vance, a thirty-two-year-old single woman who has spent eleven years caring for her ill mother and who now lives with her sister. Jackson introduces Eleanor in an extraordinary way: "The only person in the world she genuinely hated, now that her mother was dead, was her sister. She disliked her brother-in-law and her five-year-old niece, and she had no friends. […] She could not remember ever being truly happy in her adult life…" (6). Eleanor has come to Dr. Montague's attention "because one day, when she was twelve years old and her sister was eighteen, and their father had been dead for not quite a month, showers of stones had fallen on their house, without any warning or any indication of purpose or reason…" (7). Like Dr. Montague, "Eleanor had been waiting for something like Hill House" (7).

The other residents of Hill House include Theodora or Theo (whose last name is not given), and Luke Sanderson. The light-hearted Theo, who is "not at all like Eleanor" (8), has been contacted by Dr. Montague because "she had somehow been able, amused and excited over her own incredible skill, to identify correctly eighteen cards out of twenty, fifteen cards out of twenty, nineteen cards out of twenty, held up by an assistant out of sight and hearing" (8). After "a violent quarrel with the friend with whom she share[s] an apartment" (9) whose sex is undetermined, Theo impulsively decides to accept Dr. Montague's invitation to join him at Hill House. Luke, who is introduced as "a liar" and "a thief" (9), is sent to Hill House by his aunt, the owner of the property, who "would have leaped at any chance to put him safely away for a few weeks" (9).

Because Eleanor's sister is unwilling to allow her to use the car they share, Eleanor drives away in it without her knowledge. Excited by her newfound freedom, as she travels to Hill House she fantasizes about continuing "on and on until the wheels of the car were worn to nothing and she had come to the end of the world" (17); and she nearly stops "forever" at "a tiny cottage buried in a garden" (22). She eventually reaches the gated road leading to the house and, after a terse exchange with "Dudley, the caretaker" (31), is permitted to pass the gate and encounter Hill House for the first time. She shivers and thinks, "it is diseased; get away from here at once" (33). But Eleanor tells herself, "this is what I came so far to find [...] I can't go back" (35), and she enters the house. Once inside she meets the peculiar Mrs. Dudley, who cares for the house with her husband and who warns Eleanor that neither she nor anyone in the town of Hillsdale would be available to help her should she need them "in the dark" (39). Eleanor soon finds relief and comfort in the presence of Theo, whom she thinks is "not at all the sort of person who belongs in this dreary, dark place" (43).

After sundown, the two women meet Luke and Dr. Montague. Over dinner, they discuss their lives and their first impressions of the house before Dr. Montague tells "the story of Hill House" (75). The house "was built eighty-odd years ago," he explains, "as a home for his family by a man named Hugh Crain," but it was "a sad house almost from the beginning; Hugh Crain's young wife died minutes before she first was to set eyes on the house, when the carriage bringing her [there] overturned in the driveway" (75). Though "a sad and bitter man," Hugh Crain "did not leave Hill House" (76), and he kept his two daughters with him there. He married twice more, but the "second Mrs. Crain died of a fall" in a "tragically unexpected" fashion, and the "third Mrs. Crain died of what they used to call consumption" (76). After his third wife's death Crain closed the house, and his daughters grew up with their mother's cousin. The two Crain sisters "spent the rest of their lives quarreling over Hill House" (77–78). Their father died, the younger sister married, and the older one came back to live in the family home "alone for a number of years, almost in seclusion," with only "a girl from the village [of Hillsdale] to live with her, as a kind of companion" (77). After willing Hill House to her companion, the older sister "died of pneumonia [there] in the house, with only the little companion to help her" (78). The younger sister contested the will but the "companion won her case at last"

(79)—though, tormented by the younger sister and unhappy in Hill House, she eventually committed suicide.

With this dark narrative in mind, the four investigators explore the house and appear to encounter supernatural forces. They discover a cold spot at the door to the nursery, the psychic "heart of the house" (119); they hear "hammering" (130) on doors when nobody is knocking; they discover messages written on the walls: first "HELP ELEANOR COME HOME" in chalk (146), and then "HELP ELEANOR COME HOME ELEANOR" in what seems to be blood (155). Lying awake in the dark late one night, Eleanor hears what she believes to be ghostly shrieks and sobs. She reaches out for Theo's hand and grips it in terror, only to realize after the room is illuminated and that the hand she was holding was not Theo's after all (163).

As the psychic phenomena escalate, relations among the group members—especially the friendship between Eleanor and Theo—become more complex and impassioned. The interpersonal tensions increase further after Mrs. Montague arrives (with her driver and assistant Arthur in tow), intending but failing to refocus her husband's experiment by employing planchette, a Ouija Board-like device (186–87).

One evening Eleanor, who has begun to fall under the spell of the house, walks into the library and nearly plunges from its unstable circular staircase (232–37). The following morning Dr. Montague tells her that she must leave Hill House for her own safety, but she resists him and declares, "I want to stay here" (239). Finally, he and the others compel her to drive away. "But I won't go," she thinks, "I won't go, and Hill House belongs to me" (245)—just before driving the car into a tree and ending her life.

Symbols & Motifs
Personification: Hill House, a "living organism" (3), functions as if it were alive—and "not sane" (3).

It is both literally and figuratively unbalanced: as Dr. Montague explains, Hugh Crain was "a strange man" who "made his house to suit his mind," so that "every angle is slightly wrong" (105) and the result is a "deranged house" (70), a "[c]razy house" (105), a "lunatic house" (163). Hill House is not only mad but also malevolent, for "a house arrogant and hating, never off guard, can only be evil" (35); thus, "the evil is the house itself" (82) rather than in any spirits which might inhabit it. When Eleanor comes "face to face" with the house, she believes it to be "more frightening because the face of Hill House [seems] awake, with a watchfulness from the blank windows" (34). "I am like a small creature swallowed whole by a monster" (42), she thinks after passing through its front door.

Mothers and Daughters: Describing the furnishings of Hill House, Luke remarks that "[i]t's all so motherly […]. Everything so soft. Everything so padded. Great embracing chairs and sofas which turn out to be hard and unwelcome when you sit down, and reject you at once—" (209). His observation is telling, for Hill House (mis)treats Eleanor much as her mother did, controlling and eventually consuming her life. The house is consistently associated with (abused) children: the "heavy iron knocker" on its front door has "a child's face" (36); after entering the place, Eleanor, "a very silly baby" (94), imagines herself "like a child sobbing and wailing" (37); she pities Hugh Crain's "two poor little girls" for "walking through these dark rooms" (82); Dr. Montague describes his fellow researchers as "willful, spoiled children" (69) and "a pack of children" (142). The "dark" nursery has "an indefinable air of neglect found nowhere else in Hill House" (119), and the space outside it, remarkable for its "vicious cold" (120), is both literally and figuratively chilling. Hill House's role as Eleanor's alluring yet abusive surrogate mother emerges most clearly one night when she awakens to what she believes to be her bedridden mother's insistent rapping against the wall, saying sleepily, "Coming, mother, coming" (127)—only to realize that the strange sound she hears is "a noise down the hall […] near the nursery door," and "not [her] mother knocking on the wall" (127). Later she hears the "little infinitely sad cry" of a ghostly child's sobbing, "Please don't hurt me. Please let me go home" (162), and she imagines herself to be holding a child's hand. Ultimately, Eleanor, drawn by the malign maternal power of Hill House, ends her own life and accepts its invitation to "COME HOME" (146,155) forever.

Historical Context

The text's action appears to take place in the late 1950s, when the novel was published. In "The Haunting of Hill House," however, the present is dominated by the past. Though Dr. Montague is an up-to-date scholar, he nonetheless hopes to follow in the footsteps of "the intrepid nineteenth-century ghost hunters" (4) by living in and investigating Hill House—which he compares with much older haunted houses such as "Ballechin House," "Borley Rectory," and "Glamis Castle" (138). He even links it to "the houses described in Leviticus" and Homer's "House of Hades" in order to stress that "the concept of certain houses as unclean or forbidden […] is as old as the mind of man" (70).

Furthermore, as in the stories of Edgar Allan Poe, in Jackson's novel the past, present, and future seem to blend in a dreamlike, non-linear fashion—particularly within Hill House, where "[t]ime passe[s] lazily" (149) and the researchers forget which day it is (151). The house is historically marked as an outmoded late-Victorian edifice built eighty years before they arrive, yet by virtue of its supernatural associations it seems almost to transcend history. At both the beginning and the end of the novel the omniscient narrator notes that Hill House has stood "for eighty years and might stand for eighty more" (3, 246), and the repetition of this observation underscores the potentially timeless quality of the place.

Societal Context

Jackson's novel is certainly interested in relations among members of different social classes; it explores, for example, how the working-class Mr. and Mrs. Dudley interact with the middle- and upper-middle-class psychic researchers. That said, its principal concern lies not with class but with gender, and with the typically Gothic motif of women's imprisonment—not only within structures such as castles and (haunted) houses, but also within traditional "feminine" roles such as caretaker, wife, and mother. When the novel opens, Eleanor—an unmarried woman approaching middle age whose reason for existence ends with her mother's life—has been freed from eleven years of servitude only to fall under the control of her married sister, who infantilizes her and dismisses her as "still a young woman" (11) though she is in her thirties. En route to Hill House, Eleanor begins her search for a new identity, and once there she encounters various married and single women who might serve as role models: the severe caretaker Mrs. Dudley, whose face is marked by "suspicious sullenness" (37); the unmarried, seemingly carefree, and sexually ambiguous Theodora, whom she finds "charming" (43); the bossy and controlling Mrs. Montague, determined to put "things in some kind of order" (182); and the ghosts of Hill House, including Hugh Crain's ill-fated three wives and two daughters. Before killing herself, Eleanor thinks, "I am doing this all by myself, now, at last; this is me" (245). She finds herself and freedom, paradoxically, by remaining imprisoned within Hill House for eternity.

Religious Context

While not a major factor in "The Haunting of Hill House," religion links the present to the past, intensifies the novel's atmosphere of oppression and evil, and reinforces the motif of child abuse. After Luke retrieves a scrapbook that Hugh Crain created for his daughter Sophia in 1881, the researchers are horrified to discover within its pages graphic illustrations of hell and suffering alongside Crain's handwritten admonishments to his young child. It contains "a Goya etching; a horrible thing for a little girl to meditate upon," together with the injunction to "Honor thy father and thy mother" (168); a "color plate of a snake pit [...] above the message [...] 'Eternal damnation is the lot of mankind'" (168); a depiction of hell and an exhortation to "hear for a moment the agony, the screaming, the dreadful crying out and repentance, of those poor souls condemned to everlasting flame!" (169); images of "the seven deadly sins" (170) drawn by Crain himself; and, finally, his signature in blood (171).

Scientific & Technological Context

"The Haunting of Hill House" explores the conflict between science and the supernatural. This struggle is evident from the beginning of the text, when Dr. Montague is introduced as "a doctor of philosophy" who "had taken his degree in anthropology, feeling obscurely that in this field he might come closest to his true vocation, the analysis of supernatural manifestations" (4). Dr. Montague is "scrupulous about the use of his title because, his investigations being so utterly unscientific, he [hopes] to borrow an air of respectability, even scholarly authority, from his education" (4). He is a reasonably careful experimenter; for instance, he approaches the cold spot outside the nursery with a "[m]easuring tape and [a] thermometer," and "chalk for an outline" (120). Yet his efforts come to naught, as science is defeated by the supernatural. He is "considerably hampered in his work by the fact that, his hands repeatedly chilled by the extreme cold, he [can] not hold either the chalk or the tape for more than a minute at a time" (150). Moreover, the "thermometer, dropped into the center of the cold spot, refuse[s] to register any change at all" (150). When Dr. Montague publishes "his preliminary article analyzing the psychic phenomena of Hill House," his colleagues' "cool, almost contemptuous reception" of his work leads him to "finally [retire] from active scholarly pursuits" (246).

Biographical Context
Shirley Hardie Jackson was born in San Francisco in 1916 to Leslie and Geraldine Jackson. From childhood through maturity she had a difficult relationship with her mother, whose conventional approach to life clashed with her daughter's idiosyncratic personality. An affluent and upwardly mobile family, the Jacksons lived comfortably—first in Burlingame, California and then in Rochester, New York.

Jackson graduated from Brighton High School in 1934 and attended the University of Rochester until 1937, when she transferred to Syracuse University. There she joined the campus literary magazine and met her soon-to-be husband, the future literary critic Stanley Edgar Hyman. After earning Bachelor of Arts degrees and marrying in 1940, she and Hyman moved to New York City. The couple settled in North Bennington, Vermont, in 1945.

Jackson earned considerable critical and popular attention after the publication of "The Lottery," a chilling and possibly allegorical tale that appeared in The New Yorker in 1948 and continues to be widely anthologized today. After "The Lottery" came many short stories, two fictionalized memoirs about her family life: "Life Among the Savages" (1953) and "Raising Demons" (1957), and six novels: "The Road Through the Wall" (1948), "Hangsaman" (1951), "The Bird's Nest" (1954), the "Sundial" (1958), "The Haunting of Hill House" (1959), and "We Have Always Lived in the Castle" (1962). Jackson died of heart failure on August 8, 1965.

In preparing to write "The Haunting of Hill House," Jackson conducted extensive research into both ghost stories and architecture. She also considered her own beliefs about the supernatural. "No one can get into a novel about a haunted house without hitting the subject of reality head-on," she observed. "[E]ither I have to believe in ghosts, which I do, or I have to write another kind of novel altogether" (Oppenheimer 226). Jackson's hard work and open-mindedness paid off, as the novel was both a critical and a popular success. The New York Times called Jackson "the finest master currently practicing in the genre of the cryptic, haunted tale," and the Times Literary Supplement described "The Haunting of Hill House" as a "novel which has distinctiveness and genuine power." Stephen King has judged it as one of the greatest horror novels of all time, and he dedicated "Firestarter" "to Shirley Jackson, who never had to raise her voice" (Oppenheimer 227).

Jamil M. Mustafa

Works Cited
Friedman, Lenemaja. *Shirley Jackson.* Twayne's United States Authors Ser. TUSAS 253. Boston: Twayne-G.K. Hall, 1975.

Jackson, Shirley. *The Haunting of Hill House.* 1959. New York: Penguin Books, 1984.

Oppenheimer, Judy. *Private Demons: The Life of Shirley Jackson.* New York: Putnam, 1988.

Discussion Questions

1. Why does each psychic researcher decide to move into Hill House? What does each hope to discover there? Does he or she find it?
2. How does Eleanor's trip to Hill House prepare her—and us—for her experiences there?
3. How do those who visit or live in Hill House react to it? What do their reactions tell us about them, and about the house?
4. How does the story of the Crain family affect the characters' responses to Hill House?
5. Is Hill House haunted? Is it evil? Are the strange events that occur within it natural, supernatural, or both?
6. Is Eleanor sane?
7. What sort of relationship do Eleanor and Theo have? Eleanor and Luke? Eleanor and Dr. Montague? (How) do these relationships change during the course of the novel?
8. What does this novel suggest about how families function? About the meaning of home?
9. Do the characters in this novel conform to traditional gender roles?
10. Why does this novel end as it does?

Essay Ideas

1. Analyze how the psychic researchers relate to one another.
2. Analyze the significance of the novel's setting.
3. Argue for Eleanor's mental (in)stability.
4. Argue that Hill House is (not) haunted.
5. Compare this story to any text mentioned above in terms of theme, character, figurative language, or other literary elements.

Hop-Frog

by Edgar Allan Poe

Content Synopsis

Poe begins this story by introducing the king who, it is made clear, loves jokes. While some have retired their jesters, this king not only has seven ministers "all noted for their accomplishments as jokers," but also Hop-Frog, a professional jester that by virtue of his wit, physique, and dwarf stature is "a triplicate treasure in one person." Hop-Frog, so named due to his leaping, bent-over posture and inability to walk properly, was given as a gift to the king after being forcibly taken from his "barbarous region" of a home. On account of his inability to walk properly, Hop-Frog's upper body had adapted itself with enormous strength and dexterity; allowing him to perform amazing feats of entertainment and utility. Along with Hop-Frog, the king was given Trippetta, also a dwarf (graced with "exquisite beauty") forced to leave her home.

Both Trippetta and Hop-Frog are depended upon for their contributions to the king and his court. Hop-Frog's joking and entertainment abilities and Trippetta's grace and dancing abilities make them integral parts of the king's planning process when he decides to throw a masquerade ball. Upon Trippetta's careful direction, the party and hall are bedecked for the ball. When the day of the fete arrives, however, the king and his ministers all remain without an idea for their costumes. Even more boisterous and dominating than usual due to great amounts of wine, they decide to enlist the help of Hop-Frog in designing their costumes. Upon Hop-Frog's arrival, the king implores him to drink despite the knowledge that he has little tolerance for alcohol as it excites "the poor cripple almost to madness."

The scene quickly turns bad when, after Hop-Frog refuses to drink, the king becomes "purple with rage." In an attempt to save her companion, for whom she has utilized her charm and looks to protect before, Trippetta implores the king to leave Hop-Frog alone. In a sweeping movement, the enraged king throws the contents of his goblet in Trippetta's face. The room becomes impeccably silent until a "low, but harsh and protracted grating sound" begins to come from without the space. A bit alarmed, the king at first believes that the sound came from Hop-Frog but is not certain and as such, is easily swayed to the contrary by Hop-Frog himself.

Hop-Frog's countenance immediately changes as he tells the king that he will drink whatever amount of wine the king so desires and begins imparting his idea for the king's costume. The idea, termed "the Eight Chained Ourang-Outangs," requires the king and his ministers to appear as ourang-outangs who have escaped their masters. Hop-Frog ensures them that he will make them appear so life like that the guests will assume they are real and that "the beauty of the game... lies in the fright it occasions among the women." The king and his ministers are enthralled by the idea and leave themselves to the hands of Hop-Frog.

To fashion the costumes, the king and ministers are first dressed in "tight-fitting stockinet shirts and drawers." They are then coated with tar and covered with flu, a plant fiber. Finally, chains are attached to each of the men and then tied together to create a circle among them. Though their excitement is difficult to endure, the men wait until midnight to enter the ballroom; a room so carefully prepared by Trippetta as to be void of the chandelier that normally lights the room but would also have dripped wax on the attendees.

Upon their entrance, the crowd is alarmed to see these beasts and their jangling chains and the king could not have been happier at their frightened reactions. To keep the attendees captive and ensure a good show, the king made sure the doors were locked behind him and gave Hop-Frog governance over the keys. Within the tumult of the crowd, the man-beasts are thrust to the center of the room where they do not notice the creeping down of the chandelier hook upon them. With a deft movement, Hop-Frog attaches the chandelier hook to the chain connecting the king and his men. By some unseen force, the chandelier hook begins to rise and begins to pull the men closer and closer until they are face-to-face and no longer a fright to the laughing crowd.

In maneuvers of deft and careful skill, Hop-Frog makes his way over the heads of the crowd to where the ape men stand in their predicament. Upon reaching them, the dwarf leaps upon the king's head and scurries up the chain where he holds a torch and shouts, "Leave them to me! I fancy I know them. If I can only get a good look at them, I can soon tell who they are." With the whole room erupted in laughter a barely audible whistle is sounded and the chandelier chain rises quickly up about 30 feet; leaving the struggling ourang-outangs dangling.

The crowd is immediately silenced by the frightening display of the eight men and dwarf suspended above them. The silence is broken, however, by "a low, harsh, grating sound, as had before attracted the attention of the king and his counselors when the former threw the wine in the face of Trippetta." Unlike the first time, though, there was no question that the sound came from the dwarf who foamed and grated at the mouth with the countenance of a maniac towards the eight entrapped men. Hop-Frog began to yell, "Ah ha! I begin to see who these people are now!" and held the flame closer and closer to the king until the tar and flax sparked into a flame and all eight men were enveloped in fire.

With the horror-stricken crowd unable to help or speak below, Hop-Frog continues to yell:

> They are the great king and his seven privy-concillors,—a king who does not scruple to strike a defenceless girl and his seven councilors who abet him in the outrage. As for myself, I am simply Hop-Frog, the jester—and this is my last jest.

With the soon blackened corpses hanging from their post, Hop-Frog finishes his speech and climbs to the ceiling where he vanishes through the skylight. Neither Trippetta nor Hop-Frog is seen again after that night.

Symbols & Motifs

There are two instances within the story during which Hop-Frog is apparently grinding his teeth—when he decides to take revenge upon the king and again when he executes that revenge. In several of Poe's other short stories, such as "The Facts in the Case of M. Valdemar" and "Berenice," teeth are a prominent story element. Poe uses teeth as symbols of mortality (Kennedy 79).

The method by which Hop-Frog suggests that the king and his minstrels dress to look like ourang-outangs involves them being covered in tar, an element through which Poe not so discretely reminds us was a popular form of punishment. Poe even writes, "At this stage of the [dressing] process, some one of the party suggested feathers; but the suggestion was at once overruled by the dwarf." While this is clearly a foreshadowing of the terrible demise that the king and his ministers will meet, the reader and Hop-Frog are the only people privy to such an inkling; the victims are none the wiser.

Another element of this story that is repeated within other Poe stories, namely "The Murders in the Rue Morgue," is the orangutan. In both stories, the orangutan (ourang-outang as Poe writes it) entails a confusion between animal and man. In "Hop-Frog," the men are dressed as ourang-outangs in what begins as a ruse and ends with gruesome murders. In "The Murders in the Rue Morgue" the ourang-outang is responsible for gruesome murders that were originally thought to be perpetrated by man. The ourang-outang would appeal to Poe in their exotic nature; during his lifetime, sailors and world travelers began coming back to the Americas with exotic animals like apes and birds. The ourang-outang, with its clear similarities to man, made it an easy way for Poe to draw comparisons and make statements while adding further mystery to his stories.

The most obvious motif of this story is revenge. It is the king's abuse of Trippetta that drives Hop-Frog to exact revenge, a moment (as discussed above) defined by the grinding of his teeth. Hop-Frog not only gets brutal revenge on the king and his ministers, he also gets away without punishment or repercussion. Termed one of Poe's revenge tales, "Hop-Frog" is similar to "The Cask of Amontillado," in that both killers succeed in their revenge and are able to avoid any consequences of their deeds.

Historical Context

While certainly fictional and sensational, "Hop-Frog" does exhibit some elements of history

within. The presence of jesters and ministers within a king's inner circle was a common occurrence during the Middle Ages. While the role of the jester is largely assumed to be that of a clown and entertainer, the jester was more of a cunning and quick trickster who, unlike the rest of a society's citizens, was able to speak openly and honestly about taboo or forbidden subjects due to the pre-assumption that it was merely "jest." As recorded through text, the jester was integral to the monarch and also responsible for providing logical advice and insight. Hop-Frog is illuminated as just such a being—cunning and intelligent enough to gain the king's trust (in this case, much to the monarch's detriment).

Societal Context

"Hop-Frog" clearly brings issues of class and society into light. Hop-Frog is taken from his home (a terrible abduction no matter how "barbarous" his homeland) and given to the king as a gift. The triviality of the location and name of Hop-Frog's exact homeland is highlighted to further evidence his lack of human importance to the king. While Hop-Frog is a dwarf and disabled, he is no less a human and the fact that he is treated so obviously as a commodity is an injustice impossible for the reader to ignore. Further, the king's treatment of Hop-Frog and Trippetta despite their abundance of intelligence and service to him is harsh, disrespectful and tyrannical. In fact, the king, while presumably powerful and rich, is clearly not as intelligent as the marginalized Hop-Frog.

Interestingly, the king and his ministers are not the only people punished. By locking the ballroom doors and stringing the murder victims up out of reach, the ball attendees are punished as well. This leads one to believe that Poe was making wider implications of guilt upon the society who harbored such a king. The fact that Hop-Frog exerts his revenge and escapes to live his own life further illustrates Poe's feelings towards class stratification and the down-trodden or disrespected classes.

Religious Context

There is a lack of religious context within "Hop-Frog" which is most likely due to the fact that Poe chose to enumerate stories involving the methods and questions of psychology and science as opposed to the mysticism of religion.

Scientific & Technological Context

While there isn't a specific scientific or technological context, there is a pronounced psychological aspect to "Hop-Frog" as there is to many of Poe's stories. Poe was very interested in psychology and specifically phrenology (a pseudoscience purporting that different parts of the brain are responsible for different functions). In "Hop-Frog," there are several moments when Poe takes us on a "journey into the mind" (Canada 1997).

The first instance is when Hop-Frog makes the eerily swift switch from being extremely angry and obstinate to calm and obedient after the king forces him to drink and throws wine in Trippetta's face. Poe is clearly illustrating that within Hop-Frog, something has switched his countenance. The reader soon finds that this is the moment when Hop-Frog determines his plan for revenge. The murder of the king and his minstrels itself is another psychological element within the story. Hop-Frog not only seeks revenge, he seeks the very public and horrible eroding of the king. By stringing the king and his cronies up on the chandelier chain, Hop-Frog is forcing the entire captive audience to watch as he burns them. This is not only psychologically (and clearly physically) damaging to the king, but to the crowd as well who watch helplessly as the men burn above them.

Biographical Context

Edgar Allan Poe was born to actor David Poe and actress Elizabeth Poe in 1809 in Boston, Massachusetts. The author's father left the family in 1810 and in 1811, his mother died of tuberculosis. Around that time, Poe was sent to live with tobacco merchant John Allan and his wife Frances Allan who were his foster parents but never officially adopted him. Due to gambling debts and arguments with his foster father over financial support, Poe dropped out of both the University of Virginia and West Point Academy. Poe moved to Baltimore where he lived with his aunt and cousin Virginia in 1831. After finding success as an editor of the "Southern Literary Messenger," Poe moved his cousin (then wife) and aunt to Philadelphia where he published some of his most famous works such as "The Fall of the House of Usher," "Ligeia," and "William Wilson." After Virginia's death in 1847, Poe continued to travel and write. In 1849, the year during which many of his most famous poems were published ("Annabel Lee," "The Bells"), Poe disappeared after a Richmond lecture tour and was found later in an unconscious condition in Baltimore.

Throughout his life, Poe battled problems with alcohol and gambling. With the loss of his parents and the troubles he had with his foster father, Poe was something of an outsider. While he posthumously attained far-reaching fame and is credited with the creation of the literary genres pure-poetry, short story and detective fiction, he struggled during his lifetime to find lasting success, both critically and monetarily.

Comparison between Poe and his character Hop-Frog have been made based upon their common struggles with alcohol, acceptance and success. Like Hop-Frog, Poe quickly became out of control with the smallest amount of alcohol. Both Poe and his character try to avoid drinking but are not able to. The king himself, a representation of wealth, society and the temptations of alcohol, inhabits the true sources of evil and unhappiness in both Hop-Frog and Poe's lives. If such comparison's are to be made, it is interesting to note Poe's depiction of Hop-Frog as a crippled dwarf. Clearly, this illustrates the position of powerlessness and disadvantage that Hop-Frog, and by correlation Poe, were fighting against. The success of Hop-Frog in overcoming the king says much about Poe's hopes for himself.

Emily Ryan

Works Cited

Canada, Mark, ed. "Edgar Allan Poe." *Canada's America*. 1997.

Kennedy, J. Gerald. *Poe, Death, and the Life of Writing*. New Haven, CT: Yale University Press, 1987.

May, Charles E. "Edgar Allan Poe." *Magill's Survey of American Literature,* Revised Edition. Pasadena, CA: Salem Press, 2007. *Literary Reference Center.* 1 Dec. 2008.

Poe, Edgar Allen. (2006). "Hop-Frog." *Works of Edgar Allen Poe—Volume 5.* Salt Lake City, Utah: Project Gutenberg Literary Archive Foundation, 2006. *Literary Reference Center.* 1 Dec. 2008.

Discussion Questions

1. Who would you say is the protagonist of the story? Who is the antagonist?
2. Which character do you relate the most with in this story? Why?
3. Do you think Hop-Frog was justified in doing what he did to the king?
4. Did Trippetta help Hop-Frog with his revenge and escape? Provide examples as to why you do or do not think so.
5. Why does Hop-Frog choose to seek revenge on the king with a captive audience?
6. Do you think that this story reflects on any real elements of Edgar Allan Poe's life?
7. What do we know about Hop-Frog? How does this make us more or less willing to accept his decision to take revenge on the king?
8. What role did Hop-Frog play for the king? Do you think that the king trusted and relied on him?
9. Why did Poe choose to make Hop-Frog a crippled dwarf?
10. Is there any significance in the costumes that Hop-Frog creates for the king and his ministers?

Essay Ideas

1. Compare and contrast "Hop-Frog" to one or two of Poe's other short stories. How are they similar and different? Use examples from the text.
2. Poe uses a lot of symbolism in "Hop-Frog." Choose several examples of symbolism and discuss its importance to the story.
3. Poe uses a third person narrator to tell the story of Hop-Frog. Write a new version of the story through one of the main character's eyes.
4. Write an essay regarding the theme of revenge and its application in the story. Also discuss the consequences (or lack thereof) of revenge.
5. Read a biography of Edgar Allan Poe and write an essay about how Poe and Hop-Frog are similar or different.

I Stand Here Ironing

by Tillie Olsen

Content Synopsis

As its title suggests, Tillie Olsen's short story "I Stand Here Ironing," portrays a woman while she engages in ironing. The story is written from the point of view of the woman, an unnamed first person narrator, and is told as a monologue, as though the narrator directly addresses someone, perhaps a teacher or a counselor. However, as the story progresses it becomes clear that the narrator is not virtually talking to anyone but mentally rehearsing what she might say to someone who has expressed concern about her daughter. Not much happens in the story proper, as the bulk of the story is presented as the narrator's thoughts.

The story reveals the narrator's experience raising her daughter, Emily, who is currently nineteen years old. The narrator had given birth to Emily when she was nineteen, during the Depression. When Emily was eight months old, the narrator had to leave her in the care of a woman who lived downstairs because Emily's father had left and she had to support herself and Emily. After work, she would run from the streetcar, eager to pick up Emily. After awhile she found a nighttime job and was able to spend days with Emily, but she soon had to leave Emily with her father's family so she could work. When Emily was two, the narrator raised the money for Emily's return fare and, after Emily healed from chicken pox, she came home. However, her "baby loveliness [was] gone" (672).

The narrator contemplates that even if she had known when Emily was a child what she knows now she would have had no choice but to place Emily in daycare. She knew Emily did not like attending daycare because even though she did not cry for her mother, she would claim her mother looked sick or say her teachers were sick to entice her mother to stay home.

The narrator wonders how Emily achieved a gift for comedy, noting that her humor was not apparent when she had to send Emily away for the second time. After the narrator gave birth to her second child, Susan, she was persuaded to send the seven-year-old Emily to a convalescent home so the narrator could focus on caring for the new baby. Emily wrote to her once a week, and although the narrator frequently wrote Emily, she was not allowed to keep letters from home. Emily befriended a girl at the home, but the friend was moved to another housing unit at the home. Emily had explained, "They don't like you to love anybody here" (673). During her stay at the convalescent home, Emily lost her appetite and began to look increasingly frail. When Emily returned home after eight months she did not want to be held. The narrator hardly saw Emily play with friends, perhaps because they moved often. She was not successful at school, and her mother sometimes let her stay home. Also, Emily had asthma. As they grew older, conflict developed between Emily and Susan, who were opposite in appearance and mannerism.

The narrator interrupts her monologue to announce that her baby, Ronnie, needs his diaper changed. She changes his diaper, holds him, and after he falls asleep, puts him in his bed.

She says she does not remember well the war years, only recalling, "I was working, there were four smaller ones now, there was not time for [Emily]. She had to help be a mother and housekeeper, and shopper" (674). She also recalls that after some of the younger children were asleep, Emily would eat or study, while the narrator performed various domestic duties. During this time Emily would often perform comic routines or say things to make her mother laugh. The narrator thinks she may have encouraged Emily to perform in the school amateur show, which she won, and was subsequently asked to perform at high schools, colleges, and at local and state events.

The narrator interrupts her monologue to announce that Emily is running up the stairs. Emily asks her mother if she will ever finish ironing, and requests that her mother not awaken her in the morning. When her mother inquires whether Emily has exams, she replies that the exams won't matter in a few years because they will all be dead from atom bombs.

The narrator returns to the style of monologue used at the very beginning of the story, in which she appears to talk directly to someone: "She is so lovely. Why did you want me to come in at all? Why were you concerned? She will find her way" (676). She says that she will never explain the history of Emily's childhood to the person inquiring, although she immediately summarizes Emily's past in her mind. She ends her summary by acknowledging, "My wisdom came too late. She has much to her and probably little will come of it. She is a child of her age, of depression, of war, of fear" (676). At the end of the story, the narrator commands, "Let her be. So all there is in her will not bloom—but in how many does it? There is still enough left to live by. Only help her to know—help

make it so there is cause for her to know—that she is more than this dress on the ironing board, helpless before the iron" (676).

Symbols & Motifs

The iron is the most obvious symbol in the story. Throughout the story, the narrator is busy ironing. The iron symbolizes both the hard labor the narrator has endured to support her family, as well as the way in which she attempts to "iron," or come to terms with, Emily's personal history. At the end of the story, the narrator wants Emily to understand that unlike the dress on the ironing board, she is not helpless. The contrast between Emily and the dress suggests that unlike the dress, Emily is more than what her mother has shaped her to be. When Emily asks her mother if she will ever finish ironing, an implication is made that ironing could refer to domestic labor in general. This suggests that Emily knows her mother works all the time and never rests.

The clock is another prominent symbol in the story. When Emily was left at home alone one night, the door was open and the clock sitting on the floor when the narrator returned. Emily thought that if she opened the door her mother would come home sooner. She told her mother, "The clock talked loud. I threw it away; it scared me what it talked" (673). Emily told her mother that the clock talked loud again when she left to go to the hospital to give birth to Susan. The clock symbolizes the time the narrator was separated from Emily. Emily's fear of the clock suggests her loneliness, her anticipation of her mother's return, and the sense of abandonment she experienced.

Poor quality of childcare is a motif that recurs throughout the story. The narrator refers to "the teacher that was evil" at the nursery school that Emily attended when she was two (672). She remembers that the teacher made cruel remarks to the children. Additionally, the convalescent school Emily later attended was not nurturing. Emily never received a star for writing her letters even though she was led to believe she would be awarded one. Furthermore, Emily was forbidden to keep cards or letters sent from home. Emily summed up the attitude of the school administers when she told her mother, "They don't like you to love anybody here" (673).

Historical Context

"I Stand Here Ironing" was first published in 1956 (under a different title) and reflects issues during that time period as well as those during the Depression era, when Emily was born. The story shows that jobs that pay well were very difficult for women to secure during both time frames.

The narrator explains that Emily was born during the Great Depression. During the Depression people had to use whatever means they had to earn incomes. Money was scarce, and buying necessities such as food took precedence over nurturing family members. That the narrator secures employment during this era demonstrates her strength and determination.

The story proper, the time frame in which the narrator stands ironing, is set in the fifties. After the war, women were expected to stay at home and engage in unpaid labor while their husbands earned the money. If a woman worked, she was often criticized for not caring for her children or meeting her husband's needs. The story clearly shows the mother had few choices and does not suggest that a working mother is not performing her maternal roles properly. Because it explains the mother's dilemma and reveals her sympathetically, the story debunks the "good mother" stereotype that was popular during the fifties and still somewhat prevalent today.

Societal Context

The story addresses social concerns relevant to women's issues as well as to social class issues. Only stopping to change her baby's diaper, the narrator irons throughout the story. This demonstrates

the sorts of domestic labor in which the narrator engages. She works at home in addition to various jobs she has held. Although we do not get details of these jobs, it is made clear that she worked long hours for little pay, as she could not even afford a babysitter at one point. The story therefore demonstrates difficulties of working class people and exposes problems inherent in a capitalistic society that distributes wealth unequally.

The story points out social pressures placed on women to conform to society's definition of beauty. The narrator recalls that Emily "fretted about her appearance, thin and dark and foreign-looking at a time when every little girl was supposed to look or thought she should look a chubby blonde replica of Shirley Temple" (674). The narrator notes that Susan was "golden- and curly-haired and chubby, quick and articulate and assured, everything in appearance and manner Emily was not…" (674). Because her physical appearance meets society's expectations, Susan is confident and because Emily's does not, she lacks confidence. Later, the narrator says that Emily "was too vulnerable for that terrible world of youthful competition, of preening and parading, of constant measuring of yourself against every other, of envy" (675). She understands that this feeling of physical inferiority magnified Emily's low self esteem. The story criticizes the notion that women and girls are expected to maintain an appearance prescribed by society and this expectation leads to low self esteem, envy, and resentment.

Religious Context

The story does not mention God or make religious allusions. Although the narrator has had difficulty and experienced immense conflict and stress, it is never revealed that she has prayed or asked for God's help. Additionally, the person to whom the narrator pretends to be speaking has inquired about Emily. The narrator's reluctance to visit with the person to whom she addresses and the lack of help sought from divine intervention suggests that neither counseling nor prayers are helpful. Implications that neither an individual counselor nor divine intervention will help Emily and her mother invite readers to consider ways Emily and the narrator might have been helped. Emily's problems and the narrator's frustration resulted from the narrator having to work long hours to support Emily. The story suggests that problems resulting from unequal distribution of wealth and women not being able to secure jobs that pay well cannot be corrected by counseling or prayer.

Scientific & Technological Context

Although science and technology do not play significant roles in the narrative, the story alludes to both. The story centers on the mother, who stands ironing. Although an iron, as other appliances, may seem to decrease domestic work usually performed by women as unpaid labor, in the story it seems as if a modern invention is the source of her hard labor. Emily questions whether her mother will ever finish ironing, suggesting that her mother's work is never completed. This suggests that technological advances have not prevented women from engaging in manual labor inherent in domestic duties, forms of unpaid labor.

Technology is also mentioned when Emily states that everyone will be "atom-dead" in a few years. This comment criticizes the atom bomb and suggests the notion that technology has not benefited society. The development and use during her lifetime of the atom bomb apparently has affected Emily, for her mother notes that Emily has made this comment before and that she believes it is true.

Science does not seem to have helped Emily overcome sicknesses. She suffered from the chicken pox and from red measles. When Emily's mother returned from the hospital after giving birth to Susan, the red measles prevented Emily from maintaining physical contact with her. The story does not mention that Emily was given medical attention either time she was sick. These examples imply that science and technology have not lead to a cure for all ills.

Biographical Context

Born Tillie Lerner, Tillie Olsen was the second of six children. Her birth is undocumented but it is believed she was born in either Omaha or near Mead, Nebraska, in 1912 or 1913. Olsen grew up in a working class environment and as a child worked to help support her family. Her parents were social and political activists, an aspect that no doubt influenced her views.

During her teens, Olsen quit high school to work to help support her family and became politically active herself, joining and volunteering for several leftist political groups. She also became a union activist, helping and encouraging various workers to organize. She was sentenced to jail in Kansas City for encouraging packinghouse workers to organize, became ill, and returned to Omaha. She moved to Minnesota in 1932. In 1934, her short story "The Iron Throat" was published and she contracted with Random House to write a novel. Although she began the novel, titled "Yonnondio," she did not finish it until decades later. When she was nineteen, she gave birth to her first daughter, Karla. She remained politically active and in 1936 moved to San Francisco, where she held various jobs. She married Jack Olsen in 1944 and they had three daughters.

Olsen remained politically active while raising her daughters during the forties and early fifties. In 1953, when her youngest daughter began school, Olsen enrolled in a writing course at San Francisco State University. Her first collection of short fiction, "Tell Me a Riddle," which includes "I Stand Here Ironing," was published in 1961. In 1974, "Yonnondio" was published, and her collection of essays, "Silences," appeared in 1978. Olsen continued her political activities and worked to reclaim forgotten works by women writers. For example, in 1972 she wrote the forward for the *Feminist Press* reprint of Rebecca Harding Davis's "Life in the Iron Mills."

Olsen currently lives in Berkeley, California, and continues to write and to engage in political and social activism.

Laurie Champion

Works Cited

Bauer, Helen Pike. "'A Child of Anxious, Not Proud, Love': Mother and Daughter in Tillie Olsen's 'I Stand Here Ironing.'" *Mother Puzzles: Daughters and Mothers in Contemporary American Literature.* New York, Greenwood, 1989. 35–39.

Coiner, Constance. *Better Red: The Writing and Resistance of Tillie Olsen and Meridel Le Sueur.* New York: Oxford UP, 1995.

Frye, Joanne S. "'I Stand Here Ironing': Motherhood As Experience and Metaphor." *Studies in Short Fiction* 18.3 (1981): 287–92.

Olsen, Tillie. "I Stand Here Ironing." *The Story and Its Writer: An Introduction to Short Fiction.* Compact 6th ed. Ed. Ann Charters. Boston: Bedford / St. Martin's, 2003. 671–76.

Discussion Questions

1. Who do you think the narrator address?
2. Compare and contrast Susan and Emily.
3. Do you think the narrator is justified in her neglect of Emily?
4. What is the narrator's attitude regarding motherhood?
5. Is there a pattern to the types of events that seem to trigger Emily's lack of appetite?
6. Do you think Emily found success as a comedian?
7. Why do you think there were times Emily did not want her mother to touch her?
8. How might the story be different if it were told from Emily's point of view?
9. Do you think the narrator feels guilty about events that occurred during Emily's childhood?
10. Would the story change if it were set in today's society?

Essay Ideas

1. Discuss the narrative device used in the story.
2. Analyze the story from a feminist perspective.
3. Discuss the narrator as a mother figure.
4. Compare and contrast what the narrator knows now with what she knew during the time frame in which the events she recounts unfolded.
5. Explore the notion of women as victims of unpaid labor as it relates the story.

The Law of Life

by Jack London

Content Synopsis

It is winter in Alaska and Old Koskoosh throws another log on the fire. He can no longer see and so he listens. He hears his granddaughter, Sit-cum-to-Ha, harnessing the dogs and knows that the camp is breaking up. He reaches beside him to make sure there is plenty of wood. His son, the chief of the tribe, approaches him before leaving to follow the trail of the caribou as this is how they survive in the winter. Those who cannot keep up, like Old Koskoosh are left behind.

He panics at first but then realizes he will die soon either way and acknowledges that sooner or later, everybody dies. He tells his son that it is for the best, that he is tired. Old Koskoosh thinks about how old his tribe is and how many old men before him were left behind to die.

He believes that "nature does not care" about the individual. He thinks that the task of life is to perpetuate the species while the law of life is to die. He uses an example of a young woman who starts out fair and bright-eyed in life. Then she marries and has children and once this task is done, she loses the light in her eyes and like Old Koskoosh will eventually get left behind to die. He acknowledges that the law applies to all of life, not just man; mosquitoes die at first frost and rabbits, when they lose their speed, will be killed by their predators.

Old Koskoosh accepts his fate as he remembers abandoning his own father on the Klondike when

he was younger. He reminisces the time when a missionary came with his "talk-books and his box of medicines." The same law applied to him and when he died, the dogs fought over his bones.

He remembers the seven years of the Great Famine when his mother died, after the salmon run failed and there were no caribou to hunt. Only one in ten men survived the Great Famine.

During times of plenty, Koskoosh recalls the dogs becoming lazy and the men prone to fighting. He remembers his friend Zing-Ha who fell through an air hole in the Yukon and died. He reminisces about the time when they were young that they tracked a moose who was being tailed by wolves. They found moose tracks in the snow, and the bodies and bones of the wolves lay in the snow around it indicating it had trampled them in the fight for survival. They walked on and saw the trail was laced with blood and the moose tracks had gotten closer together, "slow and slovenly." Finally they came upon the battle scene and crawled under a tree to watch the moose lose. He says he thought of this moment many times in his own life, as he became tribal chief and had to make many great decisions.

Old Koskoosh throws a few more sticks on the fire and thinks that if his granddaughter had thought more of him and brought more wood, he would be able to last a few hours longer. He laments that she does not honor her ancestors but acknowledges that he was the same way when he was a child. He listens in hopes that his son will come back with the dogs to get him.

Instead, he is chilled by the foreboding howl that he hears and once again recalls the moose that was ripped apart by the wolves. He then feels a "cold muzzle" brush against his cheek and grabs a stick from the fire and waves it in the air to keep it away. But he can hear more and more wolves circling around him. He waves the flaming stick around him until he finally accepts the law of life, drops the stick and lets his head fall to his knees.

Symbols & Motifs

Fire is an important symbol in "The Law of Life" as it signifies hope. It is the one thing that keeps Old Koskoosh from death, first as a source of warmth and then as a source of protection from the wolves. In the end, Old Koskoosh accepts his fate and drops the flaming stick, the one thing keeping the wolves from devouring him.

The moose in the story is also significant. Old Koskoosh remembers tracking the moose as a child and watching its fierce fight for life as it tried to defend itself from the wolves. Like Old Koskoosh, however, the fight of the moose was unsuccessful and it, like all things, eventually succumbed to death. Both symbols illuminate the Naturalist philosophy that Nature is impartial to man and beast and all things eventually must die.

Historical Context

First published in *McClure's Magazine* in March of 1901, "The Law of Life" is one of London's stories inspired by his travels to the Yukon in 1897. London experienced firsthand the unforgiving nature of winter in Alaska in addition to learning about the practices of native tribal cultures.

Societal Context

London was profoundly influenced by a belief in naturalism, which was developed as a literary movement in the late 19th century. Naturalism, like realism, depicted events that reflected everyday life. In addition, naturalist writers focused on characters that were lower class and struggling to survive in an unforgiving universe ("Crane, London and Literary Naturalism").

Old Koskoosh embodies this philosophy in "The Law of Life" as he patiently awaits death and accepts that there is nothing he can do about it. He accepts the custom of his tribe to leave behind the elders that hold back their journey for their own survival.

> "The old men he had known when a boy, had known old men before them. Therefore it was true that the tribe lived, that it stood for the obedience of all its members, way down into the forgotten past, whose very resting-places were unremembered. They did not count; they were episodes. They had passed away like clouds from a summer sky. He also was an episode, and would pass away" (London).

He remembers abandoning his own father on the trail many years prior and understands this is time to die.

The narrator states, "Nature was not kindly to the flesh. She had no concern for that concrete thing called the individual" (London). Naturalistic texts often depict the conflicts of man against nature or man against man and present free will as an illusion (Campbell). Influenced by the theories of Darwin, naturalist writers were highly conscious of the influence that society and nature have on the individual (Crane, London and Literary Naturalism.). Koskoosh's reminiscence of the moose trying but failing to fight off the wolves and his own doomed encounter with the wolves depicts this harsh, unmerciful quality of nature.

Religious Context

"The Law of Life" does not have a specific religious context excepting the philosophy that free will does not exist and nature is indifferent to the existence of man. Many facets of naturalism are present in London's story. Naturalists attempted to link philosophy closely with science (Papineau). They believed that the scientific method could and should be used to explain all things (Papineau). Naturalists did not believe in the existence of the supernatural, only in one single world in which all things occur and from which all things are caused.

Scientific & Technological Context

"The Law of Life" does not have a specific scientific or technological context.

Biographical Context

John Griffith London was born in 1876 in San Francisco to a single mother, Flora Wellman. Later that year she married Civil War veteran John London and the London family settled in Oakland. London began to use the name Jack as a teenager. He quit school and worked various labor jobs, including oysterman and patrolman to catch poachers, before going back to school at age 19. He became a Socialist and unsuccessfully ran for Mayor of Oakland a few times. London eventually decided to become a writer to escape a life of hard manual labor (Stasz).

In 1897, he spent the winter in the Yukon, which provided inspiration for his first published stories that appeared in "Overland Monthly" in 1899. London then embarked on a prolific career that included over fifty volumes of stories, novels and essays (Stasz). The publication of the novel "Call of the Wild" in 1903, delivered fame and financial freedom to London.

London used his success to speak out on issues such as socialism, women's suffrage and prohibitions, although many of his beliefs contradicted his behaviors (Stasz). For example, London enjoyed great commercial success even though he favored Socialist ideals.

London was married twice, first to Bess Maddern with whom he had two children, and then to Charmian Kittredge. He died of kidney failure on November 22, 1916 at the age of forty (Stasz).

Jennifer Bouchard

Works Cited

Campbell, Donna M. "Naturalism in American Literature." 6 November 2007. *Literary Movements.* 25 October 2008.

Center for Naturalism. 25 October 2008.

Crane, "London and Literary Naturalism." *National Endowment for the Humanities.* 25 October 2008.

London, Jack. "The Law of Life." *The World of Jack London.* 25 October 2008.

Papineau, David. "Naturalism." 2007. *Stanford Encyclopedia of Philosophy.* 25 October 2008.

Resources for Teachers. 26 July 2001. *The Jack London Online Collection.* 27 October 2008.

Stasz, Clarice. "Jack London." 19 August 2001. *The Jack London Online Collection.* 27 October 2008.

Discussion Questions

1. Describe the protagonist of the story.
2. How does the narrator describe the tribe?
3. Identify six characters mentioned in the story and describe their relationships to one another.
4. How do these characters range in age? Why do you think the author may have done this?
5. What happened to the missionary in the story? Why was this mentioned?
6. What do the men do when times are good and food is abundant?
7. What does Old Koskoosh hope his son will do? Does he really believe it will happen?
8. Discuss Old Koskoosh's memory of tracking the moose. Why is it significant?
9. How would you describe the ending of the story?
10. What are the main themes of the story?

Essay Ideas

1. Write a journal entry from the perspective of Old Koskoosh. Delve into his thoughts about nature and feelings about survival, etc.
2. Write an essay in which you analyze the ways in which Jack London represents the philosophy of naturalism in "The Law of Life."
3. Describe and analyze London's literary style. Focus on his descriptions, the structure of his narrative and the ending of "The Law of Life."
4. Write an essay in which you analyze the significance of the moose in the story.

The Lesson

by Toni Cade Bambara

[W]e are at war, and that war is not simply a hot debate between the capitalist camp and the socialist camp over which economic/political/ social arrangement will have hegemony in the world. It's not just the battle over turf and who has the right to utilize resources for whomsoever's benefit. The war is also being fought over the truth: what is the truth about human nature, about the human potential? My responsibility to myself, my neighbors, my family and the human family is to try to tell the truth.

Toni Cade Bambara (Tate 17)

Content Synopsis

Toni Cade Bambara's short story "The Lesson" is told from the first-person point of view of Sylvia, a young African American girl. Set in New York City, the story takes place one summer afternoon. One of the strengths of the story is the narrative voice, which becomes apparent from the opening line: "Back in the days when everyone was old and stupid or young and foolish and me and Sugar were the only ones just right, this lady moved on our block with nappy hair and proper speech and no makeup" (87).

Sylvia says that Miss Moore frequently plans activities for the neighborhood children and that the parents dress up the children for the outings. After describing Miss Moore and introducing the story, Sylvia focuses on one particular day when Miss Moore takes several of the neighborhood children to F.A.O. Schwartz, a toy store in Manhattan. Sylvia's explanation of the activities of the children as they stand by a mailbox and listen to Miss Moore serves to introduce the characters: Sugar, Flyboy, Fat Butt, Q.T., Rosie Giraffe, Mercedes, Junebug, and herself. Disinterested in Miss Moore's lectures about the concept of money, Sylvia would rather go swimming or to the movies. Miss Moore explains to the children that they are poor and that "money ain't divided up right in this country" (89). Miss Moore hails two taxis, hands Sylvia five dollars, and tells her to calculate the cab driver's tip. Sylvia immediately contemplates how she will spend the money. When the cab stops, Sylvia decides the driver doesn't need the money as much as she does.

The children stand on Fifth Avenue, next to the F.A.O. Schwartz toy store. Sylvia sees a woman dressed in a fur coat despite the heat and concludes, "White folks crazy" (89). The children peer through the toy store window and excitedly begin to claim things inside. When Big Butt says he will buy a microscope, Miss Moore explains its function. She ends her biology lesson by asking the price of the microscope. Rosie Giraffe sees a glass paperweight and announces the four hundred and eighty dollar price. Miss Moore explains the purpose of a paperweight and asks the children if they have office supplies on their desks at home. Sylvia assumes that Miss Moore knows they don't have office supplies, Junebug says she doesn't even have a desk, much less something to put on it, and Flyboy says he doesn't even have a house. Miss Moore explains that it's important to have a space in which to work.

The children continue to stand outside the store and peer inside through the window. Flyboy sees a sailboat and they "all start reciting the price tag like [they] in assembly" (92). Sylvia thinks the almost twelve hundred dollar price tag "unbelievable" and feels angry (92). The children begin to discuss how much less expensive sailboats can be bought. Finally, Q. T. says, "Must be rich people shop here" (92). Sylvia asks Miss Moore what a real boat would cost, and Miss Moore challenges her to find out and inform the group. As Sylvia and Sugar lead the way to the store's entrance, Sylvia feels shame. Her feelings of inferiority remind her of the time she and Sugar, on a dare, went in a Catholic church, another incident in which she felt inferior. Both she and Sugar are too shy to enter the store, and soon the children all crowd in the doorway and almost fall over each other trying to get in. When Sugar touches the sailboat, Sylvia feels jealous and angry. She says, "I sure want to punch somebody in the mouth" (94). When Miss Moore questions Sylvia, she will not admit that she is angry.

On the train ride home, Sylvia recalls seeing at F.A.O. Schwartz a small clown that cost thirty-five dollars. She imagines the scolding she would get if she asked her mother for the clown. She contemplates what thirty-five dollars would buy on her family's budget, then questions, "Who are these people that spend that much for performing clowns and $1,000 for toy sailboats? What kinda work they

do and how they live and how come we ain't in on it? (94). She recalls that Miss Moore points out frequently that "where we are is who we are" and waits for somebody to say that the poor need to demand equality (94). She then justifies keeping Miss Moore's four dollar change from the taxi because she is "messin up [her] day with this shit" (95).

Upon returning to the neighborhood, Miss Moore lines up the children in front of the mailbox. Sylvia says "where we started from, seem like years ago, and I got a headache for thinkin so hard" (95). When Miss Moore asks the children what they think of the store, Rosie Giraffe, says, "White folks crazy" (95). Also, Sugar comments that all the children combined eat in a year the price of the sailboat, and then Miss Moore delivers the lesson: "Imagine for a minute what kind of society it is in which some people can spend on a toy what it would cost to feed a family of six or seven. What do you think?" (95). Sugar replies that "this is not much of a democracy if you ask me. Equal chance to pursue happiness means an equal crack at the dough, don't it?" (95). Sylvia feels awkward and when Miss Moore asks if anyone else learned something, Sylvia walks away. Sugar runs to Sylvia and reminds her that they have four dollars. She suggests they buy cake and ice-cream sodas and challenges Sylvia to a race to the store. Sugar runs ahead of Sylvia, but Sylvia does not compete. She says she is going to go to the West End and think the day through. The story concludes with Sylvia's thought: Sugar "can run if she want to and even run faster. But ain't nobody gonna beat me at nuthin" (96).

Symbols & Motifs

All the children except Sylvia are referred to by nicknames, some of which symbolize ideas expressed in the story. Mercedes has connotations of the luxury car Mercedes-Benz. Cars are status symbols and a Mercedes-Benz is an expensive car, thus representing the wealthy who shop at F.A.O. Schwartz and the unequal distribution of wealth in American society. The name Miss Moore suggests the idea of "more," which also represents inequality—some possess more, while others possess less. Miss Moore's name suggests also that she gives more to the children than an ordinary person might give.

The merchandise pointed out at F.A.O. Schwartz symbolizes frivolous spending. For example, the children's discussion of ways the thousand-dollar sailboat is no better than the ones they make for under a dollar signifies the ways in which those with money buy things they do not need. Also, the paperweight, although functional, is made from semi-precious stones. Furthermore, the discussion of the use of the paperweight reveals that the children would have no use for a paperweight, however inexpensive, because they lack the desk on which to set it. Additionally, the performing clown serves no purpose and further represents extravagance. Sylvia notes that the price of the clown would pay her family's rent and a payment on their piano.

The fur coat Sylvia sees a woman wearing symbolizes both frivolous spending and ostentatious flaunting of wealth. Sylvia notes that the woman is wearing the coat even though it is hot outside. Although a fur coat could be functional, in this case it is yet another example of impracticality and economic waste.

Historical Context

Toni Cade Bambara's description of herself as a "product of the sixties spirit" (Guy-Sheftall 234), seems quite accurate. Bambara wrote and participated in political and social causes during the Civil Rights Movement and during the second wave of feminism in the United States. African Americans and women were struggling to gain equality, not only economically but socially as well. African Americans and women were fighting politically to overcome the consequences of a racist and sexist society.

This time frame also encompasses the Black Arts Movement, the first movement of African American artists since the Harlem Renaissance. As during the Harlem Renaissance, African Americans united, created their own sense of community, and celebrated their ethnicity. During this era, African Americans were becoming increasingly aware of the consequences to blacks as a whole when individual blacks adhered to white middle-class values and declined to celebrate their heritage.

Bambara's works reflect feminist ideology, and celebrate African American culture and heritage. Many of her stories are told from the point of view of young African American girls, and her essays and lectures seek racial and gender equality. Moreover, Bambara was a political and social activist, participating and leading events and organizations that aimed to promote equality in terms of gender, race, and class. Although "The Lesson" primarily explores classism, it also exposes racism and serves as a fine example of the types of political and social issues that were prominent during the time Bambara was writing.

Societal Context

"The Lesson" is packed with social implications. One major point of the story is the criticism of a capitalist society, in which wealth is unequally distributed. Distribution of wealth is such an important concept that Miss Moore often tells the children that "where we are is who we are" (94), relating economic status to identity. Additionally, when they return from F.A.O. Schwartz, Miss Moore asks, "Imagine for a minute what kind of society it is in which some people can spend on a toy what it would cost to feed a family of six or seven" (95). Here, Miss Moore challenges the children to consider their capitalistic society.

Additionally, "The Lesson" supports the notion that members of society should take social responsibility. For example, Sylvia says that Miss Moore had "been to college and said it was only right that she should take responsibility for the young ones' education, and she not even related by marriage or blood" (88). Miss Moore also teaches the children that the poor should assume responsibility to eradicate economic disparity. When Sylvia questions to herself why those in her neighborhood cannot afford extravagance, she recalls that Miss Moore prescribes that the poor demand economic equality.

The story portrays the children as a social group, all living on the same block and engaging in numerous activities. It shows their impoverished living conditions: Sylvia mentions "winos who cluttered up our parks and pissed on our handball walls and stank up our hallways and stairs so you couldn't halfway play hide-and-seek without a goddamn gas mask" (87). The story juxtaposes the children's lifestyle against those who might shop at F.A.O. Schwartz, those who wear fur coats and dress "up in stockings" (89). Sylvia understands that those in her neighborhood differ from those who shop at F.A.O. Schwartz. She asks, "Who are these people that spend that much for performing clowns and $1000 for toy sailboats? What kinda work they do and how they live and how come we ain't in on it?" (94). The story reveals Miss Moore as a sort of foil to the children. For example, whereas the children use slang and dialect, Miss Moore has "proper speech." She also has "no first name" (87), while the children only have first names.

Although the story addresses classism more than racism or sexism, it is interesting to note that twice one of the children uses the phrase "white folks crazy." Near the beginning of the story, Sylvia uses the phrase in response to seeing the woman in a fur coat during the summer. Near the end of the story, when Miss Moore asks the children what they think of F.A.O. Schwartz, Rosie Giraffe says it. This comment suggests that part of the problem with unequal economics is race related. Perhaps it suggests that classism and racism are somewhat intertwined and that it is important to eradicate both.

Apparently, white people shop at F.A.O. Schwartz and represent privileged members of society.

Religious Context

At the beginning of the story, Sylvia says that Miss Moore "always looked like she was going to church, though she never did" (87). She remarks that the neighborhood adults gossip about Miss Moore because she does not attend church. Later, Sylvia equates her reluctance to enter F.A.O. Schwartz with the time she and Sugar entered a Catholic church to perform a dare. She says that she was unable to follow through on the dare because "Everything so hushed and holy and the candles and the bowin and the handkerchiefs on all the drooping heads" (93). Similarly, when the children enter F.A.O. Schwartz, they "all walk in on tiptoe and hardly touchin the games and puzzles and things" (93–94). This parallel of a church and the toy store, in addition to the fact that Miss Moore doesn't attend church, suggests that organized religion promotes capitalism. In any case, "The Lesson" does not suggest prayer or religious activity as a solution to poverty. Contrarily, it promotes political action.

Scientific & Technological Context

When the children first arrive at the toy store, Big Butt says he wants a microscope. Miss Moore uses this as an opportunity to give the children a science lecture. She defines bacteria as "the million and one living things in the air around us is invisible to the naked eye" (90). Her explanation implies that similar to living organisms only recognizable through a microscope, unequal distribution of wealth may not be apparent unless exposed by someone such as Miss Moore.

Technology is mentioned in the descriptions of the paperweight and the sailboat. The paperweight is "made of semi-precious stones fused together under tremendous pressure" (90), and the sailboat is handcrafted from fiberglass (92).

Since the paperweight and the sailboat represent extravagance, the story suggests that technology is not always used wisely, or at lease economically. Sylvia says, "Who'd pay all that when you can buy a sailboat set for a quarter at Pop's, a tube of glue for a dime, and a ball of string for eight cents?" (92). Sylvia understands that one need not employ complicated and expensive technology to make a sailboat.

Biographical Context

Toni Cade Bambara was born on March 25, 1939, in New York City. She grew up with her mother, Helen Brent Henderson Cade, and her brother in New York City and Jersey City. She lived in various cites in the United States, receiving her B.A. in Theater Arts and English from Queens College. She published her first short story, "Sweet Town," in 1959. She worked as a social worker in New York, while attending graduate school at City College. In 1961, she studied in Milan, Italy, and worked as a freelance writer. After returning to New York, she held several jobs such as Brooklyn's Colony House Director and therapist for the Metropolitan Hospital. After she received her master's degree, she taught at City College from 1965 to 1969 and at Livingston College, in New Jersey, from 1969 to 1974. In 1970 she edited the critically acclaimed "The Black Woman," while continuing her activism for the rights of African–Americans and women. The stories she published form 1959 to 1970 are published under the name Toni Cade.

In 1972, the short story collection "Gorilla, My Love" appeared and is considered among Bambara's finest work. Bambara continued writing and engaging in political activism, until her death from cancer in 1995.

Laurie Champion

Works Cited

Bambara, Toni Cade. "The Lesson." *Gorilla, My Love.* New York: Vintage, 1992. 85–96.

Comfort, Mary. "Liberating Figures in Toni Cade Bambara's Gorilla, My Love." *Studies in American Humor,* Ser. 3.5 (1998): 76–96.

Guy-Sheftall, Beverly. "Commitment: Toni Cade Bambara Speaks." *Sturdy Black Bridges: Vision of Black Women in Literature.* Ed. Roseann P. Bell, Bettye J. Parker, and Beverly J. Guy-Sheftall. Garden City, NY: Doubleday, 1979. 230–49.

Heller, Janet Ruth. "Toni Cade Bambara's Use of African American Vernacular English in 'The Lesson.'" *Style* 37.3 (2003): 279–93.

Tate, Claudia. "Toni Cade Bambara." *Black Women Writers at Work.* Ed. Claudia Tate and Tillie Olsen. New York: Continuum, 1983. 12–38.

Vertreace, Martha M. "Toni Cade Bambara: The Dance of Character and Community." *American Women Writing Fiction: Memory, Identity, Family, Space.* Ed. Mickey Pearlman. Lexington: UP of Kentucky, 1989. 154–71.

Discussion Questions

1. What is the significance of the title of the story?
2. Discuss the range of emotions Sylvia feels as she contemplates entering F.A.O. Schwartz.
3. Why do you think Sylvia does not want to race Sugar at the end of the story?
4. How does the story address racism?
5. Why do you think Bambara portrayed Sylvia as using curse words frequently?
6. Does the dialect strengthen the story? If so, how?
7. Near the end of the story, why does Sylvia walk away when Miss Moore asks her if she learned anything during the trip to the toy store?
8. At the beginning of the story, Sylvia says that the neighborhood children laugh at Miss Moore and "kinda" hate her. Why do you think the children feel this way?
9. Why do you think Sylvia feels betrayed near the end of the story when Sugar answers Miss Moore's question regarding the social implications of capitalism.
10. Do you think Sylvia's decision to keep Miss Moore's change from the taxi ride is justified?

Essay Ideas

1. Analyze the symbols in the story.
2. Explore Miss Moore's attitude about capitalism revealed in the story.
3. Analyze the characters in the story and how they interact with each other.
4. Discuss Sylvia's role as narrator of "The Lesson."
5. Using examples of her lessons to the children, analyze Miss Moore's teaching style.

The Masque of the Red Death

by Edgar Allan Poe

Content Synopsis

This short story of Poe's touches upon the grave devastation caused by plague. There is nothing one can do to prevent a hideous demise once a person has contracted the disease called "The Red Death" (red because the most significant outward signifier of the sickness was blood which would leak from the body). The story describes the end results of the plague: "sharp pains, and sudden dizziness, and then profuse bleeding from the pores, with dissolution… the whole seizure, progress and termination of the disease, were the incidents of a half hour" (238).

The story is told via a first person narrator, presumably someone inside the abbey where they take refuge. Prince Prospero, ruler of the plague-affected setting, is the protagonist of the story. The fact that his name echoes the word "prosperous" is certainly ironic as his money and power are ultimately insufficient to save him (and his friends) from the scourge of the land. The lack of care he demonstrates for the common people is emphasized by his flight from the area, "half depopulated" by the Red Death at the time of his escape (238). While the plague ravages the countryside, Prospero makes the decision to collect one thousand of his closest friends, all knights and dames, and remove them from the pestilential threat. It is clear that Prospero believes his great wealth and power will protect him from the disease even as it decimates the lower class population.

The large group travels to a deserted abbey protected by battlements, operating as physical signifiers of protection from a disease against which walls provide no real defense. Prospero's attitude that "the external world would take care of itself" speaks to his selfishness which, in his defense, was not particularly out of keeping with the dukes and princes of the day (238).

In isolation, the group is able to happily forget about the death and destruction visited upon the population at large. Unconcerned with the fact that the extensive losses of life will eventually affect the dominion in terms of both labor and food production, they pass the time engaged in various entertainments designed by Prospero himself, who brings along comedians, actors, ballet dancers, and musicians. In sharp contrast to the pain, suffering, and want certainly present in the world outside of the castle walls, inside, "there was Beauty, there was wine" (238). At almost every turn, the concepts of internal versus external realities are ironically reversed: people are not what they seem, and inside the castle there is no safety from death.

During the sixth month of their seclusion (while the plague still "raged" outside the embattlements), Prospero decides to have a masked ball. The ball is held in seven rooms, each decorated in a different color scheme. The number seven alludes to several things: the seven deadly sins, the Seven Wonders of the World, and the seven stages of life.

Prospero's "love of the bizarre" finds its fullest expression in the rooms which (unlike other palaces and suites at the time where most of the floor plan was open) followed one after the other so that the participants were afforded a look into "little more than one [room] at a time" (239). Each room contains two stained glass gothic style windows, the colors of which match the tone of the room. In the easternmost room, the color is blue, the next purple, the third green, the fourth orange, the fifth white, and the sixth violet. The seventh and last room is draped in black (symbolic of not only the "Black Death" pandemic of the 14th century, but also of death itself, as well as a statement about the characters' being 'in the dark' in terms of understanding the present threat). This is the only chamber in which (for obvious reasons) the color of the room does not match the color of the windows. The windows are red, the color of blood. Instead of lighting by candelabra, the traditional mode of lighting a chamber, each is only illuminated by the glowing coals of a brazier. The hellish quality of this light adds to the tone of the story. The effect of the brazier light was disconcerting in all rooms, but in the seventh the "blood tinted panes …produced so wild a look upon the countenances of those who entered, that there were few of the company bold enough to set foot within its precincts at all" (239). In this manner, the chamber comes to represent the Red Death that lies in wait outside the castle walls (as well as inside), a setting from which each of the members shies away.

The seventh chamber also holds a large ebony clock. The pendulum that swings as part of the mechanism of the clock represents the cycle of disease and renewal that accompany any pandemic. Personified, the clock's gongs issue from its "brazen lungs," as the device seems to patiently wait to announce that death has arrived at the party. The sound of the clock at each hour affects the partygoers deeply. Laughter and dancing cease and each grows pale and disturbed with each succeeding gong.

The eccentricities of the duke are developed via his decorations further described as "bold and fiery," "barbaric," and "grotesque." The idea that Prospero may, in fact, be mad is touched upon but dismissed by the narrator who assures the reader that only those not able to "see and touch" Prospero would hold this notion. While the specifics of the rooms are not disclosed, the reader's imagination takes hold, envisioning exactly what the narrator means when describing the scene within each chamber as "wanton" "terrible" and containing "not a little of that which might have excited disgust" (240). The westernmost chamber contains only a few brave souls and none of the dreamlike characters who populate the previous areas of the fest. In the other chambers "beat feverishly the heart of life," a line which symbolizes the passionate desire to live as much as it provides clues to the fate of the revelers already described as "feverish."

At the tolling of the twelfth hour, the partygoers notice, for the first time, a new masked figure who inspired in them "terror, horror and disgust" (241). Dressed as if ready for the grave, the figure was 'masked' as a corpse. In this scene it is fairly clear that the revelers cannot discern the real from the artificial, as the new member of the group is not wearing a mask at all but is, in fact, dying of the Red Death from which they believed themselves to be safe. Face covered in blood (the signifier of the most contagious point of the disease), the members of the party feel this guest has gone too far in dressing up as if he had the very plague they are trying to outrun.

The response of Prospero to the new character includes a "convulsion" and "reddened" brow, further signifying the presence of the Red Death in him, though he does not know it yet. Threatening the figure with death at sunrise, Prospero, standing in the blue northern chamber, orders the man to be unmasked. The figure, ignoring the duke, passes "within a yard" of him and proceeds through each chamber, making his way to the final, westernmost and darkest room. Prospero draws a knife and follows the figure to the final chamber where the masked figure turns to face Prospero who falls down dead at the sight.

The crowd surges forward and attacks the figure only to find it an insubstantial presence—a symbol of the death that lies in wait for them: "the presence of the Red Death" among them. In the end, death conquers all as, one by one, the thousand guests fall victim to the plague, and "the Red death held illimitable dominion over all" (242).

Historical Context

One of the closest parallels to the Red Death described in the story is the Black Death, a disease so named because the skin of its victims would turn black from hemorrhaging under the surface, a pandemic of the 14th century which killed approximately one third of Europe's population. There was also, as a result of the plague, a rise in persecution of religious and ethnic minorities. In the "Masque of The Red Death," the desertion of responsibility and flight of the privileged into what they felt were secure locations mirrors historical events in times of plague. Poe's story reflects not only his personal engagement with historical events but also explores the ways in which external events shape people's actions and emotions.

Societal Context

According to Harold Bloom, one of the reasons Poe's work seems to resonate with so many readers is that "Poe's writing is eerily prescient of the changes that have overtaken American society, the neurosis and misery, the sense of alienation and inner turmoil…" (12). "The Masque of the Red Death" not only echoes contemporary paranoia and fear of disease, but it also responds to the issues of Poe's own time period and historical moments in which human character was tested.

The probable source for Poe's Red Death, the Black Plague, had tremendous societal effects.

Large cities suffered the greatest casualties of the plague, while isolated rural villages were usually spared. Massive crop failures and a ban on food importation added to growing levels of panic and general lack of support for the population. Growing inflation caused the poorest of society to continue to suffer the most. Poor hygiene and close quarters made the casualties primarily lower class citizens.

There were many peasant uprisings in parts of Eastern and Western Europe as the plague ate its way through cities and towns. Some revolted because they no longer felt any compulsion to remain on their farmland, especially without the presence of an overseer or landowner who probably had the money to escape to safer environs, leaving the peasants and farmers to fend for themselves. Due to the death or desertion of large numbers of workers, competition for the remaining laborers sometimes became fierce. In most instances though, the benefit for the lower classes, including increased wages, would not be felt for a hundred years or more. In some European countries, the drop in population opened up opportunities never before imagined; in others it did just the opposite. Some rulers tightened control of already highly regulated activity, and passed more laws meant to enforce the divisions between classes. There was a general perception that institutions had failed to protect the people in any meaningful way, an idea expanded upon in the persona of Prince Prospero who turns his back on the commoners and flees with his friends. The fact that he is killed along with the rest of his upper class companions hints at Poe's feelings about the privileged class.

Religious Context

Historically, the plague was closely connected to religion and religious practice in several ways. The massive death toll and generalized fear and paranoia accompanying historical plague events ignited in the people a need for a scapegoat. Religious fanaticism was rampant and various religious groups were blamed as causes of the plague (Jews for example). Causing more harm than help, religious leaders often claimed they could cure the plague. Their failure to do so added to the increasing agitation on the part of parishioners looking for solace and safety.

The setting of the deserted abbey (a monastery or church) reveals several things. On the one hand, the opulence of the "palace" bespeaks the endowment enjoyed by its former religious occupants. On the other hand, the "battlements" support the theory that the religious building may have or was assumed to come under attack. The deserted abbey probably means one of two things, either the inhabitants had left in order to minister and provide comfort to the sick, or that they had already perished (the close quartered inhabitants of monasteries usually suffering as the first casualties of plagues).

The party is described as one which "out Heroded Herod" an allusion to a Biblical king who was so enchanted with Salome (a dancer) that he gave her whatever she fancied, in one case, the head of John the Baptist. The idea that one can go too far and that excess leads to death is also a theme in Poe's story.

Poe's own feelings about Christianity and the state of religion during his lifetime are explored by critic Allen Tate, who asserts that Poe was a man for whom "Christianity, for reasons that nobody knows anything about, had got short-circuited" (36). Richard Wilbur notes that "Poe conceived God as a poet" and that the planet had "fallen away from God by exalting the scientific reason above the poetic intuition" (53).

Scientific & Technological Context

Clearly a story about the limitations of early science, there is no real understanding of what causes the Red Death or how it is transmitted. The revelers believe they will be safe in their isolation, never thinking that one of them could have already been infected before the group went into seclusion. Historical failures of science at least tangentially relate to events of the story, including the inability of doctors to classify any other disease that might look like plague, but in fact be something innocuous. Lepers, acne sufferers and those with psoriasis were routinely murdered as potential plague carriers.

Poe often wove various concerns of his day into his stories, science and technological issues included. Common theories about phrenology, psychology, and even mesmerism often occur in Poe's texts. This text is also an example of Poe's interest in exploring historical events, bringing the distant past to life. Poe wrote and published articles on science and history regularly during his life. The concept that nature was an all-powerful force, as Tennyson wrote "red in tooth and claw" was only beginning to be seen as a force that could be 'tamed' and brought under human control via science and technology.

Biographical Context

Edgar Allan Poe was born in Boston in 1809, the son of two actors. He inherited his artistic talent from his mother, and problems with alcohol and mood disorders from his father. Abandoned by both parents, his father having left home after Poe's sister was born, and his mother dying of tuberculosis, Edgar was raised thereafter by John and Francis Allan, a wealthy couple. As Poe aged, he became increasingly moody and often argued with his foster father (Kennedy and Gioia 234). Poe published his first collection "Tamerlane and other Poems" when he was just eighteen years old. Poe left his foster family and moved in with is aunt and cousin. Poe eventually married his cousin Virginia in 1836 when she was only thirteen years old. Poe's short lived stability, a product of Virginia's influence, collapsed after her death at 24. Found "incoherent" in the streets of Baltimore in 1849, the circumstances of Poe's death remain largely a mystery, although several theories have been posited including the idea that he had contracted rabies and died as a result. Literary critic Harold Bloom refers to Poe as "perhaps, except for Mark Twain, the most popular of all American authors" (Bloom's Major...9), despite the fact that he believes "Poe is an inescapable author, but not a good one" (Major 9). Though in the minority opinion, Harry Levin noted almost half a century ago that Poe's efforts "smell [sic] of the thesaurus" (qtd. in Bloom's Major Short Story Writers 9).

Tracy M. Caldwell

Works Cited

Bloom, Harold, Ed. "Introduction." *Bloom's Major Short Story Writers: Edgar Allan Poe.* New York: Chelsea House, 1999. 9–11.

Bloom, Harold, Ed. "Introduction." *Bloom's Modern Critical Views: Edgar Allan Poe.* New York: Chelsea House, 1985.

Kennedy, X. J. and Dana Gioia. *Literature: An Introduction to Fiction, Poetry and Drama.* New York: Pearson/Longman, 2005.

Tate. Allen. "The Angelic Imagination." *Bloom's Major Short Story Writers: Edgar Allan Poe.* New York: Chelsea House, 1999. 23–30.

Wilbur, Richard. "The House of Poe." *Bloom's Modern Critical Views: Edgar Allan Poe.* Ed. Harold Bloom. New York: Chelsea House, 1985. 51–70.

Discussion Questions

1. This plague is called The Red Death. Can you think of any parallel diseases today that threaten humans of all classes? Do you think certain populations feel 'safe' from any of these diseases? Why? Are they right?

2. Prospero flees his responsibility to his subjects in order to save himself and his friends. Are there any situations you see as parallel in modern times in this country or any other in which a leader fails to take responsibility for the people he or she represents or rules?

3. Why do you think Prospero chooses to hold the masque when he does?

4. Why does the text continually refer to Prospero's eccentricities and love of the bizarre?

5. Do you think Prospero is "mad" as the narrator suggests some others believe?

6. Why do you think his friends believe him sane? Is there evidence that they don't really believe this?

7. If everyone dies at the end of the story, how can you explain the narrative point of view? Who is speaking?

8. What role does the clock play in the story?

9. Why do the rooms move from east to west? What does this symbolize?

10. Many critics see the story as a parable. If you agree, what do you think is the moral of the story?

Essay Ideas

1. Write an essay that explores Poe's use of symbols in the text. Some ideas include the uses of colors and numbers, setting, the clock, description and names.

2. Using psychological criticism, write an essay that analyzes the character of Prospero. What kind of man is he? How do the narration, and his actions and speech help to develop characterization?

3. Write an essay in which you research some possible historical influences on Poe's description of the plague.

4. Using Marxist criticism, analyze the ways in which social class issue are raised. What kinds of suggestions are made by the author and narrator about the experiences of the highest versus lower classes in society?

5. Write an essay that compares this story with another of Poe's tales. How are they alike in theme and content? How are they different?

6. Write an essay that explores how setting and description influences the tone and suspense of the story.

The Minister's Black Veil

by Nathaniel Hawthorne

Content Synopsis

This short story, set in seventeenth-century Puritan New England, centers around Parson Hooper who astounds and disturbs his congregation by adopt-ing the practice of wearing a black veil over his face. The first sermon Hooper preaches in his black veil concerns "secret sin, and those sad mysteries which we hide from our nearest and dearest, and would fain conceal from our own consciousness, even forgetting that the Omniscient can detect them" (13). The congregation is greatly affected by the sermon; each person is certain that the preacher has discovered his or her own "hoarded iniquity of deed or thought" (13).

Hooper continues to wear the veil through the rest of the day's duties, including a funeral, at which the veil seems an "appropriate emblem," and a wed-ding service, at which it decidedly does not (14). The veil makes Hooper appear so other-worldly that after the funeral members of the congregation believe they see him "and the [departed] maiden's spirit … walking hand in hand" (15). When it becomes clear to the community that Hooper plans to wear the veil indefinitely, they appoint a group to speak to him about their concerns. The group's mission is a complete failure; in the words of the narrator, "Never did an embassy so ill discharge its duties" (16). The committee perceives the veil as "the symbol of a fearful secret between him and

them," and they find themselves too intimidated to broach the subject.

Only one person is able to broach this delicate subject with Hooper, his fiancée Elizabeth. But he refuses her entreaty to remove the veil and insists that he must wear it until he dies. When Elizabeth begs him at least to remove the veil of mystery from his words, he says to her: "Know, then, this veil is a type and a symbol, and I am bound to wear it ever, both in light and darkness, in solitude and before the gaze of multitudes, and as with strang-ers, so with my familiar friends" (17). When Eliza-beth asks him what affliction causes him to wear the veil, he replies: "If it be a sign of mourning … I, perhaps, like most other mortals, have sorrows dark enough to be typified by a black veil" (18). And when she suggests that members of the com-munity may interpret the veil as a symbol of great sin, he replies: "If I hide my face for sorrow, there is cause enough … and if I cover it for secret sin, what mortal might not do the same?" (18).

Hooper begs Elizabeth to understand: "O! you know not how lonely I am, and how frightened, to be alone behind my black veil," he cries (18). Elizabeth asks that he lift the veil just once to look at her. When he refuses, she bids him farewell and slowly departs.

As the minister continues to wear the veil, day after day and year after year, the community becomes aware of his own antipathy toward it. They see that he is hesitant to pass in front of mirrors or to so much as glimpse his reflection in a pool of still water. And though this antipathy makes plausible the theory that the veil represents some terrible sin, the minister's otherwise impeccable conduct suggests that the veil must instead represent a great sorrow. As a result of this uncertainty, an "ambiguity of sin or sorrow … enveloped the poor minister, so that love or sympathy could never reach him" (19).

The minister lived his life "a man apart from men, shunned in their health and joy, but ever summoned to their aid in mortal anguish" (20). On his own deathbed, Hooper, as he had come to be called, is cared for by the town physician; Elizabeth, who had long loved him in secrecy; and the minister of Westbury, who insists that the black veil finally be lifted from Hooper's face so that there be no shadow on his memory. Hooper summons up enough energy to refuse and to make a final exhortation:

> "What, but the mystery which it obscurely typifies, has made this piece of crepe so awful? When the friend shows his inmost heart to his friend; the lover to his best beloved; when man does not vainly shrink from the eye of his Creator, loathsomely treasuring up the secret of his in; then deem me a monster, for the symbol beneath which I have lived, and die! I look around me, and, lo! on every visage a Black Veil!" (23).

Historical Context

The Puritans were a religious group, influenced by the ideas of reformer John Calvin, who wanted to purify the Anglican Church by replacing elaborate ceremony and hierarchy with emphasis on Bible reading and individual prayer. When the Stuart Monarchs of England began to persecute the Puritans in their attempt to unite their subjects in devotion to the Anglican Church, many Puritans decided to leave England for the New World. In 1630, a group of these immigrants formed a Puritan Commonwealth in present-day Boston and Salem, and the settlement grew to more than 20,000 by 1643. The Puritans immigrated to the New World "not merely to save their souls but to establish a 'visible' kingdom of God, a society where outward conduct would be according to God's laws, a society where a smooth, honest, civil life would prevail in family, church, and state" (Morgan 3). When Hooper begins to the wear the veil, he introduces the idea that even the minister may have dark sins to hide. It is not surprising that this so unsettles his congregation who depend on him to be the cornerstone of their good and orderly society.

Societal Context

Though the Puritans strove for a just and good society, they were uncomfortable when all seemed too orderly, so sure were they that hypocrites—those outwardly model citizens who were not truly saved—lurked within their congregation. The Puritan belief in the essential wickedness of humanity, "led them to discipline themselves and their children with psychologically crippling severity" (Johnson 13). This tendency toward discipline spilled over into the community as well, since a "zealous enforcement of morality on others was another way of proving to oneself" that one was indeed among the elect (Morgan 6).

Although the Puritans rejected the hierarchical philosophy of the Anglican Church which put too much distance between ordinary individuals and God, they cultivated order and discipline in their own ranks through the observance of a social hierarchy which placed God in control of men who were in turn in charge of women and children. Within the community of men, church members outranked non-members and ministers held authority over the entire community. The minister was a central figure in Puritan communities, often called upon to give advice on political and economical matters as well as the spiritual and psychological. Not surprisingly, when Hooper, the most venerated, authoritative figure in the community of Milford, begins to wear a veil which seems to symbolize some sort of imperfection, the entire community becomes uncomfortable and worried about the state of their own souls.

Religious Context

One of the core beliefs of Puritanism held that all people deserved damnation. God, in his benevolence, had chosen to absolve some of them from sin and save them before they even existed. Thus, salvation was predestined. Puritans were very concerned about how to recognize whether they were chosen to be saved. According to many Puritan clergymen, a person had to accept God's offer of salvation through grace. Keys to recognizing this grace were self-examination, reading the Bible, and listening to the minister's sermons. Some Puritans believed that conversion was a dramatic, recognizable experience, while others believed it simply happened unnoticed. After the conversion experience, one would live in a new state of redemption, recognizable by moral behavior.

In order to be a member of the Puritan church, one had to know and believe its doctrines, to live a moral life, and to prove that he or she was one of the elect. While early on, one simply had to describe his or her conversion to provide the necessary proof of election, later applicants were required to give an account of the process by which they prepared for conversion. Even if one were accepted into the church and possessed all the outward signs of election, he or she could not truly be certain of salvation until death.

The minister's black veil, especially when first worn while giving a sermon on secret sin, likely represented for the congregation their private doubts concerning their own salvation. Hawthorne writes that the veil made "the most innocent girl,

and the man of hardened breast, [feel] as though the preacher had crept upon them, behind his awful veil, and discovered their hoarded iniquity of deed or thought" (13).

Scientific & Technological Context

The Puritans kept new scientific ideas out of their communities for as long as they could. Newtonian physics, which appeared in 1687, was not seriously considered in New England until more than thirty years after its appearance, when it was explained by Cotton Mather. In 1714, Mather became the first influential Puritan to accept the Copernican theory of the universe, 178 years after Copernicus proposed it. Ultimately, Puritans' exposure to and acceptance of new scientific and rational thought which "stressed observable fact in the visible world" helped to erode "the very spiritual bedrock of Puritanism" (Johnson 203). The decline of the Puritan church was not due to the influence of science alone, however; Claudia Johnson also cites "the introduction into New England of a non-dissenting, British presence after the loss of the charter …[a] backlash against seventy years of unrelieved church intrusion into both government and private life …[t]he absolute intolerance of other Protestant religions," among other factors (200).

In "The Minister's Black Veil," Hawthorne demonstrates the Puritan belief in the supernatural by having two members of the congregation simultaneously have a "fancy … that the minister and the [deceased] maiden's spirit were walking hand in hand" (15). The entire story is imbued with the sense that the veil is a successful attempt on the part of Hooper to remind his congregation that the spiritual realm always co-exists with the reality of everyday life.

Biographical Context

Nathaniel Hawthorne was born on July 4, 1804 in Salem, Massachusetts. His father died of yellow fever in 1808, after which his mother rarely left her room. Although his extended family became involved in his upbringing, it is not surprising, given these circumstances, that isolation would be one of the themes the author would explore in his work. Hooper's veil, for example, has often been read as a symbol of human isolation and alienation. Hawthorne suggests that not even the closest of humans, husband and wife, can really see into each other's souls while they are still on this earth. Though Hooper begs Elizabeth not to leave him lonely and frightened, she cannot bring herself to live as his wife with the constant reminder of their inability to completely know and understand one another.

In the decade after he graduated from Bowdoin college, Hawthorne lived a rather reclusive life in his mother's house, struggling to support himself as a writer and contributor to periodicals, reading a great deal of material from his local library, much of it material concerning his Puritan ancestors, and making occasional excursions across the countryside, recording detailed observations as he went. Hawthorne was deeply affected by and concerned with his Puritan ancestors, particularly their darker side as represented by, among other things, the Salem Witch Trials. This concern comes through in "The Custom House," in which he wrote: "I … hereby take shame upon myself

for their sakes, and pray that any curse incurred by them … may be now and henceforth removed" (Swisher 30). The extensive knowledge he gained about New England history and culture in this period served him well as much of his creative work would have this subject matter at its core, including the short stories "The Minister's Black Veil," and "Young Goodman Brown," and his well-known novels "The Scarlet Letter" and "The House of the Seven Gables."

Kim Becnel

Works Cited

Bunge, Nancy L. *Nathaniel Hawthorne: A Study of the Short Fiction.* New York: Twayne, 1993.

Hawthorne, Nathaniel. "The Minister's Black Veil." *Hawthorne's Short Stories.* New York: Dodd, Mead & Co, 1962. 10–23.

Johnson, Claudia Durst. *Daily Life in Colonial New England.* Westport, CT: Greenwood P, 2002.

Morgan, Edmund Sears. *The Puritan Family: Religion & Domestic Relations in Seventeenth-Century New England.* Westport, CT: Greenwood P, 1966.

Wineapple, Brenda. *Hawthorne: A Life.* New York: Knopf, 2003.

Discussion Questions

1. What is the significance of the subtitle: "A Parable"?

2. Why does the black veil seem an "appropriate emblem" for a funeral?

3. Why is the veil such a disturbing symbol at the wedding?

4. Why do you think Hooper avoids looking at himself once he begins to wear the veil?

5. Why do you think the mourners at the funeral see the minister and the dead maiden's spirit "walking hand in hand"? What is the significance of this vision?

6. Why does the "deputation" sent to discuss the matter of the veil with the minister fail so terribly?

7. Why do you think Elizabeth does not at first feel the "terrors" of the veil?

8. Why does Elizabeth forsake Hooper when he refuses to let her look at his face one more time?

9. Why does she continue to love him, only secretly, after he dons the veil? Why do you think she would make sure that Hooper's face remain covered and avert her own eyes if the veil slipped?

Essay Ideas

1. What does the community's reaction to the black veil tell us about its beliefs and fears?
2. Does the veil make Hooper a better or worse minister than he had been before? Why?
3. What do you think is the author's judgment of Hooper's decision to wear the veil? Does he think that the benefits it gave to Hooper and his community outweighed the troubles it caused?
4. Why do you think the minister's election sermon resulted in "the legislative measures of that year" being "characterized by all the gloom and piety of our earliest ancestral sway?" What is the connection between the black veil and the "our earliest ancestral sway?" (20).
5. Analyze Hooper's last words: "I look around me, and, lo! On every visage a Black Veil." (23). What clues do his dying words give us as to the veil's meaning?

The Murders in the Rue Morgue

by Edgar Allan Poe

Content Synopsis

"The Murders in the Rue Morgue" opens with the unnamed narrator talking about the nature of analysis. He talks about the kind of human mind that enjoys solving puzzles, both important and trivial. He compares the mind of the chess player, which can hold all the possible piece positions and moves in his head, with the checkers player, who must use greater skills in order to win when the game has a much simpler set of rules. He then moves on to outline the ways in which the latter type of man can win at cards, not by having a better hand, or following the cards, but by reading the nature of the other players. At the end of this discussion, the narrator tells us that the story he proposes to tell us will be illuminated by this discussion of analytical skills.

He then goes on to narrate how he came, in a Paris library, to meet Monsieur C. Auguste Dupin; a man from a rich family much reduced in status. After several more meetings, and the recognition by each of a like-minded soul, together they rent an old mansion where they keep themselves secluded from the world and read, write and converse.

The narrator tells us that his new companion is fond of the night, only leaving the house once it is dark. At that time, the two men head out into Paris; talking, walking, and seeking intriguing events to which they can turn their minds.

On one such occasion, the narrator tells us, there had been a period of silence between the two men that Dupin suddenly broke with a comment that completed the thoughts of the narrator, even though the narrator had not spoken his thoughts aloud. When asked, Dupin explains how he came to follow his companion's train of thought through a series of events and causal links to be able to predict the exact course of his friend's private musings.

The narrator then tells us of the account in the newspapers, some short time after the above event, of two murders in a house on the Rue Morgue. The murders were discovered, according to the newspaper, when cries were heard from the fourth story of a house inhabited by a Madame L'Espanye and her daughter, Camille. A group of neighbors, accompanied by two gendarmes, broke into the house to discover what was occurring. As they climbed they heard two voices arguing, voices which had stopped by the time the party reached the fourth floor. In the apartment of the two women, all was in disarray. The furniture was broken and belongings had been thrown around. Strands of grey hair, seemingly torn form someone's head, were found, along with numerous valuable belongings and a quantity of money. The two women could not be found, nor could any burglars or assailants.

However, finding soot in the fireplace, the chimney was searched and the body of the daughter was found to have been pushed, feet-upwards, into the narrow opening. She was pulled free and many marks and bruises were found on her face and neck.

Having failed to find the mother in the building, she was subsequently discovered outside, in the yard, her head and body mutilated and her throat so completely torn through that when the neighbours tried to lift her body, her head fell off. No trace of any attackers could be found.

In the subsequent day's newspaper various accounts of the neighbors and other interested parties explained the reclusive life of the mother and daughter, and about the recent removal of a large amount of money from Madame L'Espanye's bank account. Various neighbours who entered the house commented on the voices which were heard as they entered the house. All agreed that there was one gruff voice, speaking French, and one shrill voice. However, they couldn't agree as to which language this second voice was speaking. The gendarme believed that the other voice was foreign, possibly Spanish. A French neighbour believed that the second voice was Italian. A Dutch passer-by thought it was French. An English neighbour thought it German. A Spanish neighbour thought it English. An Italian thought it to be Russian.

The newspaper also gave information about the state of the bodies. The daughter had been throttled to death while the mother had been mutilated and battered, with several broken bones. Her throat had been cut with something sharp which could have been a razor.

Finally, the paper reported that the bank clerk who had delivered the woman's money had been arrested, despite the fact that the money had not been stolen and there was no evidence against him.

The narrator tells us that Dupin is interested in this case and dismisses the efforts of the police as being insufficient. He determines to make his own investigation into the murders.

With permission from the police, Dupin and the narrator go to the house in the Rue Morgue and examine the premises as well as the bodies of the deceased which are still there. Having looked at everything in detail, the two men return home, with Dupin stopping at the office of one of the daily newspapers on the way home. Upon reaching home, Dupin tells the narrator that he is waiting for a man to call on them who, if not the perpetrator, is at least heavily involved with the murders. As a precaution, Dupin takes out two pistols and gives one to the narrator.

While they wait, Dupin explains the deductions which have led to him discovering the murderer. He explains that the reported testimony about the two voices heard by the neighbours means that the two women were killed by a third party, rather than some squabble between the two of them. Further, he highlights the fact that the shrill voice was interpreted as a range of foreign languages by people who had no knowledge of those particular languages, and that no sounds in that voice could be distinguished as words.

Leaving that point for a moment, he then goes on to talk about the physical evidence. Despite all windows and doors being locked in the room, Dupin had reasoned that the killer must have left by at least one of them. Upon examination he discovered that one of the windows was not nailed shut, as it appeared to be, and had a latch which would automatically lock when the window was shut. This, then, was the escape route. Examination of the outside of the building showed a lightning rod running up to the top of the building, within a long reach of the fourth story window's shutter, not only for escape but also for entrance into the apartment.

Next, Dupin draws the narrator's attention to the fact that the apartment was not robbed, and that at least some of the mess in the room could be attributed to the habits of two women living together in rooms which were never visited by others, rather than any kind of burglary.

Finally, Dupin draws attention to the unlikely and excessive natures of the murders themselves—the stuffing up the chimney of the daughter and the beheading of the mother.

He draws these facts together; the agility and strength of the attacker, the shrill voice which utters no real language, the failure to take the money which was lying in plain sight, and asks the narrator for his thoughts. The narrator supposes that it was an escaped madman, but Dupin contradicts him. Even a madman's gibberish is generally of a recognizable language, he says, and then produces a tuft of clearly non-human hair that he found clutched in the mother's fingers. This is followed by a sketch of the throttle-marks left on the daughter's neck. Even when spread around a cylindrical surface, the narrator is unable to fit his hand to the large span of the marks. Dupin then passes the narrator an article describing the aspect and nature of the orangutan, an animal which both men agree must have been the murderer.

Dupin then expands his reasoning to include the gruff voice which was overheard. He has deduced that this was the voice of the orangutan's owner who, having followed his escaped animal, chanced upon the scene of the murders and then left, to avoid being incriminated. Dupin then reveals that when he stopped at the newspaper he asked them to place an advert that an orangutan had been found, in a very different part of the city from the Rue Morgue, and that its owner—a sailor from a Maltese vessel—was sought for its return. The specifics of the owner's identity, Dupin explains, come from finding a length of ribbon such as sailors use to tie up their hair, tied in a particular Maltese knot.

As Dupin finishes telling his tale, the two men hear someone climbing the stairs. Dupin opens the door to admit a sailor. He sits and the men talk about the orangutan. Dupin says the beast is being held in a livery stable and will be returned if the sailor will identify it and pay a small price. The sailor agrees and asks what the price is. Dupin says his price is information about the two murders. As he asks this, he locks the door and Dupin and the narrator point their guns at the sailor.

The sailor stands, clutching a cudgel, but on seeing the guns, sits back down, looking forlorn. Dupin reassures him that they know he did not commit the murders, but that he wants to know the circumstances so that the innocent bank clerk can be released from prison.

The sailor tells his tale of finding the ape on an island and, upon his return to Paris, taking it to his apartment so that it might recover from a splinter in its foot. Returning from a night out on the morning of the murders, the sailor found the animal in his own bedroom, having escaped from the closet where it had been confined. The animal held a razor in its hand and was pretending to shave. Attempting to control the orangutan with a whip, he instead frightened it and sent it running from the house, razor in hand.

The sailor followed and saw the animal enter the window of the house on the Rue Morgue. Believing the ape to be trapped, with no escape but the lightning rod, he followed up to the window where he saw the orangutan holding the mother by her hair and pretending to shave her with the razor. The shrieks of the woman caused the ape to become angry and slash at her throat. The sight of blood then enraged the animal further causing it to seize the daughter by the neck and throttle her. Then, seeing, its master at the window, and attempting to hide its crime, it tore apart the furniture, inserted the girl into the chimney and threw the old lady from the window.

The ape then advanced towards the sailor and it was his exclamations of terror and the cries of the ape which the neighbours heard while they climbed the stairs. He retreated and ran home, presumably followed by the ape, who escaped into the city.

With this testimony and the gathered evidence, Dupin is now able to affect the release of the bank clerk. The orangutan itself was later caught by its owner and sold to a botanical garden.

Historical Context

Poe's short story, "The Murders in the Rue Morgue," first appeared in the April 1841 edition of *Graham's Magazine*, a periodical based in Philadelphia, of which Poe was an editor from February 1841 to April 1842. It is commonly regarded as the first real detective story and the forerunner of the tales with such detectives as Sherlock Holmes and Hercule Poirot (Symons, 307). In particular, it has several features which would become common to books of this genre: a super-intelligent 'amateur' detective who solves the case more for his own pleasure than for any real desire to 'fight crime' (Kennedy, 86); the less-intelligent side-kick who is also the narrator of the story (c.f. Dr. Watson in the Sherlock Holmes stories and Captain Hastings in the Poirot mysteries); early examples of deduction by the detective which do not affect the story but demonstrate the methods they use; and the ending in which the detective, having gathered the piece, reveals and explains the method of the crime and identifies the killer.

"The Murders in the Rue Morgue" is the first of three stories featuring C. Auguste Dupin, the other two being "The Mystery of Marie Roget" and "The Purloined Letter."

This was a time in American literature when the Romantic Movement was flourishing, and Poe's stories are seen as a part of this. This movement prized the natural over the artificial and the rural over the urban. It foregrounded human beings as the primary subject of art, and in particular the expression of emotions and instincts (Abrams, 126–129). As such, "The Murders in the Rue Morgue" is a typical 'romantic' story featuring, as it does, the horror of the murders and the instinctive analysis of Dupin.

Societal Context

Society was going through great changes at the time that Poe was writing "The Murders in the Rue Morgue." The Industrial Revolution's creation of jobs and wealth in the cities and a need for workers in the mills and factories, led to a large number of people moving from the country into cities. As a result, cities were growing at a huge rate. Decent building standards could not keep up with the influx of people, and nor could the policing of these people. The results were a growth in the number of slums, the deterioration of living standards in the cities, a growth in crime and disorder, and a resulting isolation of the individual even within a more crowded environment (Kennedy, 9). Crime is obviously central to the story, but the use of an ape would seem to suggest that Poe sees something bestial about the nature of crime in the new cities.

Another result of the industrial revolution was the increased ability for people to move around the world with the advent of railways and the growth in use of steam powered boats to cross the oceans. As a result, levels of immigration grew and in many places, sections of cities became dedicated to particular groups of foreign immigrants.

Both of these factors seem to be present in Poe's story, with an urban crime of the most horrendous nature being witnessed by a relatively large number of people; many of them foreign to the Parisian setting of the story. Only in a modern city, with the weight of people creating such close living, could there be so many witnesses of so many different nationalities.

Religious Context

The time when Poe was writing "The Murders in the Rue Morgue" was a point when certain traditional views of the world, in particular conservative religious views, and a 'resurgent evangelicalism' were being challenged by a more rational scientific view of the world which, of course, was typified by Darwin's "Origin of Species," published in 1859

(Franks, 169). Thus the time was ripe for tales of logic and ratiocination of which "The Murders in the Rue Morgue" is seen as the first. Poe's depiction of Dupin's style of analysis aligns the story with empirical theories of human consciousness which were, at the time, allied with religious scepticism and atheism (Frank, 169–72).

Other scientific theories of the time also informed Poe's writing and opposed the predominant religious views. These are examined in the Scientific & Technological Context.

In addition, Romantic literature, the movement with which Poe's writing is associated, focused on the life of the human being as a way of achieving change and progress rather than the intervention of divine forces.

Scientific & Technological Context

The scientific contexts of this story work in opposition to the religious, as it was written during a period in history when the sudden advance of scientific methods and discoveries occasioned by the industrial revolution gave a challenge to accepted religious orthodoxy.

These methods and discoveries are primarily revealed in the story during Dupin's initial presentation of his analytical skills when he deduces the train of thought that the narrator has been following. He mentions in the train of thought the name Dr. Nichols, but does not expand on this in his later description of his deduction. This mention is almost certainly a reference to a book written by a Dr. Nichols entitled, "Views of the Architecture of the Heavens," which discusses the nebular theory of the creation of solar systems. This theory talks about the slow accretion of matter around gravitational centers to create the stars and planets which make up solar systems. This opposed the religious idea of a creator forming the heavens (Frank, 172–76).

Later in the story, in order to demonstrate how his hypothesis leads him to the conclusion that the murderer was an orangutan, Dupin shows

the narrator a passage from another book written by George Cuvier. This is presumed to be his 1834 book, "Animal Kingdom" (Frank, 179). The description of the orangutan in this book refers to it as similar in many ways to man. Thus, by having this creature as the killer, Poe predates Darwin's theories of evolution by nearly twenty years in ascribing to it the violent properties of a more primitive human.

Biographical Context

Edgar Allan Poe was born as simply Edgar Poe in Boston, Massachusetts, on January 19, 1809; the child of two actors. His father abandoned the family a year later and his mother died of consumption a year after that. He was taken in by a foster family headed by a Scottish merchant named John Allan and his sickly wife, Frances. Poe was never formally adopted but took their surname as his middle name. When still a child, the Allans moved to England, where Poe was schooled for six years before they moved back to America.

Following this upbringing, it is unsurprising that sickly mother figures appear often in Poe's writing, something which can again be seen in "The Murders in the Rue Morgue" with the murders of Madame L'Espanye and her daughter.

As well as becoming famous as a writer, Poe became known for his exploration of the field of code-breaking known as cryptography. He ran public competitions in which he would solve ciphers submitted by members of the public. This led to a boom in such puzzles being printed in newspaper. It must also have been a source of his fascination with analysis and the creation of the character of Dupin.

Poe married his 13-year-old cousin, Virginia Clemm, in 1836. Their relationship was obviously close and after her death from tuberculosis in 1847, he rapidly declined. He died in 1849, after being admitted to a hospital in a delirious condition.

Contemporary newspaper reports gave causes of death which had previously been used as euphemisms for alcoholism, but no official cause of death was ever announced.

Calum A. Kerr

Works Cited

Abrams, M. H. *A Glossary of Literary Terms.* Orlando, Harcourt Brace College Publishers, 1985.

Frank, Lawrence. "The Murders in the Rue Morgue: Edgar Allan Poe's Evolutionary Reverie," *Nineteenth-Century Literature*, Vol. 50, No. 2 (Sep. 1995), pp. 168–188, University of California Press.

Friedman, William F. "Edgar Allan Poe, Cryptographer," *American Literature,* Vol. 8, No. 3 (Nov. 1936), pp. 266–280. Duke University Press.

Kennedy, J. Gerald. *A Historical Guide to Edgar Allan Poe.* Oxford, Oxford University Press, 2001.

Poe, Edgar Allan. "The Murders in the Rue Morgue," *Selected Tales*, pp. 105–135. Oxford, Oxford University Press, 1980.

Rosenheim, Shawn and Rachman, Stephen (Eds.). *The American Face of Edgar Allan Poe.* Baltimore, The Johns Hopkins University Press, 1995.

Sinclair, David. *Edgar Allen Poe.* Totowa, Rowman and Littlefield, 1977.

Symons, Julian. "Introduction" and "Notes," *Selected Tales*, pp. vii-xiii and pp. 301–316. Oxford, Oxford University Press, 1980.

The Edgar Allan Poe Society of Baltimore, 14 May 2008.

Discussion Questions

1. What does the opening discussion of the analytical mind contribute to the story?
2. How plausible is Dupin's analysis of his comrade's thought processes?
3. Why do you think Poe sets the story in Paris rather than an American city?
4. What about the story shows that it is the creation of an American rather than a European writer?
5. How effective is the newspaper as a device in the story?
6. What is the role of the narrator in the story?
7. Compare Poe's portrayal of Dupin against his portrayal of the police in the story.
8. Dupin quotes various scholars in his deductions, but often their views are adapted or changed by Poe to suit the story. How does this affect your view of the story and the character of Dupin?
9. Do you think Poe was serious when he chose the murderer to be an ape, or should the story be viewed as a kind of joke?
10. "The Murders in the Rue Morgue" introduced many literary devices for the first time. Examine these and how they are used in the story.

Essay Ideas

1. "The Murders in the Rue Morgue" is said to be the first true detective story. Examine its possible sources and the way in which it influenced later writing.

2. Compare and contrast "The Murders in the Rue Morgue" with any one of Sir Arthur Conan Doyle's Sherlock Holmes stories.

3. Why is it important to the story that the murderer is not a native of the city?

4. The window latch on which the story turns is not a feature of that kind of window but was an invention of Poe. What purpose does this invention serve and in what other ways has Poe created his ideal environment for the story to occur.

5. In what way is "The Murders in the Rue Morgue" typical of the 'Romantic' movement in American Literature.

Nine Stories

by J.D. Salinger

Content Synopsis

In "A Perfect Day for Bananafish" Salinger depicts the events leading up to a man's suicide. The story opens with a description of Mrs. Seymour Glass trying to reach her parents by telephone from a hotel in Florida where she has traveled with her husband. From her telephone conversation, it is revealed that Seymour has been having some post-war psychological problems. We do not see Mrs. Glass again until the end of the story when Seymour returns to the hotel room and finds her asleep. After Mrs. Glass's phone conversation, the story shifts to a young girl, Sybil, who finds Seymour on the beach and asks him to go swimming with her. He takes her out on a raft and at one point kisses the arch of her foot. After swimming with Sybil, Seymour returns to the hotel room, takes a gun out of his suitcase, loads it, aims it at himself and pulls the trigger.

"Uncle Wiggly in Connecticut" depicts a visit between two former college roommates, Mary Jane and Eloise. Mary Jane is a single, working girl visiting Eloise at her home in Connecticut where she lives a comfortable lifestyle with her husband Lew, young daughter Ramona, and Grace, the maid. At first it appears that Eloise has the better life, but Salinger quickly reveals that Mary Jane is the happier of the two and that Eloise has been hardened by past experience. Eloise's daughter enters the picture with her thick eyeglasses and imaginary

friend Jimmy. Ramona delights Mary Jane, but Eloise seems burdened. After several high balls, Eloise reminisces about Walt, an old boyfriend who was killed in the war. She recalls a time when she fell and hurt her ankle and Walt called it "poor Uncle Wiggly." She misses his sense of humor. After Mary Jane probes her for answers and insists that Eloise should be happy with her husband and life now, Eloise starts crying. She later barges into her sleeping daughter's room saying "poor Uncle Wiggly" while kissing her glasses and tucking her in. The story closes with Eloise asking Mary Jane if she was a nice girl back in college, as she is aware that she herself is no longer the same person.

"Just Before the War with the Eskimos" features Ginnie Maddox, a fifteen-year old girl in New York City, who plays tennis each week with Selena Graff, a girl from school whom she is reluctant to call a friend. After several weeks in which Selena sticks Ginnie with the bill for the taxicab, Ginnie asks Selena to pay her back. Selena is offended but says she has to get the money from her mother who is ill. Ginnie is adamant about the money and goes up to Selena's apartment with her to get the money. While she is waiting in the living room, Ginnie meets Selena's brother Franklin. He is still in his pajamas and enters the room complaining that he just cut his finger. Ginnie finds him goofy looking, but after talking to him she seems drawn to him. He talks about dropping out of college and his old job at the airplane factory. The doorbell rings and Franklin leaves the room to shave and get dressed. Franklin's friend Eric, a flamboyant young man, has arrived to take him to a show. He used to work with Franklin at the airplane factory during the war. After a while, Selena returns with the money for Ginnie, but Ginnie no longer wants it and is suddenly friendly with Selena. She tells Selena that she met her brother and asks if she can come over later that night.

"The Laughing Man" is a story told in the first person from the perspective of a young boy who is a member of the Comanches, an after-school boys club led by a kind law student whom they called Chief. Every day after school and on weekends, the Chief would drive the boys in an old bus to play football, baseball or take them camping. In between outings, he was famous for telling the Comanches the ongoing story of "The Laughing Man." The Chief relayed the adventures of a young boy who was kidnapped by bandits and tortured in a carpenter's vice. The vice left the Laughing Man permanently disfigured and he went the rest of his life wearing a veil made of poppy petals. The Laughing Man befriended the animals of the forest as they were the only ones who could accept him and grew up to become a bandit himself. As the saga of the Laughing Man unfolds, the Chief develops his own drama. The narrator describes how the Chief starts seeing a young woman, Mary Hudson, who later joined the Comanches on their outings. At first the boys view her as an intruder but when she proves to be a good baseball player, they accept her presence. One day, after picking up the Comanches, the Chief goes to pick up Mary but she does not appear. She appears at the game later but does not play. From their body language, the narrator can tell that Mary and the Chief are having a heated discussion and later he sees her crying. On the way home from the game, the Chief delivers his last installment of "The Laughing Man" and he brings his adventurous life to a tragic end. The

Comanche boys are devastated and although the boys do not quite realize it, they can tell that the Chief and the Comanches will never be the way they once were.

"Down at the Dinghy" is set at a lake house during Indian summer and features Sandra the maid, Mrs. Snell the housekeeper, and Boo Boo, the mother of Lionel, a four-year old boy who keeps running away. Lionel is sitting in his father's dinghy, which is tethered to the dock, and he refuses to get out. At the beginning of the story, Sandra is anxious. She is talking to Mrs. Snell who tells her that the boy is either going to tell his mother or he isn't, without saying exactly what he is going to tell. Later, Boo Boo enters the kitchen and explains to the women that Lionel will not get out of the dinghy and that he has been running away like this for the past few years. She leaves the kitchen and walks down to the lake to try to get Lionel out of the boat. She tells him that she is an admiral in the Navy and gives him a secret bugle call in an attempt to get him to open up to her. After many tries, Lionel starts to cry and Boo Boo climbs into the boat with him. He reveals to her that he is crying because Sandra called his father a "kike." Boo Boo comforts him and tells him they are going to pick his father up at the station and they will all go sailing together.

"For Esme—With Love and Squalor" is told in the first person from the perspective of a former soldier who has been invited to a wedding in England. He reflects back to the time when he was in England for special military training and met a striking teenage girl named Esme at a teahouse. She explains how she lost both of her parents and she and that her five-year old brother live with her aunt. Esme is precocious for her age and attempts to use a lot of big words, not always correctly. He tells her he is a writer and she asks him to write a story for her, one that is filled with squalor. He agrees and she says she will write him letters while he is away at war and hopes that he returns "with all of your faculties intact." The narrator then flashes to a time just after V-E Day when a soldier dubbed Sergeant X, who did not escape the war with all of his faculties intact, is recovering from a nervous breakdown. He picks up a package from a pile of unopened letters and discovers a letter from Esme. Included with the letter is her deceased father's watch, which Esme was wearing the day they met at the teahouse in England. Esme explains in her letter that she hopes it will bring Sergeant X good luck. After reading the letter, Sergeant X relaxes and becomes sleepy; a sign that her gesture has helped him.

"Pretty Mouth and Green My Eyes" tells the story of an older man and a young woman who are in bed together one night when the phone rings. Arthur, the man's friend and coworker, is on the line frantic that his wife Joanie has not come home yet. Arthur is drunk and ranting on and on about how he has wasted five years on this woman, while remembering the good times they had together. The older man tries to calm him down but to no avail. At one point, Arthur wants to come to the man's house to talk but the man talks him out of it. When he gets off the phone, the young woman tells him he was wonderful and that she feels like "an absolute dog!" and it becomes clear that the young woman is Joanie. Moments later, Arthur calls back to tell the man that Joanie has come home and expresses concern over his job stability. The man is clearly affected by Arthur's desperate attempts to seem stable and abruptly gets off the phone. He then accidentally drops his lit cigarette and snaps at Joanie when she tries to help him pick it up.

"De Daumier-Smith's Blue Period" is a humorous, first person account of a young man who grew up in Paris with his mother and step-father and, at age 19, has returned to New York after his mother's passing. His step-father, Bobby, worked as an art appraiser in Paris and the narrator became trained as an artist. Upon returning to New York, the narrator and Bobby share a room at the Ritz

and the narrator grows increasingly bored with the arrangement. He sees an advertisement for an art instructor at a new correspondence art school in Montreal and decides to apply, making up his qualifications and even inventing a relation to the French painter, Honore Daumier and a friendship with Pablo Picasso (whom he refers to as a French painter). He is offered a position by the owners of the school M. and Mme. Yoshoto.

Upon arrival at the school, the narrator is disenchanted. The school is located above an orthopedic supply store and consists of one small office with three desks. At night, the narrator lies in bed listening to the loud moans of one of the Yoshotos. The instructors spend their days correcting, not really instructing, the artwork that has been mailed in by their students. The narrator is appalled by the lack of talent of his students except for the paintings of a nun whose work he is drawn to. He sneaks her work out of the office and writes her a long letter with suggestions and compliments her skill. He wants to meet her imagining she is young and the two can run off together. After anxiously waiting for her reply, a letter arrives from the head of the convent informing him that Sister Irma can no longer attend the art school. The narrator is dejected and writes her a letter, dresses in a dinner suit and goes out for the evening. On his way back home, he looks into the window of the orthopedic supply shop and sees a girl dressing one of the mannequins. She is startled by his presence and falls over. After her fall, the narrator has a pivotal experience in which he sees the sun shining, blinding him through the store window. The moment passes and the narrator returns to his room resolving to leave Sister Irma alone. A week later the art school closes down for not having a license and the narrator returns to live with Bobby who has relocated to Rhode Island.

"Teddy" is the final, disturbing tale in the collection "Nine Stories." The protagonist is a 10-year old genius who is on a cruise with his detached parents and six-year old sister, Booper. Teddy is introduced standing on his father's luggage looking out the porthole of their cabin. His father insists that Teddy step down but Teddy ignores him and philosophizes about a basket of orange peels that was just dumped from another part of the boat into the ocean. His parents ask where Booper is and, unconcerned, Teddy tells them that she is on deck and that he gave her the camera. The father is outraged and demands that Teddy go get the camera from her, while the mother wants to see the child before her swimming lesson. When he finds Booper, she is stacking shuffleboard discs in a pile and talking to a boy named Myron. She is a precocious child and very rude to Myron. Teddy tells her to take the camera to their parents but she does not want to go. He leaves her with the camera and goes off to write in his diary.

Later, a man named Nicholson, who had heard Teddy on a tape when he was in Boston discoursing with some professors and scientists, approaches him. The two begin a conversation in which Teddy tries to explain his belief in mysticism and reincarnation. Nicholson also asks Teddy if he told the Professors when and how they were going to die. Teddy denies this inquiry but admits he told them some things in this regard. He talks about how people are too sentimental and how he does not feel that type of emotion or attachment himself. He then goes on to explain that death is nothing to fear because it is part of the natural cycle and a person will simply leave one body and enter another until they get to stay with God. He says, for example, if he were to go to the pool that morning and it happened to be empty, his sister might push him in and he would die but it would be no tragedy. Nicholson wants to continue their conversation but Teddy insists he must go to his swimming lesson and leaves. After contemplating their conversation for a moment, Nicholson jumps up and rushes to find

the swimming pool. As he gets closer, he can hear the scream of a young girl "reverberating within four tiled walls."

Symbols & Motifs

Many of Salinger's stories depict precocious young children who seem far wiser than the adults present in their lives. Yet, with the exception of Teddy, most of the children in the stories have a sense of purity and innocence about them that the adults have lost over time. In "For Esme—with Love and Squalor" it is precisely Esme's purity and kindness that saves the damaged soldier from his own jaded mind. The young girl in "A Perfect Day for Bananafish" offers Seymour a final moment of unbridled innocence before he kills himself.

Often, the children in Salinger's stories experience a coming of age, in which they are exposed to the complications of adulthood and lose a sense of their innocence. In "Down at the Dinghy," young Lionel wants to stay in the boat to escape from the nasty words used against his father. "The Laughing Man" features a young boy who exults in his afternoon outings with the Comanche Club until he witnesses the rise and fall of the group leader's relationship with a young woman. Likewise, the adult characters in many of the stories such as "Uncle Wiggly in Connecticut" and "De Daumier's Blue Period" look back to their younger years as a time of joy and happiness and seem dissatisfied with their current lives. Loveless marriages, distant parents, lost souls and disaffected youth abound in "Nine Stories."

Historical Context

J.D. Salinger's prime writing and publishing years coincided with World War II. Salinger himself landed on Utah Beach on D-Day and spent three years in the midst of combat including the Battle of the Bulge ("J.D. Salinger"). While most of his stories do not directly depict his experiences in the war, many of them deal with the conflicts related to coming home from the war. Although Post Traumatic Stress was an unheard of disorder at the time, that is exactly what Salinger's characters are experiencing. Seymour Glass is one character who cannot cope with life after war. Sergeant X, in "For Esme—with Love and Squalor," is barely able to function after witnessing the ravages of war. "Uncle Wiggly in Connecticut" features a woman whose life was never the same after her lover was killed in the war.

Societal Context

When Salinger first began publishing his work just after World War II, his fans identified with his quiet, brooding characters and their rejection of the "phonies" of the world. Those disenchanted with the materialism and corruption of modern society made Salinger and his characters American icons. This identification, however, was not sustained as political reforms and the rise of activism led to a new generation of reader in the 1960's who saw Salinger's characters as outdated and uninvolved ("Dictionary of Literary Biography"). Salinger's popularity again resurged in the 1980s and 90's and his work is esteemed on the merit of its writing and universal messages rather than as a political statement on the times ("Dictionary of Literary Biography").

Religious Context

Salinger himself was a follower of various religions. There was a period in his life when he was an avid follower of Buddhism and the works in "Nine Stories" reflect this sentiment. Ironically, many of the characters in his stories are caught up in the material world and lack any kind of spiritual awareness. The story "Teddy," however, especially demonstrates Salinger's religious convictions as the title character adopts the Buddhist philosophies of meditation and reincarnation. He says that the problem with society is that it is too full of intellect

and logic and lacking in spiritual awareness. He is not attached to the body or sentimental about the lives of other beings; convinced that after death he will be reunited with God and the infinite oneness of existence.

Scientific & Technological Context

"Nine Stories" does not have a specific scientific or technological context.

Biographical Context

Jerome David Salinger was born in Manhattan, NY on January 1, 1919, to a Jewish father and an Irish Catholic mother, whom he did not know was not Jewish until he was a teenager ("J.D. Salinger"). He attended high school at the Valley Forge Military Academy in Wayne, Pennsylvania and attended college at New York University for one year before dropping out. He took an evening writing course at Columbia University in 1939 under the tutelage of *Story* magazine editor Whit Burnett and soon became his protégé ("J.D. Salinger"). Burnett published Salinger's short story "The Young Folks" in *Story* later that year ("J.D. Salinger"). He quickly moved on to publishing in popular magazines such as *Esquire*, *Good Housekeeping*, and the *Saturday Evening Post* from 1941 to 1948 ("Dictionary of Literary Biography"). Ultimately, his work landed in the prestigious *The New Yorker* and, from that point forward, Salinger published almost exclusively in that publication.

In 1942, Salinger was drafted into the army during World War II, where he witnessed and participated in combat in the Army Signal Corp and the Counter-Intelligence Corp until 1945 ("Dictionary of Literary Biography"). After the war, Salinger published "Slight Rebellion Off Madison" in *The New Yorker* which later evolved into the novel "The Catcher in the Rye," published in 1951 ("Dictionary of Literary Biography").

The publication of "A Perfect Day for "Bananafish," in *The New Yorker* gave Salinger the recognition of a popular audience ("Dictionary of Literary Biography"). In 1953, Salinger published "Nine Stories," followed by two books about the fictional Glass family, "Franny and Zooey" in 1961 and "Raise High the Roof Beam, Carpenters" as well as "Seymour: An Introduction" in 1963 ("Dictionary of Literary Biography"). Salinger stopped publishing his writing in the 1960's; about the same time that scholars started published essays analyzing his work. He is currently one of the most widely read writers with one of the smallest bodies of work ("Dictionary of Literary Biography"). He has led a reclusive life in New Hampshire for the past 40 years.

Jennifer Bouchard

Works Cited

Dictionary of Literary Biography, Volume 2. "American Novelists Since World War II, First Series." Jeffrey Helterman, ed. Columbia: University of South Carolina, 1978, pp. 434–444.

J.D. Salinger (1919-). *American Jewish Desk Reference*, 1999. Jewish Virtual Library, 11 April 2008.

Poore, Charles. *Books of the Times*, 9 April 1953. *New York Times on the Web*, 11 April 2008.

Salinger, J.D. *Nine Stories*. Boston: Little, Brown and Company, 1953.

Welty, Eudora. "Threads of Innocence." *New York Times*, 5 April 1953. *New York Times on the Web*, 11 April 2008.

Discussion Questions

1. Which story was your favorite and why?
2. Which story was your least favorite and why?
3. Characterize Seymour Glass, the main character in "A Perfect Day for Bananafish."
4. What causes Ginnie's change of heart towards Selena in "Just Before the War with the Eskimos?"
5. How do you think Esme's actions toward Sergeant X in "For Esme—With Love and Squalor" affected his future?
6. What discoveries are made by the protagonist in "The Laughing Man?"
7. How does the outcome of the story within the story affect the Comanches in "The Laughing Man?"
8. How would you describe the ending of the story "Teddy"?
9. What are the main themes present in this story collection?
10. Why do you think J.D. Salinger stopped publishing his fiction?

Essay Ideas

1. Describe and analyze Salinger's literary style. Focus on the structure of his narratives, characters, dialogue and common themes.
2. Write an essay in which you compare and contrast the varied protagonists in "Nine Stories."
3. Analyze the effect of World War II on J.D. Salinger's writing.
4. Read some of Salinger's other writings in which Seymour Glass appears. Write an essay in which you discuss his various representations.
5. Write a tenth story to include in the collection. Stay true to Salinger's characters and themes.

A scapegoat child, described like the one pictured here, is at the center of *The Ones Who Walk Away From Omelas*, a story included in this volume. Author Ursula K. Le Guin is an American novelist whose work often depicts futuristic or imaginary alternative worlds in politics, natural environments, gender, religion, and sexuality. Photo: Library of Congress, Prints & Photographs Division, LC-DIG-ds-02108.

The Ones Who Walk Away From Omelas

by Ursula K. Le Guin

Content Synopsis

The narrator of "The Ones Who Walk Away From Omelas" quite often directly addresses the reader, inviting them to think of descriptions of Omelas, its environs and people as they see fit; this should be borne in mind when reading the synopsis.

The story opens with the city of Omelas and its preparation for one of its celebrations: The Festival of Summer. The city of Omelas is towered and stands by a sea harbor with many boats. There are expansive parks and public buildings, and the people of the city are in numerous processions, all heading towards the festival's location.

The people are eclectic—workmen, craftsmen, old, young, formally and informally dressed. Some children are naked and playing in the fields, readying their horses for the racecourse at the festival. The scene shifts to a larger view of Omelas, depicting it as encircled by huge mountains, some snow-capped, and the view between them and Omelas is clear with no pollution.

The flapping of banners and flags, and music fill the air as the people make their way through fields and the sound of bells is heard calling the inhabitants to the festival. The joyous scene is interrupted by the narrator who inquires of the reader: "How does one know joy?"; "How can the populace be described?"

The people, though happy, are not simple people. The narrator continues by mentioning how a 'fairy-tale-like' king, with all that a king should possess—slaves, fine horses, knights and regalia—would seem fitting to the scene. However, there is none of this in Omelas. The city and people don't need swords, or slaves. It is reiterated that they are not barbarians or simple folk.

The rules of the society in Omelas are not believed to be many. It is ventured that the structure of society in Omelas does not include financial institutions, secret police or weapons of mass destruction. They are as intricate and diverse as us.

The narrator then begins a philosophical debate about the people of Omelas—asserting that happiness is considered parochial and mediocre; anguish and grief intellectual and vital. A dichotomy is thus presented which glorifies pain and belittles joy and the celebration of it. The narrator again addresses the reader to inquire how to best describe the people of Omelas, and is clearly at pains to convince the audience that the populace and its children, though happy, are not naïve, nor lacking in intelligence or maturity.

Conjecture then follows: for a civilization to be happy, there needs to be a distinction between what technology is necessary for the well being of its people, and what is not necessary, or no use to a society because of its potentially destructive capabilities. There is a conclusion that, because Omelas is described as happy, there would be no cars or helicopters. However, for the sake of comfort, the citizens would have domestic appliances, transport that minimises pollution, and—more speculation—futuristic advancements: cures for diseases, pollution-free energy sources, power from the air itself—all manner of things our culture doesn't yet have. The reader is invited to contemplate all these possibilities about Omelas and its people by the narrator, who declares that some, or none, of it may be true of the city but that the readers themselves need to decide what they believe.

The narrator believes that visitors to Omelas and the Festival have been arriving in fast trains and large buses—and that this form of transport is highly regarded, as the architecture of the stations is auspiciously decorative. The reader is then addressed as possibly believing, because of the descriptions so far, that Omelas is a true fairy-tale—a utopia. If this is the case, they are invited to add an orgy—nudes offering themselves to passers-by—or some artefact that sullies the picture painted so far.

It is then decided that there should be religion but no clergy in Omelas, and that the nudes, if they exist, should not be thought of as lewd but as part of the city's culture. The need for sex without love should be looked on as a basic need and nothing to be ashamed of. What is more, any offspring of such liaisons should be welcomed and loved by all the citizens. There should be no guilt in Omelas.

But, the narrator asks, what else should or shouldn't exist in the city? No drugs: that would be puritanical, but maybe a form of liquor that alters states of mind, and enhances perception and sex but is not addictive would be available. A sense of pride and celebration is evident but as there is no militia, pride and celebration are built upon achievements other than war.

The processions have now reached the festival site and there is an air of expectancy. The smells of cooking are everywhere and the people are purchasing goods from the many vendors. The horses are almost ready to race and a boy enraptures the crowds with his flute playing, finishing and slowly

acknowledging them. The scene excites the horses and everyone present recognizes that the festival proper has begun.

The reader is then asked: "Do you believe in Omelas now; in the joy, and the wonder of the festival?" If not, the narrator continues, then one more element needs to be described.

In a small, windowless, room of one of the beautiful buildings of Omelas, a child lives. The room has a dirt floor and is kept locked. In the room with the child are two mops. We are told that the child is afraid of them and keeps as far away from them as it can. The child is malnourished, filthy, and probably imbecilic. Its physical appearance is nauseating. It is painfully thin, its muscles atrophied. It plays with its genitals, sits in its own excrement and is covered in sores.

It understands that it is a prisoner; that it was taken away from its parents, sunlight and a home but it has long since stopped crying and pleading to be freed. It has lost the ability to speak and now accepts that its current circumstances don't change.

Sometimes, the door in its cell is opened and a jug of water and some food are thrust in. Sometimes the door is opened and people stand at the door looking in. The child may be kicked by one of them so it stands to afford the onlookers a better view of itself. The watchers never speak but just look at the child with revulsion and fear.

Every person in Omelas knows about the child. Many of them have come to see it, some of them just acknowledge the fact that it is present in their city. The child's existence is explained to all other children before their teenage years. Everyone is told about it and its reason for being there. They are told that without the child and its situation, Omelas could not exist. There would be no joy, no festivals, no learning, no craftspeople or artefacts. The health and affluence of Omelas, even its weather and harvests, depend upon the child's isolation and suffering. The conditions of the child's subsistence are absolute: no one may care for it, speak to it or for it.

Many of the people who visit the child are young themselves. They experience a wide range of emotions about the experience and its implications. Feelings such as revulsion, rage, indignation and helplessness are common. Some try to reason that even though rescuing the child may seem an act of good intention, the act would destroy their city and its people. Their conclusion is that the act of rescue would be the bigger crime.

Some youngsters, when realizing the dilemma that their survival depends upon, return home weeping, depressed and brooding. Some, after a time, console themselves with thoughts that even if the child were rescued (albeit at the expense of the city), it couldn't live a normal life as it had been retarded too long in its former existence.

They, because of their knowledge of the child and its reason for being, believe that they love their way of life, their children and their culture and city even more, because they know of the dreadful alternative. They believe their art and literature; their intellectual pursuits, crafts and festivals are made better because of the knowledge of the child. The misery of the imprisoned child is contrasted with the freedom and love of the flute player.

The reader is asked, again, if, now, they believe in the people of Omelas. They are asked if, now, they seem more plausible. Then one more incredible thing is revealed to further convince the reader.

Sometimes, we are told, one of the youths who go to see the child does not return home in remorse or guilt to deliberate over its life and fate. They simply do not return home. Occasionally an adult, who has known about the child for nearly all their lives, may leave home after several days of being withdrawn and cheerless.

They walk through the beautiful streets of Omelas and continue, out through the surrounding land. They continue walking day and night, all in different directions as long as it is away from the city. They never return, and are believed to go to a place that is even harder to imagine and describe than Omelas. We are told that it may not exist but that the people who leave Omelas seem to believe in it and are intent on finding it.

Historical Context

"The Ones Who Walk Away From Omelas" first appeared in *New Dimensions 3* magazine in 1973. It won the Hugo Award for The Best Science Fiction Short Story in 1974. When it later appeared in Le Guin's own anthology ("The Wind's Twelve Quarters Volume 2"), she added a preface to explain the idea of scapegoats in literature. In the preface, Le Guin cited William James's "The Moral Philosopher and the Moral Life" and Dostoyevsky's "Brothers Karamazov" as the basis of the idea for the Omelas story.

Scapegoats, though, have existed throughout history and are a common, possibly required, theme in literature and maybe even reality. The idea of burdening a society's ills and misfortunes on an individual is supposed to have originated with a Hebrew ritual of 'placing' troubles and illnesses on a live goat, which was then driven from a village in a symbolic cleansing of the population who were then deemed pure, for a time.

Scapegoats appear in Nathaniel Hawthorne's "The Scarlet Letter" (Hester Prynne) and Arthur Miller's "The Crucible" (John Proctor; Tituba), as well as countless books, short stories and films. Scapegoats as literary devices work on many levels but play a part in conveying a sense of moral outrage or indignation to an audience and thus help in the identification of the audience with the protagonist—a necessity in literature and film.

Societal Context

Le Guin has always portrayed "The Ones Who Walk Away From Omelas," and its central theme, as a political and moral debate—questioning why some 'cities' had excess wealth at the expense of poorer neighbours.

The question raised in "The Ones Who Walk Away From Omelas" is answered by the characters, ranging from acknowledging that rescuing the child would be at too great a cost, to being unable to cope with the knowledge and leaving the society. Such a fundamental question could probably be asked throughout many times in history and of many societies. "The Ones Who Walk Away From Omelas" was written during a time when American conduct in, and March 1973 withdrawal from, the Vietnam War left it vulnerable to criticism regarding its colonialist policies. Also in that year, Richard Nixon was embroiled in the Watergate scandal and the American Indian Movement, commonly known as AIM, was involved in an occupation of land that became known as the Siege at Wounded Knee.

Although Le Guin may not have been influenced by the above incidents, it would be difficult for readers at that time not to associate scapegoats and authority in the text with real-life events, and drawing their own conclusions. As mentioned above, though, it is easily argued (and generally accepted) that if looked for hard enough, any connotations can be made from a text, with or without the author corroborating the interpretations.

Religious Context

The religious theme in "The Ones Who Walk Away From Omelas" is perhaps hard to dispute or ignore. Le Guin in her own preface to the story called it a psychomyth (or 'parable'—with all its inherent connotations). The child scapegoat, the main subject of the piece, is innocent and deliberately chosen to be sacrificed for the greater good; the message and meaning of which is to be imparted to the rest of the society.

The Omelas society being complicit in the misery and fate of the child draws parallels with some religious cultures and beliefs. For example,

in the Bible, Jesus' fellow citizens acknowledge and seal His fate, preferring Pilate to free Barabbas instead of Him. In ancient Egypt, it was accepted that a King's servants would die when he was interred to serve him in the afterlife. African society held a similar belief, with slaves being sacrificed when their master was buried. The Aztecs sometimes sacrificed thousands of people to pacify deities at annual maize rituals; the Incas did the same when a new ruler ascended the throne. Many cultures held the practice of human sacrifice as an accepted part of maintaining social balance. In "The Ones Who Walk Away From Omelas," the whole of the culture, social order, philosophy and belief systems could not exist without the unbearable experiences of the scapegoat child/saviour figure; the scapegoat must fulfill its destiny to enable its legacy to be founded.

The matter of questioning the existence and purpose of the child in the Omelas society, and the customary answers, mirrors that of the matter of 'faith' in many religious doctrines. The populace of Omelas, largely, trusts that the child has to be there and questions it no further. It is the task of the few—the ones who walk away—to philosophize further and question the 'faith' of the many.

There are many interpretations of Le Guin's story and it's possible that in some ways, "The Ones Who Walk Away From Omelas" could be construed as an inversion of our society's religious belief system—in western society, the majority are non-believers, with the minority keeping the faith; in Omelas, the ones who walk away are considered outside the status quo. And yet, they perhaps perform the ultimate act of 'faith,' when they leave to go to a place no one is sure even exists.

Scientific & Technological Context

There is little mention, or use, of science or technology in "The Ones Who Walk Away From Omelas," which perhaps helps the story ascribe itself more to the religious contexts above, as opposed to the logical, objective realms of science. What reference there is exists in the conjecture of the narrator who supposes that Omelas may have made advances not known to the reader. By implying this, the narrator suggests that Omelas could, in some ways, be technologically superior to us. The narrator, repeatedly and consistently, does tell the reader that the citizens are not simple folk, barbarians or less sophisticated and complex. This repetition, along with the mention of technological advancements, urges the reader to avoid dismissing Omelas as a primitive culture in which the sacrificial element could be expected.

In society, generally, during the period Omelas was written, there was a slight sense of frustration with science and technology. The assurance that new discoveries and inventions would solve the world's problems had not come to fruition. The moon landings and space exploration were being looked upon as wastes of money and resources, wars were still being fought, and poverty and inequality were still prevalent.

The lack of mention of technology and science in the text, though, may say more about Le Guin than the story itself and the time at which it was written. Both Le Guin's parents worked in fields other than science and even though Le Guin, generally, is included as a writer in the science fiction genre, many of her works do not feature hard science. Instead, she more often examines and writes about the human condition.

Biographical Context
Ursula Kroeber Le Guin was born in 1929 in Berkeley, California. Her father and mother were a prominent anthropologist and a writer, respectively.

Le Guin taught French at various establishments before coming to prominence as a writer. It seems obvious, in hindsight, but her parents' professions obviously had effects on her and her future emergence and development as a writer.

Le Guin's writing, throughout her career, has concentrated on people and how they act, interact and react to their environment and other people.

Her work is full of intricately described people and societies, some of them stretching across more than one novel (Rocannon's World; Planet of Exile; City of Illusions, et al) and establishing a form of canon in her work. Moral and ethical dilemmas are faced by most of her characters and this, rather than a concentration on technology, permeates her stories.

Coming to prominence at a time when most of her science fiction contemporaries were dealing in short stories and novels based on hard science and technological extrapolation, Le Guin, and her concentration on language and humanity, was writing what could, arguably, be called science fiction literature.

Apart from "The Ones Who Walk Away From Omelas," "The Left Hand Of Darkness" (1969 Nebula and Hugo Award winner), "The Dispossessed" (1975 Nebula and Hugo Award winner) and "The Word for World is Forest" (1973 Hugo Award winner) all intimately explore the human condition, moral philosophy, and sexuality.

Jim Palmer

Works Cited
Hawthorne, Nathaniel. *The Scarlet Letter*. London, Penguin Classics, 2003.

Le Guin, Ursula K. *City of Illusions*. St. Albans, Granada Publishing Ltd., 1973.

Le Guin, Ursula K. *The Dispossessed*. London, Grafton Books, 1987.

Le Guin, Ursula K. *Encyclopædia Britannica*. 17 April 2009. Encyclopædia Britannica 2006 Ultimate Reference Suite DVD.

Le Guin, Ursula K. *The Left Hand of Darkness*. London, Macdonald & Co. Ltd., 1986.

Le Guin, Ursula K. "The Ones Who Walk Away From Omelas," *The Wind's Twelve Quarters Volume 2*. London, Granada Publishing Ltd., 1978.

Le Guin, Ursula K. *Planet of Exile*. London, W. H. Allen & Co., 1983.

Le Guin, Ursula K. *Rocannon's World*. London, W. H. Allen & Co., 1983.

Le Guin, Ursula K. *The Word For World is Forest*. London, Grafton Books, 1986.

Miller, Arthur. *The Crucible*. London, Penguin Modern Classics, 1987.

Palmer, Jim. *The Works of Isaac Asimov and* Ursula K. Le *Guin: A Dichotomy in Science Fiction*. Manchester, D & H Heathcote Printers. B.A. (Hons) Dissertation, 1988.

Ursula K. *Le Guin's Web Site*, 17 April 2009.

Discussion Questions

1. The narrator asks the reader to make their own mind up about how to describe Omelas on several occasions. What reason(s) would there be for this?

2. The narrator says that they are sure the one thing that doesn't exist in Omelas is guilt. How, then, are the actions of those who walk away justified?

3. Could / does Omelas exist?

4. If Omelas did exist, what incentive would its inhabitants have to advance or improve their civilization when they already have everything they need?

5. Why is a child used as the scapegoat in Omelas?

6. All the people who walk away are described as leaving alone. Why is this important, and what could it be taken to mean?

7. The narrator suggests that the child's filthy prison is in part of beautiful building, or in a palatial home. Why is that contrast made?

8. Who, or what, is the flute player?

9. The horses in the story are portrayed as healthy, well looked after and respected. Why are they described that way?

10. Sounds of bells are mentioned several times in the narrative. What connotations do you think are being made?

Essay Ideas

1. There are several changes of tense throughout the story. Could this be taken to mean that the central idea of a scapegoat crosses time and is omnipresent? Discuss.

2. There is a definite division in the narrative after the narrator says there is one more thing to describe. Look at the differences in language, sentence structure and tone between the two halves. What does it achieve?

3. The people who walk away from Omelas are generally considered to be those who cannot live with the guilt and knowledge of the scapegoat child. Could it be argued that those who leave do so because they are, "taking the easy way out"?

4. Le Guin has always said that the idea for "The Ones Who Walk Away From Omelas" came to her from reading a road sign backwards: Salem O(regon). Based on the complexities, symbolism and nuances in the story, do you think Le Guin is being too modest? Give reasons for and against.

5. In contemporary society, are there any people who, "walk away from Omelas"?

The Open Boat

by Stephen Crane

Content Synopsis

A cook, a captain, a correspondent and an oiler try to navigate the colossal ocean waves in a ten-foot dinghy on the open ocean. Days and nights blend together and it is a constant struggle to keep the boat upright and empty of water. The cook bails out the boat while the oiler and correspondent take turns rowing the boat. The injured captain lies in the bow spouting cynical remarks and brushing away the seagulls, but also provides much needed leadership. The men in the boat envy the birds because they can evade the powerful ocean waves. The cook believes a house of refuge is on an island not too far from where they are sailing. This idea of refuge becomes their motivation to keep going as they try not to lose hope.

As they get closer to the land, it becomes more evident that the life-saving station is not active. They continue to remark, "Funny they haven't seen us" to offset their sense of doom (Crane 201). The men try to alleviate their fears by remarking that fate would not send them to their deaths this close to land. She would have killed them before they went to all this trouble, "…if I am to be drowned, why, in the name of seven mad gods who rule the sea, was I allowed to come thus far and contemplate sand and trees?" (202). They are astounded by the possibility that nature does not deem man that important.

Another opportunity for rescue arises when the men see a beach in the distance and spot a man walking and waving at them. They think they are saved until they see an omnibus and realize the man is just a tourist who thinks he is waving at fishermen. Night falls and the men are still afloat at sea. At this point in the story, Crane stops identifying the speakers in the dialogue. It is as if the words spoken could be spoken by anyone on the boat as they echo all of their thoughts and fears. The oiler's death is then foreshadowed when the other men (who have not called each other by name throughout the story) begin to refer to him gently as Billie.

The correspondent rows in the middle of the night when other men are asleep. A large movement and the whish of a fin swims by the boat repeatedly. The correspondent is again reminded of the awesome power of nature and wishes he was not the only man awake. He is reminded of a poem about a soldier dying and feels deep empathy for the subject of the poem. The correspondent finally understands the pain and loneliness of a man who is dying as he faces his own mortality.

Morning finally arrives and a deserted beach is in the distance. The men decide to make a run for it since it appears that help from a lifeboat is not coming. The waves near shore are high and rough and the men know the boat will capsize before they hit land. When a large wave crashes onto the boat, the men jump into the ocean, prepared to swim in the rest of the way. The suspense is at its height as the correspondent gets caught in a current. The other men pass him as he struggles to move forward. Eventually a wave propels him out of the current and he is thrust into waist deep water. A man onshore sees them, strips down and runs into the water to pull them in. The correspondent embraces the sand almost violently, so relieved to be on land. He then observes the oiler face down in shallow water and watches as rescuers carry his lifeless body up the beach. The land's new purpose is to be the oiler's grave.

Symbols & Motifs

The natural elements surrounding the men serve as symbols in "The Open Boat." The seagulls that swarm overhead of the boat are an ominous symbol of the rough times ahead for the men in the boat. The seaweed that occasionally lands in the boat after a crashing wave serves as a sign of land and a metaphor for how close the men are close to safety only to be faced with the dangerous ocean again. The ocean itself is the ultimate symbol of nature's power over man and an unsettling reminder that man is irrelevant in the grand scheme of the world. The open boat is a symbol of the men's vulnerability as they are exposed to the elements, at the mercy of the ocean. They do their best to ride the waves and survive in the vast ocean that hardly notices they are there.

Historical Context

The short story, "The Open Boat," is based on Stephen Crane's real experience trying to find safety after the sinking of the Steamship *Commodore*. On December 31, 1896, the *Commodore* set sail from Jacksonville, Florida headed for Cuba carrying guns and ammunition to assist the Cuban Revolution (Stephen Crane Society). Already an established author, Crane had signed on as a seaman in order to see first hand a war in action.

After a few days at sea, the ship sprang a leak and the men were forced to abandon it. Crane and three other survivors, including the captain, spent thirty hours on a small dinghy before reaching land (Crane 216). They tried to tow other men who were floating on a raft but one of them tried to board the already crowded boat in a frantic state and so the cook let go of the line to avoid capsizing the boat (216). The men on the rafts were swallowed up by the ocean when the Commodore finally went under (216). Crane recorded his experiences in an article entitled "The Sinking of the Commodore" that landed on the front page of the New York Press a week later (213). Crane's experience became the foundation for his short story that was published later that year.

Societal Context

Stephen Crane's writing was influenced by a belief in naturalism, which was developed as a literary movement in the late 19th century. Naturalism, like realism, depicted events that reflected everyday life. In addition, naturalist writers focused on characters that were lower class and struggling to survive in an unforgiving universe (Crane, London and Literary Naturalism). Naturalistic texts often depict the conflicts of man against nature or man against man and present free will as an illusion (Campbell). In "The Open Boat," Crane notes that nature, "feels she would not maim the universe by disposing of him" (Crane 207). Influenced by the theories of Darwin, naturalist writers were highly conscious of the influence that society and nature had on the individual (Crane, London and Literary Naturalism.).

Religious Context

"The Open Boat" does not have a specific religious context excepting the philosophy that nature is an awesome entity that is indifferent to the existence of man. Many facets of naturalism are present in Crane's story. Naturalists attempted to link philosophy closely with science (Papineau). They believed that the scientific method could and should be used to explain all things (Papineau). Naturalists did not believe in the existence of the supernatural, only in one single world in which all things occur and from which all things are caused. According to this philosophy, there is no free will (Center for Naturalism). All parts of the world, including human beings, are shaped by the various influences around them (Center for Naturalism). According to the tenets of naturalism, the men on the boat are not saved due to the grace of god nor due to their own actions, but simply because the world/nature caused it to happen.

Scientific & Technological Context

"The Open Boat" demonstrates Crane's awareness that technology, regardless of how sophisticated, is no match for nature. The steamship that sinks is a distinct reminder of the imperfections of man-made technology. The men on the lifeboat think they will be saved when they spot a man on the beach beside a tour bus. They are close enough to land to be seen by the man and the other tourists, but those on land cannot help because the men are caught in the ocean's grip.

Biographical Context

Stephen Crane was born in Newark, New Jersey in 1871. He was the youngest of fourteen children born to a Methodist minister father who died when Crane was nine. He attended college at both Lafayette College and Syracuse University but never completed a degree. He moved to New York City to work as a reporter and grew to develop a deep sympathy for the underprivileged. His first novel, "Maggie: A Girl of the Streets" was published in 1893 and reflected his compassion. While it did not sell well, his next novel about the Civil War, "The Red Badge of Courage," published in 1895, was a huge success. Crane was only twenty-four and already a famed novelist. Crane worked as a writer and news correspondent traveling the world for the remainder of his short life. He met his common-law wife, Cora Taylor, in Jacksonville, Florida, before embarking on the doomed Commodore ship. Unfortunately, Crane contracted tuberculosis, which led to his demise at age 29.

Jennifer Bouchard

Works Cited

Bedford/St. Martin's, 27 January 2008.

Campbell, Donna M. "Naturalism in American Literature." *Literary Movements.* 6 November 2007, 27 January 2008.

"Crane, London and Literary Naturalism," *National Endowment for the Humanities.* 27 January 2008.

Crane, Stephen. "The Open Boat." Eds. Dana Gioia and R.S. Gwynn. *The Art of the Short Story*. New York, Pearson Longman, 1992.

Crane, Stephen. "The Sinking of the Commodore." Eds. Dana Gioia and R.S. Gwynn. *The Art of the Short Story*. New York, Pearson Longman, 1992.

Stephen Crane's "The Open Boat." *National Endowment for the Humanities.* 27 January 2008.

The Stephen Crane Society, 24 July 2007. Washington State University, 27 January 2008.

Discussion Questions

1. Who is the protagonist of the story? How can you tell?
2. What does the narrator mean when he says in the beginning of the story that "none of them knew the color of the sky?"
3. How does the narrator describe the crew?
4. What does the correspondent learn about other human beings?
5. What does the correspondent learn about nature?
6. What are some keys moments that seem to indicate a shift in the journey of the men?
7. How would you describe the ending of the story?
8. What are the main themes of the story?
9. Why did Crane choose to tell the story in the third person?
10. Who do you think is the hero of the story?

Essay Ideas

1. Write a journal entry from the perspective of one of the men in the dinghy. Delve into his thoughts about nature and feelings about survival, etc.
2. Write an essay in which you analyze the ways in which Stephen Crane represents the philosophy of naturalism in "The Open Boat." Be sure to also discuss elements of the story that are anti-naturalist, if any.
3. Describe and analyze Crane's literary style. Focus on his descriptions, the structure of his narrative and the ending of "The Open Boat."
4. Research the actual events surrounding the sinking of the Commodore. Compare the real story to Crane's fictional version. Discuss why he might have changed certain elements of the story and kept others the same.
5. Write an essay evaluating the presence of leadership and teamwork in "The Open Boat."

The Pit and the Pendulum

by Edgar Allan Poe

Content Synopsis

In the short story, "The Pit and the Pendulum" the narrator begins by describing the moment in which he is sentenced to death by a group of "judges" during the Spanish Inquisition. At the moment he is condemned, his senses escaped him and he can no longer hear the judges, only can he see their lips moving. He is horrified at first and then he thinks about death and "what sweet rest there must be in the grave." After that, he is comforted and then he faints. The narrator insists that he did not lose consciousness but he "swooned' and does not remember what happened on the physical level.

The narrator then goes on to describe this stage of consciousness and his attempts to remember what occurs in the mind during this stage so as to distinguish it from death. In this attempt, his mental instability reveals itself as he remembers "tall figures that lifted and bore me in silence down…." When he regains full consciousness, he opens his eyes and his surroundings are completely dark. He begins to wonder what place or even what state of mind he is currently in. He is momentarily frozen with fear at the thought that he might be entrapped in a tomb until he realizes that he is able to sit up and move around.

The narrator recalls all of the rumors about Toledo, the prison where he must serve his sentence until his execution and realizes that he is in one of its dungeons. He tries to feel his way around the dungeon, but trips in the darkness and, overcome with exhaustion, falls asleep. When he awakens, bread and water have been placed beside him. After eating, he makes another attempt to meander the vault and slips again on the slimy floor. He is inches from falling into a cavernous pit and recalls more stories about the different methods of torture used during the Inquisition.

After another period of sleep, he awakens to more food and water but upon drinking the water, he realizes it has been drugged. He drifts off and when he wakes up, the dungeon has been lit. He can see but he is now tethered to a wood slab and can only move his head and left arm. As he studies the ceiling above him, he observes a painted figure of Time holding a large pendulum that appears to be moving slowly. Looking around the cell where he is trapped, he notices a bunch of rats climbing out of the pit and moving towards him. After about an hour of trying to scare them away, the narrator looks back at the ceiling and realizes that the pendulum has increased its sweep and is moving much faster than before. It is also descending from the ceiling and he can see that the moving "extremity was formed of a crescent of glittering steel" which is razor sharp. He realizes that this is the way in which he is going to be killed.

The narrator reasons that his torturers had planned to kill him by way of the giant pit but since he discovered it before falling in, they came up with an alternative method of execution. After hours of watching the pendulum descend closer and closer to him, it still has not come close enough to kill him. As the rats feast on the remains of his food, he determines that if he rubs the crumbs and oils on the cloth that binds him, the rats will help chew him free. After a time, the rats climb over him and eventually he is able to free himself from the tethers and the deadly pendulum. As soon as he is free, the pendulum rises back to the ceiling confirming the narrator's suspicions that he is being watched.

The narrator discovers that the light shining into the dungeon is coming from a hole between the floor and the wall. He peers into the hole and sees "demon eyes" glaring at him. Suddenly the walls grow red-hot and start closing in on the narrator. He wrestles with the choice to die by burning or the dreaded pit. Just as has lost all hope, he hears the sound of the French army barge in. The walls pull back and a general grabs him just before he falls into the pit.

Symbols & Motifs

The pendulum in the story is a clear symbol of the passing of time and the unavoidable journey towards death. Death surrounds the narrator in various forms. The fact that death does not actually befall the protagonist is unusual for Poe.

The physical and emotional torture that the narrator endures is symbolic of hell. The man receives his day of judgment and then awakens to a dark empty place. Like Poe's setting, hell is often depicted as underground, complete with fire and populated with demons. Likewise, hell is described as a place that inflicts constant physical and psychological suffering on the damned. The general who rescues the protagonist at the end of the story is symbolic of God reaching down to save the man's soul (Poe Perplex).

Historical Context

"The Pit and the Pendulum" draws on the period in history known as the Inquisition. The Inquisition

refers to a time when Rome was testing its citizens' loyalty to the Catholic Church (Edwards, Murray and Alpert). Established in the early 13th century by Pope Innocent III, the Romans became known for their efforts to suppress religious freedom and for their brutal methods of dealing with those they determined to be heretics (Edwards, Murray and Alpert). At first, those not following the Catholic Church were called upon to repent their sins during a "period of grace" (Jewish Virtual Library). After the period of grace, those who had not repented were accused of heresy and forced to stand trial where a sentence was delivered (Jewish Virtual Library). Punishments included physical and psychological torture, confinement to dungeons and being burned at the stake (Jewish Virtual Library).

In 1478, the Spanish Inquisition was established and for 350 years was known to be even more brutal. Tribunals were established in many Spanish cities and millions of Jews, Muslims, and Protestants were tried, like Poe's protagonist, and sentenced to imprisonment, torture and death (Edwards, Murray and Alpert). Between 1486–1492, 25 auto de fes were held in Toledo, the setting of "The Pit and the Pendulum" (Jewish Virtual Library). An "auto de fes" is a pubic condemnation of those found guilty and included a Catholic prayer and a reading of the sentence (Jewish Virtual Library). Four hundred sixty-seven people were burned at the stake there and many others were imprisoned. Torture and executions always took place after the "auto de fes" (Jewish Virtual Library).

The Inquisition was not limited to Europe and can be traced to such locations as Asia, Guatemala, and Brazil (Jewish Virtual Library). By the late 18th century, most inquisitions were abolished (Jewish Virtual Library).

Societal Context

"The Pit and the Pendulum" is a departure for Poe in that the protagonist prevails. Most of his stories end with the destruction of the protagonists.

Shortly after his death, Poe was accused of plagiarizing the story (Hamilton). Poe may have been inspired by the 1817 book "History of the Spanish Inquisition" by Juan Antonio Llorente. Despite the accusations, Poe took some creative license in his methods of torture (Hamilton) and his main focus was on the effects of terror and psychological torture on a man more than a period in history.

Not unusual for Poe is the use of gothic elements in his writing. Gothic literature was popular during the 1800s and included supernatural events, folklore, dungeons, tombs and medieval history (Hamilton). The dark and strange atmosphere of Gothic literature suited Poe and is certainly evident in "The Pit and the Pendulum."

Religious Context

"The Pit and the Pendulum" addresses the religious persecution that took place during the Spanish Inquisition, but it also depicts an environment that resembles certain images of hell. The fact that "an outstretched arm" pulls the narrator to safety signifies the hand of God coming to the man's rescue (Poe Perplex). This symbolic rescue is ironic considering the man being tortured is most likely not a follower of Christianity and thus, not a believer in this image of God. Poe might be suggesting that God protects all men, not just those that believe. Poe himself was raised in a devout Episcopalian household. Although it is not certain if he was a practicing Christian, he knew the Bible well and attended church sporadically in adulthood (The Edgar Allan Poe Society of Baltimore).

Scientific & Technological Context

"The Pit and the Pendulum" broke the mold for literature at the time, as did many of Poe's other short stories in that he introduces a distinctly psychological element to the narrative. The narrator of the story is being tortured, physically as well as psychologically as evidenced by his placement in a dark dungeon without any information regarding his sentence. He is in the dark, literally and figuratively, as he tries to determine where he is and how he will be punished. As he pieces together the details of his sentence, he is further tortured by the slow and mysterious methods used in attempts to torture and kill the man. First he must wander around the pitch-black dungeon barely escaping a fall into the pit as he drifts in an out of consciousness due to the drugged food and water he receives. Then a swinging pendulum drops slowly and viciously above the narrator's head as he waits for it to eviscerate him. After escaping the pendulum he must await his torturers' next attempt to kill him. Repeatedly, the narrator must suffer the mental anguish of coming face-to-face with his own mortality, knowing that at any moment some horrible method of execution will befall him.

Biographical Context

Edgar Allan Poe was born in Boston in 1809 to a traveling actor and actress. When Poe was born, his father abandoned his mother ("Edgar Allan Poe"). She died a few years later while on tour in Virginia and he was taken in by a wealthy couple in Richmond; John and Frances Allan, who could not have children. While the Allans cared for and educated Poe, they never formally adopted him and John Allan never warmed to his foster son. Once in college at the University of Virginia, Poe accrued a large gambling debt and John Allan withdrew him from school ("Edgar Allan Poe"). After a heated argument, Poe left home and moved to Boston.

In 1827, in Boston, Poe published a volume of poetry entitled "Tamerlane." The book did not sell well and, in need of money, Poe joined the army. Poe did not like the army but was promoted to the rank of sergeant major, and with the Allans' help, he enrolled in the US Military Academy at West Point ("Edgar Allan Poe"). In 1829, Poe published another book of poems "El Aaraaf" which received positive reviews. While at West

Point, Allan's wife died and he remarried. Since Poe knew he would no longer be considered as Allan's heir, Poe withdrew from West Point, and moved in with his aunt in Baltimore, Maryland ("Edgar Allan Poe").

In 1835, Poe married his chronically ill thirteen-year old cousin, Virginia. Poe worked as an editor at various magazines while trying to succeed as a writer ("Edgar Allan Poe"). He wrote only one full-length novel, "The Narrative of Arthur Gordon Pym" but his short stories became his claim to fame. Poe is given credit as the creator of the modern detective story with such stories as "The Gold Bug" and "the Murders in the Rue Morgue." Other stories, such as "The Tell-Tale Heart" and "The Cask of Amontillado" explore the inner demons of a person's mind. In 1845, he published the poem "The Raven," which brought him fame and solidified his career as a writer.

Unfortunately, alcohol abuse and financial instability continued to plague Poe throughout his life. When his wife died in 1847 of tuberculosis, Poe grew more unstable ("Edgar Allan Poe"). In 1849, Poe disappeared and a week later he was found, battered and delirious, near a Baltimore tavern. He died four days later at the age of 40 and his death remains a mystery to this day.

Jennifer Bouchard

Works Cited

"Edgar Allan Poe." *Great American* Stories. Austin: Holt, Rinehart and Winston, 1991.

Edwards, John, Alexander Murray and Michael Alpert. "The Spanish Inquisition." *BBC*, 22 May 2008.

Gioia, Dana and R.S. Gwynn, eds. "Edgar Allan Poe." *The Art of the Short Story*. New York: Pearson Longman, 1992. p.707.

Hamilton, Rosemary. "Poe Lightly." *Yale New Haven Teachers Institute*, 22 May 2008.

International Movie Database. *IMDB.com.* 20 May 2008.

Poe, Edgar Allan. "The Pit and the Pendulum." *Literature.org: The Online Literature Library*, 19 May 2008.

The Edgar Allan Poe Society of Baltimore, 22 February 2008, 20 May 2008.

"The Pit and the Pendulum." *The Poe Perplex*, 1996. United States Naval Academy, 22 May 2008.

Discussion Questions

1. What is the tone of the narrator?
2. How would you describe the mood of the story?
3. How does the setting of the story affect the mood?
4. How does Poe create suspense and enhance it throughout the story?
5. What are some actions that the narrator takes to indicate that he has not yet given up hope for survival?
6. What is the significance of the title?
7. Is the narrator a reliable source of information? Why or why not?
8. What did you think of the ending? Is it what you expected? Did you find it satisfying?

Essay Ideas

1. Describe and analyze Poe's literary style. Focus on his use of sensory images, tone, setting and voice. Use examples from the text to support your analysis.

2. Write a journal entry from the perspective of the narrator after his rescue. How has his life changed since his torturous experience?

3. Write an essay in which you discuss setting as a character in the story. Use examples from the text to support your views.

4. What might this story say about people in general? Use examples from the text to explain your thinking. In addition, discuss any people you have known, experiences you have had or other stories, movies, or works of art that may resemble this story.

5. Write a narrative essay in which you recount an incident that made you afraid. Try to make the reader relive the terror by including sensory details and carefully choosing words to describe your experience (Hamilton).

The Purloined Letter

by Edgar Allan Poe

Content Synopsis

In the short story, "The Purloined Letter," the narrator retells the account of how his friend, C. Auguste Dupin, solves a mystery regarding a letter stolen from the royal family. It begins in Dupin's Paris apartment as the narrator enjoys a pipe and the quiet company of his friend when they are interrupted by Monsieur G – –, the Prefect of the Paris police. The Prefect has come to confide in Dupin in a matter of utmost secrecy and ask for his advice.

The Prefect explains that a theft has recently occurred at the royal headquarters and diplomatically implies that the Queen has had an affair or some indiscretion that she is trying to hide from the King. Her secret was threatened when the King entered her bedroom while she was reading a revealing letter. About the same time she tried to hide the letter, the Minister D—entered the room and from the Queen's behavior figured out her secret. Determining the letter to be a great source of power over her, he found a way to swap the letter with one of similar appearance and take the original from her possession. The Minister has been blackmailing the Queen ever since.

The Prefect tells the men that he has since searched every inch of the Minister's residence but cannot find the letter. He says the Minister is a poet, which makes him a fool; the Prefect is confounded as to how his police department has not discovered

the letter yet. Dupin asks the Prefect to recount the details of his search so that he can better assist him. He explains that he and his crew took apart furniture, searched drawers, walls, floors, books, etc. He is certain that they did not miss an inch of the Minister's home. Dupin then asks the Prefect to describe the letter, which he does before leaving in disappointment that Dupin cannot be of more assistance.

One month later, the Prefect returns to visit Dupin and confesses that he still cannot find the purloined letter. Dupin asks him if he really has done all that he can. The Prefect replies that he has and says that he would pay 50,000 francs if he could get the letter. Dupin asks him to write him a check and when he does, he produces the letter for the Prefect who then leaves speechless. The narrator asks Dupin how he found the letter who goes on to explain that the Prefect underestimated the Minister's intellect because he believes that all poets are fools. Dupin, knowing this to be false, had estimated that the Minister would anticipate the Paris police ransacking his house. Therefore, Dupin knew he would not hide the letter in any of the usual places.

Dupin then explains how he went to the Minister's house himself to search for the letter. He found it in an old card rack placed in plain site, however disguised as a dirty and unimportant letter. Dupin then excuses himself but intentionally leaves his snuffbox behind so he has an excuse to return the next day. Upon his return, Dupin tells the narrator, that he paid someone to create a disturbance in the street to distract the Minister while Dupin switched the letter with a worthless one. So that the Minister would know who outwitted him, he wrote in the letter the following clue:

"– – – – Un dessein si funeste, S'il n'est digne d'Atrée, est digne de Thyeste. They are to be found in Crébillon's Atrée."

The translation of the passage is, "If such a sinister design isn't worthy of Atreus, it is worthy of Thyestes," revealing clever Dupin to be connected to, possible the brother of, the cunning Minister D–.

Symbols & Motifs

The letter in "The Purloined Letter" serves as a symbol of a privacy that has been invaded as well as a power struggle. The public release of the letter would disgrace the royal family and thus the cunning Minister uses it as a means to gain power over the Queen.

"The Purloined Letter" opens with a latin maxim, "Nil sapientiae odiosius acumine nimio," translated as "nothing is more hateful to wisdom than excessive cleverness." The story truly is a battle of wits as Dupin proves to outsmart both the Prefect and the thief.

The letter that Dupin replaces with the purloined letter so as to avoid an early detection by the Minister made reference to the brothers Atreus and Thyeste of ancient Greek lore. In the myth, the brothers were constantly in competition with one another. In an act of revenge because Thyeste had an affair with Atreus' wife, Atreus killed Thyeste's children, cooked them and served them to Thyestes

(Hunter). Eventually, Thyeste had a son who grew up and killed Atreus (Hunter). The reference to these brutally competitive brothers suggests a symbiotic relationship between Dupin and the Minister.

Historical Context

"The Purloined Letter" is one of three stories to feature C. Auguste Dupin, the world's first literary detective. He first appears in "The Murders in the Rue Morgue" written in 1841 and considered by many to be the first detective story, and "The Mystery of Marie Roget" both of which were alluded to at the beginning of the story. The actual profession of detective had just been established in the early 1800s and Poe was inspired by Francois-Eugene Vidocq who, in 1817, founded the first detective bureau (Poe and Ratiocination).

Societal Context

In a letter to James Russell Lowell, Poe used the term ratiocination to refer to "The Purloined Letter." Ratiocination is defined as the process of exact thinking or reasoning (Merriam Webster). The first detective stories are referred to as tales of ratiocination. Poe is quoted as saying, "Truth is often and in very great degree, the aim of the tale. Some of the finest tales are tales of ratiocination" (Poe and Ratiocination.) He was proud of his capacity for logic and analysis. He loved solving problems and puzzles, much like his detective Dupin (Poe and Ratiocination). However, he eventually tired of these stories and stopped writing in the genre that he created (Poe and Ratiocination).

Poe took special care to note that the villain in "The Purloined Letter" is a poet and thus, according to the Prefect, one step away from a fool. Dupin agrees but acknowledges that he himself has dabbled in the art. He therefore does not underestimate the poet's abilities at reason and is able to defeat the Minister and outsmart the Prefect. Poe is able to acknowledge society's negative views of the poet as a trivial profession, unworthy of any intellectual recognition. Yet he is also makes a statement in the sense that the character representative of the public, the Prefect, is unable to solve the crime. He cannot outsmart the poet but Dupin can due in part to his respect for the abstract reasoning abilities of a poet.

Religious Context

"The Purloined Letter" does not have a specific religious context.

Scientific & Technological Context

"The Purloined Letter" does not have a specific scientific or technological context.

Biographical Context

Edgar Allan Poe was born in Boston in 1809 to a traveling actor and actress. When Poe was born, his father abandoned his mother ("Edgar Allan Poe"). She died a few years later while on tour in Virginia and he was taken in by a wealthy couple in Richmond, John and Frances Allan, who could not have children. While the Allans cared for and educated Poe, they never formally adopted him and John Allan never warmed to his foster son. Once in college at the University of Virginia, Poe accrued a large gambling debt and John Allan withdrew him from school ("Edgar Allan Poe"). After a heated argument, Poe left home and moved to Boston.

In 1827, in Boston, Poe published a volume of poetry entitled "Tamerlane." The book did not sell well and, in need of money, Poe joined the army. Poe did not like the army but was promoted to the rank of sergeant major, and with the Allans' help, he enrolled in the U.S. Military Academy at West Point ("Edgar Allan Poe"). In 1829, Poe published another book of poems "El Aaraaf"

which received positive reviews. While at West Point, Allan's wife died and he remarried. Since Poe knew he would no longer be considered as Allan's heir, Poe withdrew from West Point, and moved in with his aunt in Baltimore, Maryland ("Edgar Allan Poe").

In 1835, Poe married his chronically ill thirteen-year old cousin, Virginia. Poe worked as an editor at various magazines while trying to succeed as a writer ("Edgar Allan Poe"). He wrote only one full-length novel, "The Narrative of Arthur Gordon Pym" but his short stories became his claim to fame. Poe is given credit as the creator of the modern detective story with such stories as "The Gold Bug," "The Murders in the Rue Morgue," and "The Purloined Letter." Other stories, such as "The Tell-Tale Heart" and "The Cask of Amontillado" explore the inner demons of a person's mind. In 1845, he published the poem "The Raven," which brought him fame and solidified his career as a writer.

Unfortunately, alcohol abuse and financial instability continued to plague Poe throughout his life. When his wife died in 1847 of tuberculosis, Poe grew more unstable ("Edgar Allan Poe"). In 1849, Poe disappeared and a week later he was found, battered and delirious, near a Baltimore tavern. He died four days later at the age of 40 and his death remains a mystery to this day.

Jennifer Bouchard

Work Cited

Blythe, Hal, and Charlie Sweet. "The Reader As Poe's Ultimate Dupe In 'The Purloined Letter'." *Studies in Short Fiction* 26.3 (Summer 1989): 311. Academic Search Premier. EBSCO. 11 June 2008.

Canada, Mark, ed. "Edgar Allan Poe." *Canada's America*. 1997, 4 March 2008.

"Edgar Allan Poe." *Great American Stories*. Austin: Holt, Rinehart and Winston, 1991, p. 93.

Gioia, Dana and R.S. Gwynn, eds. "Edgar Allan Poe." *The Art of the* Short Story. New York: Pearson Longman, 1992, p. 707.

Hunter, James. "Atreus," 3 March 1997. *Encyclopedia Mythica*, 11 June 2008.

Poe and Ratiocination. University of Paderborn. 11 June 2008.

Poe, Edgar Allan. "The Purloined Letter." *Tales of Mystery and Imagination*. London: J. M. Dent & Sons, 1912. pp. 454–471.

The Edgar Allan *Poe Society of Baltimore*, 22 February 2008, 4 March 2008.

Discussion Questions

1. What is the tone of the narrator?
2. What is the setting of the story and how does Poe reveal the action of the story?
3. Why is the letter so important?
4. What is the role of the narrator in the story?
5. Does the narrator remind you of the narrator of any other detective fiction?
6. To what lengths does the Prefect go to obtain the stolen letter?
7. How does Dupin explain the Prefect's failure to obtain the letter?
8. How is the letter retrieved?
9. What is the significance of the title, specifically the word "purloined"?
10. What do the last lines of the story imply about Dupin's relationship to the thief?

Essay Ideas

1. Describe and analyze Poe's literary style. Focus on his descriptions, the structure of his narrative and the ending of "The Purloined Letter."

2. Write a journal entry from the perspective of the Prefect after he received the letter from Dupin.

3. Write an essay in which you compare this story to a contemporary detective story. Do you see any influence of Poe in the contemporary piece? How has detective fiction changed over the past 150 years? Use examples from both stories to support your points.

4. What might this story say about people in general? Use examples from the text to explain your thinking. In addition, discuss any people you have known, experiences you have had or other stories, movies, or works of art that may resemble this story.

Runaway

by Alice Munro

Content Synopsis

"Runaway" (2004), a collection of eight short stories, is Alice Munro's tenth book. Three of the stories form a sequence charting the life of recurring heroine Juliet. Thematic resonances link all eight narratives.

In the opening title story, Carla and Clark, a young couple, live in a mobile home and earn a living looking after horses. The first part of the story is told from Carla's perspective. They are experiencing a slow summer and Clark, an Internet surfer, is becoming increasingly aggressive. They have recently lost a little white goat named Flora, to whom Carla has become particularly attached. When the story begins, their neighbor, Sylvia Jamieson, arrives back from a holiday in Greece following the death of her poet husband, whom Carla helped care for. When Carla and Clark read his obituary they learn that he had won a poetry prize. Clark sees this as an opportunity to bribe Sylvia. Carla has told Clark that Mr. Jamieson made advances towards her. She fabricated the story but has begun to believe it herself and Clark persuades her to demand compensation from Sylvia. The next part of the story is told from Sylvia's perspective. Having returned from Greece, she reflects fondly on the time she spent with Carla as they cared for Mr. Jamieson. A teacher of botany, Sylvia is used to contact with young girls, but feels a particular bond with Carla. When Carla arrives, Sylvia inquires after Flora and Carla's eyes fill with tears. She tells Sylvia that she cannot go on living with Clark. Sylvia organizes for Carla to run away to Toronto. On the bus, Carla relives her relationship with Clark and realizes that she has no life without him. He arrives at Sylvia's house, demanding to know where Carla is. In the midst of their heated discussion, Sylvia sees a mysterious shape resembling a "giant unicorn" emerging from the fog outside (39). It is Flora. This spectral appearance breaks the tension between them. As they pat the goat, the animosity dissolves. Clark returns home to find Carla who admits that she lied about Mr. Jamieson. Their life returns to normal until Sylvia writes to Carla and describes Flora's magical appearance: an occurrence that Clark has concealed from Carla. Carla burns the letter and does not ask him about Flora, but her sense of betrayal manifests itself in the "murderous needle somewhere in her lungs" (46). Sylvia moves away and Carla resumes her life, aware that she can visit the woods and perhaps find evidence of Flora's destruction. For the moment, she resists the temptation.

The next three stories centre on Juliet and are told from her perspective. "Chance" begins in 1965. Juliet, a Ph.D student, has been teaching Classics at a private school in Vancouver and the term is over. She is taking a detour to see Eric Porteous, a fisherman who lives in Whale Bay, whom she met on a train. She knows little about him, except that he has an invalid wife who is "more or less brain-dead" (48). He has written a brief letter to her to tell her that he often thinks of her. The story takes us back to their first meeting. Juliet is reading alone on the train when a man tries to strike up a conversation. After dropping several hints, Juliet tells him that she wants to read and escapes to the observation room. The train stops when it hits something. It turns out to be the body of a passenger who got off the train at a station only to throw himself in front of it. A man in the observation car leaves to look at the body and Juliet asks him to describe it; the body belongs to the man she snubbed in her carriage. Feeling guilty, she confides in Eric and they spend the rest of the evening together, ending it with a kiss. The story returns to the present. When Juliet arrives at Whale Bay, she is greeted by Eric's housekeeper who tells her that there has been a funeral; Eric's wife is dead. The housekeeper tells Juliet that Eric is at his girlfriend Christa's house. Juliet stays at Eric's house overnight and awaits his return. He arrives the next day. He tells Juliet that the housekeeper phoned him the night before and told him that she had arrived. He took a chance that Juliet would leave—"to test fate, maybe"—but felt "joy" upon seeing her (85). At the end of the story we learn that Juliet and Christa will become great friends (86).

"Soon," the next Juliet story, begins in 1969. Juliet and Eric have a baby daughter, Penelope. Juliet and Christa have become friends. Juliet goes shopping with Christa and buys a Chagall picture for her parents. It is called "I and the Village" and depicts the profiles of a white heifer and a "green-faced man who is neither young nor old" (87). It also features a woman who seems to be waiting for the man and is "hanging upside down" (87). It reminds Juliet of her parents' lives. One year later Juliet visits her parents. Her mother, Sara, has cancer and her parents have hired Irene, a home help, to whom Juliet takes an instant dislike. Juliet's father, Sam, speaks enthusiastically of Irene; she has "restored [his] faith in women" (113). Juliet feels dislocated

and senses her parents' shame over her relationship with Eric; they have not married. She finds the Chagall picture in the attic and learns that her father worried about its impression on Irene, who might be intimidated by modern art. One day, a minister calls on Sara. He criticizes Juliet for not christening Penelope and they debate the existence of God. As the minister turns to leave he has a seizure; Juliet recognises that he has diabetes and gives him some juice. He recovers and leaves the house. Sara tries to explain her particular faith to Juliet but finds that she cannot describe it: "All I can say—it's something. It's a—wonderful—something" (124). However, she can reveal that the thought of seeing Juliet sustains her: "When it gets really bad for me … I think, all right. I think—Soon. Soon I'll see Juliet" (124). In the coda to the story, we learn that Juliet returned to the house once more for Sara's funeral. Sam remarried and tore down their old house. Years later, Juliet finds a letter she wrote to Eric during her visit. She winces as she perceives how she covered up her unease. She regrets that she did not protect her mother in the same way; she responded to Sara's declaration of love with silence.

"Silence," the third Juliet story, takes place twenty years later. Juliet is on a ferry, traveling to Denman, where Penelope has been staying at a spiritual retreat for the past six months. Juliet now "appears regularly" on a television program called "Issues of the Day." She interviews people who are leading "singular or notable lives" and she directs panel discussions (126). On the ferry, Juliet reflects on her relationship with Penelope and feels that she has been in a "desert" without her daughter (128). The retreat forbids contact with the outside world but Penelope has written to Juliet, asking her to come for her. When Juliet arrives, she learns that Penelope has left the retreat. She speaks to a woman, Joan, who tells her that Penelope arrived at the retreat in "great hunger" and suggests that her upbringing lacked a "spiritual dimension" (130). Juliet returns home and a few weeks later she receives an unsigned birthday card on the day of Penelope's birthday. Reading the address, she recognizes her daughter's writing. For the next year, Penelope makes no contact but sends another card to her mother on her own birthday. The story flashes back several years to Juliet's discovery of Eric's brief affair with Christa, which had occurred while she was visiting her parents. Penelope asks to go camping with a friend and Juliet agrees, hoping to sort out her problems with Eric in Penelope's absence. Juliet feels that Eric has used Penelope's presence to avoid talking about their problems. While Penelope is away, Eric drowns at sea. Juliet and Penelope move to Vancouver where Juliet comes to terms with her grief and gets a job that leads to her career in television. Penelope seems strangely unmoved by her father's death. The story returns to the present day. Penelope has ceased sending cards and Juliet has moved. She no longer works in television. She has resumed her research into Greek literature and has a few friendships with men. One day she encounters Heather, the friend who took Penelope camping. Heather makes no reference to Juliet's estrangement from her daughter but remarks on Penelope's five children. Juliet feels that she can go on with her own life, "hoping for a word from Penelope, but not in any strenuous way" (157).

"Passion" presents Grace, a woman on an expedition to the Ottawa Valley, looking for the summer house of the Travers family. She locates the house but it is "diminished" and "irrelevant" (161). The rest of the story takes place in the summer when Grace met the Travers. It is the 1950s. Grace has left her aunt and uncle to work at a hotel at Bailey's Falls. Her uncle presumes that she will join his canning business but she is not sure what she wants to do (166). She stayed on at school for an extra year because she wanted to "learn everything you could learn for free" and is ambivalent about the prospect of marriage (166). Whilst working at

the hotel she dates Maury Travers, whose family is staying in a nearby house for the summer. Their relationship is strained by awkward physical encounters, but Grace becomes attached to Mrs. Travers, who understands her desire for knowledge. Mrs. Travers has three children. The oldest, Neil, is a doctor and from a previous marriage. Neil's father killed himself; Maury suggests that this caused Mrs. Travers' mysterious nervous condition. At Thanksgiving, the family assembles. Playing with the children outside, Grace cuts her foot just before Neil arrives. He bandages her up, but insists on taking her to the hospital. As he attends to her, Grace smells liquor on his breath. Before they leave Mrs. Travers asks Grace to keep him away from drink and says cryptically that Grace will know "how to do it" (181). Maury turns up at the waiting room but Neil instructs the nurse to tell him that they have already left. Neil drives Grace to a hotel, where he persuades the bartender to serve him although it is Sunday. As they drive away, Neil tells Grace that he has not abducted her to take advantage of her. When he hears that Grace cannot drive, he gives her the wheel. He takes over again to drive her to what appears to be a bootlegger's house. Neil picks up the liquor and drives on until he pulls over to sleep. He does not wake up and Grace takes the wheel to drive them back home. When she parks in the hotel lot, Neil stirs and reveals that he had been awake for most of the journey but did not want to put her off. They embrace tightly and Neil drives home. The next morning Grace hears that he drove his car into a bridge abutment. She receives a letter from Maury, pleading her to tell him that Neil "made her do it" and that she "did not want to go" (196). Grace replies that she went willingly. Mr. Travers gives Grace a check for one thousand dollars, which she accepts with reservations.

In "Trespasses," four people drive out of an unspecified town at midnight, looking for a place to stop where they will not be seen. The story chronicles the events leading up to this mysterious mission. A year earlier, Harry and Eileen moved to Harry's childhood town with their daughter Lauren. When Harry and Lauren are moving things into the basement, Lauren picks up a box which Harry immediately takes from her. He tells her that it contains the ashes of a baby girl Eileen gave birth to just before she became pregnant with Lauren. Distraught at the prospect of another pregnancy, Eileen left the house with the baby and went for a drive. She had an accident that killed the baby. Lauren asks if this is what Harry and Eileen fight about. Harry replies that there "'could be something about that underlying'" (204). Having struggled to fit in at her new school, Lauren accepts an invitation to the local hotel coffee shop. In the lobby, the girls push her up to the desk, where a woman named Delphine produces a chain bearing the name 'Lauren.' Lauren does not claim it but Delphine encourages her to come back the next day to see if anyone has. Lauren strikes up a friendship with Delphine, who appears curious about her life. At one point, she suggests that Lauren may be adopted because she is an only child, but insists that she is joking. One day, Delphine tells Lauren about a friend who became pregnant and had her baby adopted. Disconcerted by Delphine's insinuations, Lauren tells Eileen about Delphine. Eileen decides to send Lauren to boarding school, so that she will not have to grow up in "this crappy town" (228). Harry and Eileen wake Lauren in the middle of the night and bring her downstairs, where Delphine is waiting. They tell her that they adopted Delphine's baby after five years of trying for their own. Shortly afterwards, Eileen fell pregnant. She argued with Harry who wanted her to have an abortion and she left with the baby and had a car accident. They had called the first baby Lauren. Delphine had been searching for her baby and had naturally assumed that Lauren was her child. They go to the woods to scatter the baby's ashes. After they have dropped off Delphine, Eileen reflects that Delphine only cared for Lauren when she thought she was the child she had given up. Hearing herself alluded to as 'hers' and 'ours,' Lauren notices that her pajamas are covered in burrs and furiously tries to pick them off. She realizes that she cannot free herself yet and must "sit and wait" (235).

"Tricks" presents Robin, a twenty-six year old nurse who lives with her sister Joanne, an asthma sufferer who cannot be left alone at night. Every summer Robin visits Stratford, Ontario on her own, to see a Shakespeare play. The story flashes back a year, to when she saw "Antony and Cleopatra," and lost her purse in the theatre. While contemplating what to do, a man approached her. He offered her the money for her ticket home and invited her to his shop where he worked as a clockmaker. The man introduced himself as Daniel. He was from Montenegro. They chatted about their lives and he escorted her to the station where they kissed. They arranged to meet in a year's time, agreeing not to write. For the next year, Robin lives on memories of the kiss and, in her spare time, researches Montenegrin history. The story returns to the present. Robin returns to Stratford but is too excited to sit through "As You Like It." When she arrives at Daniel's shop, she sees him fixing a clock, but when he looks up he shakes his head at her and bares his front teeth. Taking this as a rejection, she runs away, vowing never to return to Stratford. In Part 2, the story leaps ahead. Joanne has been dead eighteen years and Robin is working with psychiatric patients. She has recently played the lead role in a local production of "Hedda Gabler." Robin arrives at the ward and sees a new patient who looks familiar. His name is Alexander and he is a deaf-mute; he is Daniel's identical twin brother. He was the man who shook his head at her. Telling herself that Shakespeare "should have prepared her" for this incredible stroke of mischance, she wonders if a relationship would have worked while they were both caring for their siblings (268). She is outraged by the trickery of chance, but also relieved of the shame she has felt since Daniel's supposed rejection.

The closing story, "Powers," is divided into titled sections. The first comprises extracts from the diary of a woman named Nancy. It is 1927, and Nancy lives in a small Canadian town. In the first entry she reports a sighting of Tessa Netterby in the store. Tessa is a local recluse who has shunned society since leaving school at fourteen under mysterious circumstances. Nancy is active in the community. She belongs to a dramatics society, which has just shelved a production of "The Gondoliers." The members of the society decide to start a book group and settle on Dante's "Divine Comedy." The next extract is from April 1st. Nancy rushes to the local doctor's house pretending to be choking but he fails to see the humor in her April Fool. Surprisingly, the doctor, Wilf, proposes to Nancy a few days later and she accepts. Ollie, his cousin, arrives to be best man. Ollie and Nancy develop a kind of bond. The next section is narrated in the third person. Nancy takes Ollie to see Tessa, who correctly guesses the contents of his pockets. Nancy tells Ollie that people travel for miles to consult Tessa about the location of lost items. Ollie asks why nobody has investigated Tessa's clairvoyance. Nancy does not answer him directly but expresses shame that she has treated Tessa "'like a freak'" (295). She admits that she introduced Tessa to Ollie because he does not think the town has "'anything … worth noticing'" (295). Letters exchanged between Nancy, Ollie and Tessa comprise the next part of the story. Nancy writes to Ollie berating him for publishing an article on Tessa. Ollie replies that Tessa will benefit from his research. Nancy warns Tessa against further involvement but Tessa writes that she and Ollie are already engaged and moving to the States. The story jumps forward to 1968. Nancy visits a Michigan hospital for the mentally ill where Tessa is staying. Tessa seems quite lucid, but tells Nancy that Ollie is dead and that somebody strangled him. The story moves forward to the early seventies. Nancy is on a cruise for the elderly and stops in Vancouver where she bumps into Ollie. We learn that Tessa has died and that Ollie has since drifted from one job to another and now lives on an isolated island, doing "this and that to make a living" (319). He remarks that he has been "incredibly lucky" in his life (321). He tells Nancy of his life with Tessa and describes how they traveled around, showcasing Tessa's gift, but relying increasingly on tricks to wow the audience. He claims that Tessa died of leukaemia. In the final part of the story, Nancy, now a widow, has a dream about Tessa and Ollie. In the dream, Ollie and Tessa are no longer able to look each other honestly in the eye. Tessa spies a pile of flies on the windowsill and delights in this sight because she "knew they were there, in the way that she knows things." After years of relying on "rehearsed tricks" she has an authentic vision (333). As she hugs Ollie, he reconsiders his recent action: he has told a doctor that Tessa is unbalanced and signed papers to admit her to a "place." Ollie tells himself that he will destroy the papers; he is still "capable of hope and honor." When Nancy awakens, she feels the "known future wither" under the "attack" of her dream (335). She is unable, however, to suppress her knowledge of Tessa's fate. She feels the presence of somebody, perhaps Wilf, drawing her away from her preoccupation with Tessa and Ollie.

Symbols & Motifs

Mythology: Most of the characters' lives turn on freak accidents and the workings of chance. Imagery from mythology signals the influence of mysterious forces. Juliet and Eric gaze at the stars in the observation car. Eric finds Orion, Sirius and Cassiopeia, and Juliet places them in their mythological context. In "Runaway" Flora meets the same end as her mythological counterparts; whether he kills her or not, Clark sacrifices her to salvage his relationship. A white heifer, another sacrificial symbol, features in the painting that Juliet buys for her parents. In losing and pining for her daughter Penelope, Juliet re-enacts the longings of Demeter for Persephone.

Ironically the name Penelope recalls Odysseus's wife, who waited patiently for her husband's return.

Journeys: Journeys feature repeatedly in the stories as a trope for self-development; most of the heroines set out to seek definition beyond the boundaries of home. Most of the stories feature an incapacitated or jeopardized character: physical disabilities or unspecified mental problems signal the threat of entrapment both for the victims and their carers.

Literary Allusions: Literary allusions pervade the text, illuminating the proximity between life and art. Robin plays Hedda Gabler "splendidly," and the audience sees only the differences between Ibsen's heroine and the "real life" Robin (263). Robin observes how her life has turned on a catalogue of chances and coincidences worthy of a Shakespeare play. Juliet's life begins to emulate the narratives of the Greek myths that so fascinate her. The drama society in "Powers" plans a production of "The Gondoliers," an opera by Gilbert and Sullivan that satirizes class distinctions and features a young woman named Tessa who marries to find that her marriage may not be what it seems.

Historical Context

The stories in "Runaway" span several decades, reaching back to the 1920s and forward to an unspecified present. In some stories, Munro provides historical markers, although the present day is often unspecified. "Powers" reaches back farthest to 1927. Each story dramatizes a character's attempt to make sense of unresolved events from the recent or distant past. Nancy's children worry that she is "Living in the Past" but she wants "not so much to live in the past as to open it up and get one good look at it" (330). Most of the stories take place in the fifties, sixties and seventies. Generational conflict registers the shift in attitudes. Juliet's parents pride themselves on their liberalism but are ashamed that their daughter is an unmarried mother.

Neither Munro, nor her characters, are particularly concerned with historical developments. Robin familiarizes herself with Montenegrin history only to feel closer to Daniel. In her present-day narrative, Juliet misses "the world news for a week at a time" (151). However, characters acknowledge the gap between then and now by noting the small changes in life. In the present-day narrative of "Tricks," Robin observes: "You can buy almost any kind of food you want …. The beach is no longer surrounded by railway sheds and warehouses—you can walk on a boardwalk for a mile along the lake" (263). Historical context has little impact on Munro's dominant themes: the uncertainties of love and the workings of chance.

Societal Context

The provinces of Canada provide the setting for most of Munro's fiction. "Runaway" is no exception. Most of the characters grow up in isolated towns where opportunities for women are limited. Gender and class boundaries inform most of the relationships in the stories. The characters themselves register and comment on these distinctions. In "Soon" Sara attributes her husband's protectiveness towards Irene to class guilt: "'You know how he is with people that are under him. He'll do anything to make sure they don't feel he's any different from them'" (101). It takes the appearance of Flora to ease the tension between Clark and Sylvia. Class and gender ideologies limit educational opportunities for the heroines. Nancy perceives that Ollie draws solace from the limits placed on her potential:

"He had an idea […] that his life would have some meaning to it. Maybe that was what drew them together. But the difference was that he would go on, he would not settle for less. As she would have to do—as she had already done—being a girl. The thought of choices wider than anything girls ever knew put him suddenly at ease" (287–8).

Juliet recalls that her professors were unable to reconcile her academic prowess with her gender identity: "Her professors were delighted with her … but they were worried, as well. The problem was that she was a girl. If she got married … she would waste all her hard work and theirs, and if she did not get married she would probably become bleak and isolated" (53). Like most Munro heroines, the young women in "Runaway" are disenchanted by the plots available to them and leave home seeking new ones. In "Passions," issues of class and gender conspire to limit the possibilities for Grace; she takes full advantage of free education, aware that she faces a choice between a career in canning or marriage. In "Tricks," Robin recalls that the "girls of the better class" were expected to leave behind high school boyfriends to find someone more suitable at college, while the others secured future husbands at school, often dropping out to marry (248). Mrs. Travers tells Grace that she does not worry about her daughter Gretchen, "Because women always have got something … to keep them going … That men haven't got" (175). Some of the men in "Runaway" sustain this view. Mrs. Travers's first husband commits suicide and his son succumbs to alcoholism, as does Ollie for a time. The fates of Munro's heroines testify that gender boundaries are losing currency in the postmodern era. By the end of the stories, most of the heroines have achieved autonomy. Robin and Juliet are alone when their stories return to the present. Grace appears to be alone when she returns to the Ottawa Valley and Lauren looks forward to the time when she too will be unfettered by relationships. As a whole, the collection dramatizes the positive aspects of isolation for women. Munro does not present her heroines as victims of postmodern, secular alienation. They find a freedom in their solitude. Juliet's contentment and self-sufficiency emerge clearly in the final paragraphs of "Silence."

Religious Context

Munro's characters try to probe the mystery behind pivotal events in their lives. Their reflections on the past do not provide answers. Events in these stories test the characters' sense of reality: Nancy's dream tells her more about Tessa and Ollie than her conversations with them; Sylvia views Flora's ghostly appearance as a "miracle" (45). The hand of chance repeatedly asserts itself, rendering any search for meaning fruitless. In such a context, religious discourses would appear to have no place. However, religious conflict lies at the center of the Juliet sequence, where it places pressure on relationships. When Eric dies, the community gather to burn his body and Eric's co-worker waives the invitation to speak. Some of the mourners are relieved, as his wife is Evangelical Anglican and he may have felt compelled to offer reassurances that "would have distressed Eric" (142). Her parents have a relaxed attitude to religion. Sara experiments with the Baha'i faith and Sam tells the neighbors that they are Druids so that they can categorize the new arrivals. As a child, Juliet attends the Anglican Church for a time, mainly because she had an Anglican friend. As an adult, she prides herself on her rationalism. In "Soon," she confidently dismisses the minister's appeals and greets her mother's intimations about her faith with silence, although she later regrets this. Juliet is forced to reconsider her position when her daughter joins a spiritual retreat and disappears. Although she derides the people at the retreat, she wonders if she should have attended to Penelope's spiritual development. The theme of spirituality comes to the fore in "Powers." The story provides no answers, however. Tessa's clairvoyance is erratic and she and Ollie resort to tricks in their act. Walking around Vancouver in the early seventies Nancy encounters a "concentration" of "youth culture." A boy and girl who call themselves Adam and Eve hand her a scroll of paper that "'contains wisdom'" (313). Nancy dismisses them but finds the paper in her pocket months later.

The legend reads: "The road is easy if you know enough to travel light" (313). The legend irritates Nancy, who has met only obstacles in her attempts to track Tessa and Ollie. However, the message seems to resonate through the story, reflecting perhaps on Nancy's life with Wilf or on Ollie, who has managed to evade responsibility. Religious questions are raised in "Trespasses" when Delphine reveals that it was a Christian group that arranged the adoption of Delphine's baby. Religion plays a lesser part once the stories reach the 'present.' Towards the end of "Tricks," Robin notices that "on a fine Sunday morning you can sit at a sidewalk table drinking fancy coffee … without any thought of worship" (263).

Scientific & Technological Context

Scientific progress is apparent but is not a major theme in the collection. In "Powers," Ollie exploits Tessa for commercial purposes, investigating her clairvoyance in the name of science. He sends her to a mental institution which uses antiquated treatments such as gas and shock therapy: measures that appear barbaric in comparison to the treatments available to Robin's patients in "Tricks."

Biographical Context

Alice Munro was born Alice Laidlaw in 1931. She grew up in a farmhouse near the town of Wingham in Ontario. She attended the University of Western Ontario studying journalism and English. For twenty years, she lived in Victoria, British Columbia, with her husband Jim, whom she later divorced. They had three daughters. During this period she wrote short stories, some of which were published in magazines. Her first collection, "Dance of the Happy Shades," appeared in 1968

and won the Governor General's Award for Fiction. Munro has published ten collections of stories. "Lives of Girls and Women" (1971) and "The Beggar Maid" (1978) are comprised of linked narratives and are often classified as novels. Some of the stories in "Moons of Jupiter" (1982) feature recurring characters. Munro is the recipient of many accolades and awards, including the Trillium Book Award for "Friend of my Youth" (1990) and the 1995 W. H. Smith Award for "Open Secrets" (1994). "The Beggar Maid" was nominated for the 1978 Booker Prize, qualifying as a novel. In 1990, Munro received the Canada Council Molson Prize for 'outstanding contribution to the cultural and intellectual life of Canada.' She received the Giller Prize for "Runaway." She remarried in 1976 and now lives in Ontario near her home town.

Rachel Lister

Works Cited

Howells, Coral Ann. "Alice Munro." *Contemporary World Writers*. Manchester: Manchester UP, 1998.

Munro, Alice. *Runaway*. London: Chatto, 2004.

Welty, Eudora. "The Reading and Writing of Short Stories." *Atlantic Monthly*, February (1949): 54–8.

For Further Study

Carrington, Ildiko de Papp. *Controlling the Uncontrollable: The Fiction of Alice Munro*. Dekalb: Illinois UP, 1989.

Miller, Judith, ed. "The Art of Alice Munro: Saying the Unsayable." Waterloo, ON: U of Waterloo P, 1984.

Rasporich, Beverley. *Dance of the Sexes: Art and Gender in the Fiction of Alice Munro*. London: Routledge, 1992.

Discussion Questions

1. In "Runaway," Sylvia describes Flora's appearance as a "miracle." Trace the seemingly miraculous or implausible events in the collection. How do you respond to the unlikely turn of events in some of these narratives? How does Munro sustain a sense of credibility?

2. Some of the heroines share a passion for literature. Trace the references to texts in the collection and consider their narrative function. Why does Munro draw attention to parities between the heroines' lives and the texts they encounter?

3. Most of the heroines in "Runaway" end up alone. What are the benefits of solitude for these women? Carla chooses to return to her husband. How did you feel about this? Compare her status at the end of the story to that of Juliet and Robin.

4. Three of the stories in "Runaway" are unified by recurring heroine Juliet. Why does Munro choose to represent Juliet's life in this way? Why did she not develop these stories into a novel? Imagine that you have read only "Silence." How would you respond to this story if you had not read "Chance" or "Soon"?

5. Some of the characters have mental or physical disabilities or are jeopardized in some way. What role do they play in the collection?

6. The women in these stories try to make sense of events that have happened in their lives. How successful are they? How satisfying did you find the endings of these stories?

7. Some of the most intriguing characters are presented through the eyes of the heroines whose impressions are mediated through the third-person narrative voice. Discuss the representation of one of the following characters: Clark, Irene, Mrs. Travers, Neil, Delphine, Ollie. How easy is it to define these characters? Why does Munro present them from a distance?

8. Why does Munro choose "Runaway" as the title? Would any other title from the collection be as effective?

9. Most of the heroines experience moments of betrayal. Trace these moments and examine their repercussions. Do the characters always recognise betrayal?

10. Trace the references to faith and spirituality. Do they create a tension in the collection as a whole? What effect do these references have on the stories themselves?

Essay Ideas

1. What role does class play in "Runaway"?

2. How does Munro represent gender difference in these stories? Are gender boundaries entirely fixed?

3. Eudora Welty stated that "Every good story has mystery—not the puzzle kind—but the mystery of allurement" (56). Does Munro achieve this with the stories in "Runaway"?

4. Analyze Munro's representation of the past in each story.

5. Most of the stories take place in the small rural towns of Canada. What do the stories suggest about the relationship between identity and place?

Sonny's Blues

by James Baldwin

Content Synopsis

James Baldwin's short story, "Sonny's Blues," is told from the first person point of view of Sonny's unnamed older brother. Although the narrator discusses Sonny throughout the story, the story reveals as much about the narrator as it does about Sonny.

The story begins as the narrator, a high school math teacher, ponders on his way to school the newspaper article he has read about Sonny's arrest for drug related crimes. He says that he felt "scared for Sonny" and that he had tried to keep from having to admit to himself that Sonny was a drug addict (103). When school is over, the narrator sits alone in his classroom and listens to his students "shouting and cursing and laughing" outside (104). He realizes that the laughter of his students is not "joyous," but "mocking and insular" (104). He listens to the students because he recognizes in them Sonny and himself. When he leaves the school building, he sees Sonny's former friend, who says he came to inform him of Sonny's plight. The friend asks what the narrator plans to do about Sonny, and the narrator says, "I haven't seen Sonny for over a year, I'm not sure I'm going to do anything. Anyway, what the hell can I do? (106). As the conversation between Sonny's friend and the narrator continues, the narrator begins to feel uncomfortable because he is being forced to address Sonny's problems. He says, "All this was carrying me some place I didn't want to go" (107).

In response to questions regarding Sonny's future, the friend informs Sonny's brother that Sonny will get out of jail and continually repeat the pattern of drug use and serving jail time. Sonny's brother views this lifestyle as a death wish and asks the friend why Sonny is "killing himself" (108). The friend replies that Sonny does not "want to die. He wants to live" (108).

Perhaps because he does not know what to say to Sonny, the narrator waits a long time after Sonny's arrest to write him a letter, and Sonny's response makes him feel remorse. Sonny writes that he can't explain how he ended up in his current predicament and asks if the narrator will meet him when he is released from jail. The narrator maintains contact with Sonny and meets him after his release. He recalls many memories of Sonny such as having been present when Sonny was born, when he spoke his first words, and when he took his first step.

Upon Sonny's release, on the way to the narrator's house where he will live for a time, he and Sonny ride in a taxi through the neighborhood in which they grew up. As they each look out the windows at the Harlem landscape, the narrator contemplates that some escape that impoverished environment while others do not. However, he understands that "what we both were seeking through our separate cab windows was that part of ourselves which had been left behind" (112). Upon Sonny's arrival to his house, the narrator fears he

185

is leading Sonny "back into the danger he had almost died trying to escape" (113). The narrator feels uncomfortable, and he and Sonny don't communicate much on the drive. He senses that Sonny also feels awkward. When Sonny asks if they are almost at the narrator's house, the narrator simply says, "Almost" and recognizes that they "were both too nervous to say anything more" (112). When they arrive at the narrator's house, Sonny is more talkative than usual and the narrator feels grateful that his wife, Isabel, seems comfortable around Sonny and is "genuinely glad to see him" (113). The narrator feels awkward, looks at Sonny "for signs" of drug use, and says he wants Sonny to be "safe" (113).

Concern for Sonny's safety reminds the narrator of his father's claim that there is no safe place for anyone. This memory marks a long flashback in the story. The narrator recalls that his father had died when Sonny was fifteen and remembers that Sonny and his father fought with each other even though Sonny "was the apple of his father's eye" (114). He remembers that last time he saw his mother alive she revealed to him that his father had a brother who sang and played the guitar. One night while the narrator's father and uncle were walking home, his uncle was run over and killed purposely and maliciously by a car driven by a white man and full of white passengers. The narrator's mother says the incident devastated his father and made him rage when the subject was mentioned. She says she is telling him the story because he has "a brother. And the world ain't changed" (118). She asks the narrator to "hold on to your brother" and tells him not to "let him fall, no matter what it looks like is happening to him and no matter how evil you gets with him" (118). The narrator promises, "I won't let nothing happen to Sonny" (118).

The narrator forgets his promise until he reunites with Sonny at his mother's funeral, during which Sonny tells him that he wants to be a musician. The narrator strives to understand and advise Sonny. He

says, "I'd never played the role of the older brother quite so seriously before" (119). The narrator continues to question Sonny about his goals, asks him what type of musician he desires to be, and demands that Sonny answer him seriously. Sonny says he wants to be a jazz musician. When the narrator asks if he wants to play the sort of music Louis Armstrong plays, Sonny says he admires Charlie Parker's style. The narrator questions, almost paternally, whether Sonny will be able to make a living as a musician and Sonny replies that it's what he wants to do. He says, "I think people ought to do what they want to do, what else are they alive for?" (121–22). Although he tries, the narrator cannot understand Sonny's goals and feels that he does not know him. When he scolds Sonny for smoking, Sonny laughs and asks the narrator if he smoked when he was his age. He pleads with Sonny to finish school and promises to help him with his goals when he graduates.

The narrator arranges for Sonny to go live at Isabel's parents, where he plays the piano, perfecting his craft. Sonny spends most of his time listening to records and then play the songs on the piano. Isabel tells the narrator that living with Sonny "wasn't like living with a person at all, it was like living with sound" (124). She says that nobody understands the music Sonny plays and that Sonny is beginning to distress the family. Although he performs everyday behaviors such as eating and walking and is not "unpleasant or rude," he seems like "some sort of god, or monster" (125). Instead of attending school, Sonny spends time in Greenwich Village with other musicians. When Isabel's mother confronts Sonny and accuses him of being unappreciative of their hospitality, he leaves and joins the Navy.

After Sonny joins the Navy, the narrator does not see him again for several years, when they are both in New York. They fight every time they visit each other. After one serious fight, the narrator goes to visit Sonny to make amends and begins to sense that Sonny feels closer to the people he lives with than he does to the narrator. They have another fight, and Sonny tells the narrator "not to worry about him any more in life" (126). As he leaves, the narrator tries to keep from crying and whistles, "You going to need me, baby, one of these cold, rainy days" (127).

The narrator does not have contact with Sonny until he writes to him after reading of his arrest in the paper. At this point, the flashback ends, and the story resumes with the narrator's explanation of why he decided to write to Sonny. He explains that his two-year-old daughter, Gracie, had died of polio and that he thinks he may have written Sonny the day Gracie was buried. He explains, "My trouble made his real" (127).

After his release from jail, Sonny lives with the narrator and his family. Almost two weeks later, the narrator is tempted to search Sonny's room for evidence of drug use. Looking out the window, the narrator notices a religious revival taking place outside. Sonny stands among the crowd and donates some change during the offering. Sonny joins the narrator inside and invites him to come watch him perform at a bar later that night. Sonny says the woman's voice who sings during the revival reminds him of what it feels like to consume heroin and says that her suffering enabled her to sing so powerfully. This comment sparks a discussion about suffering. While Sonny's brother maintains that it is best to accept suffering because there is no escape from it, Sonny says that everybody tries not to suffer. He admits that he had wanted to leave Harlem to get away from drugs but that leaving did not help. Sonny and the narrator walk together to the nightclub where Sonny will perform. Upon arrival, the narrator immediately senses that everyone at the bar respects Sonny. The narrator watches the musicians prepare to play. During the performance, the other musicians gather around Sonny. As Sonny plays, the narrator says, "I seemed to hear with what burning he had made it his, with

what burning we had yet to make it ours, how we could cease lamenting…. I understood … that he could help us to be free if we would listen, that he would never be free until we did" (140). Sonny's piano playing, or Sonny's blues, brings the narrator a sense of peace regarding Sonny, his parents, his uncle's death, and finally Gracie's death. Sonny nods at the narrator in gratitude for the Scotch and milk he has ordered him, and the narrator says the drink "glowed and shook above my brother's head like the very cup of trembling" (141).

Symbols & Motifs

Music, specifically the blues, is the most significant motif in the story. As Sonny acknowledges, his only source of meaning in life is through music. While the narrator equates jazz music with that of Louis Armstrong, Sonny, Sonny says that he admires the music of Charlie Parker. During the setting of the story, Parker was becoming famous for his bebop style that departed from traditional jazz, the sort of old school music of Armstrong. The narrator's reference to Armstrong and his unfamiliarity with Parker demonstrate his misunderstanding of Sonny as a musician. At the end of the story, Sonny and his brother connect through jazz. Moreover, the blues Sonny plays inspires the narrator to lament not only the deaths of his immediate ancestors but also the ill treatment of blacks in American society. Through Sonny's music, the narrator experiences relief from the grief he has felt for the deaths of his parents, and more recently, that of his daughter, Gracie.

Suffering is another motif that occurs throughout the story. The narrator writes Sonny shortly after his daughter is buried and acknowledges that his own suffering made Sonny's real to him. He has witnessed the hardships of his parents and heard of the atrocious death of his uncle. The narrator fears Sonny's lifestyle will kill him and seeks to reduce Sonny's suffering. Sonny and the narrator have a serious debate regarding whether people should accept suffering as part of life or try to avoid it. Additionally, suffering is the source of the voice of the woman who sings during the revival. Perhaps most importantly, suffering is the source of the blues, specifically the blues Sonny plays; therefore, the story's title, "Sonny's Blues," represents suffering.

Historical Context

The story is set during the mid-fifties, before the Civil Rights Movement. Racism was rampant in the United States during this time, and blacks were denied equal opportunities. The story exposes a segregated America, as there are no whites in the story except for reference to the men who killed Sonny's uncle. The story about the death of Sonny's uncle illustrates the sort of hate crimes that were widespread, and frequently committed without consequence, during the generation before Sonny's.

Both the narrator and Sonny have served in the military, and the narrator dates one of his reunions with Sonny as occurring long after the war was over. The reference presumably is to the Korean War, a war in which many African American men fought. Ironically, they fought abroad for American rights but received no rights upon their return home to a racist and segregated society.

Societal Context

The story exposes the impoverished living conditions of African Americans living in Harlem in the fifties and shows a segregated America. The narrator describes Sonny, and his childhood neighborhood, as the "killing streets of our childhood," with "houses exactly like the houses of our past," and sees the young boys now residing in the neighborhood as being "encircled by disaster" (112), as he and Sonny were during their childhoods. The narrator currently lives in a "rundown" housing project, described as "a parody of the good, clean, faceless life" (112). While his family lives there partly because it's close to his school, he says that "it's really just like the houses in which Sonny and I grew up. The same things happen, they'll have the same things to remember" (113).

The revival that Sonny and the narrator watch is important to their society. The narrator and everyone else watching has seen these sort of revivals all their lives, yet they still participate. Although the crowd gathered does not seem to believe the revival leaders are holy, they appreciate the gospel singing, which provides for them the same sort of spiritual sensation they gain from listening to the blues.

The family unit is another aspect of society shown in the story. Although conflict existed, Sonny and the narrator were brought up by a sense of strong family unity; moreover, one significant point of the story is the narrator's relationship with his brother, a family member. Additionally, the narrator reveals that his own family is close. He gives the impression that he and Isabel and their two sons spend quality time together.

The family unit expands at the end of the story when Sonny is surrounded by other musicians. Sonny and the other musicians form a sort of subculture in which they bond together. Also, the blues that Sonny plays brings together all African Americans in the broader sense of brotherhood that celebrates African American culture and identity.

Religious Context

The most significant religious allusion is the reference at the end of the story to "the very cup of trembling" (141). Literally, the narrator refers to the cup of Scotch and milk he has bought for Sonny, but the phrase is Biblical. The linking of the drink to the Biblical verse is ambiguous, as Keith Byerman notes, "The cup of trembling was taken from Israel when YHWH chose to forgive the people for their transgressions. But it was YHWH who had given the cup of suffering to them in the first place. Thus, it becomes important to the meaning of the story which verse is being alluded to in the metaphor. If the cup is given, then Sonny will continue to suffer and feel guilt; if the cup is taken away, then Sonny returns to a state of grace" (371).

The blues and religion offer similar spiritual benefits, and the two are compared to each other. During Sonny's performance, the narrator notices that occasionally the other musicians seem to say "amen" (140). Earlier, Sonny connects the woman singing at the revival with the feeling heroin gives and says, "Listening to that woman sing, it struck me all of a sudden how much suffering she must have had to go through—to sing like that" (132). Here, he relates the woman's gospel song to a blues song. At the end of the story, the blues provides the narrator a sort of spiritual healing that one frequently finds through religion.

Scientific & Technological Context

Although science and technology do not play significant roles in "Sonny's Blues," they are apparent. Technology is downplayed when the narrator explains that "a piano is just a piano. It's made out of so much wood and wires and little hammers and big ones, and ivory. While there's only so much you can do with it, the only way to find this out is to try; to try and make it do everything" (138). The narrator acknowledges that the musician, not the piano, creates the music. And the music, as demonstrated by the effect Sonny's music has on the narrator, is quite powerful.

Technology also is revealed in the narrator's comment about television. On the taxi ride home, he remarks that the houses in the housing project in which he lives have big windows but that they do not adequately camouflage lack of space. Instead of looking out the windows, the children watch television. Watching television becomes a means

of escape for the children, as they look at it instead of at their environment. While they watch television during the day, the children spend time on the housing project playground at night, suggesting both that they cannot see their environment due to the dark and that they are engaging in some sort of mischievous activities.

Biographical Context

Considered one of the most important African American writers of the twentieth century, James Baldwin was born August 2, 1924 in the Harlem District of New York. When James was three, his mother married a preacher, who adopted James. His mother had eight more children, and the family grew up poor. His father was a strict authoritarian and raised the family in a conservative and religious home. In junior high school, Baldwin began writing as a member of the literary club. When he was young, Baldwin worked for awhile as a preacher but when he was eighteen moved to New Jersey to work on the railroad. During the mid-forties, Baldwin moved to Greenwich Village, where he met Richard Wright. Baldwin began writing and publishing editorials, fiction, and book reviews. Baldwin left the United States in 1948 and moved to France because of rampant racism in the United States. Baldwin published his first novel, "Go Tell It on the Mountain," in 1953. Baldwin was active during the Civil Rights Movement, often returning to the United States to participate in political events and social rallies.

Baldwin has a distinguished oeuvre, writing in various genres such as fiction, poetry, drama, and nonfiction and publishing over twenty books and numerous shorter pieces. Many of his writings address the need for racial equality in America, and he is highly regarded as a spokesperson against racism. Baldwin died on December 1, 1987, in Saint-Paul de Vence, France.

Laurie Champion

Works Cited

Albert, Richard N. "The Jazz-Blues Motif in James Baldwin's 'Sonny's Blues.'" *College Literature* 11.2 (1984): 178–84.

Baldwin, James. "Sonny's Blues." *Going to Meet the Man*. New York: Dial Press, 1965. 101–41.

Byerman, Keith E. "Words and Music: Narrative Ambiguity in 'Sonny's Blues.'" *Studies in Short Fiction* 19 (1982): 367–72.

Champion, Laurie. "Assimilation Versus Celebration in James McPherson's 'The Story of a Dead Man' and James Baldwin's "'Sonny's Blues.'" *Short Story* 8.2 (2000): 94–106.

Sherard, Tracey. "Sonny's Bebop: Baldwin's 'Blues Text' As Intracultural Critique." *African American Review* 32 (1998): 691–705.

Discussion Questions

1. The narrator's desire to keep Sonny "safe" contradicts Sonny's father's proclamation that nobody is safe. What do you think the story suggests about trying to protect ourselves and other people against harm?

2. What role does music play in the story?

3. Is it significant that the narrator writes to Sonny only after his daughter, Gracie, dies?

4. The narrator comments on how comfortable his wife, Isabel, seems around Sonny. Why is Isabel able to fell comfortable around Sonny while the narrator is not?

5. Compare and contrast Sonny's lifestyle with the narrator's. Does the story suggest one lifestyle is preferable?

6. Other than to explain to the narrator that he must take care of Sonny, why do you think the narrator's mother tells him the story of his uncle's death?

7. What change takes place in the narrator when he hears Sonny play the blues?

8. What role does Sonny's drug addiction play in the story?

9. When Sonny and the narrator pass through their childhood neighborhood, what type of thoughts are evoked in the narrator?

10. The narrator recalls memories of his father and memories of stories his mother told him about his father. Compare and contrast Sonny with the descriptions of his father.

Essay Ideas

1. Using details about their childhood, their family history, and their current situations, analyze Sonny and the narrator as characters.

2. Explore ways incidents from the narrator's and Sonny's lives can be viewed as the sort of lyrics that make up a blues song.

3. Discuss Sonny's brother's role as narrator. Does the narrator seem reliable? How might the story be different if told from Sonny's point of view?

4. Compare and contrast "Sonny's Blues" to the Biblical Cain and Able story.

5. Analyze "Sonny's Blues" as an African American short story.

The Story of an Hour

by Kate Chopin

Content Synopsis

With stylistic efficiency, Kate Chopin introduces her central character (Mrs. Louise Mallard) and two crucial plot details (Louise's heart condition, and the very recent death of her husband), in the story's abrupt, attention-grabbing opening sentence—a sentence whose reference to "heart trouble" (352) seems doubly meaningful and ironic by the time the tale concludes. Also ironic is the care taken by Louise's sister Josephine in breaking "as gently as possible" (352) to Louise the news of Mr. Mallard's death; this "great care" (352) not only contrasts with the sudden revelation that will occur at the story's conclusion but also seems full of irony in light of Louise's subsequent reaction to Josephine's news. Josephine is accompanied by Richards, a family friend who will also appear at the story's conclusion, thus adding to the work's symmetrical structure. It was Richards who had first received word that Brently Mallard had been killed in a train wreck, and it was Richards who (ironically) had "hastened" to inform Louise of the accident (352). If he had taken further time to determine the accuracy of the report, the story might have developed very differently than it does, but this is a story that very much concerns life's unpredictability.

Louise responds to the news with intense emotion and shuts herself in her room. As she stares out a window she faces a scene of natural beauty

and vitality that seems, at first, merely to contrast with her own bereaved suffering; soon, however, it becomes clear that all the imagery of "spring life" is not simply ironic but also suggests to Louise the possibilities of a new, more vital existence. The complex, ambiguous tone of this section of the story is implied by the mixed imagery of "patches of blue sky showing here and there through the clouds" (352): Louise's life is momentarily dark, but new options are beginning to dawn. She weeps, but she weeps as a child does (another image suggesting vitality and potential growth). Louise is young and strong in spite of her present grief and past "repression" (353) and as she gazes off into the sky, Chopin skillfully creates a sense of suspense as both Louise and the reader wonder what is beginning to happen. The language of the story becomes sensual and its tone becomes mysterious as Chopin expertly delays the revelation.

Finally, both Louise and the reader discover that at some very deep level of her being she feels liberated by her husband's death. The language becomes even more sensual as she embraces her new freedom of soul. Ethical considerations seem irrelevant to her as she contemplates her feelings, but Chopin is careful to make clear that Louise did (and does) not hate Brently and that, in fact, Brently was a loving husband. To have made him an ogre would have cheapened the profundity of Louise's revelation and would have simplified the story's meanings. The story would have been a melodrama in which an oppressed wife is freed from a tyrannical husband. Instead, Louise realizes that she will genuinely mourn at Brently's funeral, but for the moment she can only imagine and embrace the freedom and autonomy her future now seems to offer her. She understands that even a loving relationship can be confining for one or both partners, even when they think they have the best of intentions toward each other. Significantly, Chopin makes clear that men can feel as confined as women; the story is not a simple bit of partisan propaganda for one side in the so-called war of the sexes. Its concerns go deeper and are more fundamental, although of course Chopin knew that women were much more likely to feel oppressed in her culture than men.

The essential honesty of the story (often a trait of Chopin's best writing) continues when Louise concedes that although she had usually loved Brently, often she had not. Her feelings for Brently, however, suddenly seem less important than the prospect of her bright future of freedom. When Josephine begs Louise to open the door, afraid that her sister will make herself sick, the irony is palpable; Josephine has no idea how well Louise is really feeling. She is imagining her autonomy in the days ahead. Eventually she opens the door and embraces her sister, feeling victorious. As they walk down the stairs together, Richards awaits them below. At just that moment, however, they hear the front door opening. Who should enter but Brently? He had been nowhere near the train wreck. He cannot understand Josephine's shriek or Richard's hasty effort to block Louise's view of him. Richards, however, fails, and the physicians summoned to help Louise later explain that she died of a happiness too great for her weak heart to sustain.

In alluding to Louise's heart trouble, which had also been mentioned in the very first sentence, the story neatly comes full circle. Its ending catches us by surprise, but many details scattered throughout the work make the ending seem inevitable, not a mere trick. In an astonishingly brief tale, Chopin manages to create a complex central character and to suggest her complex inner life. The sudden twist at the end owes much to the influence of Guy de Maupassant, one of Chopin's favorite writers, but the story does not seem hackneyed or trite. It displays many virtues typical of Chopin's talent: its phrasing is clear, clean, economical, and tinged with subtle symbolism and evocative imagery. The dialogue is credible, and the irony provides the kind of ambiguity that prevents the work from descending into melodrama. Chopin does not simplify her characters or their circumstances, and she resists the temptation to score cheap polemical points. Her story, which never fails to provoke real pleasure and lively discussion, is one of the best brief tales in American literature and deserves its prominent place in so many anthologies.

Historical Context

First published in 1894, "The Story of an Hour" reflects many of the historical conditions of its time. The most obvious of these (besides the subordinate roles of women) is the importance of railroads in nineteenth-century American life; Chopin was writing at a time when rail travel was the most modern form of transportation, and the fact that Brently Mallard travels by train implies how American society at this time was evolving rapidly under the forces of industrialization. Reference to the "telegram" (352) has the same effect, since the telegraph was the latest form of advanced communication. The fact that Brently is out working while his wife is at home may be due, primarily, to Louise's "heart trouble" (352). It may also reflect the fact that in the growing industrial, commercial, urban economy of this time, middle- or upper-class women were less likely to engage in the kind of labor that had been demanded of women who lived on farms or on the frontier. The story implies an urban setting and thus reflects the growing trend, during this period, for people to live in large cities, with their diverse economic classes (reflected in the "peddler … crying his wares" [352]) and professions (reflected in "the doctors" (354) who appear in the story's final sentence).

Societal Context

The most obvious social context for Chopin's story is the growing emphasis, in the nineteenth century, on various forms of emancipation for women. Women's "movements" of various sorts had now been formally organized and were advocating for various rights, especially the right to vote. Women writers, especially women intellectuals and proponents of feminism, were increasingly well known and influential, and access by women to advanced education was becoming increasingly common. Legally and culturally, however, the lives of women were still much constrained when compared with those of men, and Chopin's story reflects both these constraints and the growing desire of many women for "liberation" of various kinds. Chopin is careful, however, to prevent her story from becoming a mere political tract; even the presentation of Louise, although basically sympathetic, is not without ironies and double edges. In the final analysis the story fails to offer an explicit political argument; instead it merely presents a complex situation and allows readers to draw their own conclusions.

Religious Context

At first glance, religion seems irrelevant to this story. No one prays on learning of Brently's death; no one seeks to offer Louise religious consolation; Louise herself never turns to God for guidance; indeed, God is never mentioned in the tale. These facts, however, are themselves significant, for Chopin was living in a culture still steeped in Christian religious traditions; thus the absence of any explicit religious reference in the story implies

a society in which religion had begun to lose its formerly strong grip on at least some segments of the population. The story seems to reflect the growing influence of secularism in nineteenth-century culture—the same culture that produced such influential agnostic or atheistic voices as Darwin, Marx, and Freud, all of whom helped undermine confidence in religion, at least among the educated. Chopin herself was familiar with Darwin and had left the Catholic church in which she had received her early training, and her writings in general often reflect skepticism concerning orthodox, organized religion. Louise Mallard seems more influenced by the consolations of nature (especially as she stares out the window) than by any theological or supernatural meditations. When she imagines her future she does not think either of heaven or of hell but of the earthly pleasures of spring and summer days; having achieved a kind of freedom through Brently's death, she seems unconcerned with any supernatural fate that might follow her own eventual passing. Her new perception of her life descends upon her like a secular annunciation or non-religious epiphany. She never seems to worry how God might judge her new, possibly "monstrous joy (353)." She feels that she has now received a sublime but highly personal revelation in which traditional religion plays no part; she plans from now on to "live for herself" (353)—not for Brently, and not for God. When she thinks of her "soul" she thinks of it in conjunction with her "body," and she thinks of both as "free" (353) by which she seems to mean free not only of Brently but of any other external obligation. Josephine's hackneyed reference to "heaven" (354) thus seems irrelevant to Louise. Ironically, one of the few explicitly religious words in the story involves Louise's "quick prayer" (353) that life (that is, physical, earthly life) might be long. When she finally emerges from her room she resembles a classical, non-Christian "goddess of Victory" (354) just before she meets her crushing defeat. Chopin does not end the story, however, as another, more religious writer might have done: she provides no explicit judgment or moralization, and she suggests no sense that Louise has been punished for her sins. In substance, as in style, the story suggests that in this case, religion simply is not relevant.

Scientific & Technological Context

Reference has already been made to the significance of railroads and telegraphy in the society Chopin describes. These technological advances were part of a growing trend toward modernization of every aspect of American society during the era in which the story was written. Juxtaposed with these technological developments, the reference to the "peddler … crying his wares" (352) almost seems a throwback to an earlier, less modern form of economy. Meanwhile, although the opinion offered by the doctors at the very end of the story may seem crude by the standards of science in our own day (when a complete autopsy would be able to determine the precise physiological cause of Louise's death), the mere fact that "doctors" (354) are readily available in Chopin's story to offer an opinion reflects the growing emphasis in her culture on professional medicine and the growing prestige of science. Indeed, it is partly the prestige of medical professionals in this era that makes the doctors' pronouncement seem so limited, blinkered, and ironic.

Biographical Context

The most striking link between this story and Chopin's own life is that Chopin's father was himself killed in a railroad accident when Kate was a very small child. Kate's widowed mother never remarried, and most of the early crucial influences on Kate's life came from resourceful, independent women. Although Kate's own marriage to Oscar Chopin seems to have been a happy one, his early death gave her the kind of widowed independence Louise Mallard can only begin to imagine. Like her mother, Kate never remarried, and her writing career became both a means of supplementing her income and a means of expressing herself in ways Louise might someday have hoped to do. Ironically, just as Louise was cut down unexpectedly at precisely the moment when she seemed to stand on the threshold of her greatest independent achievements, so Chopin's own successful writing career suffered an abrupt reversal with the publication of her novel "The Awakening" (1899). Although this book is now considered her crowning achievement, in its own day it caused a scandal by depicting a woman (like Louise Mallard) who is unhappy in marriage and who seems to welcome the prospect of freedom from matrimony. Reaction to the novel was harshly negative, and although Chopin continued to live and write for a few years after its publication, neither her career, nor her spirits, ever fully recovered from the shock she suffered when the torrent of negative reviews appeared. Like Louise Mallard, she was struck down just when she seemed, to all appearances, a goddess of Victory.

Robert C. Evans

Works Cited

Chopin, Kate. "The Story of an Hour." *The Complete Works of Kate Chopin*. Ed. Per Seyersted. 2 vols. Baton Rouge: Louisiana State University Press, 1969. 2:352–354.

Evans, Robert C., ed. *Kate Chopin's Short Fiction: A Critical Companion*. West Cornwall, CT: Locust Hill Press, 2001.

Discussion Questions

1. Can males appreciate and enjoy this story as much as women can?

2. In what ways is the ending of the story satisfying or unsatisfying?

3. How does Chopin create sympathy both for Brently and for Louise? Do you fail to feel sympathy for either character? If so, why?

4. How are the lives of both Brently and Louise restricted?

5. Is this story still relevant, or has society changed so much that the "message" of the story is outdated?

6. Why is it significant that the Mallards are apparently from the upper or upper-middle class? How might Louise's situation and reactions be different if she were poor?

7. Apparently Louise and Brently have no children; how does that probability influence Louise's thoughts about her future?

8. For many years this story was largely unknown; now it appears very widely in anthologies of literature. What are some possible reasons for this relatively new recent interest in the work, and what are some possible reasons for the fact that it was overlooked for so long?

9. Some readers might charge that the story has been revived only because it is "politically correct." Would you agree or disagree with such a charge? If you disagree, how would you defend the story?

10. The original title of this story was "The Dream of an Hour." Which title, in your opinion, is more effective, and why?

Essay Ideas

1. Compare and contrast Mrs. Mallard and the main characters of some of Chopin's other works, such as Edna in Chopin's famous novel "The Awakening."

2. Using a guide to criticism of the story (such as the one included in Evans 2001), explore the different, even contradictory, ways in which the story has been interpreted and discuss the strengths and weaknesses of at least three interpretations.

3. Discuss the various techniques Chopin uses to create sympathy for Louise. In addition, discuss the various techniques Chopin uses to maintain a fundamentally objective tone.

4. Discuss the structure of the story, in particular how it moves from external to internal and then back to external again.

5. Investigate the social and legal status of widows in Chopin's culture and discuss the kind of life Mrs. Mallard might have been able to lead as a widow.

Sweat

by Zora Neale Hurston

Content Synopsis

"Sweat" reveals the plight of Delia Jones, a wash-woman who picks up dirty clothes, takes them home, and washes them. The story opens late one Sunday night in spring, while Delia is busy washing clothes. She sorts clothes and hums, while questioning the whereabouts of her husband, Sykes, to whom she has been married fifteen years. Although Delia knows that Sykes is committing adultery with a woman named Bertha, she is not concerned that he may be spending time with his mistress but that he has taken her horse and cart, her means of transportation. Delia suddenly is alarmed when she feels something slide across her shoulders. She realizes it is a bullwhip and sees Sykes standing at the door and laughing maliciously. Sykes admits to Delia that he knows she fears snakes, so he slid the bullwhip across Delia to make her think it was a snake and scare her. Both literally and figuratively, the bullwhip represents Sykes's power over Delia. It is as if he is "whipping" her into submission and yielding complete control over her. Delia scolds him for scaring her and asks where he has been with her horse. Instead of answering, he chides her for bringing home white people's laundry. This opening scene establishes that Delia financially supports the family and that Sykes abuses her, takes advantage of her, and spends her money. While Delia is busy "sweating," Sykes is riding the horse and cart for which she has paid. Additionally,

it is implied that he is out with Bertha, who also reaps rewards of Delia's labor because Sykes pays her rent and buys her things.

Sykes tries to aggravate Delia, but she patiently continues her task of washing clothes. Every comment Delia makes to Sykes, he refutes angrily. Finally, Delia says, "Ah ain't for no fuss t'night Sykes" (26), but he continues to provoke her. For example, when she reminds him she has just returned from church, he accuses her of committing sin by washing clothes on Sunday. However, when he threatens her physically, her "habitual meekness seemed to slip from under her shoulders like a blown scarf" (27). Significantly, the meekness slips from the very shoulders around which the bullwhip was slid. Delia reminds him that she has paid for the house and supported them with her "sweat" (27). When she picks up a skillet and holds it up defensively, Sykes is surprised. The narrator says that her unexpected response "cowed him and he did not strike her as he usually did" (27). Apparently, Delia suspects that Sykes will try to take the house from her or try to kill her so he can have the house. When Delia tells Sykes that he has not paid for anything and says that his mistress is not going to live in her house, her suspicion is confirmed. Sykes tells her that if she does not quit upsetting him, "They'll be totin' you out sooner than you expect" (28). Sykes leaves the house angrily, and Delia knows he will be gone all night. The narrator informs readers that

Sykes has physically abused Delia since shortly after they married. Delia no longer hopes for love or companionship from Sykes, but she desires to retain the house she has bought.

Near the end of July, on her way to deliver clean laundry, Delia rides her horse and cart by Joe Clarke's house, where several men sit on the porch. They remark amongst themselves about Delia's hard work and Sykes's abuse of her. Delia nods at the men as she passes by, but she does not hear them talking. The men criticize Sykes's treatment of Delia and for having an extramarital affair. They agree that there should be a law against Sykes's behavior. One man suggests that they take Sykes and Bertha to the swamp and beat them and kill Sykes. The narrator says, "A grunt of approval went around the porch. But the heat was melting their civic virtue" (31). As the men begin to eat a watermelon, Sykes and Bertha appear. Returning from delivering the laundry, Delia drives by and sees Sykes with Bertha. Sykes feels "pleased" that Delia sees him with Bertha. He offers to buy Bertha anything she wants from the local store, and after they leave, the men make derogatory remarks about Bertha. Sykes has been paying for Bertha to rent a room in a house in town. Sykes promises Bertha that as soon as he forces Delia to leave the house, she can move in with him.

Delia and Sykes fight continuously until August. One evening Delia comes home and finds Sykes standing in the doorway. As she enters the house, stooping under his arm, he pushes her. He points to a soapbox, in which he has caged a rattlesnake, mockingly telling Delia that he has brought her something. The story implies that Sykes brings the snake in the house either to scare Delia so she will leave the house and he can bring Bertha to live in it with him or so the snake will bite Delia and kill her. Delia is scared and asks him to remove the snake from the house but he refuses. The townsmen hear about Sykes's snake and come to see and inquire about it. The snake remains at the house despite Delia's continued pleas to remove it. When Sykes threatens Delia physically, she says, "Ah hates you, Sykes" (35). She continues her insult, saying she hates him to the degree she used to love him. Delia's harsh words surprise Sykes and he has difficulty finding "the proper fury to try to answer Delia" (36). He insults her appearance and says that she could not hate him any worse that he hates her. They continue the bitter argument, and Sykes leaves for the night.

After returning from church the next day, Delia begins her weekly laundry routine. Unbeknownst to Delia, Sykes has put the snake in the laundry hamper in hopes it will bite her. When she opens the hamper, she sees the rattlesnake and runs outside. Feeling unsafe on the ground, she climbs in the barn loft for awhile, eventually falling asleep. Early the next morning, just as the sun is beginning to rise, she hears a noise, peeks from the barn, and sees Sykes destroying the box in which the snake was kept before he put it in the laundry hamper. She watches as Sykes enters the house and then climbs down from the loft and sits beneath the bedroom window. Inside, as Sykes is in the kitchen looking for a match to light a lantern he hears the snake rattling. Because he is unable to see in the dark, he cannot discern where the snake is positioned. He runs to the bedroom. From outside, Delia hears him scream and call her name. He crawls on his hands and knees as she reaches the door and she sees his swollen neck and eye. She decides that it is too far to take him to Orlando for treatment. As Sykes lies dying at the end of the story, Delia "waited in the growing heat while inside she knew the cold river was creeping up and up to extinguish that eye which must know by now that she knew" (40). Significantly, Sykes knows that Delia sees him dying but is unwilling to save his life.

Symbols & Motifs

The snake is the most obvious symbol in the story. As in traditional myth and folklore and in the

Bible, the snake represents evil. The snake is an archetype figure; that is, it has similar connotations across cultures. Even nonpoisonous snakes are feared universally, and rattlesnakes are feared for sound reasons, as their bites are deadly. Snakes also symbolize power and dominance, a representation especially significant in "Sweat" when compared to the bullwhip, a devise literally used for control. While at first Sykes scares Delia with a bullwhip (the representation of a snake), he later places a real snake in a hamper so it will bite her. Both the bullwhip and the snake have connotations of power and control. Additionally, snakes are phallic symbols, and the snake in the story represents Sykes's male dominance.

The story's title, "Sweat," is another symbol in the story. Sweat represents the hard labor Delia has performed in order to buy the house and support herself and Sykes. This is especially relevant given that Sykes does not work at all. Delia reminds Sykes that she has been washing laundry for fifteen years and laments, "Sweat, sweat, sweat! Work and Sweat, cry and sweat, pray and sweat!" (27).

Poetic justice is a major motif in the story. Delia tells Sykes, "Oh well, whatever goes over the Devil's back, is got to come under his belly. Sometime or ruther, Sykes, like everybody else is gointer reap his sowing" (29). At the end of the story, Sykes's death is justified in that the very snake he puts in the house to kill Delia kills him instead. Essentially, his intent to kill Delia backfires on him and justice is served.

Darkness and light are presented at the end of the story. Delia enters the house, finds a match, and lights the lantern. Running from the snake, "the wind from the open door blew out the light and the darkness added to her terror" (38). Sykes enters the dark house, while Delia sits outside the bedroom window. The window shade keeps the morning light from shining through the house as Sykes hears the rattlesnake. Fearing the snake, Sykes says, "If Ah could on'y strack uh light!" (39). Hearing the

snake again, he cries out, "Oh, fuh de light!" (39). After Sykes is bitten by the snake the sun begins to shine inside the house. The sun continues to rise as Sykes calls out to Delia for help. Sykes stands both literally and figuratively in the dark, which represents his evilness. Only as he lay dying does the light appear, suggesting that the evil is gone.

Historical Context

"Sweat" was originally published in the magazine *Fire!!* in 1926, during the Harlem Renaissance. The Harlem Renaissance was a movement during the early 1900s, in which many African American artists gathered in the Harlem district of New York. These artists celebrated their heritage and began to create art for an African American audience. Many African American magazines provided opportunities for African American short story writers to publish their works. Other women writers who participated in the Harlem Renaissance include Jessie Redmon Fauset, Dorothy West, Marita Bonner, Alice Dunbar-Nelson, Anita Scott Coleman, and Nella Larsen.

Because of her portrayals of strong African American women and exposure of sexism and racism, Hurston was the forerunner for African American women writers during the sixties and seventies when America experienced the second wave of feminism. Until this time, most of Hurston's works were out of print and she was a forgotten writer. However, she was rediscovered when writers such as Alice Walker and Toni Cade Bambara acknowledged her influence and proclaimed the significance of her writings.

The story is set during a time when women were denied opportunities equal to those of men. African American men were also denied opportunities equal to those of white men, so African American women were victims of both sexism and racism. It was difficult for women, especially African American women, to get jobs, and the jobs they were able to secure paid poorly. Generally, women could not borrow money, nor did they own property. "Sweat" portrays Delia as a strong, independent woman, who despite the above mentioned limitations, was able to buy a house and support herself economically.

Societal Context

Hurston was trained as an anthropologist. Much of her work realistically documents the folklore, local customs, and culture of African Americans in Eatonville, Florida during the early twentieth century. "Sweat" is representative of Hurston's characterizations of African Americans. In "Sweat," the black community is separated from the white community, for whom Delia works. The story represents a sense of community; for example, the scene in which the men sit on the porch and gossip about Delia and Sykes demonstrates characteristics of small town life. Also, the men judge Sykes and speak of the unjust treatment he gives to Delia. The men on the porch serve as a sort of jury for the community. They plot ways to avenge the ill treatment of Delia, and they even consider killing Sykes.

Hurston grew up in an all black community, and so she had little contact with whites during her childhood. This sense of an all black community is portrayed throughout her works. Although Hurston has been criticized for stereotyping African Americans in her writings, she does not write in the protest fiction tradition as do many other writers such as Richard Wright and Chester Himes. Instead, her writings, as seen in "Sweat," celebrate African American heritage and culture in ways reflective of comments she makes in her well known essay "How It Feels to Be Colored Me": "I am not tragically colored. There is not great sorrow dammed up in my soul, nor lurking behind my eyes. I do not mind at all. I do not belong to the sobbing school of Negrohood who hold that nature somehow has given them a lowdown dirty deal and whose feelings are all hurt about it. Even in the helter-skelter skirmish that is my life, I have seen that the world is to the strong regardless of a little pigmentation more or less. No, I do not weep at the world—I am too busy sharpening my oyster knife" (153).

Even though, as mentioned above, Delia supports herself and owns a house, which demonstrates her strength and independence, it is interesting to note that she has submitted to Sykes throughout their marriage. His surprise at her expression of anger suggests either that she has never rebutted him or has done so rarely. Most likely, her submission to Sykes results from social expectations that were prevalent during the setting of the story. During this time, men were considered the heads of families and wives were expected to obey their husbands. However, Delia eventually confronts Sykes, an act that shows her ability to violate patriarchal social codes.

Religious Context

At the beginning of the story, readers are informed that Delia attends church regularly. She has switched congregations so she does not have to attend church with Sykes. Comparison is made between Delia's plight and Jesus' crucifixion: "Delia's work-worn knees crawled over the earth in Gethsemane and up the rocks of Calvary many, many times during these months" (33). Gethsemane is the garden where Jesus prayed the day before he was crucified, and the reference to Delia's crawling up Calvary alludes to the climbing up the hill of Jesus when he carried his cross to his crucifixion. This reference implies that Delia is a Christ figure and suggests that she is symbolically crucified by Sykes. In religious context, the snake represents Satan, and since Sykes brings in the snake, he is bringing Satan into the house. The darkness in which Sykes is surrounded at the end of the story suggests his spiritual blindness.

Scientific & Technological Context

Science and technology play roles in this story in terms of the medical attention Sykes could have received. Because Sykes's life might have been saved through medical intervention, Delia is given a choice whether or not to take him to the hospital. Also, Delia's role as washwoman has technological significance in that it demonstrates the type of hard labor in which women engaged before modern inventions such as washing machines and dishwashers. Although an automobile is mentioned in the story, Delia probably cannot afford one. This reference to technology demonstrates Delia's economic depravity and highlights her need to "sweat" in order to support herself.

Biographical Context

The daughter of Reverend John Hurston and Lucy Potts Hurston, Zora Neale Hurston was born on 7 January 1891, in Macon County, Alabama. In 1894, she moved to Eatonville, Florida, an African American community near Orlando. She attended Barnard College in New York City, where she studied anthropology. She collected folklore and researched African American life.

Hurston was an active participant in the Harlem Renaissance and is well known for her vibrant personality and charm. In 1935, Hurston published "Mules and Men," considered the first collection of African American folklore. Hurston published many novels, an autobiography, and several short stories and essays. Her most critically acclaimed novel is "Their Eyes Were Watching God." Hurston did not have economic success as a writer and worked in various domestic jobs throughout her later life. She died impoverished in 1960. As mentioned above, after initial publication, Hurston's works were ignored and she remained an unrecognized writer until her works were rediscovered in the seventies. Her short stories were not collected in a single volume until the mid-nineties, when Henry Louis Gates, Jr. edited "The Complete Stories of Zora Neale Hurston." In 1973, Alice Walker placed a tombstone on Hurston's unmarked grave.

Laurie Champion

Works Cited

Champion, Laurie. "Socioeconomics in Selected Short Stories of Zora Neale Hurston." *Southern Quarterly* 40.1 (2001): 79–92.

Hurd, Myles Raymond. "What Goes Around Comes Around: Characterization, Climax, and Closure in Hurston's 'Sweat.'" *Langston Hughes Review* 12.2 (1993): 7–15.

Hurston, Zora Neale. "How It Feels to Be Colored Me." "I Love Myself When I Am Laughing. And Then Again When I Am Looking Mean and Impressive: A Zora Neale Hurston Reader." Ed. Alice Walker. Old Westbury, NY: Feminist Press, 1979. 152–56.

Hurston, Zora Neale. "Sweat." Ed. Cheryl A. Wall. New Brunswick: Rutgers University Press, 1997. 25–40.

Meisenhelder, Susan Edwards. "Hitting a Straight Lick with a Crooked Stick: Race and Gender In the Work of Zora Neale Hurston." Tuscaloosa: University of Alabama Press, 1999.

Wall, Cheryl A., ed. "Sweat." New Brunswick: Rutgers University Press, 1997.

Discussion Questions

1. What role do the townsmen play in the story?
2. Discuss the significance of the snake in the story.
3. Does Hurston's use of dialect strengthen the story?
4. Do you agree with Clarke's comment regarding Sykes: "Tain't no law on earth dat kin make a man be decent if it ain't in 'im" (31)?
5. Compare and contrast the characters Delia and Bertha.
6. Do you think Sykes deserves to die?
7. Explore the irony in the story.
8. Why do you think Delia tries to remain "blind and deaf" (33)?
9. Find examples of Delia's expressions of anger toward Sykes. Does she become more aggressive toward him as the story progresses?
10. The narrator mentions the hot weather several times. Is it important to the story that it is hot?

Essay Ideas

1. Discuss whether Delia acted ethically when she did not seek aid for Sykes at the end of the story. Do her actions conflict with her Christian beliefs?
2. Explore Delia as a victim of domestic violence.
3. Discuss the role economics plays in the story.
4. Describe Delia from a feminist perspective.
5. Discuss elements of folklore Hurston weaves into the story.

The Swimmer

by John Cheever

Content Synopsis

Set during a midsummer Sunday, John Cheever's short story, "The Swimmer," begins with the narrator describing the afternoon as one of those in which "everyone sits around saying, 'I drank too much last night'" (713). The protagonist, Neddy Merrill, who has a youthful slenderness, although he is not young, attends a cocktail party hosted by the Westerhazys. He sits at the edge of the pool and sips a glass of gin. For no apparent reason, Neddy calculates that he could travel the eight miles home by swimming in the pools of people who live between the Westerhazys' house and his home. After he swims across the Westerhazys' pool, he walks across the lawn and tells his wife, Lucinda, that he will swim home. He contemplates the path home he will take and feels like "a pilgrim, an explorer, a man with a destiny" (715). After swimming across several pools, he reaches the Bunker's house, where a party is taking place. Enid Bunker welcomes Ned, and Ned greets several of the guests. Although he stays long enough to drink a gin and tonic, he does not want to delay his journey. Ned sees a de Haviland plane circling in the air and hears thunder. He swims across the Bunkers' pool, walks through their driveway, and heads toward the Levys' house, where he swims across their pool and pours himself a drink.

When Ned is almost halfway home, he hears thunder for the second time. He sees the de Haviland still circling above, hears a train, and wonders what time it is. It begins to grow dark, and it begins to storm. Ned stays in the Levys' gazebo until the storm passes. On the way to the Welchers' pool, he walks through the Lindleys' riding ring and notices the horses gone and the grass overgrown. When he discovers that the Welchers' pool is dry, the break in the "chain of water" causes him to feel "disappointed and mystified" (717). The house looks abandoned, and he sees a For Sale sign. He recalls that it seems like he has last spoken to the Welchers only a week ago, but he wonders if his memory is correct: "Was his memory failing or had he so disciplined it in the repression of unpleasant facts that he had damaged his sense of the truth?" (718).

At this point in the story, the narrative switches to second person, and the author/narrator seems to speak directly to the reader. We are informed that we may have seen Ned if we'd gone for a ride that day. "Close to naked" and looking "pitiful" (718), Ned stands waiting to cross the road. Returning to the third person, the narrator reveals that Ned is unprepared for the situation in which he finds himself. He is mocked repeatedly and from a passing car someone throws a beer can at him. He cannot understand why he does not simply return to the Wasterhazys' house. Traffic slows enough to allow him to run to the median, where he stands and becomes exposed to further ridicule.

At the Lancaster Recreation Center, he follows the policies of the public swimming pool before he swims. The lifeguards shout at him to leave the water because he has no "identification disk" (719). He leaves the recreation center and enters the Halloran estate. He calls out to the Hallorans, who are wealthy friends of his, to them to let them know he is present. Aware that the Hallorans swim in the nude, Ned removes his swimming trunks. He announces that he is "swimming across the country" (720). He swims across the pool, and Mrs. Halloran tells him that she is sorry about his misfortunes. Ned says he doesn't know to what she refers. When she informs him that she heard that he has sold his house, he denies it. Ned thanks the couple, and Mrs. Halloran bids him farewell.

Ned puts back on his swim trunks and they seem loose. He feels tired and weak and his body aches. He wants a drink of whiskey to "refresh his feeling that it was original and valorous to swim across the country" (721). He walks to the Hallorans' daughter's house. The Hallorans' daughter, Helen, asks him if he has eaten lunch at her parent's house, and he says no but admits that he visited them. He asks Helen for a drink. Helen says that they haven't had alcohol in the house since her husband, Eric, had an operation three years earlier.

Ned's conversation with Helen motivates him to question his memory. Ned begins to suspect that he has hidden from himself the painful facts that he has sold his house and that his children are in trouble. Helen tells him there is a party at the Biswangers' and says he can probably get a drink there. He swims across the Sachs' pool, says he will call them soon, and walks to the Biswangers', where Grace Biswanger, who is hosting a party calls him "a gate crasher" (722). He orders a whiskey and senses that his social status has fallen because the bartender is rude to him. After swimming across the Biswangers' pool, Ned considers that the next pool belongs to Shirley Adams, with whom he has had an affair; however, he is unable to remember whether the affair was last week or last year. He walks through her gate self-confidently. She asks him if he will "ever grow up" and tells him she will not give him any money (723). He asks for a drink, but she refuses because she says she is not alone. He swims across her pool but has difficulty climbing out, as his muscles are weakening. He climbs out of the pool by using the ladder. He sees a young man in the bathhouse, notices that the stars are out, and begins to cry. Ned has never felt so unhappy in his life. He is exhausted and his nose and throat are sore. He wants dry clothes, a drink, and companionship. Nevertheless, he swims across the Gilmartin's pool, even though he could simply walk a more direct route to his house. Instead of diving in, he climbs the stairs into the pool. Next he swims across the Clydes' pool even though he is exhausted. After swimming across the Clydes' pool, his last stop, "he had done what he wanted, he had swum the country, but he was so stupefied with exhaustion that his triumph seemed vague" (724).

Walking up his driveway, Ned sees that his house is dark. He wonders if his wife and children have gone to bed or if they are out for the evening. He notices that the storm has loosened a rain gutter. The house is locked, and Ned wonders if the cook or maid locked it but remembers that he hasn't had a maid or cook in sometime. He looks through the window and sees an empty house.

Although "The Swimmer" can be interpreted literally, many critics suggest that much of the story consists of Ned's imagination. For example, Hal Blythe and Charlie Sweet consider whether the story might be considered a fantasy and suggest that it consists of "a montage of Neddy Merrill's physical and social decline, and his odyssey takes place not on a particular midsummer Sunday afternoon, but over the course of a few years' worth of Sunday afternoons in which he repeats the essential pattern of his suburban life" ("Man-Made" 415).

Symbols & Motifs

Water is the most prominent symbol in the story. Traditionally, water symbolizes cleansing or a rebirth experience. In this story, water might represent a sort of rebirth for Ned. At the beginning of the story, Ned is disillusioned and unable to comprehend that he has moved and that he is experiencing financial problems. However, by the end of the story, it is apparent that he has been in a state of self-denial. On the other hand, water represents Ned's downfall, for at the beginning of the story he believes that he is a welcomed member of the middle-upper-class society but by the end of the story it becomes clear to him that he has become a social outcast.

The story also represents a traditional journey story, as Ned travels from the Westerhazys' house to his home. As in the traditional journey stories, Ned's adventure is a learning experience. Although Ned might not seem illustrative of the hero typical of journey stories, he experiences change as a result of his traveling. He transforms from believing that he is still a part of the suburban lifestyle to acknowledging that he is estranged from his former cohorts.

The consumption of alcohol recurs throughout the story. The first line of the story presents the notion of drinking too much. Heavy alcohol consumption is a way of life for the characters, who attend each other's social events. The drinking suggests that the characters feel discontent or bored with their upper-middle-class lifestyles. At the Bunker's social gathering, Ned sees the "smiling bartender he had seen at a hundred parties" (716), implying that the parties among this social group are all alike. Ned has a drink at almost every house at which he stops and looks forward to his next drink. For example, on his way to Helen Sachs' he craves a drink: "Whiskey would warm him, pick him up, carry him through the last of his journey, refresh his feeling that it was original and valorous to swim across the country" (721).

He craves alcohol to stimulate him both physically and mentally. In addition to traveling from pool to pool, Ned moves from drink to drink, symbolically swimming in alcohol.

Historical Context

"The Swimmer" was first published in Cheever's collection "The Brigadier and the Golf Widow" in 1964. The story portrays the lifestyle of a specific social stratum in post World War II America, when more people began to migrate to the suburbs.

Even though many of Cheever's stories are set during the turbulent times of the sixties and seventies during the Civil Rights Movement and Feminist Movement, Cheever's stories do not reflect politics directly. As R. G. Collins points out, Cheever has been "repeatedly attacked by what might be thought of as socially-conscious critics, who felt that his very subject matter confirmed his irresponsibility, since he failed to involve himself with the social realism of proletarian life" (3). During the sixties and seventies, much political and social change occurred in America. People began to fight for the rights of minorities and women. Political rallies were held, some rioting occurred, and other forms of demonstration took place across the country. Legislation was developed to protect minorities and women and to attempt to ensure equality. Cheever's characters seem oblivious to the political climate of the sixties and seventies. Instead, they seem concerned with social status, hosting parties, and consuming alcohol. Much of the tension in his fiction involves internal conflict.

Cheever's short fiction plays a significant role in the historical development of the American short story. Cheever's stories appeared so frequently in *The New Yorker* that his fiction has been defined as representative of what many critics call a vintage *New Yorker* story: "the maximum exploration and exploitation of a single dramatically presented incident, more or less strictly observing the unities of time and place and rich in implication, both in depth of characterization and in a larger implied story which had a past and predicted a future" (Garrett 53). As George Garrett points out, "The vintage *New Yorker* story has become a model for the modern short story" (53). Summing up definitions of *New Yorker* story, he says, it "was a fiction of manners, and its purpose, classical from tip to toe, was to instruct as it delighted" (54). As do many of Cheever's short stories, "The Swimmer" represents this definition of a vintage *New Yorker* story.

Societal Context

Cheever is well known for his portrayal of upper-middle-class suburban Americans. Frequently, he shows characters who cannot grasp a significant meaning in life and those who experience a mid-life crisis. Because Ned visits many people throughout the story, "The Swimmer" provides an excellent glimpse into the lifestyles of upper-middle-class suburban Americans. The story becomes almost a smorgasbord of these characters. Planning his route home, Ned lists the people he will encounter: "First there were the Grahams, the Hammers, the Lears, the Howlands, and the Crosscups. He would cross Ditmar Street to the Bunkers and come, after a short portage, to the Levys, the Welchers, and the public pool in Lancaster. Then there were the Hallorans, the Sachses, the Biswangers, Shirley Adams, the Gilmartins, and the Clydes" (714). Except for the public pool reference, the list of names provides an overview of the people with whom Ned socializes. In fact, the list of names reads almost like an invitation list for a party.

The story demonstrates Ned's digression from a prominent member of society to a person who is alone and has no home. As Ned encounters most of the characters listed, readers see that they live similar meaningless lifestyles. Significantly, at the end of the story Ned's house is "empty" (725), symbolic of his own life, as well as that of the acquaintances he has encountered throughout his journey.

When he makes his first stop at the Grahams', Ned already stands outside his social circle. Because he wants his journey uninterrupted, Ned does not want to spend time socializing with the people he encounters. However, he understands "like any explorer, that the hospitable customs and traditions of the natives would have to be handled with diplomacy if he was ever going to reach his destination" (715). This description likens Ned to an anthropologist, who looks at a society from the perspective of an outsider. However, the passage also demonstrates that Ned understands the need to perform socially accepted behavior. Later, Ned encounters the Biswangers, who frequently invite him and Lucinda to dinner even though they always decline. The Biswangers are "unwilling to comprehend the rigid and undemocratic realities of their society. They were the sort of people who discussed the price of things at cocktails, exchanged market tips during dinner, and after dinner told dirty stories to mixed company" (722). Importantly, "They did not belong to Neddy's set" and "Grace Biswanger was the kind of hostess who [invited] the optometrist, the veterinarian, the real-estate dealer, and the dentist" (722).

Significantly, the Biswangers' bartender snubs Ned, and Ned notes that "His was a world in which the caterer's men kept the social score, and to be rebuffed by a part-time barkeep meant that he had suffered some loss of social esteem" (723). As represented from the beginning of the story, Ned experiences a reverse social initiation: at the beginning of the story he is a welcomed party guest and thinks he owns a home and is the member of a content family, but by the end of the story he is shunned by his peers and realizes his house is empty and his family is gone.

Religious Context

When Ned sees his former lover, Shirley Adams, he wonders if "God forbid," she will cry. She asks, "Good Christ. Will you ever grow up?" (723).

Except for references to God made in vain, religion is conspicuously absent in the story. Rather than attending church or family picnics as religious and conservative families might do, the characters host parties in which adults gather outside and consume alcohol. Interestingly, the story takes place on a Sunday. The parties might be viewed as Sunday rituals, much like church services, performed routinely. Like church services, the parties are weekly social events.

Symbolically, Ned's experience has religious connotations. If the water symbolizes rebirth, Ned's immersions signify baptisms. This interpretation implies that Ned's journey represents a spiritual experience. In Christianity, baptism transforms one from unenlightenment to enlightenment, and Ned's immersions in water similarly transforms him from a state of unawareness to one of awareness. Also, the doctrines of Christianity and many other religions strive to bring individuals from darkness to light. Contrastingly, Ned begins his journey in the afternoon and ends it at night, suggesting that he moves from the light to the dark. Nonetheless, Ned's move from lightness to darkness brings about increasing awareness: although his symbolic baptism leads him into darkness, it enlightens him because he is forced to acknowledge that his family has gone and his house is empty. He comes to understand that he is no longer a part of the social group to which he once belonged.

Scientific & Technological Context
Science and technology are portrayed indirectly in "The Swimmer" as the means in which the story reveals an individual trying to cope with a meaningless life. Technological advances have provided opportunities for people to have swimming pools installed in their residences. Swimming pools provide the map for Ned's journey. Additionally, references to a train and plane represent technology. Amidst the approaching dark clouds, Ned sees an airplane circling and can "almost hear the pilot laugh with pleasure" (716). Simultaneously, he hears the whistle of a train and wonders what time it is. He considers the people who might be waiting for the local train, and his description offers readers a realistic glimpse of the types of people who ride the trains into the city: "a waiter, his tuxedo concealed by a raincoat, a dwarf with some flowers wrapped in newspaper, and a woman who had been crying…" (717). The sight of the plane and the sound of the train represent the reality that occurs while Ned is engaged in thought. Contrasting Ned's fantasy world, in which he swims home, a plane and a train are practical forms of transportation, representative of reality.

The storm presents a scientific element in the story. Ned contemplates storms: "Why did he love storms, what was the meaning of his excitement when the door sprang open and the rain wind fled rudely up the stairs, why had the simple task of shutting the windows of an old house seem fitting and urgent, why did the first watery notes of a storm wind have for him the unmistakable sound of good news, cheer, glad tidings?" (717). Ned relates storms to good news; however, bad news follows this particular storm, for after the storm Ned begins his downward spiral.

Biographical Context
John William Cheever was born on May 27, 1912, in Quincy, Massachusetts. When he was seventeen, he was expelled for smoking from Thayer Academy in South Braintree, Massachusetts. Cheever wrote "Expelled," a short story about his expulsion, which was published in *The New Republic* in 1930. During the early thirties, Cheever lived in Boston with his brother Fred after the two of them returned from a trip to Europe. Cheever moved to New York City in 1934, where he worked for the motion picture studio MGM and wrote fiction. He married Mary Winternitz in 1941, and the two of them had three children. According to several sources, Cheever had an unhappy marriage and

his personal relationships were affected by his alcoholism and his bisexuality.

During World War II, Cheever served in the military. In 1956 and 1957, he taught creative writing at Barnard College, and in the early-to-mid seventies, he taught at the University of Iowa, Boston University, and Sing Sing prison.

Cheever's earlier short stories were published in magazines such as *The New Republic* and *The Atlantic*. In the mid-thirties, he began to publish fiction regularly in "The New Yorker." Cheever continued for decades to contribute short fiction regularly to "The New Yorker," and his stories are considered a prototype of what critics refer to as a "*New Yorker* story." His first short story collection, "The Way Some People Live," appeared in 1943. Cheever published several collections of short stories, as well as many novels. Cheever is one of America's most prolific short-story writers and is often compared to John Updike and Saul Bellow for his contributions to American fiction, both in the short story and novel genres. His most critically acclaimed novels are "The Wapshot Chronicle" and "The Wapshot Scandal." Cheever continued to write until his death of cancer, on June 18, 1982.

Cheever has received many prestigious awards. He received a Guggenheim Fellowship in 1951. His novel "The Wapshot Chronicle" (1957), won the National Book Award. "The Stories of John Cheever" received the Pulitzer Prize, the American Book Award, and the National Book Critics Circle Award, a remarkable achievement for a short story collection.

Laurie Champion

Works Cited

Blythe, Hal, and Charlie Sweet. "Cheever's Dark Knight of the Soul: The Failed Quest of Neddy Merrill." *Studies in Short Fiction* 29 (1992): 347–52.

——. "Man-Made Vs. Natural Cycles: What Really Happens in 'The Swimmer.'" *Studies in Short Fiction* 27 (1990): 414–18.

Cheever, John. "The Swimmer." *The Stories of John Cheever.* New York: Ballantine, 1980. 713–25.

Collins, R. G. "Introduction." *Critical Essays on John Cheever.* Ed. R. G. Collins. Boston: G. K. Hall, 1982. 1–20.

Garrett, George. *John Cheever and the Charms of Innocence: The Craft of The Wapshot Scandal.* Critical Essays on John Cheever. Ed. R. G. Collins. Boston: G. K. Hall, 1982. 51–62.

Kozikowski, Stanley J. "Damned in a Fair Life: Cheever's 'The Swimmer.'" *Studies in Short Fiction* 30 (1993): 367–75.

O'Hara, James E. *John Cheever: A Study of the Short Fiction.* Boston: Twayne, 1989.

Waldeland, Lynne M. "Cheever, John." *American National Biography* Online. Feb. 2000.

San Diego State Univ. 22 Jan. 2006.

Discussion Questions

1. What do you think motivates Ned to travel home via the swimming pools of residents who live between the Westerhazys' and his home?

2. How might the story be different if told from a point of view other than Ned's?

3. What do you think is the source of Ned's discontentment?

4. What is the significance of the characters' alcohol consumption?

5. Is it important that Ned has had an affair? Why or why not?

6. What changes occur to Ned physically throughout the story?

7. Might part of Ned's experiences be merely his imagination?

8. Why do you think Ned continues his journey even though he lacks strength?

9. Why do you think Ned is mocked when he stands trying to cross the street?

10. Do you agree with Ned's ex-lover that he needs to grow up?

Essay Ideas

1. Discuss "The Swimmer" as a traditional journey story.
2. Explore the lifestyle(s) of the characters in the story.
3. Analyze the different emotions Ned experiences while on his way home.
4. Discuss Ned's experiences as representative of a particular stage he is going through (for example, a mid-life crisis).
5. Compare and contrast the characters Ned encounters while swimming home.

The Tell-Tale Heart

by Edgar Allan Poe

Content Synopsis

In the short story, "The Tell-Tale Heart," the narrator recounts his act of grisly murder against an old man in an effort to prove his sanity. The narrator insists from the start that he is not mad, just "very, very dreadfully nervous" (Poe 721). He says that he did not have a motive for killing the old man other than his disgust at the man's pale blue filmy eye. He describes the eye as "the eye of a vulture" and an "Evil Eye" and he confesses that it frightened him; once he got it into his head to kill the man, he could think of nothing else (721).

Throughout the narrative, the speaker pauses in his story telling to defend his sanity and uses the details of his wise, methodical killing as proof. He claims to have come into the man's room every night at midnight, ever so slowly and quietly. He says he would take an hour just to stick his head in the door. Once in the room, he would open his lantern slightly so he could watch the old man sleeping. He did this every night for a week but since the old man's evil eye was always closed at this time, the narrator could not bring himself to kill him.

On the eighth night, the narrator claims to have been more cautious than usual, but the old man wakes up when the narrator opens his bedroom door. The narrator describes hearing the old man groan with terror and expresses his recognition of the sound as he has had many horror-filled nights

himself. Without realizing it, the narrator is further revealing his own madness. Eventually, the narrator opens the lantern a crack and a beam of light lands on the open eye of the old man. In addition, he thinks he can hear the old man's beating heart, which he attributes to his "over-acuteness of the sense" (723). As the heartbeat grows faster, the narrator can take it no longer and attacks the old man smothering him with the bed. For many minutes, the heart continues to beat before the man dies.

In a misguided attempt to further demonstrate his sanity, the narrator describes in detail how he dismembered the corpse and placed the parts under the planks of the floor. He insists he was clean and precise and when the police knock on the door at a late hour, the narrator is confident that there is no evidence of his crime. He invites the officers in to search the house and then offers to sit and converse with them in the very room where he killed and buried the old man. As their visit progresses, however, the narrator becomes anxious and wishes them gone. His acute senses cause a ringing in his ears that will not cease. When he can take it no longer, he pulls up the planks and shows the men his crime and proclaims that the ringing in his ears was the beating of the old man's heart.

Symbols & Motifs

The heart in "The Tell-Tale Heart" serves a dual purpose. It is the source of the narrator's anxiety as he is watching the old man and its loud beating, which is most likely the beating of his own heart, is the impetus that drives him to kill. The heart also represents the narrator's inner demons, which are revealed, unintentionally, in the telling of the story. The narrator's own nervousness and guilt over his actions causes him to confess his crime.

Most of the story is set late at night and Poe focuses on the horrors of the dark. Not just the old man, but the narrator too, is frightened of the dark and recalls nights when he sat up groaning in fear of the noises and echoes present at night. The dark represents the unknown and it is in that unknown realm when a person's senses and their fears are more acute.

Madness is an important motif in the story as the narrator insists that he is not mad while detailing his act of murder upon a man with whom he had no other problem than his ugly eye. The narrator grows more anxious as the story progresses and his madness is fully revealed at the end of the story when he rips up the floorboards and claims to hear the beating of the dead man's heart.

Historical Context

Edgar Allan Poe was a key contributor to the Dark Romantic movement in literature in the mid-19th century in addition to such authors as Nathaniel Hawthorne and Herman Melville. Dark Romanticism evolved as a reaction to the optimistic Transcendental movement which espoused the belief that man could achieve enlightenment through a connection with nature. Poe and his more pessimistic contemporaries believed that man was more prone to sin and self-destruction as is evidenced by the narrator in "The Tell-Tale Heart." Dark Romantics also believed the world was shrouded in mystery and elements of the supernatural were not uncommon in the literature of the period; especially in Poe's work.

Societal Context

Poe took a specific interest in psychology and was a believer in the field of phrenology. Phrenology focused on the idea that certain areas of the brain had specific functions (Canada). His works often explored the inner workings of the human mind; in particular its dark side. Many of Poe's short stories have characters whose madness or wild imaginings lead to their self-destruction (Canada).

Religious Context

"The Tell-Tale Heart" does not have a specific religious context.

Scientific & Technological Context

"The Tell-Tale Heart" does not have a specific scientific or technological context.

Biographical Context

Edgar Allan Poe was born in Boston in 1809 to a traveling actor and actress. When Poe was born, his father abandoned his mother ("Edgar Allan Poe"). She died a few years later while on tour in Virginia and he was taken in by a wealthy couple in Richmond; John and Frances Allan, who could not have children. While the Allans cared for and educated Poe, they never formally adopted him and John Allan never warmed to his foster son. Once in college at the University of Virginia, Poe accrued a large gambling debt and John Allan withdrew him from school ("Edgar Allan Poe"). After a heated argument, Poe left home and moved to Boston.

In 1827, in Boston, Poe published a volume of poetry entitled "Tamerlane." The book did not sell well and, in need of money, Poe joined the army. Poe did not like the army but was promoted to the rank of sergeant major, and with the Allans' help, he enrolled in the U.S. Military Academy at West Point ("Edgar Allan Poe"). In 1829, Poe published another book of poems, "El Aaraaf," which received positive reviews. While at West Point, Allan's wife died and he remarried. Since Poe knew he would no longer be considered Allan's heir, Poe withdrew from West Point, and moved in with his aunt in Baltimore, Maryland ("Edgar Allan Poe").

In 1835, Poe married his chronically ill thirteen-year old cousin, Virginia. Poe worked as an editor at various magazines while trying to succeed as a writer ("Edgar Allan Poe"). He wrote only one full-length novel, "The Narrative of Arthur Gordon Pym" but his short stories became his claim to fame. Poe is given credit as the creator of the modern detective story with such stories as "The Gold Bug" and "The Murders in the Rue Morgue." Other stories, such as "The Tell-Tale Heart" and "The Cask of Amontillado" explore the inner demons of a person's mind. In 1845, he published the poem "The Raven," which brought him fame and solidified his career as a writer.

Unfortunately, alcohol abuse and financial instability continued to plague Poe throughout his life. When his wife died in 1847 of tuberculosis, Poe grew more unstable ("Edgar Allan Poe"). In 1849,

Poe disappeared and a week later he was found, battered and delirious, near a Baltimore tavern. He died four days later at the age of 40 and his death remains a mystery to this day.

Jennifer Bouchard

Works Cited

Canada, Mark, ed. "Edgar Allan Poe." *Canada's America.* 1997. 4 March 2008.

Edgar Allan Poe. *Great American Stories.* Austin: Holt, Rinehart and Winston, 1991. p.93.

Gioia, Dana and R.S. Gwynn, eds. "Edgar Allan Poe." *The Art of the Short Story.* New York: Pearson Longman, 1992. p.707.

International Movie Database. IMDB.com. 4 March 2008.

Poe, Edgar Allan. "The Tell-Tale Heart." Eds. Dana Gioia and R.S. Gwynn. *The Art of the Short Story.* New York: Pearson Longman, 1992. P.721–725.

The Edgar Allan Poe Society of Baltimore. 22 February 2008. 4 March 2008.

Discussion Questions

1. What is the tone of the narrator?
2. How does the setting of the story affect the mood?
3. To what does Poe compare the sound of the heartbeat? Why is this significant?
4. What effect is Poe creating by having the narrator watch the old man sleep for eight days before carrying out his plan?
5. Why does the narrator let the police officers freely search the house?
6. Why is the narrator unable to kill the old man before the eighth night?
7. What is the narrator's motive for the murder?
8. What explanation does the narrator offer in place of the idea that he is mad?
9. How is the crime discovered?
10. What is the significance of the title?

Essay Ideas

1. Describe and analyze Poe's literary style. Focus on his descriptions, the structure of his narrative and the ending of "The Tell-Tale Heart."
2. Write a journal entry from the perspective of one of the police officers after they have arrested the narrator. Note the speech and behavior of the narrator from the time he answered the door to the time he revealed the body.
3. Research mental illnesses such as schizophrenia and paranoia. Do you think the protagonist suffers from such a condition? Write an essay in which you defend your answer using examples from the text.
4. What might his story say about people in general? Use examples from the text to explain your thinking. In addition, discuss any people you have known, experiences you have had or other stories, movies, or works of art that may resemble this story.

To Build A Fire

by Jack London

Content Synopsis

"To Build A Fire" is one of the first of Jack London's short stories set in the Klondike during the Gold Rush years, and is arguably his most famous. The story has only two characters, a man and his dog. The man is a newcomer to the Klondike and is setting out from town to join his compatriots, referred to 'the boys' at a specified point on the Yukon River. The dog is with him, although the relationship between the man and the dog is more business-like than companionable.

Before he sets out on the trail, the newcomer is warned by a more experienced Klondike traveler, referred to as the old-timer from Sulphur Creek, that no man should travel alone when the temperature drops below −50 degrees. As he hikes along the trail, faintly visible under the trees along the winter in the dim light of the Yukon winter, the man dismisses the old-timer's advice. The man estimates the temperature to be about −75, and yet he is traveling at a good pace and estimates reaching 'the boys' by six o'clock.

Despite his confidence, the newcomer is wary of the many springs that dot the trail and appear as snow-covered ice, yet are filled with flowing water if the ice breaks through. He knows that if he stumbles into one of these springs, he must stop to build a fire and dry out his socks and moccasins. In this cold, he is well aware of the danger of frostbite and frozen limbs. He walks with a keen eye for slight depressions in the snow; a sure sign of an ice covered spring. But, just past noon when he is most confident of arriving at the meeting place, he sinks into the snow and crashes through the ice. He is wet up to his shins.

He does not panic, but calmly and methodically goes about building a fire to dry out his clothes. He forgets, however, the one rule of survival in the Yukon; never build a fire under snow covered tree limbs. Once his fire takes hold and the warm air rises, the boughs overhead shed their burden of snow. It falls and snuffs out the flames he has painstakingly started burning. He is now concerned and wonders if maybe the old-timer was right about having a trail partner. He begins to build a second fire out in the open. But now his fingers are so frozen, he fails to light a match. In desperation, he tries to light the whole pack of matches but succeeds only in dropping them in the snow.

The dog has been patiently waiting, hoping for a warm fire also and cannot understand why this human is unable to build a fire. The newcomer, now grasping the severity of his situation, considers killing the dog to warm his hands in the entrails. However, he does not have enough feeling in his hands to grasp his knife. In the end, the newcomer lays down allowing himself to drift into the sleep. The dog, smelling death, runs into the forest in the direction of other humans and other fires.

Symbols & Motifs

The singular motif in "To Build A Fire" is survival. This motif is expressed through the imagery of cold, especially as portrayed in the man's experience of frostbite, freezing extremities, and the freezing amber tobacco juice ice clinging to his beard. The man's confrontation of his own mortality in the Klondike—namely his hubris in going out on the trail alone and reliance on knowledge and skill is contrasted with the dog who relies on survival by his instincts. The nonspecific symbolism in the story is consistent with London's writing style which was based on realism. This realism, as well as the adventures played out in his stories, was the basis of his success as a writer and his appeal to publishers in the growing market of mass media and magazine publishing.

Historical Context

The historic context of "To Build A Fire" is rooted in the confluence of geography, namely the largely unexplored (at the time of London's writing) Yukon territory, and economy, specifically the Panics of 1893 and 1896. These financial crises caused widespread unemployment, recession, and numerous bank failures in the United States. The arrival of two ships, one in San Francisco and one in Seattle, in July 1897 bearing miners and their bags of gold, created an overnight sensation. It can be argued that these financial crises were the catalysts of the Gold Rush as thousands faced with the specter of poverty and financial ruin stampeded to the Klondike willing to risk life and limb for the prospect of quick wealth. Jack London himself was a victim of the national economic collapse and went to the Yukon with his brother-in-law to seek riches in the goldfield. Ultimately, most of the stampeders, as the mining adventurers came to be known, never realized their vision of quick wealth. By the time they arrived in the goldfields, most of claims along the creeks and riverbanks were already claimed (Waltham, 2007). The real wealth to be realized was in the retail trade with enterprising outfitters providing supplies and services needed by miners and travelers. This business was driven in part by the Canadian Mounted Police who, acknowledging the risk of survival in the remote and uninhabited territory, would not let prospectors cross over the Canadian border without a year's worth of supplies. As a result, business entrepreneurs trumped the prospectors in finding riches in the Yukon (Adventure Learning Foundation, 2009).

Societal Context

The society of the Yukon was characterized by a lust for adventure, risk-taking, and desperation. The lure of the Yukon was shared equally by professional men, business men, teachers, ne'er-do-wells and those generally down and out on their luck. Many women joined in the stampede as wives, husband-seekers, or business entrepreneurs in their own right. Living on the edge of survival created a society that was raw, free-wheeling and very much of-the-moment. With only three characters, the traveler, his dog, and reference to the old-timer, London shows the elemental nature of this society where traditional codes of behavior do not apply. Instinct and experience are the keys to survival not social values or laws of men. In fact, traditional law enforcement was minimal as the territory was too vast and the resources of the Canadian government, in the form of the Canadian Mounted Police, too scarce to be of great effect.

Religious Context

The lack of overt religious reference in the story is significant given the story's theme of survival, confrontation of mortality, and death. This however, is consistent with Jack London's life which does not give evidence of any specific religious belief or spiritual philosophy.

Scientific & Technological Context

The climate of the Klondike provides the geographic context for the story. There is a conspicuous lack of reference to science or technology. London relies on folklore and the observations of nature to inform his character and the character's subsequent actions. For example, the relative temperature is measured by specific natural phenomena, e.g. spittle freezing in the air before it hits the ground, breath freezing in the moustache and beard to such an extent that the man cannot open his mouth to bite his biscuit, and the presence of amber ice from dribbling tobacco juice down his chin. The knowledge needed to survive in the Yukon was largely based on folklore and the raw experience of survival in an inhospitable climate. In his journey, the main character relied on clues from the landscape. He surmised the location of deadly iced over springs by observing "the snow above the hidden pools had a sunken, candied appearance." His trail was a faint line. He had no compass, no maps, or any other tools to guide him or protect him. This lack of technology underscores the primitive society that characterized life in the Yukon. For the man in the story, and other Gold Rush stampeders, it was a contest of man vs. nature, each in its most primeval form.

Biographical Context

Jack London was born in San Francisco on January 12, 1876. His mother, Flora Wellman, was not married at the time of his birth and claimed his father to be William Chaney. Chaney denied the paternity. Wellman, in desperation, gave the baby to Virginia Prentiss, an ex-slave, who remained a powerful figure in London's life. Following recovery from an attempted suicide, Wellman married John London, a partially disabled Civil War veteran. The baby, now known as Jack London was re-united with his mother and the family eventually settled in Oakland, CA. At the age of 13, London quit school and went to work at a local cannery. It was grueling manual labor for 12–18 hour shifts. He quit this job and found subsequent work as an oyster pirate, then an oyster pirate patrol man, and then a worker on a Japanese sealing schooner. After quitting that job and returning to the United States, he became a vagrant, eventually ending up serving time in the Erie County (New York) penitentiary. He returned to California, finished high school, and at the age of 21, enrolled at the University of California at Berkeley. Financial circumstances prevented him from graduating from Berkeley and in 1897, he joined his brother-in-law, James Shepard and headed to the Klondike and the Yukon Gold Rush. Although he only spent one year at Berkeley, the experience profoundly influenced his thinking and his politics. London developed a philosophy of life centered on social Darwinism and socialist political ideology.

London's experience in the Klondike, like many others, ended in failure. He returned to Oakland in 1898 with a determination to "sell his brains" to earn a living. His experiences in the Klondike provided the basis for his short stories and novels. London was fortunate that the era of magazine publishing was blossoming at the same time he determined to make a living as a writer. His short stories, characterized by adventure and realism, were highly marketable and London soon was making a lucrative living as a writer.

London was married twice, first to Bess Maddem (1900–1904) who bore him two daughters, Joan and Little Bess. They divorced and in 1905 he married Charmian Kittredge. In 1905, he purchased 1000 acres in Glen Ellen, Sonoma County, California and began building Beauty Ranch. His dream was to make the ranch self-sustaining. To this end, he read and studied agriculture and animal husbandry. He continued to write novels, short stories, and news articles to support his family and his ranch activities. His adventures now included sailing and traveling to the South Pacific and Hawaii. He began construction of a 15,000 square foot mansion, to be called Wolf House. Tragically, the mansion burned to the ground just weeks before London was able to move in.

London died in 1916, at the age of 40. Many questions surround his death. His early life of adventure and risk taking as well as alcoholism took a toll on his body. He was suffering extreme pain from uremic poisoning and speculation exists that he either accidentally overdosed on morphine prescribed for his pain, or he deliberately overdosed. London is buried on his Glen Ellen Ranch, now maintained as Jack London State Historic Park.

Michele L. Kreidler

Works Cited

Adventure Learning Foundation. "Klondike Gold Rush Yukon Territory 1897." 2009. 14 Feb. 2009.

London, Jack. "To Build A Fire." *The Collected Jack London.* Ed. Steven J. Kasdin. New York: Marlboro Books, 1991.

Marciano, Alain. "Economists on Darwin's theory of social evolution and human behavior." *European Journal of History of Economic Thought.* 2007: 4(4), 681–700. EBSCO Online Database Academic Search Premier. 19 Feb. 2009.

Waltham, Tony. "Klondike Gold." *Geology Today.* 2007: 23(6), 219–226. EBSCO Online Database Academic Search Premier. 14 Feb. 2009.

Discussion Questions

1. Was the character in the story, "the man," prepared to make this journey? What could he have done differently?
2. The man was warned not to travel alone if the temperature was below −50 degrees. Why did he chose to travel alone?
3. What is the role of the dog in the story?
4. How does London use sensory elements in the story to describe the cold?
5. At what point in the story did the man realize he was going to die?
6. What was the man's reaction to realizing he was in mortal danger?
7. Did the man prepare himself for death? In what ways?
8. What do we know about the Old-Timer? What role does he play in the story?

Essay Ideas

1. "To Build A Fire" has only two characters in the story—the dog and the man. The climate, specifically the cold, has a significant role in the story. Can you say the cold also serves as a character in the story? Why or why not?
2. Portions of the story are told from the point of view of the dog. Is this significant to the story? In what ways?
3. We assume at the conclusion of the story that the dog survived. Why did London spare the dog's life? Is this significant to the story?
4. Jack London espoused the philosophy of 'social Darwinism.' How is this philosophy expressed in the story?
5. The man was warned about traveling in the severe cold. He was also new to life in the Yukon. Did he deserve to die? Why/why not?

Jack London was an American author, journalist and social activist. Best remembered as the author of *The Call of the Wild*, London's work was influenced by the Naturalism and Realism Movements in literature; two of his short stories are included in this volume: *The Law of Life* and *To Build a Fire*. Photo: Library of Congress, Prints & Photographs division, LC-DIG-ggbain-00676.

Vegetable Love

by Max Apple

Content Synopsis

There are only two principal characters in this short story: Ferguson and Annette Grim. Set sometime after 1971, Ferguson, the protagonist of this story, is a 28-year-old loner, a CPA at a local office, and law school student. Annette, the unlikely object of his affection, works for Prudential Insurance, typing up amendments to policies. Figured as opposites, one a happy meat eater, one a militant vegetarian, the story unravels as an exploration of love structured around the symbolic eating patterns of the two and the ways in which food represents love. Annette's point blank statement "I never make love to meat eaters" (78) becomes the catalyst and challenge to Ferguson who quickly makes Annette the center of his life. Meeting in a supermarket sets the perfect stage for the story's focus. Their chance encounter in which Annette accidentally rams her shopping cart into Ferguson's groin presages the pain he will feel in the doomed relationship. Annette's first response to damaging Ferguson is to slide her hand "under his zipper" to soothe the pain, an action which while seeming to mean little to her, means worlds to him (78). Much of the text is symbolic, from the ways in which Ferguson "blocks" the way to Annette's destination, to the "mushrooms" and "nuts" that populate their initial confrontation to their very names, one of which suggests a forbidding trap.

Despite the fact that Ferguson is depicted as a rather carnal person in terms of his love for meat, which he devours with a certain lustfulness, he initially embraces Annette's way of life as a way of relating to her and becoming more attractive to her. Annette's stoic and ascetic lifestyle, reflected in the food she keeps in her apartment—brewer's yeast, a coconut, and moldy beans—does not change at all. In her cupboards are spices, a record player, oats, wheat germ and a color poster of yogurt (78). The conflation of eating with sexuality is highlighted at several points. After one early sexual encounter between the two, Ferguson, while "gratified by her flesh," leaves Annette in bed and goes in search of further sustenance (78). He even perceives his meat consumption as "cheating" on Annette. The connection between meat and carnality is again developed later when, after tasting a mere bite of hamburger, he feels he has received enough protein and energy to "force her somewhat" into having sex with him while "suffered the carnivore upon her" (79).

In the course of the first month of their relationship, Ferguson grows smaller, losing fourteen pounds. This loss is both physical and symbolic. At this point, the loss is depicted as a positive thing in which Ferguson sheds not only extra pounds, but also some of his preconceptions. However, it also sets the stage for the larger losses of self he will suffer before finally reaching peace with himself.

Annette never directly attempts to change Ferguson's eating habits. She works by example and subtle commentary. Ferguson is responsible for measuring his progress through her eyes. She "expressed no pride in him, but she did not reject him either" (80). When he met Annette, Ferguson weighed a hefty 194 pounds. By the third month he drops down to 155 "and [is] shrinking" (79). His friends, who appear concerned, move from suggesting he see a doctor to suggesting he see a psychiatrist.

Ferguson decides to propose to Annette about three months after they begin their relationship. Annette has a "spot" identified by her as the "center of [her] consciousnesses" located within her right ribcage (79). After consulting this spot to seek an answer to his marriage proposal, she replies "'I have this strange feeling that even though I love you too, we aren't ready for each other" (80). She tells Ferguson that until he finds his spot, which only "partly has to do with what you eat or don't eat," they can have no real permanent future (80).

Annette refuses to attend Ferguson's graduation from law school because she has no respect for the profession and objects to what she perceives will be a Texas style meat-a-thon at the graduation banquet. Her decision not to support Ferguson leads to their first real fight. Though Ferguson decides he will not partake of the meat at the dinner, he has a

change of heart. Instead of a fruit plate, the dinner he ordered, he is given steak. The meat he is offered has subtle sexual qualities that add to its tempting presence, "butterflied so that it spread open" before him, he is unable to resist and in Biblical language he ate and "saw that it was good" (81). He returns that evening to his own apartment alone, sporting an almost post-coital "ruddy healthy glow" (81).

When Ferguson goes to Annette's apartment the following day, she has disappeared without a trace. His 'infidelity' in which he consumes a steak with sexual relish in order to get back at Annette causes him to believe this is what precipitates her leaving him. This is proven to be false when he finds from the landlord she had given notice a full two weeks before packing up her mung beans and leaving. She had also given a similar notice at her job. Without any sense of closure, Ferguson becomes obsessed. In spite of the evidence presented to him, "She did not fool him" and "he knew…that had he not left her for that Thursday night banquet he would not be alone now" (82). He resolves, after a two-day fast, to begin the search for his 'spot' as a kind of way of understanding Annette's disappearance.

For the remainder of the story, Ferguson all but disappears, starting with a thirty-day rice diet after which his weight plummets to 147 pounds. After his 34 days of penance fail to bring back Annette, Ferguson realizes that "it was something else" besides his steak that precipitated her move (83). At 142 pounds, Ferguson experiences hallucinations. At 134 pounds, Ferguson changes. He continues to seek his spot for Annette, but keeps eating as a vegetarian for himself. He becomes "strong and bony as a fist," ultra productive, doing "the work of five men," his co-workers call him "the computer" a nickname that changes along with Ferg's body to become "the pocket calculator" (84). When Ferguson plummets to 128 pounds after five months, his boss insists he take a vacation during which he travels to Dallas, a location Annette's landlord suggested.

While searching for Annette, Ferguson visits Pelops Arms, a restaurant where he meets Kathleen Simpson, a quasi-vegetarian to whom Ferguson discloses all the details of his relationship. Kathleen agrees to help Ferguson in his quest and takes him to the rather symbolically named "Garden of Eden" store. Eventually Ferguson wanders to the only historical landmark he knows in the city, the grassy knoll where J.F.K's assassin supposedly stood. His thought process about that fateful day takes him to the point of questioning whether or not the great people of history had spots. His conclusion that "if important people had spots and listened to them, things would not go wrong in the world" (87) leads to his epiphany that, far from being the norm, having a "spot" like Annette is rather an oddity. Ferguson, on the heels of this realization, shouts to the traffic from the top of the knoll to Annette: "You were my spot and your spot didn't know it" (87).

Ferguson runs, and runs, and runs until he finds Kathleen Simpson. Telling her he had, in fact, found Annette, he asks Kathleen to join him, running with him "to Houston for dinner and then through Mexico to the Pan American Highway, along the banks of the Amazon, over the Chilean Andes, right into Buenos Aires" (88). With only a moment's hesitation, Kathleen drops her apron and order pad and runs along with Ferguson "side by side" (88). In an interview, Apple discusses the ending of the story: "the man and the waitress put on their running shoes and go off to Mexico. It means that his quest is for nothing less extravagant than the meaning of life. But if I put it like that, who'd want to read it? Who'd want to write it?" (qtd. in Plymell).

Historical Context

The late sixties and early seventies birthed a consciousness about food that often went hand-in-hand with a political statement about consumer society. Starting with hippie culture and moving forward

to feminism, food and consumption came to mean not only what one put in one's mouth, but also was a symbol of one's attitude towards all things commercial. Annette, aside from representing the new ideas about eating and living, also reflects, in a certain sense, the emerging 70s Feminist Movement. Annette is described as a woman of utility and self-discipline; she "was eighty percent protein and water. She used no deodorants, nor did she shave her legs or underarms or cut her hair…She hadn't had a cold since the day after Nixon announced the bombing of Hanoi and Haiphong" (79). Ferguson, on the other hand, is "full of dead meats artificial flavors and additives" (79).

The notion of fast food introduced by Annette during a conversation with Ferguson reflects the growing popularity at the time of hamburger franchises like McDonald's. From 1900–1960 meat consumption in the United States reached an all time high due to advanced techniques for refrigeration and transportation. Two books published around the time the story is set reveal the basis for some of Annette's philosophies. Lappe's Diet for a Small Planet was published in 1971, launching the vegetarian movement in the U.S. Peter Singer's Animal Liberation (1975) also had an effect on meat consumption, and provided the impetus for the U.S. animal rights movement and the foundation of PETA.

Societal Context

"Vegetable Love" is essentially a satiric parody of "American obsessions with health and diet," particularly in the 1970s" (Gioia 78). Yet the story is also a kind of romantic, if twisted, exploration of love and development of identity, exploring the ways in which lovers influence each other's actions in both positive and negative ways. Notable for its male protagonist, Ferguson, the story offers a male's view of rather obsessive love. The social shift to a more consumer-driven economy in 1970s America is reflected in Ferguson and Annette. The tenor of their relationship changes after Ferguson's proposal. They became "potential parents, potential owners of houses, cars and major appliances" (81), a hint at the consumer culture already growing in America.

The social difficulties of finding love and companionship are central to this piece. The title recalls Andrew Marvel's "To His Coy Mistress," a poem written in the seventeenth century which lines echo many of the ideas in the text, most importantly: "My vegetable love should grow/ vaster than empires and more slow." The poem's carpe diem theme in which a man attempts to convince a virgin to give in to sexual desire, uses the argument that time is short and people must explore and enjoy all the pleasures the body has to offer. In its convincing tone, argument and the sense that the woman is reluctant to change her virginal ways, the poem reflects some of the themes of the story. Marvel's speaker's focus on the body of his lover upon which he would lavishly spend "Two hundred [years] to adore each breast/ but thirty thousand to the rest" as well as other images exploring the speaker's passion as devouring relate to the same bodily emphasis explored in "Vegetable Love."

Religious Context

Annette pronounces to Ferguson "to me the body is a temple. Would you bring a steak into a temple?" (78). In fact, a temple was often the site of ritualistic sacrifice and offering in which meat was given up to the gods in return for favors and as tribute. When Ferguson points out this fact, Annette replies that such offerings represent not 'true' religion but "paganism"—another reference to carnality. In the absence of any specific religious preferences given by the characters themselves, the story becomes an exploration of spirituality in general as well as the clash between science and religion. Annette is described as "converting" Ferguson to her way of life, much like a religious

conversion. (78). Annette's spot is an interestingly physical manifestation of the only religion she seems to embrace: the cult of self. She states "This is its place, my body's soul lives here. This is not the spirit or soul that maybe doesn't exist. This is a real one. You can find it without God or Jesus," (79) reflecting the difficulties of believing in a religion removed from the self in which one has no real control. Charles Plymell states, "Annette is religious about her vegetarianism, as a sign on her wall reminds Ferguson: 'The more flesh, the more worms.'"

Scientific & Technological Context

Increased knowledge about the preparation and processing of meat, as well as the conditions under which animals were kept before slaughter influenced many people to embrace vegetarianism. New scientific understanding of digestion, additives and their effects on the body is also used in the text as evidence given by Annette for eschewing all meat consumption. Annette addresses the new convenience foods by suggesting they have become necessary in order for meat eaters to make up for the time they waste digesting meat, saying that fast food shops "are to the modern meat eater what fire was to his apelike ancestor" (80). Ironically, in opposition to what Annette deems as kind of barbaric custom, many anthropologists agree vegetarianism was the diet of pre-modern humans. This would position vegetarianism as an evolutionary throw-back rather than the wave of the future she seems to believe she is riding. Parallel to the advances of the day in which scientists were "finding out the secret codes of genetic reproduction," Ferguson wonders if one day the spot will also be located technologically, a "fingernail of RNA itself like a fingernail of DNA" (84). But locating Ferguson's own spot "doctors could not help, nor because of the personal and secular nature of the spot could theologians, or friends or entertainment or art" (84).

Biographical Context

Apple grew up in Grand Rapids, Michigan in a Yiddish-speaking home, received his Ph.D. in English from the University of Michigan in 1970 and currently serves as Fox Professor of English at Rice University. His early life with immigrant grandfather Rocky and eccentric grandmother "Gootie" have served as points of reference for his memoirs. His first two books, *The Oranging of America* and *Zip* "established his reputation for wildly inventive, satirical observations of American life" (Gioia and Gwynn 77). One critic points out his lure for readers in his stories which "give us a feel for our own loony culture" (Gioia and Gwynn 77). Apple's popularity stems from "charming nostalgia that Apple generates for these characters and their times, even as they are butts of ridicule. It is a quality that makes [*The Oranging of America*] far more than just another cute barrage of pot shots at the ravaged American dream" (qtd. in Johnson). Victoria Price notes four major themes that run through Apple's work: American fascination with the "new;" the need for safety versus the need to explore the unexplored; the space between the American Dream and American reality; and the "ambiguity inherent in American enterprise."

Tracy M. Caldwell

Works Cited

Apple, Max. "Vegetable Love." *The Longman Anthology of Short Fiction: Stories and Authors in Context*. Eds. Dana Giola and R.S. Gwynn. New York: Longman, 2001.78–88.

Gioia, Dana and R. S. Gwynn, Eds. *The Longman Anthology of Short Fiction: Stories and Authors in Context*. New York: Longman, 2001.

Johnson, Anne Janette. "Max Apple." *Contemporary Authors Online*. Literary Resource Center. Gale. 12 September 2005.

Plymell, Charles. "Max Apple." *Dictionary of Literary Biography, Volume 130: American Short-Story Writers Since World War II*. Ed. Patrick Meanor. Literature Resource Center, Gale Group. 12 Sept. 2005.

Price, Victoria. Critical Survey of Short Fiction, Second Revised Ed. *MagillOnLiteraturePlus*. EBSCO. 12 Sept. 2005.

Discussion Questions

1. What is important about how the characters meet? Can you envision another place they might have first encountered one another that would have led to the same kind of theme?

2. What is Annette's "spot?" Can you think of a religious cognate for the idea of finding a spot?

3. Why is it so hard to Ferguson to find his spot? Do you think the thing he finds is truly his spot?

4. How does Annette feel about Ferguson's bodily metamorphosis? Is she supportive of the changes he has made? Why or why not?

5. Why do you think Ferguson feels so strongly about Annette attending the banquet? Is he right in feeling that she should be there?

6. How involved is Annette in their relationship? Give examples to support your assertion.

7. Explain the epiphany Ferguson has on the grassy knoll. What does JFK's death have to do with his situation? Why choose that historical figure?

8. Does this seem like a realistic story? In what ways can you identify with the characters? What is your experience of the result of changing yourself in order to please someone you love?

9. Where is the climax of the piece? Where is the resolution? Do you feel satisfied with the ending Apple provides?

10. What is the theme of the story? Is there more than one possible theme?

Essay Ideas

1. Write an essay that compares and contrasts Annette and Ferguson. Argue whether or not their relationship was doomed from the start that their relationship was probably doomed from the start.

2. Explain how setting contributes to the development of themes in the story.

3. Explain the symbols in the text including names, the title, bodily metamorphosis, food, and running.

4. Analyze the role of irony in the story using three specific examples.

5. Analyze the characterization of Ferguson. How is his character developed? Does he seem to be a hero or antihero?

What We Talk about When We Talk about Love

by Raymond Carver

Content Synopsis

Raymond Carver's short story, "What We Talk about When We Talk about Love," is set in Albuquerque and takes place during one afternoon. The story involves discussions between two couples about the essence of romantic love. Mel McGinnis, a forty-five year old cardiologist, is married to Terri. Nick, the thirty-eight-year-old narrator of the story, is married to Laura, a thirty-five-year-old legal secretary. The story proper involves the four of them while they sit at a table and drink gin. Because not much happens in terms of plot development, the gist of the story consists of dialogue between the characters.

The socializing between the couples centers on alcohol consumption, and without it they are at a loss for words and action. Throughout the story, references are made to the alcohol the characters drink. At the beginning of the story, a reference to alcohol helps set-up the plot. Nick says, "The gin and the tonic water kept going around, and we somehow got on the subject of love" (128). Later, Mel presents a toast of gin "to true love" (132). While Mel and Terri are talking about Ed, "Terri drank from her glass…. She poured the last of the gin into her glass and waggled the bottle. Mel got up from the table and went to the cupboard. He took down another bottle" (131). In the middle of

his story about the elderly couple, Mel says, "Let's drink this cheapo gin the hell up…. Then we're going to dinner, right? … But we're not going until we finish up this cut-rate, lousy gin" (135). After Mel zealously explains the impermanent nature of love, Terri asks him if he is drunk, he refutes her, and she tells him not to act drunk. Near the end of the story, Nick says, "Maybe we were a little drunk by then. I know it was hard keeping things in focus" (138). Near the end of the story, when Mel suggests they go eat, Nick says, "Eat or not eat. Or keep drinking. I could head right on out into the sunset" (139). At the end of the story, Mel spills his glass of gin and says, "Gin's gone," and Terry says, "Now what?" (139).

While not much happens between the characters sitting at the table, the theme concerns the stories about love the characters tell. Two of the stories told serve as framed narratives, or stories-within-stories. Terri and Mel tell Nick and Laura about Terri's past relationship with Ed, the man she lived with before she married Mel. Terri maintains that Ed loved her even though he abused her physically and emotionally. She gives examples such as the night Ed dragged her by the ankles and screamed curse words at her. Mel says that Ed was crazy and that he frequently harassed and threatened Mel. Terri says, "We lived like fugitives. We were afraid" (131). When Terri left Ed, he drank rat poison to attempt suicide, and he eventually shot himself and spent three days in the hospital before he died. Mel did not want Terri to visit Ed in the hospital, but she did, and was with him when he died. Terri describes the sentiments between her and Ed as representing love and adds, "Sure, it's abnormal in most people's eyes. But he was willing to die for it. He did die for it" (131). On the other hand, Mel says, "If you call that love, you can have it" and "I sure as hell wouldn't call it love" (131).

Prior to telling the second framed narrative in the story, Mel announces the story he is about to tell "ought to make us feel ashamed when we talk like we know what we're talking about when we talk about love" (134). He uses the story as an example of "what real love is" (132). The story concerns an elderly couple whom Mel treated in the hospital. A drunken teenager had hit their camper on the interstate and they suffered from serious fractures and internal injuries. The couple spent two weeks in ICU. They were both wearing body casts, with holes cut for their eyes, nose, and mouth. Mel explains that the old man became depressed not because he was injured but because he could not see his wife through the holes in his cast. When Mel finishes this story, he asks the other characters if they understand his point.

While Mel and Terri argue, and the stories told during the conversations demonstrate extreme examples of the nature of love, Nick and Laura demonstrate a more subtle love for each other. Nick and Laura have been married almost a year and a half, and they frequently touch each other or give facial gestures that express endearing sentiments. When Mel says he will explain love, Nick and Laura touch knees, and Nick places his hand on her thigh. While Mel and Terri discuss Ed's abuse of Terri, Nick reaches to hold Laura's hand, and she smiles at him. When Laura announces that she and Nick understand love, she looks at

Nick to explain. He answers by kissing Laura's hand. Nick describes his relationship with Laura: "In addition to being in love, we like each other and enjoy one another's company. She's easy to be with" (131).

After the story about the elderly couple, Mel says that he wants to call his children, but Terri warns him that Marjorie, his ex-wife, might answer the phone. Terri explains that Mel is supporting Marjorie, her boyfriend, and his children. Mel says he wants to release a swarm of bees in Marjorie's house, and Terri says that Mel wishes Marjorie would get remarried or die. Instead of calling his children, Mel suggests that the characters go out to eat. Although they seem to reach a consensus to go out, Terri says she will serve cheese and crackers. The plot is circular, for the story ends where it began, with the two couples still sitting at the table.

Symbols & Motifs
The title of the story, "What We Talk about When We Talk about Love," sums up the surface level subject of the story. The title echoes Mel's comment that the old couple's feelings for each other should make everyone feel ashamed when they talk as if they understand love. That a version of Mel's comment is used as the title of the story suggests that the old couple experiences genuine love, while the characters who discuss love merely talk about it but do not fully understand or experience it.

As in many of Carver's stories, consumption of alcohol is prevalent in the "What We Talk about When We Talk about Love." Alcohol consumption is significant because the story demonstrates how it might influence both what the characters say and their attitudes. The characters are drinking during the day, suggesting that drinking is part of their routine, and although the story does not state how often the couples visit each other, it implies that they drink together frequently.

Storytelling is a motif that runs throughout the story. The narrative involves "framed" stories. The story about Terri and Ed and the story about the old couple who Mel treats at the hospital are the notable framed narratives. During these stories, listeners ask questions and interrupt. Storytellers digress until prompted to finish their stories and make sure the points of their stories are understood. In this way, the framed narratives within "What We Talk about When We Talk about Love," the framing story, can be viewed as demonstrative of the way we tell stories.

Minor symbols include the bees and the roles referred to during the discussion of the feudal system. The bees might symbolize Mel's rage toward his ex-wife and his need for revenge. The knights, serfs, and vassals might symbolize various hierarchical relationships among people, suggesting that love between two people entails some sort of hierarchical association. Even though Mel mispronounces "vassal," he says "everyone is always a vessel to someone" (136).

Historical Context

The story was first published in the 1970s, during the beginning of the American short story renaissance. Among other Carver stories, "What We Talk about When We Talk about Love" is usually classified as minimalist fiction. Minimalism is a writing style in which most of the plot occurs beneath the surface. Among other attributes, minimalist fiction is realistic, often depicts working-class characters, and frequently presents open-ended conclusions. Chekhov is exemplary of a minimalist fiction writer and often credited with originating the technique. Hemingway is credited with developing the American minimalist short story, and his well known "iceberg theory," in which he says that seven-eighths of the action of a story takes place under the surface of the plot, provides a good definition of minimalism. Carver acknowledges Hemingway and

Chekhov as important writing influences, and he revived the minimalist short story tradition in America more significantly than any other writer during the 1970s. Other contemporary American minimalist short story writers include Ann Beattie, Tobias Wolff, Frederick Barthelme, Amy Hempel, and Grace Paley. Carver made his writing debut during an important time period in the history of the American short story. American short stories were gaining critical acclaim due to many factors, including the increasing popularity of university fiction writing workshops, increased critical attention given to the genre, and the rise in prestigious awards and grants given to American short story writers.

Societal Context

This is a character-driven story that explores ways humans interact and their roles in society: spouse, ex-spouse, doctor, patient, friend, etc. The story departs from most of Carver's short fiction, which depicts working class characters. Although Mel resents supporting his ex-wife, he is a cardiologist, and he and Terri do not seem to struggle financially. Likewise, Nick and Laura do not mention financial difficulties. The story is a realistic portrayal of a sort of day-in-the-life of two couples who are close friends. It shows ways friends communicate with each other, as well as demonstrating various ways humans experience romantic love.

Mel's references to the drunk driver reveal attitudes about drunk driving prevalent in today's society. When discussing feudal times, Mel says the armor prevented knights from getting hurt. He adds, "No drunk teenagers to tear into your ass" (136). This comment refers to the driver who collides with the old couple and suggests, by referring to medieval times, that the couple's love for each other is timeless. The discussion about the knights, vassals, and serfs has social connotations because it explains a society composed of a clearly structured class hierarchy.

Religious Context

Although Mel spent five years studying at a seminary before becoming a cardiologist and believes "real love [is] nothing less than spiritual love" (128), the story is not religious. In fact, it is significant that the characters do not add religious references as a context in which to discuss love. Nobody quotes the Bible or other religious sources when trying to define love. Prayer is only mentioned when Mel says he is "praying" that his ex-wife will either remarry or get stung to death by bees (139). The term "praying" is used casually and has no real religious bearing. The characters seek a secular definition of love, and the story about the old couple proves a fine example. It is interesting to note that Mel changed from seminary school to medical school, two fields that seem opposed when considering that one seeks divine intervention and the other depends on human knowledge and skill to cure humanity.

Scientific & Technological Context

Science and technology are portrayed in this story as Mel's role as a cardiologist and as reflective of modern times in which we drive cars. Mel describes his role as cardiologist in technical terms: "I'm just a mechanic. I go in and I fuck around and I fix things" (136). Significantly, his job as heart specialist is a significant factor that leads to his meeting of the old couple because he helps them survive their catastrophic injuries. Also, cars represent technology because the story is told in a context in which cars are a major source of transportation. If not for cars, the old couple would not have been injured and Mel would have never met them. Although science and technology are not thematically significant in and of themselves, they provide the means for the gist of the story. Rather than focusing directly on science or technology, the heart of the story concerns the way humans relate to each other, both as friends and as romantic partners.

Biographical Context

Raymond Carver was born in Clatskanie, Oregon on May 25, 1938 and was raised in Yakima, Washington. After graduating from high school, he worked in a sawmill with his father. In 1957, he married Maryann Burk, and by the time he was twenty, he and Maryann had two children. In 1958, he moved to California, where he worked blue-collar jobs such as gas station attendant and janitor. He earned a bachelor's degree in English from Humboldt State College. Shortly afterward, he attended the Iowa Writers Workshop. He began to drink heavily during this time, and in 1977, he recovered from alcohol abuse. Shortly after he quit drinking, he met the poet Tess Gallagher, whom he later married.

Carver's background provides clues to many of the subjects and themes he writes about. Carver grew up in a working-class environment, and, like himself, his father was an alcoholic. Similarly, many of Carver's characters are alcoholics and many struggle financially. Frequently, details in Carver's fiction demonstrate ways alcohol weakens, if not diminishes, one's quality of life. Also, many of the problems Carver's character face are intensified due to economic circumstance. Carver comments on the connection between his life and his fiction: "Most of what I write is about myself, even though I never write anything autobiographical.... A writer writes about what he knows, and in most cases that's himself." He says that his stories link himself "to a world that is part real, part imagination" (Tromp 79).

John Gardner, the author of the critically acclaimed "On Moral Fiction" and "The Art of Fiction," and Gordon Lish, "Esquire" fiction editor at the time Carver began writing fiction, served as Carver's mentors during his early writing career. His first nationally recognized publication was "Neighbors," which appeared in "Esquire." Carver wrote exclusively in the short fiction and lyric poetry genres. Many critics agree that Carver was instrumental in bringing about the American short story renaissance and maintain that he is the most distinguished American short story writer since Hemingway. He has received numerous prestigious awards such as a Guggenheim, two National Endowment of the Arts Awards, and Pulitzer Prize nominations. Raymond Carver died at age fifty, on August 1988, from cancer.

Laurie Champion

Works Cited

Campbell, Ewing. *Raymond Carver: A Study of the Short Fiction*. New York, Twayne, 1992.

Carver, Raymond. "What We Talk About When We Talk About Love." *Where I'm Calling From: New and Selected Stories*. New York: The Atlantic Monthly Press, 1986.

Champion, Laurie. "What We Talk About When We Talk ('About Love'): Carver and Chekhov." *Journal of the Short Story in English 28* (1997): 24–36.

Siebert, Hilary. "Raymond Carver." *A Reader's Companion to the Short Story in English,* ed. Erin Fallon, et al. Westport, CT: Greenwood, 2001. 95–104.

Stull, William. "Raymond Carver." *Dictionary of Literary Biography Yearbook: 1988.* Ed. J. M. Brook. Detroit: Gale Research, 1989. 199–213.

Tromp, Hansmaarten. "Any Good Writer Uses His Imagination to Convince the Reader." Interview with Raymond Carver. *Conversations With Raymond Carver.* Ed. Marshall Bruce Gentry and William L. Stull. Jackson: University Press of Mississippi, 1990. 72–83.

Discussion Questions

1. Do you agree with Mel that Terri and Ed did not experience a relationship based on love?
2. Do the characters in the story define love the way you would define it?
3. What type of emotions does Mel display during the story? Does his mood change as the story progresses?
4. Do you think the conversation between the characters is influenced by the fact that they are drinking gin?
5. The story suggests that people often fall in love more than once in their lifetimes. Do you agree or disagree with this concept?
6. What does the story imply is the nature of the relationship between Nick and Laura?
7. Why do you think Terri wanted to be with Ed when he was in the hospital?
8. Does the story have a sense of closure?
9. What is the significance of Nick's role as narrator of the story?
10. Sometimes literature raises questions rather than providing answers. Does "What We Talk about When We Talk about Love" explain or raise questions about the nature of romantic love?

Essay Ideas

1. Analyze ways the story about Terri and Ed and the story about the elderly couple relate to the discussions between Terri, Mel, Nick, and Laura.
2. Compare and contrast the various manifestations of love the story reveals.
3. Explore ways the main characters interact with each other.
4. Discuss the story as a "minimalist" story, one in which most of the action occurs beneath the surface.
5. Analyze the significance of drinking alcohol in the story.

Where I'm Calling From

by Raymond Carver

Content Synopsis

In the short story, "Where I'm Calling From," Raymond Carver provides a bird's eye view of life at an alcohol treatment center. Carver's narrator affects a matter-of-fact, but sincere, voice. He is an Average Joe except that he is in rehab "drying out" (Carver 581). The narrator's story begins with a description of the other people in the rehab center, focusing mainly on the story of Joe Penny with whom he is currently sitting on the front porch of Frank Martin's facility.

Through his description of J.P. and the other characters, the narrator reveals elements of himself even before he talks about himself and how he ended up in rehab directly. J.P. has the shakes; the narrator has a jerk in his shoulder. He explains how a "big fat guy" they call Tiny had a seizure after two weeks in rehab. Tiny had nicked his face shaving that morning but, "Just about everybody at Frank Martin's has nicks on his face" (Carver 582). The narrator describes how Tiny was sitting at breakfast telling old drinking stories and making everybody laugh when all of a sudden he was on the floor "heels drumming the linoleum" (582). Tiny's seizure is significant because the narrator fears that what happened to Tiny will happen to him.

As the narrator and J.P. sit on the porch, J.P. recounts his life story. When he was a child, he fell in a well and remained there terrified until his father came with a rope and rescued him. When he finished high school, he fell for a young woman chimney sweep and discovered he wanted to be one too. Eventually J.P. and the woman got married, had children and J.P joined the family chimney sweep business. J.P. recounts his happiness during this time but he nonetheless began to drink more and more until he was drinking all day long. J.P. then pauses in his story but the narrator encourages him to go on as it serves as a good distraction from the narrator's own problems. J.P. talks about how he and his wife fought all of the time and eventually she started seeing someone else. Once he got arrested for drunk-driving, which prevented him from driving his work truck, he decided to enter Frank Martin's facility. The narrator then says that everyone at Frank Martin's is there by choice.

The narrator then recalls his second entrance into Frank Martin's and reveals that he was drunk and said goodbye to his girlfriend who was also drunk. He remembers that as he was getting settled in, he saw two big guys drag J.P. into Frank Martin's by force. He realizes that they must have been his father-in-law and brother-in-law.

While the narrator and J.P. are sitting on the porch, Frank Martin comes outside to smoke his cigar. He points out that Jack London lived nearby and that alcohol killed him. He warns them that London was a great man but even he "couldn't handle the stuff" (Carver 588). Before going inside, Frank Martin tells them that he can help them if they let him. J.P. tells the narrator that Frank Martin makes him feel like a bug and that he wishes he had a name like Jack London.

The narrator remembers when his first wife brought him to Frank Martin's the first time and then just six months later when his girlfriend brought him to Frank Martin's for the second time. He mentions that she has a "mouthy teen-age son" and that she recently got a bad diagnosis from a Pap Smear (588). He and his girlfriend have not spoken since she dropped him off. The next day, which is New Year's Eve, the narrator calls his wife, rather than his girlfriend, but there is no answer.

J.P.'s wife comes to visit him the next day and the narrator has a flashback of his own failed marriage, from when he and his wife were happy newlyweds. He wants to connect with her again, but he does not know what to say or how to tell her where he is calling from; the reader is left with the image of the narrator removing change from his pocket.

Symbols & Motifs

In telling J.P.'s story, the narrator's voice switches back and forth from 'I' to 'We' to remind the reader where the narrator is coming from; the narrator is not one of us, he is one of them: "Like the rest of us at Frank Martin's, J.P. is first and foremost a drunk" (Carver 581). The narrator empathizes with J.P. because he is like him.

The narrator relays the events of J.P.'s life story and how he ended up at Frank Martin's. He begins with the time when J.P. fell in a well as a child. This is an apt metaphor for hitting rock bottom; J.P.'s fears while waiting for help are expressed. J.P. then tells the narrator how he met his wife and found a career as a chimney sweep. His life was good, but for some reason, he began drinking more. The narrator interrupts this story about J.P. asking rhetorically, "who knows why we do what

we do?" then returns to his story (Carver 585). These types of interruptions in narrative reveal more about the narrator of the story than the person he is talking about.

After relaying J.P.'s story, the narrator jumps back into the "I" voice and shares some background on how he ended up at Frank Martin's two times. He depicts the drive to Frank Martin's with his girlfriend and how they drank champagne on the ride there (Carver 589). He and his girlfriend haven't talked since he got to Frank Martin's and it seems that neither one of them can understand what the other is going through. The narrator assumes his "we" voice when he talks about J.P, further revealing his connection to his fellow drunks. They understand one another; they understand how it can happen, how people can slip. When talking about his past relationships, he must revert back to the "I" voice because he is alone in the world of memory.

The narrator also references the Jack London story, "To Build a Fire"; a survival story of man against nature. He recalls how the London character is almost able to get a fire going before it goes out and he ultimately loses against nature (594). Through this reference, the narrator is able to reveal his fear of failure without admitting it directly.

Like Jack London, and Tiny and J.P., the narrator's story is one of survival but also one of love and longing. The title suggests the narrator's attempt to explain what he is going through. His memories of marriage, his depiction of his girlfriend, his hesitation of which woman to call for support, all contribute to his experience. His memories and observations of the world reveal his inner battles and his inability to find a comfortable place in the world.

Historical Context

One June 2, 1977, after ten years of excessive drinking, Raymond Carver quit. He admitted to being out of control and recognized that drinking had ruined his health, family and writing (Luce). In the year before he quit, Carver's wife took their children and left him and he was hospitalized four times for alcoholism (Luce). After he quit, Carver credited Alcoholics Anonymous for helping him and began a fresh start; what he called his "other life" (Luce).

In the three years after Carver got sober, he wrote and published about 12 new stories dealing with marriages falling apart and the painful struggles of alcoholism, including "Where I'm Calling From" (Luce). Carver and his wife did get back together for a time, but the two eventually separated and divorced in the 1982 (Luce). In the meantime, Carver had met the poet Tess Gallagher and the two became a pair for the remainder of his life.

Carver admitted that although he had moved past his dreary life as an alcoholic: "In this second life, this post-drinking life, I still retain a certain sense of pessimism" (Luce). The ending of "Where I'm Calling From" hints at this. While there is a sense of hope, the narrator is left in limbo; unsure of who he will reach out to and unsure if that person will reach back or if he will be left alone.

Societal Context

Raymond Carver's writing is considered an offshoot of American realism (Robinson). The focus of his stories is on ordinary people living ordinary lives that are often disrupted by marital problems, alcoholism, and dissatisfying jobs (Robinson). Tom Luce describes Carver's characters as living "unheroic lives, most simple and most ordinary and therefore most terrible" (Luce). The subject matter of Carver's work reflects the lives of real people living in the 1970s and 80s.

Although Carver himself did get divorced, the characters in his stories never quite get to that point. According to Marilynne Robinson, Carver demonstrates marriage as, "desperately vulnerable to derangement and bad luck, but always precious in itself, its lost pleasures always loyally remembered" (Robinson). In "Where I'm Calling From," the narrator is estranged from his wife but still dependent on her, and at the end of the day, she is the one he tries to call.

Religious Context

"Where I'm Calling From" does not have a specific religious context.

Scientific & Technological Context

"Where I'm Calling From" does not have a specific scientific or technological context.

Biographical Context

Raymond Carver was born in Clatskanie, Oregon in 1938 to a working class family (Goia and Gwynn). He spent most of his childhood in Yakima, Washington where his father worked as a sawmill worker (Goia and Gwynn). Carver married young and had two children. To support his family, Carver worked at a lumber mill and other manual labor jobs including picking tulips and cleaning toilets ("Rough Crossings"). Many of Carver's characters reflect the struggling working class people he spent most of his life around.

Carver attended Chico State College for a time where he studied with famed writer John Gardner. Carver then attended Humboldt State College (now University of California, Humboldt) where he graduated in 1963 (Goia and Gwynn). He also participated in the Writers' Workshop of the University of Iowa but was unable to finish and had to return to California due to family financial problems (Goia and Gwynn).

In 1967, the author met Gordon Lish, the editor at Esquire and then Knopf, who would eventually publish many of Carver's stories and helped establish his place in the literary world ("Rough Crossings"). Carver became known as a minimalist (although Carver did not like the term) and it appears that Lish may have been more responsible for Carver's minimalist stories than Carver himself ("Rough Crossings"). In 1968, he published a collection of poems "Near Klamath" (Goia and Gwynn). Throughout the 1970s, Carver taught at a series of universities for brief periods but marital problems and struggles with alcoholism flanked his success. In 1977, Carver quit drinking, a feat he considered to be his greatest accomplishment (Goia and Gwynn). He also published his first collection of short stories, "Will You Be Quiet, Please?" that same year; the collection was nominated for a National Book Award ("Rough Crossing"). Carver divorced his first wife and received a full time teaching appointment at Syracuse University in 1980 (Goia and Gwynn).

Carver published another collection of short stories, "What We Talk About When We Talk About Love," in 1981. Two years later, he received the Mildred and Harold Strauss Living Award, which allowed him to devote all of his time to writing (Goia and Gwynn). The author moved back to Washington and married his longtime girlfriend, poet Tess Gallagher, in 1988 (Goia and Gwynn).

Unfortunately, Carver died the same year due to lung cancer after a lifetime of smoking. His last story, "Errand," won the O. Henry Award later that year ("Rough Crossings").

Jennifer Bouchard

Works Cited

Carver, Raymond. "Where I'm Calling From." *The Best American Short Stories of the Century*. Ed. John Updike. Boston: Houghton Mifflin, 2000. P. 581–594.

Goia, Dana and R.S. Gwynn, eds. "Raymond Carver." New York: Pearson Longman, 1992. 347.

Luce, Tom. *Carver: The Raymond Carver Website*. 1997. Whitman College, 21 February 2008.

Robinson, Marilynne. "Marriage and Other Astonishing Bonds." *The New York Times,* 15 May 1988. 21 February 2008.

"Rough Crossings: The Cutting of Raymond Carver." *The New Yorker*. 24 December 2007. 21 February 2008.

Discussion Questions

1. What is the role of the narrator in this story?
2. What is the tone of the story?
3. How does the setting of the story affect the mood? What time of year is it?
4. What is the significance of Tiny's seizure for both the narrator and Tiny himself?
5. Why did Frank Martin mention the fact that Jack London lived nearby?
6. Compare and contrast the narrator to J.P. Who seems more likely to recover?
7. How would you describe the atmosphere at Frank Martin's?
8. What are some of the other patients like? What do they talk about?
9. How would you describe the ending of the story?
10. What are the main themes of the story?

Essay Ideas

1. Describe and analyze Carver's literary style. Focus on his minimalist descriptions, the structure of his narrative and the voice of the narrator of "Where I'm Calling From."
2. Discuss the voice of the narrator and how he uses the story of J.P. to reveal his own situations and problems.
3. Read the story "To Build a Fire" by Jack London. Write an essay in which you compare the protagonist of that story to the narrator in "Where I'm Calling From." Discuss why Carver made special mention of this story in his own.
4. Write an essay in which you compare this story to Carver's own personal struggles with alcoholism. What does he reveal through his characters about the nature of this struggle?
5. Write a story that, through the telling of another person's story, you reveal your own story.

Eudora Welty was a Pulitzer Prize winning American author and short story writer about the American South; two of her stories are included in this volume: *Why I Live at the P.O.* and *a Worn Path*. Photo: Library of Congress, Prints & Photographs Division, LC-USZ62-109631.

Why I Live at the P.O.

by Eudora Welty

Content Synopsis

"Why I Live at the P.O." takes place on the Fourth of July in China Grove, Mississippi. It is narrated by the first-person voice of Sister and takes the form of a dramatic monologue. Sister lives with her grandfather—Papa-Daddy—her Mama and her Uncle Rondo, who takes some mysterious medication every Fourth of July. The family constitutes "the main people" of China Grove (Collected 56). Much to Sister's chagrin, Stella-Rondo, the second daughter of the family, returns home that day. Stella-Rondo left China Grove to marry a man named Mr. Whitaker, a man who once courted Sister. The narrator tells us that Stella-Rondo stole Mr. Whitaker by telling him that her older sister was lop-sided. Stella-Rondo has returned with a child, Shirley T., whom she insists she has adopted. The rest of the family appears to believe her but Sister is convinced that the child is the offspring of Stella-Rondo and her old beau. Stella-Rondo also brings back her trousseau, which includes a pink kimono.

Throughout the story, Stella-Rondo and Sister argue. Stella-Rondo tells various family members that Sister has criticized them behind their backs, twisting Sister's words. She tells Papa-Daddy that Sister ridiculed his beard and Uncle Rondo that Sister laughed at him for wearing her pink kimono. Uncle Rondo punishes Sister by throwing firecrackers into her room the next morning. Sister

often appeals to the reader to witness what she actually said. Throughout the story, the family supports Stella-Rondo, reminding Sister that at least Stella left home and managed to find a man. Sister reminds them that as China Grove's postmistress of Mississippi's second smallest post office she has her own form of independence and has control of the family's communication with the outside world. Sister casts aspersions about Shirley T.'s state of mind because she has not spoken a word since her arrival. She reminds Mama of how Mr. Whitaker used to drink. Mama approaches Shirley T. who starts to sing Popeye the Sailor Man, proving Sister wrong. An argument builds concerning the parentage of Shirley T. and the whereabouts of Mr. Whitaker. Sister insists that Stella-Rondo has been deserted by Mr. Whitaker. The family refuses to contemplate this possibility. By the end of the story, Sister has become so infuriated by the apparent favoritism shown towards Stella-Rondo that she moves out, taking anything that she has purchased or nurtured in the house. She goes to live at the P. O., which she insists is "ideal" for her (56). However, the family boycotts the P.O. so that there is little business for her to attend to. She ends the story vowing never to listen to Stella-Rondo again.

Symbols & Motifs

The P.O. is the most important symbol in the story. For Sister, it signifies the possibility of

241

independence. However, her autonomy as post-mistress is countered by the fact that she must rely on her family's support to maintain the business. The other family members boycott the P.O. to show their disdain for Sister. The radio and the sewing-machine motor which Sister takes to the P.O. symbolize modernity for the family. Various items symbolize the underlying tensions between the family members. The pink kimono, the trousseau, and Shirley T. herself, represent the sexual experience that Stella-Rondo both flaunts and denies. Uncle Rondo's firecrackers, an obvious phallic symbol, represent the threat of masculine sexuality but also the experience which Sister feels she has been denied by Stella-Rondo. The names Shirley T. and Popeye the Sailor Man are cultural references, again reminding Sister of her ignorance of the outside world.

Societal Context

Race and gender ideologies are firmly entrenched in China Grove. Stella-Rondo has risen in status because she has married and moved away. Papa-Daddy states that she "deserved credit for getting out of town" (48). The oppressive gender ideology which underpins Southern society is clearly in place. As an unmarried woman, Sister has few options and Papa-Daddy reminds her of this when he threatens to take the P.O. away from her. Despite their insularity, the family observes collective notions of social propriety. Southern manners demand that Stella-Rondo deny Shirley T.'s true parentage and that the family colludes in this deception.

Much of Welty's fiction challenges hegemonic gender ideology by satirizing masculine assertions of power and control. The representations of masculinity in this story are no exception. Although Sister and Stella-Rondo have to compete for Mr. Whitaker, "the only man to drop down in China Grove," it is male vanity which emerges most clearly (54); both Uncle Rondo and Papa-Daddy

punish Sister when they think that she has criticised their appearance.

Social trends enter the family when Stella-Rondo returns. She has named her daughter after Shirley Temple, whose appearance was celebrated as the paradigm of beauty for white American girls. It is significant that Shirley Temple disproves Sister's theory concerning her mental state by singing the theme tune to Popeye the Sailor Man: not only does she prove herself capable of speech, but she asserts her familiarity with popular culture.

There is only a brief reference to race relations in China Grove. In telling language, Sister informs us that the family's servants have been "turned loose" for the day as they could not be "held" on the Fourth of July (50). She adds incidentally that Jaypan, one of the servants, fell in the lake that day and nearly drowned; this story is clearly of little significance to Sister.

Historical Context

There are few historical references in the story; we learn that Sister made the largest contribution to the sewing-machine motor which she bought "back in 1929" and there is a fleeting reference to Uncle Rondo's service in France, presumably in World War One (54). The story was published during the Second World War, when women were sampling a new kind of independence; going out to work for the first time. After the War, both the feminist movement and the Civil Rights Movement would change the oppressive race and gender ideology so deeply entrenched in the South. World events hold little interest for Sister who remains preoccupied with her status in the family. However, her triumphant tone at the end of the story is countered by a sense of alienation from the rest of the world.

Religious Context

The characters often try to score points with each other by appealing to a moral code: Stella-Rondo reminds Sister that she gave her word of honor not to query Shirley T.'s parentage; Mama tells Sister: "I prefer to take my children's word for anything when it's humanly possible" (50). However, there are no direct references to religion in the story and social ideology seems to determine the reactions of the characters. Although Welty grew up in a "religious-minded society," she did not belong to a "churchgoing family." She reveals that her "reverence" for life emanated from her experience of earthly wonders such as the "frescoes of Piero, of Giotto" but that she greatly appreciated the language and imagery of the Bible which resonates throughout the literature of Southern writers (One Writer's Beginnings 33). Much of Welty's fiction is informed by her knowledge of classical and mythical narratives.

Scientific & Technological Context

The family is bound together by a sense of their insularity from the modern world which lies beyond China Grove. Sister takes great pleasure in reminding the family of her control over their mail and feels that by leaving for the P.O. she is cutting them off from the outside world. As she prepares to leave for the P.O. she takes the most modern items with her such as the radio and the sewing-machine motor she bought for her mother in 1929: items which represent the possibility of technological advancement.

Biographical Context

Welty was born in 1909 in Jackson Mississippi, where she was based for most of her life. She lived in her family's second home until her death in 2001. She grew up with her parents and two brothers and wrote from an early age. She estimates that she was nine years old when she won the Jackie Mackie Jingle Contest, for which she was awarded $25. After attending the University of Wisconsin, she went to Columbia University in New York to study advertising for one year. She returned to Mississippi where she worked as

a journalist, reporting on Southern life. It was at this period of her life that she took most of her photographs, some of which would be published in her two collections of photography. In 1940, she began to work with the editor Diarmuid Russell. Her stories began to appear in "The New Yorker" and "The Atlantic Monthly." Her story "Lily Daw and the Three Ladies," appeared in "The Best American Stories of 1938." Her first collection of short stories was published in 1941, entitled "A Curtain of Green." Her first novel, "The Robber Bridegroom," was published the following year. "The Wide Net," another story collection, appeared in 1943. In 1946, Welty's second novel, "Delta Wedding," was published. In 1949, "The Golden Apples" appeared. This cycle of seven linked stories remains her most radical experiment with form and her favorite work of fiction. The stories are linked by the fictional setting of Morgana, a range of recurring characters, a network of mythological references and intertextual engagement with the poetry of W.B. Yeats. "The Golden Apples" enacts in its form Welty's preoccupation with connection and 'confluence,' one of her favorite words. "The Bride of Innisfallen," another collection of short stories, was published in 1955.

In 1980, her story collections appeared together in one volume, "The Collected Stories of Eudora Welty," along with "The Golden Apples." Welty's two comic novels followed in 1954 and 1970: "The Ponder Heart" and "Losing Battles" respectively. She also wrote a children's book, "Pepe the Shoe Bird" (1964). Her book of essays and reviews, "The Eye of the Story," was published in 1978. The essays deal with a range of subjects, from her own writing methodology to personal recollections and celebrations of favorite writers such as Chekhov, Austen, Porter, Cather and Faulkner. In 1983, she received the Pulitzer Prize for her final novel, "The Optimist's Daughter." In the same year her autobiography, "One Writer's Beginnings," was published to much acclaim. Welty is revered for her lyrical narrative style, her keen ear for dialogue and her evocation of place. She was the recipient of many awards and honors. She won O. Henry Awards for several of her stories, including "The Demonstrators," "The Whole World Knows," and "A Worn Path." In 1972, she was elected to the American Academy of Arts and Letters and in 1979, she received the National Medal for Literature. She received honorary degrees from a number of universities, including Harvard and Yale. In her introduction to "A Curtain of Green," Katherine Anne Porter noted, "[t]here is in none of these stories any trace of autobiography in the prime sense, except as the author is omnipresent, and knows each character she writes about only as the artist knows the thing he has made, by first experiencing it in the imagination" (xxii).

Rachel Lister

Works Cited

Bunting, Charles T. "'An Interior World': An Interview with Eudora Welty." *Southern Review* 8 (1972): 711–35.

Porter, Katherine Anne. "Introduction." *A Curtain of Green.* New York: Harcourt, 1941 xi–xxiii.

Welty, Eudora. *A Writer's Beginnings.* Omnibus BBC. 1985.

_____. *The Eye of the Story: Collected Essays and Reviews.* 1979. London: Virago, 1997.

_____. "Why I Live at the P.O." *The Collected Stories of Eudora Welty.* 1981. London: Penguin, 1983, 46–56.

Discussion Questions

1. How reliable is Sister as a narrator? Identify the strategies she deploys to convince us of her credibility. How effective are they?

2. What impression does this story create of life in the small towns of the South?

3. Discuss the significance of the names in the story.

4. How does Welty generate and sustain the much celebrated oral quality to Sister's narration?

5. "I've always got the P.O." (55). What is the significance of the P.O. for the family? To what extent does it function as a symbol of autonomy for Sister?

6. Katherine Anne Porter wrote that Welty "has simply an eye and an ear sharp, shrewd, and true as a tuning fork" ("Introduction" xx). Identify visual images and aural effects which support this evaluation.

7. Throughout the story, the narrator glosses over stories and histories that do not directly concern her: the near-drowning of Jaypan, the African-American servant; Uncle Rondo's time served in France and his doses of "medication." What impact do these brief references have on the main narrative line?

8. At the end of the story, Sister tells us: "I want the world to know I'm happy" (56). How convinced are you of her contentment?

9. In her introduction to "A Curtain of Green," Katherine Anne Porter delivers a notably dark interpretation of the story: she states that Sister is suffering from "a terrifying case of dementia praecox" (xx). Why might Porter reach this conclusion? Do you agree with this diagnosis?

10. Welty stated that: "Whereas in a novel you have time to shade a character, allow him his growth, in a short story a character hardly changes from beginning to end. He's in there for the purpose of that story only, and any other modification is ruled out" (Southern Review 717). With reference to her use of language, can you detect any changes in Sister's sensibility or outlook?

Essay Ideas

1. In a television interview for BBC's "Omnibus" in 1985, Eudora Welty identified the central theme of her fiction as the "common dilemma of trying to communicate with your fellow human beings … [of] understanding yourself in relation with the world and with other people." By what means does she dramatize this dilemma in "Why I Live at the P.O."?

2. Welty wrote that the evocation of place is the "most honest and natural way" of convincing the reader that a work of fiction is "true" ("Place in Fiction" 121). In light of this statement, consider Welty's representation of place in "Why I Live at the P.O."

3. To what extent might one define "Why I live at the P.O." as a comedy? You might consider the farcical and absurdist elements in the story.

4. In his reading of "Why I Live at the P.O.," Chester E. Eisinger observes that "the story becomes a performance" (Eisinger 9). What features of the story support this interpretation?

5. Consider the role of gender ideology in "Why I Live at the P.O."

A Worn Path

by Eudora Welty

Content Synopsis

The story takes place on a December day and dramatizes the thoughts of Phoenix Jackson, an old African-American woman, as she makes a familiar journey through the woods of the Natchez Trace. Phoenix makes her way through thickets and across creeks with the aid of a cane, commenting aloud on her progress and communicating with the wildlife. After crossing a creek, she rewards herself by sitting down and has a dream vision of a little boy who brings her a plate of marble cake. She wakens and walks across a field where she sees a scarecrow. When she reaches the road she encounters a black dog. She hits it with her cane and falls into a ditch. She has another dream which makes her reach up her hand but there is no response. She wakes up to see a white hunter approaching with a gun and another dog. He helps her up and tells her to go home but she replies that she must go to town. He laughs that "you colored people" would not miss an opportunity "to see Santa Claus!" (Collected 145). A nickel falls out of the man's pocket. While he sees to the dogs, Phoenix picks it up and takes it. When the man returns he points his gun at Phoenix, who remains unfazed. They part.

As Phoenix reaches the city she asks "a lady" to tie up her shoe before entering a "big building" (147). The lady complies and Phoenix enters the building where she sees a diploma hanging on the wall which "matched the dream that was hung up in her head" (147). The attendant identifies Phoenix as a charity case but a nurse explains that Phoenix has come for medication for her grandson who suffers from a sore throat. Phoenix seems to enter a kind of trance and does not respond to the nurse's inquiries until she asks if her grandson is dead. Only then does she reply that she had forgotten why she had made the trip in the first place. The nurse reminds her that her grandson swallowed some lye several years ago. She assures the nurse that her grandson is not dead but that he still struggles to breathe and speak. The nurse gives her the medicine she came for, calling it an act of "charity" (148). The attendant gives Phoenix a nickel for Christmas and Phoenix places it in her palm alongside the nickel she took from the hunter. She decides to buy her grandson a paper windmill and turns away to begin the journey home.

Symbols & Motifs

The name "Phoenix" evokes images of the mythical bird which rises from the flames and regenerates. Welty develops this association, figuring the recovery of Phoenix's memory as "a flicker" and "a flame" of "comprehension" (148). Birds feature prominently in the story; some symbolize the fragility of Phoenix and her grandson and others are more sinister and seem to presage death. In the opening paragraph, the narrative voice describes Phoenix as a "solitary little bird." Later, Phoenix sees a bob-white "stuffed" in the hunter's bag, "its beak hooked bitterly to show it was dead." This image resonates backwards and forwards (145). Phoenix talks to the "little bob-whites" at the beginning of the story and at the end she compares her grandson to a "little bird" with his beak open, waiting to be fed (142, 148). When Phoenix pockets the hunter's nickel, a bird flies by and she remembers that God is watching her. When Phoenix encounters a buzzard, a bird of prey, she asks him "Who you watching?" (144). The mourning dove evokes the threat of death, as does the scarecrow which Phoenix initially takes for a ghost.

The chains which Phoenix seems to feel about her feet, the thorns, and the barbed wire symbolise the continuing oppression which restricts the social mobility of the African-American people in the South. Symbols in Phoenix's dreams figure the possibility of social justice, equality and prosperity for all: The hand that Phoenix reaches up in the hope of receiving help and the marble cake which is offered by the little boy. The two nickels and the windmill are more tangible symbols of promise, if only on a small scale. The diploma represents not only the end of the journey for Phoenix but also the educational opportunity that she has been denied. As in many of Welty's texts, some of the experiences and tropes in this story are reminiscent of fairy tales: A female subject makes her way through a wood on a mission to help the afflicted; she faces a series of challenges and temptations; she meets and overcomes a threatening male.

Societal Context

Racial conflict emerges clearly in Phoenix's encounters with white people. She defines the white woman whom she asks to tie her shoe as a "lady." In asking her to perform this task, she places the white woman in a position of servitude that is assigned to African-Americans. A similar role reversal is played out in Phoenix's dream. She responds to the little boy's offer of marble cake with measured compliance:

"That would be acceptable" (143). The white hunter tries to assert his power over Phoenix by pointing his gun at her and by reminding her of her vulnerability. Although the white man does not physically harm Phoenix, his words betray the prejudices which remain entrenched in the South: his presumption that "colored people" visit town to see Santa Claus and his coded threat; "stay home and nothing will happen to you" (145). Phoenix is acutely aware of the opportunities she has been deprived of by the white race: She describes herself as "an old woman without an education" (148).

Historical Context

Alfred Appel views "A Worn Path" as "an effort at telescoping the history of the Negro woman" (166). Phoenix has certainly experienced much of this history firsthand. When she stoops to drink from a well, she states: "Nobody know who made this well, for it was here when I was born" (144). In effect, Phoenix presumes that nobody predates her. She does not contest the hunter's estimate that she must be "a hundred years old" and she tells the nurse that she was "too old at the Surrender" for an education (148). It is therefore apparent that she has experienced life before, during and after the Civil War. As Nancy K. Butterworth notes, race relations did not improve in the South before the Civil Rights movement. Welty's story registers the lack of change. Phoenix's description of herself as "an old woman without an education" reflects disillusionment with the absence of progress.

Religious Context

The thorns which momentarily impede Phoenix have obvious religious connotations. When she steals the money, she registers this theft as a sin against God, but does so impassively. Although Welty grew up in a "religious-minded society" she did not belong to a "churchgoing family." She reveals that her "reverence" for life emanated from her experience of earthly wonders such as the "frescoes of Piero, of Giotto" but that she greatly appreciated the language and imagery of the Bible which resonates throughout the literature of Southern writers (One Writer's Beginnings 33). Much of Welty's fiction is informed by her knowledge of classical and mythical narratives. Nancy Butterworth notes that Phoenix has been compared to a number of mythical "fertility figures" such as Persephone and Adonis.

Scientific & Technological Context

As "the only two left in the world," Phoenix and her grandson have little knowledge of scientific and technological advancements (148); she predicts that her grandson will find it difficult to believe that a windmill might really exist. She is given a glimpse of medical advancements through her visits to the hospital in the city and is determined that her grandson will benefit from them.

Biographical Context

Welty was born in 1909 in Jackson, Mississippi, where she was based for most of her life. She lived in her family's second home until her death in 2001. She grew up with her parents and two brothers and wrote from an early age. She estimates that she was nine years old when she won the Jackie Mackie Jingle Contest, for which she was awarded $25. After attending the University of Wisconsin, she went to Columbia University in New York to study advertising for one year. She returned to Mississippi where she worked as a journalist reporting on Southern life. It was at this period of her life that she took most of her photographs, some of which would be published in her two collections of photography. In 1940, she began to work with the editor Diarmuid Russell. Her stories began to appear in "The New Yorker" and "The Atlantic Monthly." Her story "Lily Daw and the Three Ladies" appeared in "The Best American Stories of 1938." Her first collection of short stories was published in 1941, entitled

"A Curtain of Green." Her first novel, "The Robber Bridegroom," was published the following year. "The Wide Net," another story collection, appeared in 1943. In 1946, Welty's second novel, "Delta Wedding," was published. In 1949, "The Golden Apples" appeared. This cycle of seven linked stories remains her most radical experiment with form and her favorite work of fiction. The stories are linked by the fictional setting of Morgana, a range of recurring characters, a network of mythological references and intertextual engagement with the poetry of W.B. Yeats. "The Golden Apples" enacts (in its form) Welty's preoccupation with connection and 'confluence,' one of her favorite words. "The Bride of Innisfallen," another collection of short stories, was published in 1955.

In 1980, her story collections appeared together in one volume, "The Collected Stories of Eudora Welty," along with "The Golden Apples." Welty's two comic novels followed in 1954 and 1970: "The Ponder Heart" and "Losing Battles" respectively. She also wrote a children's book, "Pepe the Shoe Bird" (1964). Her book of essays and reviews, "The Eye of the Story," was published in 1978. Essays deal with a range of subjects, from her own writing methodology to personal recollections and celebrations of favorite writers such as Chekhov, Austen, Porter, Cather and Faulkner. In 1983, she received the Pulitzer Prize for her final novel, "The Optimist's Daughter." In the same year, her autobiography, "One Writer's Beginnings," was published to much acclaim. Welty is revered for her lyrical narrative style, her keen ear for dialogue and her evocation of place. She was the recipient of many awards and honors. She won O. Henry Awards for several of her stories, including "The Demonstrators," "The Whole World Knows," and "A Worn Path." In 1972, she was elected to the American Academy of Arts and Letters and in 1979, she received the National Medal for Literature. She received honorary degrees from a number of universities, including Harvard and Yale. In her introduction to "A Curtain of Green," Katherine Anne Porter noted, "[t]here is in none of these stories any trace of autobiography in the prime sense, except as the author is omnipresent, and knows each character she writes about only as the artist knows the thing he has made, by first experiencing it in the imagination" (xxii).

Rachel Lister

Works Cited

Appel, Alfred Jr. *A Season of Dreams: The Fiction of Eudora Welty (Southern Literary Studies)*. Baton Rouge: Louisiana State UP, 1965.

Butterworth, Nancy K. "From Civil War to Civil Rights." *Eudora Welty: Eye of the Storyteller.* Ed. Daun Trouard. Kent, OH: Kent State UP, 1989. 165–72.

_____. "A Worn Path." *The Collected Stories of Eudora Welty.* 1981. London: Penguin, 1983, 142–49.

_____. "Is Phoenix Jackson's Grandson Really Dead?" *The Eye of the Story: Collected Essays and Reviews.* 1979. London: Virago, 1997, 159–62.

Discussion Questions

1. In her own commentary on "A Worn Path," Welty reveals that she based the story on a sighting of "a solitary old woman" walking on a winter's day and "persisting in her landscape" (Eye 161). By what means does Welty dramatize Phoenix Jackson's persistence?

2. Welty writes that she "invented" for Phoenix "some passing adventures—some dreams and harassments and a small triumph or two, some jolts to her pride, some flights of fancy to console her, one or two encounters to scare her, a moment that gave her cause to feel ashamed, a moment to dance and preen" (Eye 161). Identify these moments and discuss their impact on the narrative as a whole.

3. Discuss the ways in which Welty raises questions of education in "A Worn Path."

4. What is the significance of the bird imagery which features in the story?

5. Discuss the significance of Phoenix's dreams.

6. Readers and scholars frequently contacted Welty to ask if Phoenix's grandson is really dead. She replied that this is not really significant; to dwell on such speculation is to miss the point of the story. Why might she respond in this way?

7. What is the significance of Phoenix Jackson's age?

8. Discuss Welty's engagement with fairy-tale tropes and narratives. How does Welty emulate and subvert the premises of this genre?

9. Discuss Phoenix's commentary on her journey. What does it reveal about her state of mind?

10. "My senses is gone. I too old" (Phoenix Jackson, "A Worn Path" 144). Explore the representation of the senses and memory in "A Worn Path": How does Welty dramatize their powers and their limitations?

Essay Ideas

1. In her autobiography, One Writer's Beginnings, Welty wrote: "Travel itself is part of some longer continuity" (97). Analyze "A Worn Path" in the light of this statement.

2. Welty wrote that, "ambiguity is a fact of life" (Eye 160). Identify and analyze moments of ambiguity in "A Worn Path."

3. Welty stated that, "In the case of the short story, you can't ever let the tautness of line relax. It has to be all strung very tight upon its single thread usually, and everything is subordinated to the theme of the story: Characters and mood and place and time; and none of those things are as important as the development itself" (Bunting 717). By what means does she achieve the effect of "tautness" in "A Worn Path"?

4. What do Phoenix's journey, dreams and encounters tell us about race and gender

5. relations in the South?

6. Welty identifies the "subject" of the story as "the deep-grained habit of love" (Eye 161). How does she dramatize love in "A Worn Path"?

Nathaniel Hawthorne was an American novelist and short story writer. His fiction is considered part of the Dark Romanticism Movement, and often includes psychologically complex moral messages; two of his works are included in this volume: *Young Goodman Brown* and *The Minister's Black Veil*. Photo: Library of Congress, Prints & Photographs Division, LC-USZ62-2358.

Young Goodman Brown

by Nathaniel Hawthorne

Content Synopsis

Nathaniel Hawthorne's "Young Goodman Brown" is a short story set in Puritan New England which traces the journey of Goodman Brown as he reluctantly heads into the forest one evening, presumably for some kind of meeting with witches, leaving his wife, Faith, behind at home.

Goodman Brown meets a "fellow-traveler" with a staff resembling a great black snake who convinces him to keep walking into the forest despite his protestations that none of his ancestors had ever walked the path that he was about to tread. The traveler, a kind of demonic figure, explains to Goodman Brown that he "helped [his] grandfather, the constable, when he lashed the Quaker woman so smartly through the streets of Salem" and that it was he who brought Goodman Brown's own "father a pitch-pine knot … to set fire to an Indian village" (196). Further, the traveler goes on to say that he is well acquainted with many people in New England, including deacons and even the governor.

Goodman Brown persists in his arguments, telling the traveler that if he continues on this journey, he will never be able to face his minister again. When the traveler erupts into laughter, Goodman Brown exclaims: "There is my wife, Faith. It would break her dear little heart; and I'd rather break my own" (197). To this, the traveler responds; "I would not for twenty old women like the one hobbling before us that Faith should come to any harm" (197).

Goodman Brown recognizes Goody Cloyse, a pious woman who had taught him his catechism, ahead on the path. He hides so that she will not see him tarrying in the woods so late in the evening, but it is Brown himself who receives a surprise when he overhears Goody Cloyse talking to the traveler as to an old friend, remarking that she is on her way to the meeting.

Goodman Brown exclaims: "Not another step will I budge on this errand. What if a wretched old woman do choose to go to the devil when I thought she was going to heaven: is that any reason why I should quit my dear Faith and go after her?" (198). The traveler instructs Goodman Brown to rest awhile, going ahead on his own but leaving behind his staff. As he is resting, Goodman Brown believes he overhears the minister and Deacon Gookin discussing "deviltry" as they head down the path.

Goodman Brown vows to resist the devil and begins to pray; however, a black cloud sweeps in and with it the sound of voices. Goodman Brown believes that he recognizes the voices of townspeople, both "saints and sinners." He knows one voice in particular, his Faith's. Just after he calls her name and hears a scream, the black cloud drifts away and down flutters one of Faith's pink ribbons.

Young Goodman Brown cries: "My Faith is gone .... There is no good on earth; and sin is but a name. Come, devil; for to thee is this world given" (201). Goodman Brown, now "maddened with despair," flies to a clearing in which he finds a group of people he thinks he recognizes, including Deacon Gookin and "Indian priests, or powwows, who had often scared their native forest with more hideous incantations than any known to English witchcraft" (202).

A voice calls "Bring forth the converts!" and Goodman Brown feels himself led to a blazing rock by Deacon Gookin and the minister to join the other proselytes. The voice begins, there "are all whom ye have reverence from youth . Ye deemed them holier than yourselves, and shrank form your own sin, contrasting it with their lives of righteousness and prayerful aspirations heavenward. Yet here are they all in my worshipping assembly" (204).

Goodman Brown sees his wife Faith, and the demonic figure exhorts: "Depending upon one another's hearts, ye had still hoped that virtue were not all a dream. Now are ye undeceived. Evil is the nature of mankind. Evil must be your only happiness. Welcome again, my children, to the communion of your race" (204).

Goodman Brown shouts to Faith, "look up to heaven, and resist the wicked one," after which he immediately finds himself alone, somehow transported back to the rock on which he had previously rested (205).

The narration leaves unclear whether Goodman Brown's experience was real or dream. Regardless, it has dramatic consequences for the rest of his life. Goodman Brown can never trust anyone again: "And when he had lived long, and was borne to his grave a hoary corpse, followed by Faith, an aged woman, and children and grandchildren, a goodly procession, besides neighbors and not a few, they carved no hopeful verse upon his tombstone, for his dying hour was gloom" (206).

Historical Context

The Puritans were a religious group, influenced by the ideas of reformer John Calvin, who wanted to purify the Anglican Church by replacing elaborate ceremony and hierarchy with emphasis on Bible reading and individual prayer. When the Stuart Monarchs of England began to persecute the Puritans in their attempt to unite their subjects in devotion to the Anglican Church, many Puritans decided to leave England for the New World. In 1630, a group of these immigrants formed a Puritan Commonwealth in present-day Boston and Salem, and the settlement grew to more than 20,000 by 1643. The Puritans immigrated to the New World "not merely to save their souls but to establish a 'visible' kingdom of God, a society where outward conduct would be according to God's laws, a society where a smooth, honest, civil life would prevail in family, church, and state" (Morgan 3). Religion and government in Puritan society were inextricably linked.

In 1692, the "visible Kingdom of God" was plunged into turmoil when several members of the Salem church began to accuse others of witchcraft. Part of what makes the Salem Witch Trials such a disturbing and intriguing phenomenon is that they occurred at a time in which "advances in science and the expansion of trade were undermining superstition everywhere" (Hill 1). Although thousands of people were killed between 1500 and 1650 in the European witch-hunts, by 1692, in Europe as well in the new world, the number of witch trials had drastically dwindled and many, if not most of them, resulted in the acquittal of those accused. Not so in Salem; the trials there resulted in the deaths of almost thirty people.

"Young Goodman Brown" is set in this dark period of Puritan history. The story makes reference to two historical figures from the witch trials, Goody Cloyse and Goody Cory, as well to another historical incident, the lashing of a Quaker woman which occurred in Salem in 1693.

Reading Goodman Brown's dissent into darkness and distrust with these references in mind, we are reminded of the sad reality that an overzealous desire for goodness and purity can be so perverted as to ultimately result in violence and death.

Societal Context

The Puritans strove for a just and good society, but they were constantly on the lookout for hypocrites, those who, though outwardly model citizens, were not truly saved. This belief in the essential wickedness of humanity, "led them to discipline themselves and their children with psychologically crippling severity" (Johnson 13). It also played an integral role in the witch-trial incident, which, according to some scholars, illustrates "the human tendency to separate evil from good and project that evil into the enemy, and then to destroy it by destroying the enemy" (Hill xviii).

Although this may indeed be a general human tendency, it must have been particularly strong in the Puritan spirit, not only because of their religious doctrine, but also because they were in fear of losing their way of life. Frances Hill reminds us that the witch-hunts "took place against the background of a Puritan theocracy threatened by change, in a population terrified not only of eternal damnation but of the earthly dangers of Indian massacres, recurrent smallpox epidemics, and the loss of the charter from England" (Hill xviii). No doubt, they hoped that purging the sinners from their midst would please God and allow them to retain their status as his chosen people.

The human tendency to perceive evil in others is a central theme of "Young Goodman Brown." Regardless of whether Goodman Brown's experience in the woods was dream or reality, he is rather easily convinced that the holiest members of his community have been consorting with the devil. Never again able to believe in the goodness of his neighbors or even his own family, he is doomed to a lonely life. The story warns us that if one looks too hard for hypocrites, one will surely find them.

Religious Context

One of the core beliefs of Puritanism held that all men deserved damnation. God, in his benevolence, had chosen to absolve some of them from sin and save them before they even existed. Thus, salvation was predestined. Puritans were very concerned about how to recognize whether they were chosen to be saved. According to many Puritan clergymen, a person had to accept God's offer of salvation through grace. Keys to recognizing this grace were self-examination, reading the Bible, and listening to the minister's sermons. Some Puritans believed that conversion was a dramatic, recognizable experience, while others believed it simply happened unnoticed. After the conversion experience, one would live in a new state of redemption, recognizable by moral behavior.

In order to be a member of the Puritan church, one had to know and believe its doctrines, to live a moral life, and to prove that he or she was one of the elect. While early on, one simply had to describe his or her conversion to provide the necessary proof of election, later applicants were required to describe the process which led them to that conversion as well. Even if one were accepted into the church and possessed all the outward signs of election, he or she could not truly be certain of salvation until death.

In "Young Goodman Brown," Hawthorne suggests that this doubt about one's own salvation and the true state of the other souls in the congregation can cause one to become fixated on evil and to distrust the motives of everyone around him. Frances Hill writes that "Young Goodman Brown" "articulates the profound Puritan terror of evil as embodied by the devil but also rooted deep in the soul, perpetually threatening to destroy men's and women's feeble attempts to be godly" (Hill 314).

Scientific & Technological Context

The Puritans kept new scientific ideas out of their communities for as long as they could. Newtonian physics, which appeared in 1687, was not seriously considered in New England until more than thirty years after its appearance, when it was explained by Cotton Mather. In 1714, Mather became the first influential Puritan to accept the Copernican theory of the universe, 178 years after Copernicus proposed it. Ultimately, Puritans' exposure to and acceptance of new scientific and rational thought which "stressed observable fact in the visible world" helped to erode "the very spiritual bedrock of Puritanism" (Johnson 203). Of course, the decline of the Puritan church was not due to the influence of science alone; Claudia Johnson also cites "the introduction into New England of a non-dissenting, British presence after the loss of the charter,[…][a] backlash against seventy years of unrelieved church intrusion into both government and private life, […][t]he absolute intolerance of other Protestant religions," among other factors (200).

Because of their emphasis on spectral evidence, the witch trials are interpreted by some as a sort of backlash against the new modes of empirical and rational thought that threatened Puritans' deeply-rooted beliefs in the power of supernatural forces. Hawthorne's "Young Goodman Brown" aptly demonstrates the ambiguity of spectral evidence as the narration purposefully leaves readers unsure of what exactly happens to Goodman Brown on the night he ventures into the woods. The story also makes clear that for those who believe in it, spectral evidence is powerful indeed, for Goodman Brown's entire perspective is forever altered as a result of this one night's experiences.

Biographical Context

Born in 1804, Nathaniel Hawthorne was the great-great-grandson of John Hathorne, magistrate at the examinations of accused witches. "Young Goodman Brown" is set in Salem Village near the time of the witch trials. Hawthorne establishes the time by referring to historical incidents, such as the Quaker woman being lashed in Salem's streets which occurred in 1693, and by having two of the characters in the story, Goody Cloyse and Goody Cory, carry the names of historical figures connected to the trials. Frances Hill writes that Hawthorne's mention of the incident involving the Quaker woman as well as his mention of an Indian village which was set on fire during King Philip's War, "reminds us of the guilt he felt not just for the iniquities of his great-great-grandfather but for those of his father, William Hathorne, a chief persecutor of Quakers, and of William Hathorne Junior, John Hathorne's brother, a military officer who befriended Indians, tricked them, and sold them into slavery" (314–15).

In the decade after he graduated from Bowdoin college, Hawthorne lived a rather reclusive life in his mother's house, struggling to support himself as a writer and contributor to periodicals, reading a great deal of material from his local library, much of it material concerning his Puritan ancestors, and making occasional excursions across the countryside, recording detailed observations as he went. Hawthorne was deeply affected by and concerned with his Puritan ancestors, particularly their darker side as represented by, among other things, the witch trials. This concern comes through in "The Custom House," in which he wrote: "I … hereby take shame upon myself for their sakes, and pray that any curse incurred by them … may be now and henceforth removed" (Swisher 30). The extensive knowledge he gained about New England history and culture in this period served him well as much of his creative work would have this subject matter at its core, including the short stories "The Minister's Black Veil," and "Young Goodman Brown," and his well known novels "The Scarlet Letter" and "The House of the Seven Gables."

Kim Becnel

Works Cited

Bunge, Nancy L. *Nathaniel Hawthorne: A Study of the Short Fiction.* New York: Twayne, 1993.

Hill, Frances. *The Salem Witch Trials Reader.* Cambridge, MA: Da Capo, 2000.

Hawthorne, Nathaniel. "Young Goodman Brown." *Hawthorne's Short Stories.* Dodd, 1962. 193–206.

Johnson, Claudia Durst. *Daily Life in Colonial New England.* Westport, CT: Greenwood P, 2002.

Morgan, Edmund Sears. *The Puritan Family: Religion & Domestic Relations in Seventeeth-Century New England.* Westport, CT: Greenwood P, 1966.

Wineapple, Brenda. *Hawthorne: A Life.* New York: Knopf, 2003.

Discussion Questions

1. What might the wilderness and Young Goodman Brown's journey into it represent?
2. How does Hawthorne establish the setting of the story?
3. What is the symbolic significance of Faith's pink ribbons?
4. What is the significance of Faith's remark that a "lone woman is troubled with such dreams and such thoughts, that she's afeard of herself, sometimes"?
5. Why do you think Hawthorne crafts the story so that Goodman Brown is never quite sure that he recognizes people from the congregation in the forest?
6. Why does it bother Goodman Brown so much to see "saints and sinners" gathered together in the forest?
7. What do you think Hawthorne means when he writes that Goodman Brown was "the chief horror of the scene"?
8. What kind of commentary, if any, is Hawthorne making on the Salem Witch Trials with this story? What statement is he making about the validity of "spectral evidence"?
9. Why do you think the devil appears in the form of Goodman Brown's ancestors?
10. How does the story portray Native Americans? What statement do you think Hawthorne is trying to make through this portrayal?

Essay Ideas

1. Analyze the rhetorical strategies of the devil figure. How is he able to convince Goodman Brown to keep walking into the forest?
2. Compare and contrast "Young Goodman Brown" with another of Hawthorne's short stories, "The Minister's Black Veil." What themes or messages do the stories share?
3. Compare and contrast this story with others you have read that are set during the time of the Salem Witch Trials. What makes Hawthorne's vision of Puritan psychology unique?
4. What is Hawthorne saying about Puritan society through this story?
5. Why does Hawthorne intentionally leave readers unsure whether Goodman Brown had "fallen asleep in the forest and only dreamed a wild dream of a witch-meeting"?

You're Ugly, Too

by Lorrie Moore

Content Synopsis

Lorrie Moore's short story "You're Ugly, Too" centers on Zoë Hendricks, an American history professor at Hilldale-Versailles College outside of Paris, Illinois. In addition to teaching American history courses, Zoë writes articles and edits them meticulously, intentionally working during different times of the day to add different perspectives to her work. This is her fourth year of teaching at this college, and she is bored with her job. She often sings lines from "Getting to Know You," in class or offers students sips of her hot chocolate. She once had more patience with students, even allowing them to call her at home. Now she is sarcastic and condescending to the students and notices that she has developed "a crusty edge, brittle and pointed" (70). For example, one student tells her that she acts as if her opinion is more important than everyone else's in the class, and she says that she is paid to act that way. Additionally, she says her students "seemed actually to know very little about anything…" (69).

Every Tuesday, Zoë calls her sister, Evan, who lives in Manhattan. This Tuesday, she tells Evan that she is bored, and Evan says that her tediousness is part of a pattern in which she feels unsettled after returning from vacations. Later in the conversation, Zoë announces that she is coming to visit Evan, and Evan invites her to her Halloween party. Zoë says that she will dress as a bonehead.

Evan says she wants to introduce Zoë to a man she thinks she might find attractive, and Zoë advises Evan not to get married.

Zoë has dated three men since she began teaching at Hilldale-Versailles. One became upset because Zoë brushed an ant off her sleeve in his car. Another man said things that would "startle her" (73). The most recent one she dated was a professor who flirted with the wives of his colleagues during double dates.

Zoë is in the midst of undergoing hospital tests because she has a "mysterious growth in her abdomen" (73). When she has an ultrasound, the technician can't tell her anything. She is reminded of the joke that describes a doctor who tells his patient that he has only six weeks to live. When the patient requests a second opinion, the doctor says, "'You're ugly, too'" (77).

Evan is happy to see Zoë when she arrives in Manhattan. Zoë tells her that she got sick on the plane. Evan confides in Zoë regarding her relationship with Charlie, her live-in boyfriend. She says that she feels as if she and Charlie are middle-aged and that they watch fuzzy TV because they have no cable. She describes in detail how Charlie takes off his clothes at night, and Zoë tells her maybe she and Charlie "should just get it over with and get married" (79). Zoë elaborates that although Evan and Charlie may think that living together offers "the best of both worlds" that situation "can suddenly twist and become the worst of both worlds" (79). Evan announces that she and Charlie are getting married and asks Zoë to be her maid of honor.

Zoë begins to tell Evan a story about an award-winning violinist who dated a man who mocked her musical talent and required her to attend his softball games. The violinist later committed suicide. However, Zoë does not reveal to Evan the truth about the woman. Instead of revealing that she committed suicide, she tells Evan that the woman learned to like softball. Zoë attends a movie, where she begins to feel "strangely self-conscious sitting alone" (81).

At Evan's Halloween party Zoë meets Earl, the man who Evan had mentioned on the phone. Earl is dressed as a nude woman. On the balcony, Zoë notes that because she is uncomfortable talking to men, she concocts things to say in her mind, imagining that she marries the man with whom she converses, has children, and divorces him. She tells Earl that she and her sister had speech impediments when growing up. When Zoë begins to tell him the joke about the doctor who informs his patient he has only six weeks to live, Earl interrupts and tells his own joke, which also involves a doctor and patient. However, unlike Zoë's joke, Earl's is sexist. When Earl asks her if she is involved in a relationship, she says no and invents a story about having recently dated a man who was a weed expert.

Zoë leaves the balcony, goes to the bathroom and pulls a hair out of her chin, which causes a sore and bleeding. She places a wad of toilet paper on the sore. When she returns to the balcony, Earl asks her what she believes about love. He interrupts the conversation to inform her that something is on her chin. Zoë removes the wad of toilet paper and continues the discussion. She tells Earl the story about the violinist that she began to tell Evan earlier. When telling Earl the story, she reveals that the woman committed suicide. Earl loses interest in discussing the topic of love and informs Zoë

that she should wear more blue to show her coloring. Zoë responds by asking if the word "fag" means anything to him. Earl reacts to the question by saying that he should not attempt to meet career women. The conversation stops, and Zoë walks behind him and shoves him. He is offended, and she assures him that she was only kidding. At the end of the story, Zoë smiles and wonders how she looks.

Symbols & Motifs

Typical of Lorrie Moore's writing style, "You're Ugly, Too" reflects jokes, puns, and other witty devices. The title of the story refers to a joke Zoë thinks of when she visits the doctor. When Zoë begins to tell the joke to Earl, he proceeds to tell a joke that he thinks is a version of the one Zoë started. However, his joke is not similar to the one Zoë began, but his is sexist and offends Zoë. Other comic devices include the sarcastic and flippant comments Zoë makes to her students. Also, Moore makes up and changes words to create humor. For example, she lists sonograms, mammograms, and candygrams. She also tells Earl that she and Evan had to go to "peach pearapy" to treat their speech impediments (83). Zoë says that she survived her reluctance to talk by telling jokes because she had the lines memorized. The humor gives the story a light-hearted tone. When Earl tells his sexist joke, it jars both Zoë and the reader because it contradicts the way humor is used throughout the story. The humor also helps to build Zoë's character. It helps make her a likeable character. Finally, humor adds to the entertainment quality of the story.

The nature of romantic relationships is referred to both directly and indirectly throughout the story. Evan describes her relationship with Charlie, Zoë summarizes several past attempts she has made to date men, and Earl asks Zoë directly what she thinks of love. In one of her descriptions of a man she dated, Zoë notes that he flirted with married women, who reciprocated. Also, the framed story, the tale about the violinist, is used to illustrate how romantic love contributes to a woman's suicide. The story portrays romantic love cynically and suggests that content couples are the exception, not the rule.

Historical Context

The story alludes to history in relation to Zoë's role as a history professor. She teaches courses such as one entitled "The Revolution and Beyond" and is writing a book entitled "Hearing the One About: Uses of Humor in the American Presidency." The title of the book echoes the title of "You're Ugly, Too," which also refers to a joke. Zoë can recite the soundtrack of "The King and I" and wonders, "Is this history?" (68). The students know little history or geography. They make remarks such as "all those states in the East are so tiny and jagged and bunched up" (69). Zoë's "students were by and large good Midwesterners, spacey with estrogen from large quantities of meat and cheese. They shared their parents' suburban values; their parents had given them things, things, things. They were complacent. They had been purchased. They were armed with a healthy vagueness about anything historical or geographic" (69). The references to history suggest that it is difficult for people to put things in historical perspective. It implies that suburban values have influenced the current generation to focus on materialism and the present rather than contemplating philosophical ideas and examining events in relation to past events.

Societal Context

"You're Ugly, Too" is packed with references to society and social roles. The story implies that sometimes people do not want to change with the times. For example, Zoë recalls that when she taught in New Geneva, Minnesota, she noticed that one wasn't "supposed to notice that the town had overextended and that its shopping malls were raggedy and going under" (70). She says the townspeople

expected women "to be Heidi. You were supposed to lug goat milk up the hills and not think twice" (70). The comments about New Geneva suggest that people sometimes resist change and that they remain stagnant in their social customs and beliefs.

The story illustrates the plight of women in contemporary society. Zoë is the only woman faculty member of the history department. The narrator says, "Generally, the department of nine men was pleased to have her. They felt she added some needed feminine touch to the corridors—that faint trace of Obsession and sweat, the light clicking of heels. Plus they had had a sex-discrimination suit, and the dean had said, well it was time" (67). Zoë's male colleagues appreciate her "feminine touch" rather than her scholarly endeavors or her teaching strengths.

The story also illustrates other ways sexist attitudes still exist in today's society. For example, Zoë notes that "all men, deep down, wanted Heidi. Heidi with cleavage. Heidi with outfits" (72). Additionally, Zoë does not attend an art museum in Manhattan because "women alone in art museums had to look good. They always did. Chic and serious, moving languidly, with a great handbag" (80). She refuses to succumb to this stereotype. Considering the idea of beauty, Zoë says, "Look it up in the yellow pages and you found a hundred entrees, hostile with wit, cutesy with warning. But look up Truth-ha! There was nothing at all" (809). Here, she notes that society is more concerned with a notion of beauty than it is with seeking truth. Perhaps the most blatant demonstration of sexist attitudes is presented in the joke Earl tells. His joke describes a doctor bragging because he "finally fucked" his secretary (84). This reinforces stereotypes of women as being objects for male's sexual fantasies.

Throughout the story, social aspects involving ways people interact with each other are revealed. Zoë, who is five years older than Evan, attempts to fulfill the socially prescribed duty of a big sister: "Zoë tried to sound like an older sister; an older sister was supposed to be the parent you could never have, the hip cool mom" (79). The relationships between men and women are explored repeatedly in the story. Interpersonal relationships are also depicted in the description of the Halloween party Evan hosts. The interactions that occur during the party reveal ways individuals come together and act during a social event.

Religious Context

Although religion is not a major aspect of "You're Ugly, Too," the story makes some allusions to religion and spirituality. Zoë buys an Oriental rug designed with Chinese symbols. The salesperson claimed the symbols stood for "'Peace' and 'Eternal Life'" (74), but Zoë begins to doubt whether they do. She decides the symbols might just as easily represent Bruce Springsteen. The connection between peace and eternal life and Bruce Springsteen reveals Zoë's flippant attitude about spirituality. Spirituality is also depicted in reference to the baroque mirror in Zoë's hallway. A colleague told her that the mirror "would keep away evil spirits" (75). However, the mirror frightens her because she does not recognize the image of herself when she stands in front of it. Perhaps the "evil spirits" are the pressures for women to maintain bodies that society deems beautiful, and the mirror invites rather than repels evil spirits. Christianity is alluded to when Zoë describes that her former boyfriend used to put his hands on her navel and say "evangelically, 'Heal! Heal for thy Baby Jesus' sake!'" (76). The comment is made in jest, suggesting that religion is to be ridiculed.

Scientific & Technological Context

Most of the references to science and technology in "You're Ugly, Too" concern Zoë's medical condition, for which she is having tests performed. Zoë has a cynical attitude toward the medical profession. Contemplating her scheduled ultrasound tests, she thinks, "According to her doctor and her doctor's assistant, she had a large, mysterious growth in her abdomen. Gall bladder, they kept saying. Or ovaries or colon" (75). This assessment reminds her of the time a vet diagnosed that her dog either "has worms or cancer or else it was hit by a car" (76). While the technician performs an ultrasound, Zoë asks, "Do you suppose … that the rise in infertility among so many couples in this country is due to completely different species trying to reproduce?" (76). Here, she uses a scientific example to imply that human beings in a relationship are so diverse that they might as well be different species.

Also, Earl makes scientific observations. When he explains to Zoë his job as a photographer, he says that he believes it may be dangerous "spending all your time in a darkroom with that red light and all those chemicals. There's links with Parkinson's you know" (85). At the end of the story, Earl explains how bugs maintain population control: "They're sprayed with bug hormones, female bug hormones. The male bugs get so crazy in the presence of this hormone, they're screwing everything in sight: trees, rocks—everything but female bugs. Population control. That's what's happening in this country…. Hormones sprayed around, and now men are screwing rocks. Rocks!" (91). This comment follows Earl's announcement that he should avoid relationships with career women. In context with his attitude about career women, the comment about men "screwing rocks" suggests that Earl views women as a hormone drugged bug might view a rock. This comment parallels the joke Earl tells about the doctor and reinforces his sexist attitude.

Biographical Context

Born January 13, 1957, in Glen Falls, New York, Marie Lorena Moore was nicknamed Lorrie by her parents. Moore completed high school early and attended St. Lawrence University, where she served as editor of the literary journal. When she was nineteen, she won the fiction contest sponsored by *Seventeen* magazine, which led to her first publication.

After graduating college, Moore worked as a paralegal in Manhattan. In 1980, she enrolled in the MFA program at Cornell. She began to publish stories in magazines such as *Story Quarterly* and "*Ms.*" In 1983, her first short story collection, "Self-Help," which consisted mostly of stories comprising her master's thesis, was published by Knopf. In 1984, she began teaching at University of Wisconsin, often returning to Manhattan for visits.

"You're Ugly, Too" was the first story of Moore's to appear in "The New Yorker." She has since contributed many stories to "The New Yorker" and other distinguished magazines and journals. She has published several volumes of short stories and two novels. Her stories are frequently included in "The O. Henry Awards" and "The Best American Short Stories;" annual collections in which the best stories for each year are anthologized. Moore was chosen as guest editor for the 2004 volume of "The Best American Short Stories." Additionally, she has received several prestigious awards for her writing, including a National Endowment for the Arts and a Guggenheim. Moore currently teaches at the University of Wisconsin, where she serves as Delmore Schwarz Professor of the Humanities.

Laurie Champion

Works Cited

Lee, Don. "About Lorrie Moore." *Ploughshares* 24 (1998): 224–29.

Moore, Lorrie. "You're Ugly, Too." *Like Life: Stories.* New York: Plume, 1988.

Weekes, Karen. "Identity in the Short Story Cycles of Lorrie Moore." *Journal of the Short Story in English* 39 (2002): 109–22.

_____. "Postmodernism in Women's Short Story Cycles: Lorrie Moore's Anagrams." *The Postmodern Short Story: Forms and Issues.* Ed. Farhat Iftekharrudin, Joseph Boyden, Mary Rohrberger, and Jaie Claudet. Westport, CT: Praeger, 2003. 94–106.

Discussion Questions

1. Why do you think Zoë is sarcastic to her students?
2. Why does Zoë shove Earl at the end of the story?
3. Compare and contrast the men Zoë has dated in the story.
4. What is the relationship between Zoë and Evan? How do they relate to each other?
5. What is Zoë's attitude toward men?
6. What is the significance of Zoë's and Earl's Halloween costumes?
7. Analyze the character of Zoë. What are her traits and emotions?
8. How does the story Zoë tells about the violinist relate to the themes of "You're Ugly, Too"?
9. What does Zoë imply when she asks Earl near the end of the story if the word "fag" means anything to him?
10. What is the significance of Zoë's medical condition?

Essay Ideas

1. Analyze "You're Ugly, Too" from a feminist perspective.
2. Discuss the use of humor in "You're Ugly, Too."
3. Explore ways "You're Ugly, Too" portrays relationships between men and women.
4. Compare and contrast "You're Ugly, Too" with one of the stories listed under "complementary texts."
5. Analyze the symbols in "You're Ugly, Too."

BIBLIOGRAPHY

Abrams, M. H. *A Glossary of Literary Terms*. Orlando, Harcourt Brace College Publishers, 1985.

Adams, Michael. "T. Coraghessan Boyle (1948–)." *DLB Yearbook: 1986*. Ed. J. M. Brook. Detroit: Gale, 1987. 281–86.

Albert, Richard N. "The Jazz-Blues Motif in James Baldwin's 'Sonny's Blues.'" *College Literature* 11.2 (1984): 178–84.

Appel, Alfred Jr. *A Season of Dreams: The Fiction of Eudora Welty (Southern Literary Studies)*. Baton Rouge: Louisiana State UP, 1965.

Apple, Max. "Vegetable Love." *The Longman Anthology of Short Fiction: Stories and Authors in Context*. Eds. Dana Giola and R.S. Gwynn. New York: Longman, 2001.78–88.

Atwood, Margaret. *Bluebeard's Egg and Other Stories*. 1983. New York: Fawcett Crest, 1986.

Auerbach, Jonathan. *The Romance of Failure: First-Person Fictions of Poe, Hawthorne, and James*. New York: Oxford UP, 1989.

Baldwin, James. "Sonny's Blues." *Going to Meet the Man*. New York: Dial Press, 1965. 101–41.

Bambara, Toni Cade. "The Lesson." *Gorilla, My Love*. New York: Vintage, 1992. 85–96.

Bamber, Martyn. "The Virgin Spring." *Senses of Cinema*. August 2004. 12 December 2005.

Bauer, Helen Pike. "'A Child of Anxious, Not Proud, Love': Mother and Daughter in Tillie Olsen's 'I Stand Here Ironing.'" *Mother Puzzles: Daughters and Mothers in Contemporary American Literature*. New York, Greenwood, 1989. 35–39.

Bierce, Ambrose. "An Occurrence at Owl Creek Bridge." *Elements of Literature: Fifth Course, Literature of the United States*. Holt, Rinehart and Winston, 2003. p. 469–473.

———. *Elements of Literature: Fifth Course, Literature of the United States*. Holt, Rinehart and Winston, 2003. p. 466–467, 474–476.

Bloom, Harold, Ed. "Introduction." *Bloom's Major Short Story Writers: Edgar Allan Poe*. New York: Chelsea House, 1999. 9–11.

———. "Introduction." *Bloom's Modern Critical Views: Edgar Allan Poe*. New York: Chelsea House, 1985.

Blotner, Joseph. *Faulkner: A Biography*. New York: Random House, 1984.

Blythe, Hal, and Charlie Sweet. "Cheever's Dark Knight of the Soul: The Failed Quest of Neddy Merrill." *Studies in Short Fiction* 29 (1992): 347–52.

———. "Man-Made Vs. Natural Cycles: What Really Happens in 'The Swimmer.'" *Studies in Short Fiction* 27 (1990): 414–18.

Boyle, T. C., Ed. *Doubletakes: Pairs of Contemporary Short Stories*. Massachusetts: Thompson Wadsworth, 2004.

———. "Greasy Lake." *The Longman Anthology of Short Fiction: Stories and Authors in Context*. Compact ed. Ed. Dana Gioia and R. S. Gwynn. New York: Longman, 2001. 129–36.

Brereton, Bridget and Kevin A Yelvington. "Introduction: The Promise of Emancipation." *The Colonial Caribbean in Transition: Essays on Post-emancipation Social and Cultural History*. Ed. Bridget Brereton and Kevin A. Yelvington. Gainesville, FL: UP of Florida, 1999. 1–25.

Brereton, Bridget. "Family Strategies, Gender and the Shift to Wage Labour in the British Caribbean." *The Colonial Caribbean in Transition: Essays on Post emancipation Social and Cultural History*. Ed. Bridget Brereton and Kevin A. Yelvington. Gainesville, FL: UP of Florida, 1999. 77–107.

Brinkley, Douglass. *American Heritage History of the United States*. New York: Viking, 1998.

Brown, Stewart. "Introduction." *The Oxford Book of Caribbean Short Stories*. Ed. Stewart Brown and John Wickham. NY: Oxford UP, 1999. xiii–xxxiii.

Bunge, Nancy L. *Nathaniel Hawthorne: A Study of the Short Fiction*. New York: Twayne, 1993.

Bunting, Charles T. "'An Interior World': An Interview with Eudora Welty." *Southern Review* 8 (1972): 711–35.

Burrows, Victoria. *Whiteness and Trauma: the Mother-Daughter Knot in the Fiction of Jean Rhys, Jamaica Kincaid, and Toni Morrison*. NY: Palgrave Macmillan, 2004.

Butterworth, Nancy K. "From Civil War to Civil Rights." *Eudora Welty: Eye of the Storyteller*. Ed. Daun Trouard. Kent, OH: Kent State UP, 1989. 165–72.

———. "A Worn Path." *The Collected Stories of Eudora Welty*. 1981. London: Penguin, 1983, 142–49.

_____. "Is Phoenix Jackson's Grandson Really Dead?" *The Eye of the Story: Collected Essays and Reviews.* 1979. London: Virago, 1997, 159–62.

Byerman, Keith E. "Words and Music: Narrative Ambiguity in 'Sonny's Blues.'" *Studies in Short Fiction* 19 (1982): 367–72.

Campbell, Donna M. "Naturalism in American Literature." 6 November 2007. *Literary Movements.* 25 October 2008.

_____. "Naturalism in American Literature." *Literary Movements.* 6 November 2007, 27 January 2008.

Campbell, Ewing. *Raymond Carver: A Study of the Short Fiction.* New York, Twayne, 1992.

Canada, Mark, ed. "Edgar Allan Poe." *Canada's America.* 1997. 4 March 2008.

Carrington, Ildiko de Papp. *Controlling the Uncontrollable: The Fiction of Alice Munro.* Dekalb: Illinois UP, 1989.

Carver, Raymond. "Cathedral." *The Longman Anthology of Short Fiction: Stories and Authors in Context.* New York: Longman, 2001. 269–279.

_____. "What We Talk About When We Talk About Love." *Where I'm Calling From: New and Selected Stories.* New York: The Atlantic Monthly Press, 1986.

_____. "Where I'm Calling From." *The Best American Short Stories of the Century.* Ed. John Updike. Boston: Houghton Mifflin, 2000. P. 581–594.

Cash, Jean W. *Flannery O'Connor: A Life.* Knoxville: U of Tennessee P, 2002.

Champion, Laurie. "Assimilation Versus Celebration in James McPherson's 'The Story of a Dead Man' and James Baldwin's "'Sonny's Blues.'" *Short Story* 8.2 (2000): 94–106.

_____. "Socioeconomics in Selected Short Stories of Zora Neale Hurston." *Southern Quarterly* 40.1 (2001): 79–92.

_____. "What We Talk About When We Talk ('About Love'): Carver and Chekhov." *Journal of the Short Story in English 28* (1997): 24–36.

Charters, Ann, ed. *The Story and Its Writer: An Introduction to Short Fiction*, 3rd ed. Boston: Bedford Books of St. Martin's Press, 1991.

_____. "John Updike." Biographical note in *The Story and Its Writer: an Introduction to Short Fiction.* Boston: Bedford books of St. Martin's Press, 1991.

Cheever, John. "The Swimmer." *The Stories of John Cheever.* New York: Ballantine, 1980. 713–25.

Chopin, Kate. "The Story of an Hour." *The Complete Works of Kate Chopin.* Ed. Per Seyersted. 2 vols. Baton Rouge: Louisiana State University Press, 1969. 2:352–354.

Clark, Beverly Lyon. *Flannery O'Connor.* Georgetown University. 15 January 2008.

Coiner, Constance. *Better Red: The Writing and Resistance of Tillie Olsen and Meridel Le Sueur.* New York: Oxford UP, 1995.

Collins, R. G. "Introduction." *Critical Essays on John Cheever.* Ed. R. G. Collins. Boston: G. K. Hall, 1982. 1–20.

Comfort, Mary. "Liberating Figures in Toni Cade Bambara's Gorilla, My Love." *Studies in American Humor,* Ser. 3.5 (1998): 76–96.

Cooke, Nathalie. *Margaret Atwood: A Critical Companion.* Westport, Connecticut and London: Greenwood Press, 2004.

Crane, Stephen. "The Open Boat." Eds. Dana Gioia and R.S. Gwynn. *The Art of the Short Story.* New York, Pearson Longman, 1992.

_____. "The Sinking of the Commodore." Eds. Dana Gioia and R.S. Gwynn. *The Art of the Short Story.* New York, Pearson Longman, 1992.

Daniel, Reginald G. *More than Black?: Multiracial Identity and the New Racial Order.* Philadelphia: Temple University Press, 2002.

Drake, Robert. "The Bleeding Stinking Mad Shadow of Jesus in the Fiction of Flannery O'Connor." *Comparative Literature Studies,* Vol. 3, No. 2, 1966, pp. 183–96.

Evans, Robert C., ed. *Kate Chopin's Short Fiction: A Critical Companion.* West Cornwall, CT: Locust Hill Press, 2001.

Faulkner, William. *Go Down, Moses.* New York: Random House, 1942.

Frank, Lawrence. "The Murders in the Rue Morgue: Edgar Allan Poe's Evolutionary Reverie," *Nineteenth-Century Literature,* Vol. 50, No. 2 (Sep. 1995), pp. 168–188, University of California Press.

Friedman, Lenemaja. *Shirley Jackson.* Twayne's United States Authors Ser. TUSAS 253. Boston: Twayne-G.K. Hall, 1975.

Friedman, William F. "Edgar Allan Poe, Cryptographer," *American Literature,* Vol. 8, No. 3 (Nov. 1936), pp. 266–280. Duke University Press.

Frye, Joanne S. "'I Stand Here Ironing': Motherhood As Experience and Metaphor." *Studies in Short Fiction* 18.3 (1981): 287–92.

Garrett, George. *John Cheever and the Charms of Innocence: The Craft of The Wapshot Scandal.* Critical Essays on John Cheever. Ed. R. G. Collins. Boston: G. K. Hall, 1982. 51–62.

Gioia, Dana and R.S. Gwynn, eds. "Edgar Allan Poe." *The Art of the Short Story.* New York: Pearson Longman, 1992. p. 707.

_____. *The Art of the Short Story.* New York, Pearson Longman, 1992.

_____. *The Longman Anthology of Short Fiction: Stories and Authors in Context.* New York: Longman, 2001.

_____. "Raymond Carver." New York: Pearson Longman, 1992. 347.

Grenander, M. E. "Ambrose Bierce." *Dictionary of Literary Biography, Volume 186: Nineteenth-Century American Western Writers.* Ed. Robert Gale. Pittsburgh: University of Pittsburgh, 1997.

Guy-Sheftall, Beverly. "Commitment: Toni Cade Bambara Speaks." *Sturdy Black Bridges: Vision of Black Women in Literature.* Ed. Roseann P. Bell, Bettye J. Parker, and Beverly J. Guy-Sheftall. Garden City, NY: Doubleday, 1979. 230–49.

Hamilton, Rosemary. "Poe Lightly." *Yale New Haven Teachers Institute*, 22 May 2008.

Hawthorne, Nathaniel. "The Minister's Black Veil." *Hawthorne's Short Stories.* New York: Dodd, Mead & Co, 1962. 10–23.

_____. *The Scarlet Letter.* London, Penguin Classics, 2003.

_____. "Young Goodman Brown." *Hawthorne's Short Stories.* Dodd, 1962. 193–206.

Hayes, Kevin J., ed. *The Cambridge Companion to Edgar Allan Poe. Cambridge Companions to Literature.* Cambridge: Cambridge UP, 2002.

Heller, Janet Ruth. "Toni Cade Bambara's Use of African American Vernacular English in 'The Lesson.'" *Style* 37.3 (2003): 279–93.

Helterman, Jeffrey, ed. *Dictionary of Literary Biography, Volume 2.* "American Novelists Since World War II, First Series." Columbia: University of South Carolina, 1978, pp. 434–444.

Hill, Frances. *The Salem Witch Trials Reader.* Cambridge, MA: Da Capo, 2000.

Howells, Coral Ann. "Alice Munro." *Contemporary World Writers.* Manchester: Manchester UP, 1998.

Hunter, James. "Atreus," 3 March 1997. *Encyclopedia Mythica*, 11 June 2008.

Hurd, Myles Raymond. "What Goes Around Comes Around: Characterization, Climax, and Closure in Hurston's 'Sweat.'" *Langston Hughes Review* 12.2 (1993): 7–15.

Hurston, Zora Neale. "How It Feels to Be Colored Me." "I Love Myself When I Am Laughing. And Then Again When I Am Looking Mean and Impressive: A Zora Neale Hurston Reader." Ed. Alice Walker. Old Westbury, NY: Feminist Press, 1979. 152–56.

_____. "Sweat." Ed. Cheryl A. Wall. New Brunswick: Rutgers University Press, 1997. 25–40.

Jackson, Shirley. *The Haunting of Hill House.* 1959. New York: Penguin Books, 1984.

Johnson, Anne Janette. "Max Apple." *Contemporary Authors Online.* Literary Resource Center. Gale. 12 September 2005.

Johnson, Claudia Durst. *Daily Life in Colonial New England.* Westport, CT: Greenwood P, 2002.

Kennedy, J. Gerald. *A Historical Guide to Edgar Allan Poe.* Oxford, Oxford University Press, 2001.

_____. *Poe, Death, and the Life of Writing.* New Haven, CT: Yale University Press, 1987.

Kennedy, X. J. and Dana Gioia, Eds. *Literature: An Introduction to Fiction, Poetry and Drama*, 4th Ed. New York: Pearson Longman, 2005.

Kincaid, Jamaica. "Girl." *At the Bottom of the River.* NY: Farrar, 1983. 3–5.

_____. "My Brother." *Transition: An International Review.* Winter 1996: 4–34.

_____. "A Small Place." *Life Notes: Personal Writings by Contemporary Black Women.* Ed. Patricia Bell-Scott. NY: Norton, 1994. 300–308.

Knapp, Bettina L. *Edgar Allan Poe.* "His Life and Legacy." New York: F. Ungar, 1984.

Kozikowski, Stanley J. "Damned in a Fair Life: Cheever's 'The Swimmer.'" *Studies in Short Fiction* 30 (1993): 367–75.

Kurlansky, Mark. *A Continent of Islands: Searching for the Caribbean Destiny.* Reading, MA: Addison-Wesley, 1992.

Lee, Don. "About Lorrie Moore." *Ploughshares* 24 (1998): 224–29.

Le Guin, Ursula K. *City of Illusions.* St. Albans, Granada Publishing Ltd., 1973.

_____. *Planet of Exile.* London, W. H. Allen & Co., 1983.

_____. *Rocannon's World.* London, W. H. Allen & Co., 1983.

_____. *The Dispossessed.* London, Grafton Books, 1987.

_____. *The Left Hand of Darkness*. London, Macdonald & Co. Ltd., 1986.

_____. "The Ones Who Walk Away From Omelas," *The Wind's Twelve Quarters Volume 2*. London, Granada Publishing Ltd., 1978.

_____. *The Word For World is Forest*. London, Grafton Books, 1986.

Leverenz, David. "Poe and Gentry Virginia." *In The American Face of Edgar Allan Poe*, ed. Shawn Rosenheim and Stephen Rachman. Baltimore: Johns Hopkins UP, 1995. 210–36.

Levin, Harry. *The Power of Blackness: Hawthorne, Poe, Melville*. New York: Knopf, 1958.

London, Jack. "The Law of Life." *The World of Jack London*. 25 October 2008.

_____. "To Build A Fire." *The Collected Jack London*. Ed. Steven J. Kasdin. New York: Marlboro Books, 1991.

May, Charles E. "Edgar Allan Poe." *Magill's Survey of American Literature*, Revised Edition. Pasadena, CA: Salem Press, 2007. *Literary Reference Center*. 1 Dec. 2008.

May, John R. *The Pruning Word: The Parables of Flannery O'Connor*. Notre Dame, IN: Notre Dame P, 1976.

Meisenhelder, Susan Edwards. "Hitting a Straight Lick with a Crooked Stick: Race and Gender In the Work of Zora Neale Hurston." Tuscaloosa: University of Alabama Press, 1999.

Miller, Arthur. *The Crucible*. London, Penguin Modern Classics, 1987.

Miller, Judith, ed. "The Art of Alice Munro: Saying the Unsayable." Waterloo, ON: U of Waterloo P, 1984.

Moore, Lorrie. "You're Ugly, Too." *Like Life: Stories*. New York: Plume, 1988.

Morgan, Edmund Sears. *The Puritan Family: Religion & Domestic Relations in Seventeenth-Century New England*. Westport, CT: Greenwood P, 1966.

Munro, Alice. *Runaway*. London: Chatto, 2004.

O'Connor, Flannery. "A Good Man is Hard to Find." Eds. Dana Gioia and R.S. Gwynn. *The Art of the Short Story*. New York, Pearson Longman, 1992.

_____. "Everything that Rises Must Converge." *The Complete Stories*. New York: Farrar, Straus, and Giroux, 1964. 405–420.

_____. *The Habit of Being. Letters*. Ed. Sally Fitzgerald. New York: Farrar, Straus, and Giroux, 1979.

_____. "The Element of Suspense in 'A Good Man is Hard to Find'" Eds. Dana Gioia and R.S. Gwynn. *The Art of the Short Story*. New York, Pearson Longman, 1992.

O'Hara, James E. *John Cheever: A Study of the Short Fiction*. Boston: Twayne, 1989.

Olsen, Tillie. "I Stand Here Ironing." *The Story and Its Writer: An Introduction to Short Fiction*. Compact 6th ed. Ed. Ann Charters. Boston: Bedford/St. Martin's, 2003. 671–76.

Oppenheimer, Judy. *Private Demons: The Life of Shirley Jackson*. New York: Putnam, 1988.

Papineau, David. "Naturalism." 2007. *Stanford Encyclopedia of Philosophy*. 25 October 2008.

Paravisini-Gebert, Lizabeth. *Jamaica Kincaid: A Critical Companion (Critical Companions to Popular Contemporary Writers)*. Westport, CT: Greenwood, 1999.

Peck, David. "A & P." *Masterplots II: Short Story Series*. MagillOnLiteraturePlus. EBSCO. 15 Aug. 2005.

Poe, Edgar Allan. "The Cask of Amontillado." *In The Fall of the House of Usher and Other Writings: Poems, Tales, Essays and Reviews*, ed. David Galloway. London: Penguin, 2003. 310–16.

_____. *The Fall of the House of Usher and Other Writings*. Ed. and intro. David Galloway. London: Penguin Classics, 1986.

_____. "The Fall of the House of Usher." In *The Fall of the House of Usher and Other Writings: Poems, Tales, Essays and Reviews*, ed. David Galloway. London: Penguin, 2003. 90–109.

_____. "The Gold-Bug." In *The Fall of the House of Usher and Other Writings* 283–319.

_____. "The Murders in the Rue Morgue," *Selected Tales*, pp. 105–135. Oxford, Oxford University Press, 1980.

_____. "The Pit and the Pendulum." *Literature.org: The Online Literature Library*, 19 May 2008.

_____. "The Purloined Letter." *Tales of Mystery and Imagination*. London: J. M. Dent & Sons, 1912. pp. 454–471.

_____. "The Tell-Tale Heart." Eds. Dana Gioia and R.S. Gwynn. *The Art of the Short Story*. New York: Pearson Longman, 1992. pp. 721–725.

_____. (2006). "Hop-Frog." *Works of Edgar Allen Poe—Volume 5*. Salt Lake City, Utah: Project Gutenberg Literary Archive Foundation, 2006. *Literary Reference Center*. 1 Dec. 2008.

Porter, Katherine Anne. "Introduction." *A Curtain of Green*. New York: Harcourt, 1941 xi–xxiii.

Price, Victoria. Critical Survey of Short Fiction, Second Revised Ed. *MagillOnLiteraturePlus*. EBSCO. 12 Sept. 2005.

Rasporich, Beverley. *Dance of the Sexes: Art and Gender in the Fiction of Alice Munro*. London: Routledge, 1992.

Ridout, Alice. "Temporality and Margaret Atwood." *University of Toronto Quarterly* 69.4 (fall 2000): 849–871. Academic Search Premier. 6 December 2005.

Robinson, Marilynne. "Marriage and Other Astonishing Bonds." *The New York Times*, 15 May 1988. 21 February 2008.

Rogers, Michael. Interview with John Updike. "The Gospel of the Book: LJ Talks to John Updike." *Library Journal* 124.3 (1999): 114–117.

Rosenheim, James. *The Cryptographic Imagination: Secret Writing from Poe to the Internet*. Baltimore: Johns Hopkins UP, 1997.

Rosenheim, Shawn and Rachman, Stephen (Eds.). *The American Face of Edgar Allan Poe*. Baltimore, The Johns Hopkins University Press, 1995.

Salinger, J.D. (1919-). *American Jewish Desk Reference*, 1999. Jewish Virtual Library, 11 April 2008.

_____. *Nine Stories*. Boston: Little, Brown and Company, 1953.

Sherard, Tracey. "Sonny's Bebop: Baldwin's 'Blues Text' As Intracultural Critique." *African American Review* 32 (1998): 691–705.

Siebert, Hilary. "Raymond Carver." *A Reader's Companion to the Short Story in English,* ed. Erin Fallon, et al. Westport, CT: Greenwood, 2001. 95–104.

Silverman, Kenneth. *Edgar A. Poe: Mournful and Never-ending Remembrance*. New York: Harper Perennial-Harper Collins, 1991.

Sinclair, David. *Edgar Allen Poe*. Totowa, Rowman and Littlefield, 1977.

Stull, William L. "Prose as Architecture: Two Interviews with Raymond Carver." *Clockwatch Review* Inc., 1995–96. 25 Sept. 2005.

_____. "Raymond Carver." *Dictionary of Literary Biography Yearbook: 1988*. Ed. J. M. Brook. Detroit: Gale Research, 1989. 199–213.

Sutton, Rosemary. *The Red Shoes: Margaret Atwood Starting Out*. Toronto: HarperCollins, 1998.

Symons, Julian. "Introduction" and "Notes," *Selected Tales*, pp. vii–xiii and pp. 301–316. Oxford, Oxford University Press, 1980.

Tate, Allen. "The Angelic Imagination." *Bloom's Major Short Story Writers: Edgar Allan Poe*. New York: Chelsea House, 1999. 23–30.

Tate, Claudia. "Toni Cade Bambara." *Black Women Writers at Work*. Ed. Claudia Tate and Tillie Olsen. New York: Continuum, 1983. 12–38.

Tromp, Hansmaarten. "Any Good Writer Uses His Imagination to Convince the Reader." Interview with Raymond Carver. *Conversations With Raymond Carver*. Ed. Marshall Bruce Gentry and William L. Stull. Jackson: University Press of Mississippi, 1990. 72–83.

Ulin, David L. Interview with T. Coraghessan Boyle. *The Bloomsbury Review* 9.6 (1989): 4–5, 16. *Rpt. in* Short Story *Criticism*. Vol 16. Ed. David Segal. New York: Gale, 1994. 149–52.

Updike, John. "A & P." *Literature: An Introduction to Fiction Poetry and Drama*, X. J. Kennedy and Dana Gioia, Eds. New York: Pearson and Longman, 1985.

Vertreace, Martha M. "Toni Cade Bambara: The Dance of Character and Community." *American Women Writing Fiction: Memory, Identity, Family, Space*. Ed. Mickey Pearlman. Lexington: UP of Kentucky, 1989. 154–71.

Walker, I. M., ed. *Edgar Allan Poe: The Critical Heritage*. New York: Routledge & Kegan Paul, 1986.

Wall, Cheryl A., ed. "Sweat." New Brunswick: Rutgers University Press, 1997.

Walters, Dorothy. *Flannery O'Connor*. Boston: Twayne, 1973.

Weekes, Karen. "Identity in the Short Story Cycles of Lorrie Moore." *Journal of the Short Story in English* 39 (2002): 109–22.

_____. "Postmodernism in Women's Short Story Cycles: Lorrie Moore's Anagrams." *The Postmodern Short Story: Forms and Issues*. Ed. Farhat Iftekharrudin, Joseph Boyden, Mary Rohrberger, and Jaie Claudet. Westport, CT: Praeger, 2003. 94–106.

Welty, Eudora. *A Writer's Beginnings*. Omnibus BBC. 1985.

_____. *The Eye of the Story: Collected Essays and Reviews*. 1979. London: Virago, 1997.

_____. "Why I Live at the P.O." *The Collected Stories of Eudora Welty*. 1981. London: Penguin, 1983, 46–56.

_____. "The Reading and Writing of Short Stories." *Atlantic Monthly*, February (1949): 54–8.

_____. "Threads of Innocence." *New York Times*, 5 April 1953. *New York Times on the Web*, 11 April 2008.

Wilbur, Richard. "The House of Poe." *Bloom's Modern Critical Views: Edgar Allan Poe.* Ed. Harold Bloom. New York: Chelsea House, 1985. 51–70.

Wilson, Sharon Rose. *Margaret Atwood's Fairy-Tale Sexual Politics.* Jackson University Press of Mississippi, 1993.

Wineapple, Brenda. *Hawthorne: A Life.* New York: Knopf, 2003.

Woodberry, George E., and R. W. B. Lewis. *Edgar Allan Poe.* New York: Chelsea House, 1997.

Zimmerman, Shannon. "Boyle, T. Coraghessan (1948–)." *The Facts on File Companion to the American Short Story.* Ed. Abby H. P. Werlock. New York: Facts on File, 2000. 66–68.

INDEX